REASON &
RELIGIOUS BELIEF

An Introduction to
the Philosophy of Religion

Third Edition

MICHAEL PETERSON
Asbury College
WILLIAM HASKER
Huntington College
BRUCE REICHENBACH
Augsburg College
DAVID BASINGER
Roberts Wesleyan College

New York   Oxford
OXFORD UNIVERSITY PRESS
2003

OXFORD UNIVERSITY PRESS

Oxford   New York
Auckland   Bangkok   Buenos Aires   Cape Town   Chennai
Dar es Salaam   Delhi   Hong Kong   Istanbul   Karachi   Kolkata
Kuala Lumpur   Madrid   Melbourne   Mexico City   Mumbai
Nairobi   São Paulo   Shanghai   Taipei   Tokyo   Toronto

Published by Oxford University Press, Inc.
198 Madison Avenue, New York, New York, 10016
http://www.oup-usa.org

Library of Congress Cataloging-in-Publication Data
Reason & religious belief: an introduction to the philosophy of religion / Michael
Peterson . . . [et al.].—3rd ed.
     p.   cm.
   Includes bibliographical references and indexes.
   ISBN 0-19-515695-1 (pbk.: alk. paper)
     1. Religion—Philosophy.   2. Christianity—Philosophy.   I. Title: Reason and religious
   belief.   II. Peterson, Michael L., 1950–

BL51 .R326   2003
210—dc21

                                                                                    2002066347

Printing number: 9 8 7 6 5 4 3 2
Printed in the United States of America
on acid-free paper

CONTENTS

Contents

Contents

Contents

PREFACE TO THE THIRD EDITION

We continue to be pleased by the widespread use of *Reason and Religious Belief*. After more than a decade and two previous editions, this new edition attempts to remain at the forefront both by including all of the standard material needed in a basic philosophy of religion course and by incorporating much new material not found in previous editions. Suggestions from both users and reviewers made it reasonable to do this more substantial revision while at the same time keeping the result linked to our other Oxford text, *Philosophy of Religion: Selected Readings*, 2nd edition. We particularly appreciate Robert Miller, our editor at Oxford University Press, who provided insightful help and much encouragement to continue the work begun in the first edition.

Asbury College	M.P.
Huntington College	W.H.
Augsburg College	B.R.
Roberts Wesleyan College	D.B.

PREFACE TO THE
SECOND EDITION

We have been very gratified by the reception that the first edition of Reason and Religious Belief received. Suggestions and criticism from many of those who used the book have been helpful in preparing this revision. In addition, we decided to add several topics not covered in the previous edition.

We offer this edition of Reason and Religious Belief in the hope that it will continue to be helpful to those interested in a first course in philosophy of religion. In doing so, we remain committed to the primary task undertaken in the previous edition: to analyze important concepts and evaluate major arguments in the field, with the aim of finding the most reasonable position on the issues.

Asbury College	M.P.
Huntington College	W.H.
Augsburg College	B.R.
Roberts Wesleyan College	D.B.

PREFACE TO THE FIRST EDITION

Reason and Religious Belief grows out of our many years of collective experience reflecting upon the issues in philosophy of religion and teaching them to undergraduate students. So, in our writing, we have been especially conscious of the need to communicate the issues in ways that students can understand.

Perhaps more than anything else, though, the book was born out of longstanding friendship and intellectual interaction among the four of us. We dare to hope that the enjoyment and even the excitement of the type of philosophical discussion we have shared will show through these pages and become contagious. Our different interests and specializations within the philosophy of religion are welded together by our complete agreement on the nature of the philosophical task in general: to analyze important concepts and evaluate major arguments, with the overall aim of finding the most reasonable position on any issue.

No project of this magnitude can be successful without help from others. We wish to thank the Faculty Research and Development Committee of Asbury College for providing a small grant to defray the costs of producing this manuscript. And we are grateful to Robert Audi and George Mavrodes for reading and making valuable suggestions on earlier drafts of the manuscript.

Asbury College   M.P.
Huntington College   W.H.
Augsburg College   B.R.
Roberts Wesleyan College   D.B.

INTRODUCTION

Interest in philosophy of religion has exploded in the past quarter of a century. Professional philosophers have brought new techniques to bear on traditional problems and are pioneering new territory as well. *Time* magazine reported this resurgence of interest in the philosophical examination of religious beliefs, stating that "God is making a comeback." Clearly, both the vitality and the level of sophistication in this burgeoning area of scholarship indicate the seriousness and importance of the issues.

This text has been written as an introduction to the basic issues and options in the exciting field of philosophy of religion. We try to provide a very accessible, comprehensive treatment of philosophy of religion—one that is current, historically informed, theologically sophisticated, and philosophically challenging. We do not assume any background in philosophy on the part of the reader, making it suitable for undergraduate, graduate, and seminary students with no previous exposure to philosophy. The text should be accessible even to thoughtful, diligent readers apart from any formal course setting. Although this text is designed as a basic presentation of matters in philosophy of religion, there is a good deal of general philosophy along the way, supplying helpful background about major philosophers and their ideas.

The strategy of this introductory text is to distill and discuss the main issues in the field, extracting the intellectual dialogue with which the more difficult primary literature is occupied. The anthology *Philosophy of Religion: Selected Readings* (Oxford University Press, 2000; hereafter PRSR2e) is closely correlated with the structure of the present text and serves as a tool to help students follow the dialogue emerging from the original sources.

We invite students to participate in that great debate about religion that has occupied many great philosophers through the centuries. Our primary emphasis is on the *structure* of the issues. We want students to understand precisely the shape of each issue, its logic, what is at stake, and the main options. Our goal is to help students be able to form reasonable opinions about the issues and to continue to think about them in meaningful and helpful ways.

Since there is obvious pedagogical advantage in finding a point of contact with students, we begin each chapter with a concrete story, example, or quotation and then gradually develop the larger issue. We try to draw students naturally into the discussion and encourage thoughtful response, striving throughout for clarity and friendliness of presentation.

Although there is something of a logical order in the sequence of the first several chapters, instructors using this text can assign chapters in almost any order, as the topics are somewhat independent. Obviously, supplementary readings of original works can be coordinated with the individual chapters. Study questions are included at the end of each chapter in order to facilitate classroom discussion as well as private review. Suggested reading is included for each topic so that students can pursue the issues in their own research.

Since the long-standing interest among Western philosophers has been in theism, this text is devoted largely to the issues related to the view that there exists a Supreme Spiritual Being, transcendent from the world, who is omnipotent, omniscient, and perfectly good. This, of course, is the view known more precisely as *classical theism,* which is shared by the major theistic religions (Judaism, Christianity, and Islam). Although we treat issues pertaining to classical theism, we do consider some issues pertaining to specifically *Christian* theism because contemporary analytic philosophers of religion pay so much attention to it. At appropriate points, we also explore how the issues here apply to other major religions and theological conceptions, thus acquainting students to some degree with Hinduism, Buddhism, and other non-Western traditions. At points, we also explore the feminist voice on key issues.

Although we make the most minimal assumptions about students' familiarity with the religious tradition or theological conceptions that are examined, it is helpful to be somewhat acquainted with Western religious faith and the sorts of beliefs that are characteristic of theistic religions generally. However, we supply enough exposition of these beliefs along the way that even the neophyte can quickly grasp the ideas involved. Beyond this, we do not assume that readers are theists or religious believers of any persuasion.

This text is designed to cover all of the issues that are treated in standard philosophy of religion texts and several topics that are rarely treated but that many instructors want. Chapter 1 begins by surveying the pervasive religiosity of the human race and explaining what a philosophical examination of religion is. Chapter 2 examines what is perhaps for many people their most familiar and concrete contact with religion—religious experience. We examine such questions as whether there is a common core or structure to all religious experiences and whether these experiences can serve to justify religious beliefs. We move beyond experience in chapter 3 and consider whether religious commitments are subject to rational evaluation. After looking at two extreme positions—hard rationalism and fideism—we adopt a posture that we call "critical rationalism." Critical rationalism is committed to the analysis and evaluation of religious beliefs but does not maintain that these beliefs are subject to conclusive proof or disproof. Then we devote chapter 4 to the attributes traditionally associated with the theistic deity, attributes that define more precisely the Being who is the subject of further argument and debate. We do not neglect, however, the trenchant critique of the traditional concept of deity offered by process thinkers.

The following three chapters address, in one way or another, the matter of argumentation about God's existence. In chapter 5, we present and examine the standard arguments for the existence of God, the main fare of natural theology. These arguments continue to fascinate and challenge those who think about whether it is possible to provide rational support for theistic belief. Reflecting on this whole enterprise in Chapter 6, we take up the issue of whether belief in God needs to rest on rational argument or whether it can be "basic" in the framework of our beliefs. Chapter 7 then poses, develops, and evaluates the problem of evil as the most serious rational objection to belief in God.

In the remaining chapters, we discuss a variety of important issues. Chapter 8 is entirely new in this edition and recognizes the energetic discussion of God's relation to the world that has taken place since the early 1990s. What is the nature and extent of divine knowledge? And of divine action in the contingent world? Following naturally upon the previous chapter, chapter 9 discusses the concept of miracle. Since most theistic religions have historically involved a belief in miracles, this chapter examines the key philosophical problems related to that concept: the difficulty of definition, the issue of whether miracles are possible, and the issue of if we can identify whether a miracle has occurred. Chapter 10 focuses on the problem of life after death. In this chapter, we show how concepts of postmortem survival vary with views of the human self and scrutinize several arguments for the reality of life after death.

At the next stage of our discussion, we pause to reflect on the very fact that we are employing human language in relation to the divine. In chapter 11, we raise the question of how human words can meaningfully apply to God, and we work through various important theories of religious language, including the more recent feminist theories. We incorporate in this new edition the discussion of a feminist perspective. Chapter 12 looks closely at the relation of religion and science, a topic not frequently covered in philosophy of religion texts. The aim in this chapter is to bring some order to the discussion by looking at various ways the relation of these two important human activities has been conceived. In the succeeding chapter we take up an increasingly pressing issue: the problem of religious diversity. This matter alone is inspiring numerous new courses in colleges and universities. In chapter 13, we explore problems related to the truth and salvific character of the various living religions. In chapter 14, we examine the connection between religion and ethics, raising such questions as whether ethical norms can originate in God and whether religion offers a distinctive vision of human moral fulfillment. Chapter 15, the final one in the book, serves as a capstone to our study of the philosophy of religion. It summarizes the main lessons that can be learned and invites readers to continue exploring the issues in the fascinating field of philosophy of religion.

In an introductory treatment of intellectually important issues, we are convinced that the impact on readers is determined not so much by *what* particular issues are selected for treatment as by *how* those issues are handled. Hence, the approach we have taken here is of major consequence. We have sought to strike a balance between pure neutrality on the one hand and outright advocacy on the other. While we attempt to be fair to various positions, we sometimes indicate which one among alternatives seems most reasonable to us. This approach is more personal than "pure neutralism" and, we believe, helps enlist readers in the activity of critical thinking about the issues.

We believe that a serious study of philosophy of religion is both intellectually stimulating and personally rewarding, and we have diligently tried to design this text to facilitate such outcomes. If we have met our philosophical and pedagogical objectives in sufficient measure, then we dare to hope that our readers will find this exploration of the philosophy of religion to be genuinely worthwhile.

CHAPTER 1 THINKING
ABOUT GOD:
THE SEARCH FOR
THE ULTIMATE

Religion is a powerful force in human life. The evidence for this fact is both clear and abundant:

- Cro-Magnon societies buried persons in fetal position, surrounding them with useful objects—weapons, necklaces, and cooking utensils—as though they might experience another life.
- An aboriginal tribe prays to the great spirit of the sky to be favorable toward them and not withhold rain.
- In Japan, a Zen Buddhist meditates on the unity between the "I" and the "not-I."
- During the Islamic holy month of Ramadan, a devout Moroccan family practices fasting from dawn to sundown.
- On Easter Sunday, Christian believers all over the world celebrate the Resurrection of Jesus just as Christians have done for two thousand years.

From the birth of civilization, a multitude of religions has developed, each very complex. We know that prehistoric tribes manifested their religious impulse in animistic and totemistic practices. Contemporary world religions have highly developed concepts of God or Ultimate Reality: for Jews it is Yahweh, for Christians it is the Triune God, for Muslims it is Allah, for Hindus it is Shiva or Vishnu, for Theravada Buddhists it is Nirvana.[1]

There is also much evidence that countless numbers of people in today's world are not religious at all. Millions adhere to no religious tradition, practice no forms of worship or meditation, and thus seem to possess no religious faith. There are also individuals and organizations that actually promote some version of atheism or at least the rejection of religion. Well known in popular culture is the Association of American Atheists.[2] There is also the American Humanist Association, which was organized by philosopher Paul Kurtz.[3] Yet such groups, which expressly reject all forms of religion, witness in a peculiar way to its impact on human life.

DEFINING RELIGION

What exactly is religion? Arriving at a precise definition of *religion* is notoriously difficult, since each proposed definition seems subject to counterexample. C. P. Tiele wrote, "Religion is, in truth, that pure and reverential disposition or frame of mind which we call piety." F. H. Bradley stated that "religion is rather the attempt to express the complete reality of goodness through every aspect of our being." "Religion," claims James Martineau, "is the belief in an ever living God, that is, in a Divine Mind and Will ruling the Universe and holding moral relations with mankind." Clearly, each of these authors specifies a different characteristic: Tiele accents the attitude of piety, Bradley links religion with goodness, and Martineau features belief in ethical monotheism. Other definitions touch upon traits such as ritualistic acts, prayer and communication with gods, and so on.[4]

Wisdom counsels us, however, not to elevate any isolated feature to the status of a universal definition. Religions are more complex than that. There are shamanistic religions, for example, that seem not to involve feelings of genuine piety so much as prudential or utilitarian acts of obeisance. Thus, Tiele's definition is incomplete. Likewise, there are polytheistic religions (such as those of ancient Egypt and Greece) that do not recognize a single divine ruler of the universe. Thus, the definition given by Marineau fails to cover all religions. Realistically speaking, counterexamples for most definitions of religion can be found.

Speaking too generically about religion is imprecise and distorts the rich and complicated details of actual religions. For example, religion is almost always associated with the supernatural or the divine, but not always. The notion of a supernatural realm does not occur, for example, in the nontheistic schools of Buddhism and functions in very different ways in Taoism, Hinduism, and Islam, for example. The great differences among religions make it difficult to find a least common denominator or to talk of religion in general.

On the other hand, focusing on one specific religion ignores or underestimates some of the very broad traits that all religions seem to share. Ninian Smart argues that all religions have an experiential dimension, ranging from a quiet sense of the presence of the divine in ordinary life to the mystical consciousness of union with the divine. Each religion has a mythic dimension that that conveys a large-scale understanding of God or Ultimate Reality to the faithful in terms of symbolic speech and stories. In each religion, the ethical dimension concerns the sphere of moral action and practical life orientation. Ritual is a dimension of all religions that pertains to the prescribed behaviors, both public and private, related to worship of the divine.

The last dimension, the social, pertains to how a religion organizes all sorts of interpersonal relationships.

In spite of the difficulties in defining and applying the term "religion," we can propose a tentative, working definition. For our purposes, we assume that *religion is constituted by a set of beliefs, actions, and experiences, both personal and corporate, organized around a concept of an Ultimate Reality.* This Ultimate Reality may be understood as a unity or a plurality, personal or nonpersonal, divine or not, differing from religion to religion. Yet is seems that every cultural phenomenon that we call a religion fits this definition. The prescribed actions vary from ritualistic patterns to ethical living; the desired emotions vary from feelings of piety and humility to a sense of optimism about life and the universe.

As the title of this texts suggests, our study of philosophy of religion is directed at *beliefs*, specifically at *religious* beliefs. But how shall we think about this? *Beliefs*, we shall say, are statements (i.e., propositions) that are accepted as true; they are truth-claims. In a certain sense, every religion rests on beliefs. These religious beliefs tend to revolve around five basic areas. First, humans find themselves in a predicament (e.g., sin for Judaism and Christianity, *samsara* for Hinduism, mortality for Taoism). Second, humans need a way to resolve the predicament (e.g., salvation, liberation). Third, there exists something transcendent that assists us or is the goal of our existence (e.g., Ultimate Reality, God, Brahman, Nirvana). Fourth, this "something" can be known or approached in some specified way (e.g., holy scriptures, shamans). Fifth, we must do something to achieve salvation or liberation (e.g., have faith, deny self, engage in meditation, follow the Five Pillars of Islam).

Such beliefs in a given religion account for the particular actions and emotions that it endorses. These beliefs may be made official and presented in the form of doctrine and teaching, or they may be somewhat implicit in the daily practice of the religion. Yet the numerous details of any religion are, in a real sense, an extension of how the fundamental beliefs about Ultimate Reality are interpreted and expressed in real life.

Accordingly, when we find a group of human beings involved in a network of beliefs, actions, and experiences that focus on some Ultimate Reality, we are justified in saying that we have an instance of religion. Obviously, some cultural phenomena embody all of the relevant features to a remarkable extent and thus provide clear, uncontroversial examples. Roman Catholicism and Orthodox Judaism are unmistakable instances of religion according to our definition. Other practices less obviously possess the set of relevant characteristics but are still arguably cases of religion, such as certain forms of Buddhism and even Unitarianism. It has even been argued that secular humanism and communism are religions, or at least strongly exhibit some religious characteristics.

Of course, we cannot fully understand a given religion—its preferred attitudes and emotions, its prescribed rituals, its important stories and myths, and its recommended way of life—simply by looking at it. Many subtle factors—psychological, sociological, anthropological, and historical—are not obvious to the untrained eye. That is why an expert, say, in the psychology of religion or the sociology or religion, can reveal fascinating insights to the novice. However, these disciplines do not ask questions about the meaning, truth, consistency, or explanatory adequacy of the religious belief systems they study. That is the purview of philosophy of religion.

WHAT IS PHILOSOPHY OF RELIGION?

Since philosophy is the discipline that closely examines *beliefs*, we may rightly expect it to be interested in *religious beliefs*. Philosophers often raise critical questions about whether certain beliefs are *meaningful, true, probable,* or *plausible*. They seek to *clarify* beliefs and are concerned about whether beliefs are *consistent* and *coherent*. They are interested in whether beliefs have *explanatory power* and what their *implications* are. We will find philosophers of religion asking these same kinds of questions about religious beliefs.

Philosophers of religion also bring insights and interests from other areas of philosophy (e.g., *epistemology, metaphysics,* and *ethics*) to bear on their consideration of religion. For example, philosophers of religion might think about the epistemology of religious belief, pondering questions about the sources and justification of religious knowledge. Or they might analyze various metaphysical theories of the nature of God and the structure of the divine attributes, or the metaphysics of human free will in relation to divine sovereignty. They might even trace the connection between a given religious tradition and a certain ethical way of life.

The particular approach one takes to philosophy of religion depends on precisely how one conceives of the philosophical task in general. The *traditional* conception of philosophy, dominant throughout the history of Western thought, was that philosophy should be used in the service of comprehensive, systematic perspectives on life and the world—even those perspectives that are religious or theological in orientation. The name *natural theology* became a label for the enterprise that presumed that belief in the existence of God and other religious beliefs could—and indeed should—be established by philosophical argument.[5]

During the twentieth century, philosophy of religion among English-speaking philosophers took a turn that was greatly influenced by the *analytic* movement. Narrowly conceived, this approach restricts the task of philosophy solely to the clarification and analysis of the logic of our ideas, as it denies that philosophy can address questions of truth or falsity in our beliefs.[6] More broadly conceived, the analytic approach is certainly concerned with clear analysis and logical rigor, but as a prelude to more substantive considerations of truth and reasonableness and even the more synthetic activity of constructing a point of view.

The present study is basically analytic in its style, seeking to clarify and analyze important concepts and arguments. Yet it is not narrowly analytic, for it seeks to point out, where possible, those positions which seem most correct and fruitful. In this way, our current venture preserves much of the spirit of the traditional approach, without adopting wholesale the old model of natural theology.

While our explanation of the relationship of philosophy to religion is somewhat loose and approximate, it is on equal footing with philosophy of art, philosophy of science, philosophy of history, and a number of other studies in which philosophy thoroughly inspects a specific subject matter. Obviously, all such studies are doubly difficult to define because both the nature of philosophy and the discipline under study can be conceived in a variety of ways. Here we simply assume that the enterprise of philosophy is to be conducted according to our foregoing description. Therefore, we are now in a position to propose a working definition for *philosophy of religion: the attempt to analyze and critically evaluate religious beliefs.* In order to make our study more manageable, we now need to narrow the set of religious beliefs that we will investigate in the chapters to follow.

THE GOD OF THEISM

All major religious systems merit serious philosophical investigation. Worthwhile exercises in philosophy of religion can be conducted by inquiring into the specific beliefs of any one given religion or by comparatively studying various religions. For the past twenty-five hundred years in Western culture, the chief interest of philosophers who study religion has been the theistic concept of deity. *The theistic deity is conceived as a transcendent spiritual being who is omnipotent, omniscient, and perfectly good.* We might call this view *classical theism* or *standard theism.* Theism itself, of course, is not a religion but expresses an important belief framework of three living religions. Amid their differences, Judaism, Christianity, and Islam share this basic view of God.

William Rowe calls the core beliefs of standard theism *restricted theism.* Restricted theism conjoined with other distinctive beliefs that arise from the creeds, doctrines, and sacred texts of a particular living religion give us a specific form of what he calls *expanded theism.*[7] Contemporary Anglo-American philosophers of religion continue to be interested in issues surrounding restricted theism as well as those that relate to various versions of expanded theism. In this vein, the present study treats a variety of key issues related to theistic belief.

Some people contend that purely intellectual interest in God (in this case, the God of theism) misses the heart of true religion. They maintain that the abstract analysis of religious concepts and the logical examination of theological beliefs fail to appreciate the intimate, personal involvement of religious faith. Insisting that "the God of the philosophers" is not "the God of faith," they often argue that rigorous intellectual investigation has nothing to offer to devout faith. However, while intellectual interest—and, in the present case, philosophical interest—in religion is not the same thing as passionate religious commitment, it is our belief that faith cannot be totally divorced from reason.

Although religious faith certainly involves an element of personal trust in God, that trust is normally based on a number of *beliefs* about what God is like and how a person becomes properly related to God. It is surely true that having faith in God and living in a manner that manifests that attitude amount to *more* than intellectually adopting beliefs such as "God exists" and "God is perfect in power, knowledge, and goodness." But having faith in God is *at least* a matter of accepting such beliefs. In some cases, religious believers may not have a clear and self-conscious understanding of their own beliefs or may not be particularly adept at articulating them. However, this does not alter the fact that religious faith rests on beliefs about the kind of object in which one has faith.[8]

Besides, the instant a believer makes some sort of claim of faith, some statement about her relation to the God she worships, she has automatically entered the arena of rational discussion and dialogue. Likewise, anytime someone denies some particular religious belief or rejects all religious beliefs generally, that stance is also open to *rational evaluation and discussion*. Wittingly or unwittingly, the believer as well as the nonbeliever has stated some intellectual beliefs, has uttered truth-claims that are subject to being criticized as well as defended. Even the belief that faith is immune from critical examination and must be either accepted or rejected on other grounds must itself be rationally evaluated.

Actually, it is not just outsiders or critics who have the right to examine the belief-component of religious faith. Believers themselves may want to seek further understanding of their faith by deeply probing its beliefs. In fact, all major religions recognize their own intellectual dimension, or belief-component, and therefore have self-critical traditions. In addition, they recognize that they must confront criticism from outside. They realize that if religion in modern life is to have any relevance to people who are intellectually honest and morally sensitive, it must be open to continued scrutiny. Over the centuries, the theistic view of God has produced a rich legacy of dialogue and debate, an ongoing discussion in which the reader of this text is invited to participate.

THE RELIGIOUS AMBIGUITY OF LIFE

We have now reached a working definition of religion, become acquainted with the role of philosophy of religion, and narrowed the scope of our study to theism. But how shall we proceed? Specifically, how might we characterize the initial situation in which we find ourselves as we start thinking philosophically about theistic belief? We might remind ourselves of the dual facts with which we opened this chapter: that many people embrace religion and that many do not. Since we are going to narrow our discussion to theistic religion, we could readily say that many people accept theistic belief and many people do not. Opinion is obviously divided.

We need to make a further distinction between two general categories of people: *reflective* and *unreflective*. Admittedly, people exhibit the tendency to be rationally reflective in varying degrees: some are highly reflective, some seem not to be reflective at all, and others fall somewhere in between. Believers and nonbelievers alike fall into such categories. Clearly, many people have not seriously pondered the important questions related to the coherence, plausibility, and truth of theism, and yet they have decided either to accept or reject a theistic orientation. Some say that they just believe in an all-powerful and all-good God, or that prayer is valid, or that miracles happen—and that this is the end of the matter for them. Others claim that they do not believe in God, or that prayer is pointless, or that the idea of miracles seems silly—and that this is the end of the matter for them. But neither the believers nor the unbelievers here have made a serious attempt to reflect on the grounds for their opinions. What we have, then, is *unreflective belief* and *unreflective nonbelief*, respectively.

The present study cannot be concerned with unreflective belief or disbelief. Philosophy is preeminently an enterprise of *reflective reason*, which seeks to get beyond superficial approaches to important issues. It seeks to look responsibly at all relevant arguments, clarify key ideas, and carefully trace out implications of beliefs. Accordingly, we are interested here in how things look "upon reflection." Interestingly, and perhaps disturbingly for some, we get a mixed opinion even from reflective people about the truth of theism. It is not just that unreflective people split on the issue; reflective ones divide as well. Seemingly responsible, earnest, thoughtful people who look hard at the evidence and arguments do not agree!

Most *reflective believers* with a theistic orientation realize that the truth of God's existence is not immediately obvious. For some, God's "hiddenness" constitutes a problem and challenges us to search for him. St. Anselm (1033–1109) wrote: "Lord, if thou art not here, where shall I seek thee, being absent? . . . And, by what marks, under what form, shall I seek thee? I have never seen thee, O Lord my God; I do not know thy form. What, O most high Lord, shall this man do, an exile far from thee?"[9] Anselm stands in a long line of thoughtful believers who have sought to give a rational account of why they believe in God and hold other theistic ideas. They attempt to search out God's existence, to try to construe the facts to see if they point us to God and help us make sense of related religious beliefs—an exercise that Anselm himself called "faith seeking understanding."[10] Not all theists, of course, claim God to be hidden, and not all agree on the degree of divine hiddenness. Some claim to have strong experiential grounds for belief or to have witnessed miracles. Yet some of the most honest and sensitive theistic literature revolves around the theme of the hiddenness of God. In our contemporary period, this theme is becoming more commonly discussed.

Reflective nonbelievers also agree that the existence of God is not plainly evident. However, in attempting to be reasonable and reflective about the matter, they have concluded that there are no good grounds for believing in God and often cite positive grounds for disbelief. In "A Free Man's

Worship," Bertrand Russell stated that the universe appears to be ultimately meaningless:

> That man is the product of causes which had no prevision of the end they were achieving; that his origin, his growth, his hopes and fears, his love and beliefs, are but the outcomes of accidental collocations of atoms, that no fire, no heroism, no intensity of thought and feeling, can preserve individual life beyond the grave; that all the labors of the ages, all the devotion, all the inspiration, all the noonday brightness of human genius, are destined to extinction in the vast death of the solar system, and that the whole temple of Man's achievement must inevitably be buried beneath dispute, are yet so nearly certain, that no philosophy which rejects them can hope to stand. Only within the scaffolding of these truths, only on the firm foundation of unyielding despair, can the soul's habitation henceforth be safely built.[11]

For Russell, as well as for numerous other thoughtful nonbelievers, the prima facie nonexistence of God is "upon reflection" taken as a correct conclusion.

OUR TASK

We indicated earlier that the present study attempts to think critically about the issues related to the theistic concept of God. We acknowledge that these issues are not only very complex but are matters on which reasonable, responsible persons can legitimately disagree. In a universe that can be honestly and sensitively characterized by "mystery" or "divine hiddenness" or perhaps even "divine absence," we should not expect unanimity of opinion on the existence and nature of Ultimate Reality. There is a long tradition of theistic thinkers who believe that they can make good rational sense of the existence of God, faith, prayer, miracle, and other theistic concepts. By contrast, down through the centuries there has been a notable array of people with very fine intellects who believe that such concepts must be rejected.

Therefore, as we embark on our journey, we are committed to a posture that respects serious and responsible thought, regardless of the outcome. That does not mean, however, that we will adopt a purely neutral stance as we sort through the arguments and counterarguments. We believe that respect for the rational process also demands that we indicate at points where we stand on key issues. This is not to succumb to blind bias, which lies at the opposite extreme from pure neutrality, but it is to attempt to model a kind of interested objectivity. The form of objectivity that we seek strives to be fair to various positions and to acknowledge when appropriate which one seems most reasonable among alternatives.

The present venture, then, is open to all who are seeking understanding and who are committed to subjecting all beliefs, religious or otherwise, to rigorous philosophical examination. The results of this process are hard to predict. For some, it will lead to the modification of certain views. For others, it could lead to either the acceptance or rejection of theism. For still others, it may lead to deeper commitment.

STUDY QUESTIONS

1. Formulate your own definition of "religion." Test your definition to see if it applies to various cultural phenomena normally labeled religious.

2. Try to define "philosophy." What are some of its main concerns?

3. What is the philosophy of religion? Explain how approaches to philosophy of religion are influenced by different approaches to philosophy itself.

4. Discuss the importance of considering matters of consistency, coherence, plausibility, truth, and meaning with respect to religious beliefs.

5. What is meant by the "hiddenness of God"? Evaluate the significance of this concept.

6. Is it possible to remain completely neutral in the study of religion? Is it desirable to remain neutral? What kind of objectivity should we seek in the rational investigation of religion (or any important subject)?

7. At the outset, what issues in religion would you identify for philosophical analysis and discussion? Prior to reading this book, have you ever read any material that subjects religious belief to rational scrutiny?

8. Try to state in your own words the basic position of classical theism. Discuss its relationship to some specific concrete religions.

9. Show how some major issues in philosophy of religion arise on the basis of certain events and experiences in ordinary life.

10. Explore the objection that philosophical interest in religion misses the essence of religious faith. Do you think that religion or religious faith is subject in any way to rational investigation?

NOTES

1. For an excellent study of the religions of the world, past and present, see Ninian Smart, *The Religious Experience*, 4th ed. (New York: Scribners, 1991).

2. See, for example, the *American Atheist* magazine. See also Robert G. Ingersoll, *Atheist Truth vs. Religion's Ghosts* (1900; reprint, Austin, Texas: American Atheist Press, 1980).

3. See the listing for this organization in the *Directory of American Philosophers*, 1996–1997, ed. Archie Bahm, 18th ed. (Bowling Green, Ohio: Philosophy Documentation Center, 1996), p. 186. For the general position of humanistic atheism, also see P. Kurtz, ed., *Humanist Manifestos I and II* (Buffalo, N.Y.: Prometheus Books, 1973).

4. The preceding definitions are cited in William P. Alston, "Religion," in the *Encyclopedia of Philosophy*, (New York: Macmillan, 1967), 7: 140.

5. There are also other disciplines that are thought to have a supportive function for theistic belief. *Dogmatic (confessional, sacred) theology* begins from the assumption that a certain religious tradition is authoritative. Dogmatic theologians seek to provide ways of elucidating and systematizing accepted doctrines but do not challenge their acceptance. Philosophy of religion is also distinct from *apologetics*, which seeks to secure a given religious position. Apologetic projects may be either negative or

positive: *negative apologetics* seeks to show that certain criticisms of a specific religious position fail, whereas *positive apologetics* seeks to show that the position is reasonable or credible. Apologetics often has a very practical side, lending itself readily to the activity of persuasion. While philosophical awareness and logical skill are relevant to the enterprises of dogmatic theology and apologetics, the latter activities are not philosophical in the fundamental sense of beginning from a position of relative openness to alternative views and willingness to critique their own most basic commitments.

6. One of the classic sources in the analytic tradition, which denies substantive content to philosophy, is A. J. Ayer, *Language, Truth, and Logic* (New York: Dover, 1936). A classic source that promotes philosophy as the enterprise of elucidation and not of advancing truth-claims is Ludwig Wittgenstein, *Philosophical Investigations,* trans. G.E.M. Anscombe (New York: Macmillan, 1953).

7. William Rowe, "Evil and the Theistic Hypothesis: A Response to Wykstra," *International Journal for Philosophy of Religion* 16 (1984): 95.

8. This point is expanded in H. H. Price, "Belief 'In' and Belief 'That,'" *Religious Studies* 1, no. 1 (1965): 1–27.

9. St. Anselm, *Proslogium,* in *St. Anselm, Basic Writings,* trans. S. M. Deane, 2nd ed. pt. 1, (LaSalle, Ill.: Open Court, 1974), pp. 3–4.

10. Ibid.

11. Bertrand Russell, *Why I Am Not a Christian and Other Essays on Religion and Related Subjects,* ed. Paul Edwards (New York: Simon and Schuster, 1957), p. 107.

SUGGESTED READING

Alston, William. "Problems of Philosophy of Religion." In the *Encyclopedia of Philosophy.* Vol. 6. New York: Macmillan, 1967.

Burtt, Edwin A. *Types of Religious Philosophy.* Rev. ed. New York: Harper and Brothers, 1951.

Hick, John. *An Interpretation of Religion: Human Responses to the Transcendent.* New Haven, Conn.: Yale University Press, 1989.

Lewis, H. D. "History of Philosophy of Religion." In the *Encyclopedia of Philosophy.* Vol. 6. New York: Macmillan, 1967.

Livingston, James C. *Anatomy of the Sacred: An Introduction to Religion.* New York: Macmillan, 1989.

Morris, Thomas. *Making Sense of It All.* Grand Rapids, Mich.: William B. Eerdmans, 1992.

Quinn, Philip, and Charles Taliaferro, eds. *A Companion to Philosophy of Religion.* Oxford: Blackwell, 1997.

Schellenberg, J. L. *Divine Hiddenness and Human Reason.* Ithaca, N.Y.: Cornell University Press, 1993.

CHAPTER 2   RELIGIOUS EXPERIENCE: WHAT DOES IT MEAN TO ENCOUNTER THE DIVINE?

In many religions, believers not only claim to experience some Ultimate Reality but feel that such experiences give significant meaning and direction to their lives. In the eighth century B.C., the Hebrew prophet Isaiah recorded his experience of God.

> In the year that King Uzziah died, I saw the Lord seated on a throne, high and exalted, and the train of his robe filled the temple. Above him were seraphs, each with six wings, . . . calling to one another: "Holy, holy, holy is the Lord Almighty; the whole earth is full of his glory." . . . "Woe to me!" I cried. "I am ruined! For I am a man of unclean lips, and I live among a people of unclean lips, and my eyes have seen the King, the Lord Almighty."[1]

One of the more famous experiences of the divine is found in the writings of the North African Christian theologian, Augustine (354–430).

> I was asking myself these questions ["Why not make an end of my ugly sins at this moment?"], weeping all the while with the most bitter sorrow in my heart, when all at once I heard the sing-song voice of a child in a nearby house. Whether it was the voice of a boy or a girl I cannot say, but again and again it repeated the refrain "Take it and read, take it and read." At this I looked up, thinking hard whether there was any kind of game in which children used to chant words like these, but I could not remember ever hearing them before. I stemmed my flood of tears and stood up, telling myself that this could only be a divine command to open my book of Scripture and read the first passage on which my eyes should fall.[2]

Some experiences make less or even no appeal to sensory data but nonetheless provide focus to human life. Consider the following Hindu description of an awareness of the universal Self.

Not by sight is It grasped, not even by speech,
Not by any other sense-organs, austerity, or work.
By the peace of knowledge, one's nature purified—
In that way, however, by meditating, one does behold
Him who is without parts.[3]

How are we to understand religious experiences? In this chapter we will explore what a religious experience is, whether we can use religious experience to justify our religious beliefs, and whether described religious experiences have a common core.

TYPES OF RELIGIOUS EXPERIENCE

An *experience* is an event that one lives through (either as a participant or an observer) and of which one is conscious or aware. For example, to experience a World Series baseball game is to play in it, attend and watch the game, or (in an extended or mediated sense) see it on television or hear it on the radio. *Religious experiences* differ, in part, from ordinary experiences in that what is experienced is taken by the person to be some supernatural being or presence (God either in himself or as manifest in some action), a being related to God (a manifestation of God or personage such as the Virgin Mary), or some indescribable Ultimate Reality (such as the nondual Absolute [Brahman] or Nirvana).

It is important to distinguish religious experience from gaining a religious insight.[4] Religious experience, as we understand it, requires that persons have or believe that they have an encounter with some transcendent reality, whereas those having a religious insight need not believe that they are encountering some transcendent reality. For example, one might get an insight into the way sin proliferates and conquers us by noting, when digging in one's garden, that if the roots of a nearby tree are not continually removed from the soil, they gradually spread and choke out the vegetable plants. Although some concept of God is necessary to understand the concept of sin (which is an offense against God), the gardener need not believe that he or she has experienced God to achieve this religious insight. Some event in our ordinary experience might suffice to trigger an insight into our spiritual condition or the relation of God to the world without our ever experiencing or believing that we have experienced God in that event. Of course, a religious experience can be the source of religious insight. Both Isaiah and Augustine claimed that their experiences of God gave them understanding both about the nature of God and about their own sinfulness. But one can have religious insight without either experiencing God or believing that God exists, whereas to have a religious experience requires that God or some transcendent reality either be the object of the experience or taken to be such.

We should note, however, that religious traditions often treat both insight and religious experience as important, if not necessary, to achieve the ultimate goal of liberation or salvation. For example, Buddhists hold that since our human predicament or bondage (suffering or *dukkha*) is caused by ignorance, insight into the nature of reality is necessary to liberate us. By seeing that all, including ourselves, is insubstantial, impermanent, changing, one is freed from the ignorance that takes things as objects worthy of desire. Cravings and desires (*tanha*) can be eliminated ultimately only by terminating their root causes, which—according to the twelve-spoked wheel of dependent origination—include sensation, consciousness, and ultimately ignorance. Thus, religious experience can be directed properly to the cessation of sensation and conceptualization, to realizing mindlessness, wherein no cognitive activity, including insight, remains.

> By the transcendence of all conceptualizations of form, by the disappearance of conceptualizations based upon sense-data, by paying no attention to conceptualization of manifoldness, having attained to the sphere of infinite space [the practitioner] remains therein, thinking "space is unending." By entirely transcending the sphere of infinite space [infinite consciousness; of nothing at all; of neither conceptualization nor nonconceptualization], having attained to the sphere of infinite consciousness [nothing at all; neither conceptualization nor nonconceptualization; the cessation of sensation and conceptualization] [the practitioner] remains therein.[5]

We claim to experience God or Ultimate Reality in a variety of ways. Richard Swinburne (b. 1934) suggests five types of religious experience, classified *from the perspective of the experiencer.*[6] These types he considers mutually exclusive and totally exhaustive of the possibilities.

1. *Experience of God or Ultimate Reality mediated through a common, public, sensory object.* For example, one might claim to see God in an icon, sunset, or ocean. Icons or sunsets are not God, but that in and through which God or the transcendent is encountered.

> Crossing a bare common, in snow puddles, at twilight, under a clouded sky, . . . I have enjoyed a perfect exhilaration. . . . In the wood, is perpetual youth. Within these plantations of God, a decorum and sanctity reign, a perennial festival is dressed. . . . Standing on bare ground,—my head bathed by the blithe air, and uplifted into infinite space—all mean egotism vanishes. I become a transparent eyeball; I am nothing; I see all; the currents of the Universal Being circulate through me; I am part or particle of God.[7]

2. *Experience of God or Ultimate Reality mediated through an unusual, public, sensory object.* For example, one might claim to experience the transcendent through an appearance of the Virgin at Lourdes, a figure seen in a cloud formation, or in a bush that burned but was not consumed.

> Now Moses was keeping the flock of his father-in-law, Jethro. . . . And the angel of the Lord appeared to him in a flame of fire out of the midst of a bush; and he looked, and lo, the bush was burning, yet it was not consumed. . . . God called to him out of the bush, "Moses, Moses!"[8]

The appearance would be public, in that many people present could (in theory) observe what is happening and experience God through it. However, the appearance is unusual, for few assert they have seen the Virgin at Lourdes, and only Moses claimed to witness a burning bush that was not consumed.

One might also claim to experience something unusual, which someone else in the same situation might take to be common or ordinary. Swinburne provides the example, described in the New Testament, of the encounter by two persons of a man walking to Emmaus. The two eventually understood this companion to be the risen Jesus Christ, whereas another "might have had the same visual sensations . . . and yet not had the religious experience."[9]

3. *Experience of God or Ultimate Reality mediated through private sensations that can be described in normal sensory language.* For example, a person might claim to experience God in a dream or vision, as did Peter who, in a trance, saw a cloth filled with unkosher animals lowered from heaven.[10] Visions, dreams, utterances, and the like, despite being described in sensory language, are available only to one person.

> I was sitting in a certain chapel, and while I was taking pleasure in the delight of some prayer or meditation, I suddenly felt within me an unwonted and pleasant fire. When I had for long doubted whence it came, I learned by experience that it came from the Creator and not from creature, since I found it ever more pleasing and full of heat.[11]

4. *Experience of God or Ultimate Reality mediated through private sensations that cannot be described in normal sensory language.* Here one feels or claims to experience something, but it cannot be spoken about; it is ineffable. For example, St. Teresa of Avila (1512–1582) relates the following experience.

> I was at prayer on a festival of the glorious Saint Peter when I saw Christ at my side—or, to put it better, I was conscious of Him, for neither with the eyes of the body nor with those of the soul did I see anything. I thought He was quite close to me and I saw that it was He Who, as I thought, was speaking to me. . . . All the time Jesus Christ seemed to be beside me, but as this was not an imaginary vision, I could not discern in what form: what I felt very clearly was that all the time He was at my right hand, and a witness of everything that I was doing.[12]

5. *Experience of God or Ultimate Reality that is not mediated by any sensations.* The person claims to be intuitively and immediately aware of God or the One. A Western mystic, Nicholas of Cusa (1401–1464), writes,

> I behold Thee, O Lord my God, in a kind of mental trance, for if sight be not sated with seeing, nor the ear with hearing, then much less is the intellect with understanding.[13]

This type is most richly illustrated by the higher meditational states of Hinduism and Buddhism.

> Of one who has entered the first trance the voice has ceased; of one who has entered the second trance reasoning and reflection have ceased; of one who has entered the third trance joy has ceased; of one who has entered the fourth trance the inspirations and expirations have ceased; of one who has entered the realm of the infinity of space the perception of form has ceased;

of one who has entered the realm of the infinity of consciousness the perception of the realm of the infinity of space has ceased; of one who has entered the realm of nothingness the perception of the realm of the infinity of consciousness has ceased.[14]

In reality perhaps few religious experiences fall cleanly into one given type, for experiences contain richly diverse elements. For example, Nicholas commends beginning meditational experience with an icon, though the ultimate experience of God is nonsensory.

> But I perceive, not with my fleshly eyes, which look on this icon of Thee, but with the eyes of my mind and understanding, the invisible truth of Thy face, which therein is signified, under a shadow and limitation. Thy true face is freed from any limitation, it hath neither quantity nor quality, nor is it of time or place, for it is the Absolute Form, the Face of faces.[15]

Hence, it is less important to try to categorize each experience than to understand more generally the diversity of ways persons understand their religious experiences. Mystical experience (generally categorized as types 4 or 5) provides one kind of religious experience but does not exhaust all possibilities.

Given this typology of how people *understand* their religious experiences, the question remains concerning what people *really* experience. Do they *really* experience God, or do they only interpret certain experiences or feelings religiously? Philosophers have suggested three different perspectives on the structure of religious experience.

RELIGIOUS EXPERIENCE AS FEELING

In his influential nineteenth-century writings, Friedrich Schleiermacher (1768–1834) contended that religious experience is not an intellectual or cognitive experience, but "a feeling of absolute or total dependence upon a source or power that is distinct from the world."[16] It is self-authenticating, intuitive, and unmediated by concepts, ideas, beliefs, or practices. Since it is a feeling preceding conceptual distinctions, we cannot describe it. It is an affective rather than a cognitive experience.

This view influenced many, including Rudolf Otto (1869–1937). He agrees that some aspects of God can be grasped by reason. By analogy we can ascribe to God attributes such as spirit, purpose, good will, omnipotence, and selfhood. "All these attributes constitute clear and definite *concepts:* they can be grasped by the intellect; they can be analyzed by thought; they even admit of definition."[17] Yet in respect to God's deeper nature—his holiness— God cannot be rationally known; God is ineffable. We must apprehend God's holiness by something that goes beyond the rational, namely, by feeling.

Otto understands religious experience as a feeling, or better, a complex of feelings. This feeling comes in many forms.

> The feeling of [the *mysterium tremendum*] may at times come sweeping like a gentle tide, pervading the mind with a tranquil mood of deepest worship. It

may pass over into a more set and lasting attitude of the soul, continuing, as it were, thrillingly vibrant and resonant. . . . It may burst in sudden eruption up from the depths of the soul with spasms and convulsions, or lead to the strangest excitements, to intoxicated frenzy, to transport, and to ecstasy.[18]

Otto calls this the experience of the numinous and finds it manifested in three specific types of feeling. We experience the feeling of dependence, that we are mere creatures, "submerged and overwhelmed by [our] own nothingness in contrast to that which is supreme above all creatures."[19] We can also experience the feeling of religious dread (awe) and of being over-powered before the *mysterium tremendum*. We shudder and quake at the "sight" of God. And finally, we have a feeling of longing for the transcendent being that fascinates us. Built into us is a restlessness, a longing for God.[20]

William James (1842–1910) contends that since "feeling is the deeper source of religion,"[21] philosophical and theological reflection are secondary products, outgrowths of religious experience. Without religious experience, we would have no theologies or religious philosophies. "The attempt to demonstrate by purely intellectual processes the truth of the deliverances of direct religious experience is absolutely hopeless."[22]

James correctly contends that there would be no philosophy of religion if people had no religious experience. At the same time, for religious experience to generate the myths, dogmas, and theologies that are the stuff of philosophy of religion, religious experience cannot be "private and dumb, and unable to give an account of itself."[23] That is, it is hard to see how one can generate the cognitive religious truth-claims found in theology and religious philosophy out of noncognitive feelings. If both the experienced and the experience are ineffable, and if the latter is so fundamental that it precedes cognitive distinctions, what religious truths can follow upon it? Even attempts to describe the experience by analogy presuppose that the event can be cognitively understood, so that one can appreciate which analogies are appropriate to the experience and which are not.

A second objection is that defenders of this view have misunderstood the nature of feelings and emotions. Emotions

> are not more fundamental than beliefs or behavior. Indeed, emotions, like beliefs and acts, depend on concepts. Emotions are in part constituted by concepts and judgments. To say that a concept is constitutive of an emotion is to say that the emotion cannot be specified without reference to that concept. . . . In order to specify an emotion it is necessary to specify the quality of the feeling, the object of the emotion and the rational grounds by which the subject justifies the emotion. We can now see that among those grounds are the subject's beliefs about the causes of his state.[24]

But if concepts in part constitute emotions, religious experience cannot be completely divorced from the cognitive.

At the same time, however, one might contend that both objections place too much emphasis on the cognitive aspect of religious experience. In some traditions religious experience involves a gradual weaning of the individual from cognitive consciousness to a state which, at best, can be described as pure consciousness or pure emptiness (*shunya*). In Buddhism, for example, the goal is to transcend all conceptualization in order to attain to the sphere of pure consciousness, and from there to the state of emptiness. Experiencers do not seek knowledge, but to free themselves from the cravings and desires of being a self. Once one realizes that there is no self, one can remove the cravings and desires that flow from desire for self and consequently remove the suffering that pervades our existence. Religious experience, at this stage, is fundamentally directed toward liberation, not cognitive understanding. Indeed, by overcoming the subject-object distinction, cognitive understanding is rendered impossible. Religious experience in this tradition is not feeling, but it is ultimately noncognitive.

RELIGIOUS EXPERIENCE AS PERCEPTUAL EXPERIENCE

A second view is that religious experiences are a type of perception. William Alston (b. 1921), for example, holds that many experiences of God have the same structure as perception.[25] We can discern three elements in our ordinary, sensory perception (for example, seeing a cat): the perceiver (the person who sees the cat), the perceived object (the cat that is seen), and the phenomenon (the appearance of the cat). Similarly, there are three elements in many experiences of God: the religious experiencer, what is experienced (God), and the appearance or presentation of God to the perceiver. Philosophers debate precisely how perception is to be analyzed. In particular, they raise questions concerning the status of the phenomenon. But philosophers generally agree that in perception objects present themselves to us in ways that enable us to know them. The cat looks like a cat; it is not taken as a cat. Similarly, in experiences of God, God presents himself in ways that enable us to know God and his actions. God appears as God; God is not taken as God.

Some might think it strange to understand religious experience or experiences of God as a kind of perception. It appears that ordinary perceptual or sense experience differs in important ways from experiences of God. Sense perception is a common experience, "insistently and unavoidably present in all our waking hours," whereas religious experience is unusual, perhaps even rare; sense perception is "vivid and richly detailed, bursting with information" about the world, whereas the experience of God is "dim, meager, and obscure," yielding apparently little information about God; all humans have the capacity for sense perception, but many seem not to have the capacity for religious experience.[26] These differences, however, do not show that the experience of God has a structure unlike perception. For one thing, neither the frequency of an experience nor the amount of information it yields tells us anything about its structure. Furthermore, some people have limited sensory and hence perceptual capacities because they cannot see or hear, but this fact casts no doubt on the claim that seeing and hearing are forms of perception. Similarly, that many do not have religious experiences is irrelevant to the claim that the experience of God is structured like perceptual experience.

Some philosophers, however, point to one significant difference that allegedly shows that the experience of God is not a type of perception. It concerns the nature of the perceptual appearance or presentation (the phenomenon). Ordinary perception is sensory; the perceived object presents itself as bearing certain sensory qualities. For example, the desk in front of me appears brown, hard, rectangular, and wooden. But those who have experiences of God sometimes report that what they perceive, namely, God, bears perceptual qualities that are *not* sensory. The qualities they experience in God are divine goodness, power, love, sovereignty, and giving strength.[27] The problem is this: If the characteristics of what is allegedly perceived (the phenomenon) in the experience of God differ so much from the sensory phenomena of ordinary perceptual experience, is not the structure of the experience of God so different that it is a mistake to understand the experience of God perceptually?

Alston admits that the perceived qualities of experiences of God—properties such as power, beauty, and goodness—are not sensory. For example, they may concern God's dispositions or the attitudes behind his actions. However, for Alston that does not mean that these properties cannot be the content of a perception. He distinguishes between phenomenal qualities (the way something looks to me at the moment) and objective qualities (the way we expect an object to look under normal circumstances). When we describe an experienced object, he claims, frequently our description refers to its objective qualities given under normal circumstances and not its phenomenal or immediately perceived qualities. If you asked me to describe my house, I would not list the particular sense data that I am now receiving—that my house appears to me dark brown and beige, darker in the shadows, trapezoidal beneath the roof, and so on. If we give descriptions of perceived objects in terms of how they look to us at the moment, the description would be both indefinitely large (in order to reflect the large quantity of received sensory data) and so unique (since I perceive objects under indefinitely many lighting conditions and from indefinitely many angles) that we could not construct usable concepts from such diverse patterns. Rather, we often speak about the thing's objective or dispositional qualities by using assumed or unstated *comparative* concepts.[28] That is, when I describe an object, I state how it would look under *normal* conditions. For example, to the question "What is the color of your house?" I would respond that it is beige, though at night it would not appear beige.

To put this point more simply, just ask yourself about the shape of your classroom door. More than likely you will say that the door is rectangular. Yet rectangularity is not its phenomenal property at the moment; rather, from where you are sitting it probably appears trapezoidal. But you usually give its objective property (rectangularity) when asked what the door you see is like.

In a similar fashion, God's qualities of power, goodness, and love are reported using not phenomenal or sensory language, but comparative concepts. They characterize how God could be expected to appear under certain "normal" conditions (his objective rather than phenomenal properties). If we describe our experience of God using comparative concepts, the way we report our experience of God distinctly parallels how we report objects of sense perception. Just as we frequently report our perception of things not by talking about how the things appear at the moment but rather by using comparative concepts referring to how they would look in normal circumstances (their objective properties), so our reports of our experience of God appeal to comparative rather than phenomenal concepts.

An objection might be raised to the effect that we know how houses, cars, and trees would appear in normal circumstances because we could, if pressed, provide the relevant phenomenal description. The objective properties are at some time phenomenal. But how do experiencers of God know how God would appear under normal circumstances, since they cannot provide a phenomenal description of God?

Alston suggests that we cannot anticipate ahead of time, apart from experience, what something would look like. Without experience we would not know that "trees are recognizable by their look, while physicists are not."[29] What prepares us for our experience of God is our experience with humans who are more or less good; this experience gives us some idea of what it is like to experience God showing his goodness. But does knowing how good people act give us an expectation of how we should experience *God's* goodness? Here again we would be moving from the one point of comparison that contains sensory information (how good people act) to a point that lacks it (how God acts). It would seem that we should have some idea of the phenomenal conditions under which we could experience God in order to anticipate how God would manifest his goodness under normal circumstances.

Alston replies that one who experiences God need not determine the phenomenal conditions, for it is not uncommon for persons to have perceptual experiences of things without being able to specify what they would look like under normal circumstances. But having some notion of how God would be perceived under normal circumstances is essential for suggesting that experience of God parallels ordinary perceptual experience, since in ordinary perceptual cases we can specify what objects normally look like. In short, the absence of phenomenal concepts in experiences of God may raise questions about whether experience of God is a kind of perceptual experience.

The question concerning how God would appear gives rise to a second problem. Whereas human sensory perception is generally consistent, so that we can check the accuracy of any particular perception by appealing to other perceptual experiences, religious experiences are extremely diverse. Thus, the accuracy of any particular experience cannot be so easily confirmed. Religious experiences are conditioned by distinctive cultural and religious perspectives, so that what people in various religions experience widely differs.

The Ultimate Reality that a Hindu experiences is very different from the personal God a Christian experiences. But we cannot easily confirm which is correct independent of the distinctive religious systems. This, of course, does not show necessarily that religious experience is not perceptual; it may only mean that religious experiences are more open to individual interpretation. We will return to the problem of diverse experiences later in this chapter.[30]

RELIGIOUS EXPERIENCE AS INTERPRETATION BASED ON RELIGIOUS BELIEFS

Defenders of a third view reject the thesis that religious experiences are perceptual experiences. According to Wayne Proudfoot (b. 1939), to call an experience a perception entails a claim not only about the person's awareness of the event (something must have been presented to or appeared to the perceiver), but also about the cause of the experience. For our experiences really to be perceptions, the perceived object must be there and make a causal contribution (of the right sort) to our experience of it. For example, to say that a person sees a cat is to grant both that a cat exists and that the cat causally contributes to the person's seeing it. If the cat neither exists nor in some way causes the perception, then we do not say that the person perceives or sees the cat but that the person hallucinates a cat or mistakes something else for a cat.

If religious experience is a kind of perceptual experience, the same conditions must hold true for it. What is perceived must exist and make a causal contribution of the right sort to our experience of it. However, because we want to be liberal in allowing that people have religious experiences, understanding religious experiences as perceptions would commit us to the belief that the objects of or alleged causes of those religious experiences really exist. That is, we could not admit that people had religious experiences without admitting that what they perceived existed. To avoid this unsatisfactory result, Proudfoot holds that our characterization of religious experience must be broad enough to permit someone to admit that people have religious experiences that they describe in terms of experiencing something divine, without having to grant that anyone actually experienced a divine object.

For Proudfoot, a religious experience is an experience that the person who has it *takes* or interprets as religious. The experience is not religious because it has religious content (which is the case in the perceptual view) but because of the belief structure that a person brings to whatever experience he or she has, because it is based in the person's religious belief.

Proudfoot distinguishes the *description* of the experience from the *explanation* of it. In describing the experience, the perspective of the subject dominates. Religious experiences cannot be described apart from the experiencer's *belief* system, including the belief that the best way to explain the experience is that the experienced object exists and caused the experience. In describing religious experience, to reduce it to any other kind of experience is to misidentify the experience. As such, scientific accounts that dispense with the supernatural element are irrelevant to *describing* the experience, for whereas science attempts to explain the experience in terms of its natural causes, those who have the religious experience require that a supernatural explanation be part of its description. In this purely descriptive sense, Proudfoot echoes Alston's perceptual account of religious experience.

However, for Proudfoot, the fact that experiencers describe the experience in terms of the supernatural does *not* mean that this is how the experience is to be *explained* or understood. Here is where Proudfoot departs from Alston's perceptual account. In the case of Augustine, it might just have happened that, apart from any divine activity or intention, a child nearby was playing a game, of which the sing-song—"take it and read"—was a part. What makes the experience a religious experience is that Augustine understood these words in light of his religious beliefs that God exists and can communicate through spoken and written words. In other words, an experience is a genuine *religious* experience for a person because it is a product of his or her belief system, regardless of the conditions that hold in reality. All that is required is that experiencers describe or interpret their experience in terms of categories and beliefs about the supernatural. Hence, religious experience is constituted by concepts and beliefs and shaped by language. It is not an objective report about the cause of an experience but a theoretical commitment to a certain set of religious beliefs and practices. This means that descriptions of religious experiences fit no single pattern; different belief structures give rise to different accounts of religious experiences.

But can a person experience God? If each person's concepts and beliefs shape his or her religious experience, how can we determine which account—the natural or the supernatural—provides the best explanation? Proudfoot is not interested in this sort of question. External causes, like the supernatural, are irrelevant. Since "the concepts and beliefs under which the subject identifies his or her experience determine whether or not it is a religious experience, we need to explain why the subject employs those particular concepts and beliefs. We must explain why the subject was confronted with this particular set of alternative ways of understanding his experience and why he employed the one he did. What we want is a historical or cultural explanation."[31]

Proudfoot's account clearly differs from the perceptual account. In the perceptual account, we want to know what caused or brought about the religious experience. But Proudfoot is interested in why the person invokes this particular belief system to describe the experience. What is there about the person's upbringing, acquaintances and experiences, and present life that bring him or her to claim that this experience cannot be explained naturally? In effect, we want to know a person's psychological history. Whereas the perceptual account may help us understand something about the divine, Proudfoot wants to help us understand religious people and how they come to their beliefs. In the perceptual account, there may be grounds to evaluate the veracity of claims of religious experience; for Proudfoot veracity is not an issue.

CAN RELIGIOUS EXPERIENCE JUSTIFY RELIGIOUS BELIEF?

We cannot doubt that people have religious experiences. But what interests the philosopher of religion most is whether these experiences can provide the basis or grounds for making knowledge claims about reality. Some theists contend that religious experience plays a valuable role in justifying religious beliefs. As one bumper sticker puts it, "God is not dead—I talked with him this morning!" But whether the alleged experience of God can be used to ground our beliefs depends, in part, upon how one characterizes religious experience.

Suppose that religious experiences are *merely* feelings. Schleiermacher thought that not only could he generate the structure of religious belief by an appeal to these feelings, he also could justify that structure by the same feelings. But can feelings justify cognitive belief? The difficulty arises from the claim that both God (as transcendent) and our experience of God (as feeling, unstructured by concepts and beliefs) are ineffable. But for the experience to have cognitive significance, it must be mediated by rational beliefs and concepts.

Otto faces a similar problem. He grants that the conceptual descriptions of the numinous are not "genuine intellectual 'concepts,' but only a sort of illustrative substitute for a concept."[32] He calls the concepts used to describe the experience "ideograms," imperfect analogies drawn from our ordinary experience, yet he designates certain concepts as appropriate for marking the numinous. To distinguish what appropriately designates it from what does not implies that there is some conceptual system by which the numinous can be grasped. The experience of the numinous, therefore, must have some intellectual content.

In short, those who describe religious experience as mere feeling encounter a dilemma. If the religious experience is ineffable, then it cannot be used to ground religious beliefs, for it provides no content for the grounding. If, however, the experience has conceptual content, then it cannot be independent of conceptual expression and immune from criticism. Those who make religious experience into mere feeling cannot have it both ineffable and the foundation for religious conceptual systems.

Suppose that one characterizes religious experience as Proudfoot does, namely, as experience that is interpreted by the experiencer as caused by something supernatural but whose explanation may be quite different. Then the very designation of an experience as religious requires that experiencers have certain beliefs about what they take to be its cause. The invocation of beliefs about the identification of the cause is part of the description of the experience. This means that religious experience is not a phenomenon that can be used to establish or ground religious beliefs. Since the religious experience is constituted by the beliefs, it cannot be used to justify those beliefs, for example, about the existence of a supernatural cause. To do so would be to argue in a circle: the experience is religious because someone has religious beliefs that are included in the description of the event as being caused by

God, and that person has good reason to believe that his or her beliefs about God are true because of this religious experience.

The consequence of this view is that religious experience is meaningful insofar as it finds its place within a particular religious worldview or belief system. The experience is religious and makes sense because a person already has a set of beliefs that includes the supernatural. The existence of the supernatural is not properly inferred from the experience but is part of its very description and, hence, a presupposition of the experience.

The critical question here concerns what justifies our belief in something we take to be an object of experience. It appears that justification in terms of our experience needs to be understood in terms of what best explains this and similar experiences. If the best explanation for a perceptual experience of a cat is in terms of a cat, then that experience might provide evidence for the existence of a cat. Similarly, if the best explanation for a religious experience is in terms of a supernatural cause, then that experience might provide evidence for God's existence. Others may offer a completely naturalistic explanation of the experience. However, the more experiences that can be explained cogently by appeal to the supernatural, and the more these experiences fit in with a coherent belief structure, the more one is justified in believing that this explanation of the experience is correct. This reply suggests that some religious experiences can be reasonably considered authentic perceptual experiences, and this brings one closer to Alston's position.

Those who hold that religious experience is a perceptual experience argue that religious experience can be used to justify religious beliefs in the same way that we commonly use our perceptions to justify our beliefs about the world. For example, we are justified in believing that there is a robin on the lawn when we see a robin on the lawn and have no reason to think that the perceptual conditions are unusual or our perceptual apparatus is not working properly. Similarly, religious persons are justified in believing that God exists, loves them, or answers their prayers on the basis of their religious experiences.

THE PRINCIPLE OF CREDULITY

But could we be mistaken about our religious experiences, and, if so, how can they provide evidence to justify religious belief? Of course we can be mistaken, but this is neither contrary to our normal perceptual experience nor sufficient to deny that religious experience justifies religious belief. When people say they see a robin outside, we ordinarily grant that there is a robin that they see. Swinburne calls this the *Principle of Credulity:* When it seems to someone that something is the case, it probably is so, unless special considerations mitigate the claim.[33] The way things appear to be provides good grounds for believing that this is the way things are. We are justified in holding the belief until someone introduces contrary considerations that would cast doubt upon either this particular perception or the accurate functioning of our perceptual apparatus. We could be mistaken about the experience, but the Principle places the burden of proof on those who would claim that the experience was not genuine.

Similarly, if some religious experience or experience of God is a perceptual experience, we can apply the Principle of Credulity to that religious experience as well. In the absence of special considerations, the religious experience should be taken by experiencers as providing good grounds for the belief that God exists or has certain experienced properties. As in ordinary perceptual experience, experiencers could be mistaken in their belief about what they experienced, but persons are entitled to their belief about God until they are given good reason to think that the belief conflicts with other justified beliefs (for example, about God's nonexistence) or that their perceptual apparatus is defective. The religious experience provides a *prima facie* justification for beliefs about God; the claim must be judged on its own merits.

But can we accept the Principle of Credulity? Do not special considerations cast doubt on the applicability of the Principle to religious experience? Michael Martin (b. 1932) objects that many people have tried to have religious experiences but have failed. Hence, he posits a negative Principle of Credulity: If it seems to someone that something is absent, then probably it is absent. For him, the perceptual experience of God's absence is as telling as the perceptual experience of God's presence is for others.[34]

A second criticism, developed by C. B. Martin (b. 1924), is that in order to be justified in making knowledge claims based on perceptual experience, the experience must be checkable or verifiable. When someone claims to see a robin on the lawn, that person is justified in holding the belief that a robin actually is on the lawn only if that person or others can check out the perception by other perceptions. But the special consideration involved in religious experience is that it lacks verifiability. "If the believer says, 'I had a direct experience of God at 6:37 p.m., May 6, 1939,' this is not an empirical statement in the way other [perceptual experience] statements are."[35] Martin sees this as a product of the religious believer's attributing religious experience either to a kind of sixth sense that differs from the other five but borrows language from them in a way that can only be metaphorical or to a unique way of knowing that only those who have it can understand (just as only sighted people can understand what it is for something to be blue). In both cases, Martin claims, the experience cannot be checked, so that the believer is not justified in making knowledge claims on the basis of that experience.

Martin notes that those who have religious experiences often claim indubitability for their experience. But claims of perceptual indubitability are more like claims about appearances (what appears to the perceiver to be the case) than about something perceived. That someone has an appearance of a blue ball is indubitable. But from the fact that a person has an appearance of a blue ball he cannot conclude that there really is a blue ball that he sees. Hence, believers are caught in a dilemma. Either claims based on religious experience are indubitable and hence are only about what appears (appearance claims) and not about any object of the experience (like God), or they are about God but unverifiable. In neither case can knowledge claims about God's existence and character follow from religious experiences.

William Wainwright (b. 1935) replies that it is true that some "disanalogies" hold between some religious experience and other perceptual experiences. For one, religious believers generally disregard differing claims. If others disagree with their claims, then perhaps those critics did not use proper meditative techniques. Believers may change their mind about their experience when faced with opposing claims, but they need not do so. For another, the religious experiencer does not make verifiably predictive claims (at least verifiable in this life). Wainwright argues, however, that these disanalogies occur because of the nature of the object perceived. Since God differs from the sense objects we normally perceive, one cannot require that everyone perceive God in the same way or that the experience of God yield verifiable predictions. Religious experience is more analogous to perceiving a person than to perceiving inanimate sensory objects; one person might perceive another person as dispassionate and distant, a second might perceive that same person as warm and friendly.[36]

Beyond this, Wainwright contends that there are tests for checking religious experience claims. One kind of test involves evidence to show that God exists, such as provided by the arguments for God's existence. Alston similarly holds that there may well be independent reasons, supplied by natural theology and historical claims within religions, for epistemically preferring one form of religious experience to others.[37] Of course, someone like Martin might not accept this evidence, but the critical rationalist does not require that an argument be convincing to everyone to hold that it provides justificatory evidence. The point here is that tests will be part of a larger framework of beliefs that one takes to be justified.

Wainwright's other tests relate indirectly to the religious experience: whether it produces for the believer a life marked by virtues, the effect the believer has on others, the profundity of what the believer says, the coherence with orthodox religious claims, its coherence with the experiences of others, and the pronouncements of an authority.[38]

It might be objected that these tests are indirect, whereas we test ordinary perceptual experience more directly. I check to see if my visual sensation of a computer in front of me is true by reaching out and touching it. But if there is doubt that the first sensory experience puts us in contact with the physical object, so that it needs to be supported by a second sensory experience, the same can be said about the second sensory experience, and we are committed to an infinite regress. Rather, we confirm our experiences by "tapping into our general background-belief system that was built up on sense perception, precisely the source of the belief under investigation."[39] We may check someone's report that he saw a fighter plane flying over his house by checking air traffic reports at that time and the person's eyesight. In the same way, we confirm someone's religious experiences by the background system that was built up by that person's and others' religious experiences. To allow this background of related experience in sensory perception but not in religious experience constitutes a double standard.

DIVERSITY OF RELIGIOUS EXPERIENCES

One of Wainwright's tests is the coherence of the beliefs that arise from believers' religious experiences. Some would object that the beliefs of those who
have religious experiences do not cohere with each other. Whereas the way
we report both ordinary perceptual experiences and the objects of those
experiences is fundamentally uniform, reports about religious experiences
themselves and what is allegedly experienced significantly disagree among
different religious traditions. For example, Christians describe the God they
encounter as triune, personal, and really distinct from themselves, whereas
Hindus characterize Brahman as the whole of reality and describe the relation of the self (*atman*) to Brahman nondualistically. Can incompatible descriptions of what is experienced be reconciled?

Perhaps these differing descriptions cannot be reconciled. However, this
is not fatal to the Principle of Credulity. The principle does not require that
all perceptual descriptions be veridical. Where perceptions yield conflicting
testimony, we must turn to other experiences and rational arguments to determine the truth of the various claims. That is, where incompatible accounts
are given, additional considerations can be introduced to help decide which,
if any, of the religious experiences are veridical. Although the reports provide a prima facie ground for their acceptance, not all beliefs based on such
experiences are true. Just as we at times doubt perceptual claims for good
reasons (seeing the mirage of a water puddle in the road on a hot day), we
might do the same for claims based on religious experience. Consonance
with other justified beliefs about God and religious practices might be one
way to winnow out less reliable claims.

At the same time, the presence of conflicting claims does raise questions
regarding whether one can use such experiences to justify religious beliefs.[40]
It suggests that religious experiences lack a general reliability. Indeed, these
experiences seem to rely rather heavily upon the personal religious backgrounds of the respective reporters of the experiences. In such cases naturalistic accounts in terms of culture rather than supernaturalistic accounts in terms
of some divine being or reality might better explain the religious experiences.

The objection from conflicting claims must be carefully put if it is to be
telling. It is very important to note that it is not mere diversity of religious
experiences that poses a problem, but the incompatibility of the religious
claims based on them. For one thing, it is perfectly reasonable that people
may have differing experiences. Ordinary perceptual experience is very diverse; people experience different things or the same thing from differing
perspectives. For another, varying descriptions of what is experienced does
not of itself pose a problem for justification. For example, although two people will describe a painting in front of which they are standing in different
ways, the existence of the painting will not be in doubt. Similarly, that religious experiencers give different names to what is experienced, or that different people experience different beings (Mary, Krishna, angels) or receive
different revelations regarding their personal lives does not establish that

their respective experiences are incompatible or incapable of justifying any claim to the existence of what they perceived. All that follows is that they are different. Rather, the problem arises only on the incompatibility of claims made about Ultimate Reality on the basis of religious experience. That is, for the objection to hold, it must be shown that the Ultimate Reality allegedly experienced by one person is *incompatible* with that allegedly experienced by another, not merely different from it.

Even here, Alston notes, what is missing is some non–question-begging criteria that would enable us to discriminate among the religious experiences. The fact that we cannot specify such criteria, he argues, does not imply that persons should believe that their experiences of God are unreliable. What he suggests is that believers can be justified in sitting tight with their own beliefs, provided they well guide their life activity.

IS THERE A COMMON CORE TO RELIGIOUS EXPERIENCE?

The discussion of the objection to religious experience from allegedly conflicting claims about reality based on religious experience raises a fundamental issue, namely, whether there is a common core to religious experience. On the one hand, some argue that the diversity objection fails because all religious experiences of Ultimate Reality have something in common. Differences are to be explained by the fact that experiencers proceed to give detailed interpretive accounts that, by invoking concepts, models, and metaphors from their respective religious traditions, introduce incompatibility into the descriptions of the experience. The differences are imported from the religious doctrines they hold and are not necessarily to be found in the experiences or stimuli themselves.[41] Once the interpretations are removed, a common core remains.

This is particularly evident, according to some thinkers, in mystical experiences that involve an immediate and noninferential consciousness of some Reality, prior to any subject-object differentiation. The mystic achieves union with Ultimate Reality either epistemologically (there is no *experienced* subject-object distinction) or ontologically (there is no *real* distinction between experiencer and object). Although mystics later interpret this experience through the use of rational concepts and categories, this already departs from the ineffability of the original experience.

The view that religious experiences have a common core—a core that transcends the boundaries of diverse religions, denominations, and cultures—is espoused by writers such as William James, Walter T. Stace (1886–1967) and more recently Caroline Franks Davis (b. 1957). Stace is concerned particularly about mystic experiences. His goal is to give a phenomenologically objective description of the mystic experience. He notes that one must be careful to distinguish between the experience and the interpretation of the experience. The interpretation is introduced to enable the person to understand and communicate the experience. Stace wants to ascertain what occurs in the experience itself. He lists seven distinctive core features of the mystic experience.

1. the Unitary Consciousness; the One, the Void; pure consciousness;
2. nonspatial, nontemporal;
3. sense of objectivity or reality;
4. blessedness, peace, and so forth;
5. feeling of the holy, sacred, or divine;
6. paradoxicality;
7. alleged by mystics to be ineffable.[42]

Nonetheless, one might ask whether this very classification invokes interpretation, especially when Stace speaks about the One or the Void (with a capital letter) as fundamental to this experience? Stace replies that one must distinguish levels of interpretation.

> If a mystic speaks of the experience of "an undifferentiated distinctionless unity," this mere report or description using only classificatory words may be regarded as a low-level interpretation. But this is being more fussily precise than is usually necessary, since for all intents and purposes it is just a description. If a mystic says he experiences a "mystical union with the Creator of the universe," this is a high-level interpretation since it includes far more intellectual addition than a mere descriptive report.[43]

His point is that the preceding seven characteristics are solely descriptive. Interpretation enters later in attempts to identify the One with, for example, the God of Christianity or Brahman of Hinduism.

However, admitting that interpretation occurs in a basic description, even if only at a low level, appears to be fatal to the contention that one can discern a cross-cultural, universal core. This becomes clear when, in making the distinction between extrovertive and introvertive mystical experiences, Stace suggests that the introvertive kind is a more complete version of the extrovertive, since "consciousness or mind is a higher category than life."[44] To speak of categories and to evaluate them introduces interpretation into the most important of the alleged core elements.

Taking the opposite position, Steven Katz (b. 1944) argues that no experience is unmediated by concepts and beliefs. We process all experience through our beliefs, learned categories, and conceptual framework. Even self-consciousness—the paradigm of intuitive experience—is conceptually conditioned. Consequently, religious and cultural beliefs condition religious experience, to the extent that persons in different religious traditions actually experience differently. There is not *one* religious experience, but a plurality of diverse experiences. Katz appeals to his own Jewish tradition to support his thesis.

> All these [Jewish] cultural-social beliefs and their attendant practices . . . clearly affect the way in which the Jewish mystic views the world, the God

who created it, the way to approach this God, and what to expect when one does finally come to approach this God. That is to say, the entire life of the Jewish mystic is permeated from childhood up by images, concepts, symbols, ideological values, and ritual behavior which there is no reason to believe he leaves behind in his experience. Rather, these images, beliefs, symbols, and rituals define, *in advance,* what the experience *he wants to have,* and which he then does have, will be like.[45]

That is, our prior beliefs, formed by interaction with our religious tradition, shape our religious experience by preforming the schema by which we perceive and understand it.

As confirmation of this position, note the role of gurus and teachers of the mystical tradition. Small groups of devotees, led by a master or teacher who instructs them in a specific method for achieving the desired goal, closely hold the relevant wisdom. Hence, the methods and beliefs instilled by the teacher condition the mystic experience. The master sanctions, if not determines, the attainment of genuine mystic insight. For example, it was Hung-jen, the fifth Zen Buddhist Patriarch, who recognized that the poem of Hui-neng, the uneducated rice-pounder,

> The Bodhi is not like a tree,
> The clear mirror is nowhere standing
> Fundamentally not one thing exists;
> Where, then, is a grain of dust to cling?

showed superior insight to that of the learned Shen-hsiu, who wrote,

> This body is the Bodhi-tree
> The soul is like a mirror bright;
> Take heed to keep it always clean
> And let not dust collect on it.[46]

How, then, does one account for the apparently similar descriptions of religious experience given by Stace? First, Katz holds that the similarity is only apparent. Although the descriptions of the experiences use the same terminology, the terms may not have the same meaning in all reports. That two persons from different traditions, for example, describe their experience as paradoxical does not mean that it is paradoxical in the same way or that the same content stands in the relationship of paradox. Indeed, the terms *paradox* and *ineffable* serve to "cloak the experience from investigation and to hold mysterious whatever ontological commitments one has," rather than to "provide *data* for comparability."[47] Second, the terms used to characterize the experience are too general and vague, so that they fail to carefully delineate the mystical experiences. James's suggestion that every mystical experience is ineffable and noetic (yields knowledge) leaves open whether the ineffability is the same and whether the noetic quality has the same content in every case. The truth-claims of Madhyamika Buddhism, with its emphasis on the emptiness of Reality, differ markedly from the truth-claims of Christianity about God and God's relation to his created world. The Realities in the two cases cannot be identified.

> Henry Suso's "intoxication with the immeasurable abundance of the Divine House . . . entirely lost in God [of Christianity]," the *Upanishads* "*sat* [what is] . . . is expressed in the word *satyam*, the Real. It comprises this whole universe: Thou art this whole universe," as well as the Buddhist's "dimension of nothingness" all can be included under these broad phenomenological descriptions of "Reality," yet . . . it is clear that Suso's Christian God is not equivalent to the Buddhist's "nothingness," and that the experience of entering into the Divine House is not equivalent to losing oneself in Buddhist "nothingness." It becomes apparent on reflection that *different* metaphysical entities can be "described" by the same phrases if these phrases are *indefinite* enough.[48]

Katz's analysis has not gone unchallenged. One criticism is that his view cannot account for some fundamental features of mystical experience. Mystics claim to be able to achieve a state in which self-awareness and awareness of objects cease. Yogis, for example, meditate on various things, such as physical objects, invisible things, the self, and finally consciousness. Gradually they attain to *samādhi*, a form of inward concentration in which progressively all conscious content—consciousness of all distinctions among perceptual objects, of inner states such as joy, of oneself as a distinct being, of objects of meditation as distinct from oneself, and, ultimately, of consciousness itself—is removed. In the final intuitive state, pure consciousness unifies all—past, present, and future.

The very attaining of pure consciousness defies Katz's analysis. To reach enlightenment, mystics often specify a path or a set of techniques by which they intentionally "forget" or bracket their previous experiences and categories of understanding. The Hindu school of Yoga, for example, specifies eight methods or types of practices directed toward the realization of pure consciousness. The first five, sometimes referred to as external aids, include a life-style of self-restraint and abstention (practicing celibacy, never stealing, and committing no injury), moral observances (practicing contentment, doing penance, and studying), practice of bodily postures, and breath control. The last three involve concentration on objects (*dhārana*), meditation (*dhyāna*), and contemplation (*samādhi*). Adherents claim that following such disciplines ends their automatic perceptual and conceptual responses to what they experience. Ultimately, the yogi achieves pure consciousness, in which all categories, ideas, and external input are forgotten. In the final stages the subject-object, knower-known dualism that characterized our treatment of religious experience earlier in this chapter is replaced by a more unitary experience, devoid of distinctions.

The methods used, such as concentration for extended periods on a particular object—or, in the case of some Zen Buddhists, wall meditation—have been duplicated in the laboratory. Participants whose eyes were exposed only to a patternless field (by taping halves of Ping-Pong balls over them or by mounting a tiny projector on a contact lens so that the same object always appears) did not report seeing nothing (which still involves making conceptual distinctions) but described an end of seeing, "a complete disappearance of the sense of vision for short periods."[49]

In short, if forgetting and the like are possible, and if the mystic can attain a state of pure consciousness with neither object nor content of consciousness, then Katz's thesis must be reconsidered. Since all categories and experiences are transcended, there is nothing in the higher-stage mystical states to be conditioned by prior conceptual categories or experiences.

In conclusion, the issue of a common core to religious experience is significant for addressing whether religious experience can be used to justify religious belief. If Stace is correct, then the differences in religions need not affect the more basic contention that religious experience can justify a basic core of beliefs. There is no ultimate incompatibility. What it does not do, however, is by itself provide grounds for more developed or detailed (ramified) religious beliefs. A more comprehensive case would have to be structured to move beyond the common core. If Katz is correct that religious experience not only exhibits great diversity but is conditioned by the experiencer's prior beliefs, religious experience may be so conditioned by prior concepts that it cannot provide a sound basis for religious beliefs. At the same time, however, one might note that all our perceptual experiences occur in the context of prior beliefs about the world, but this does not prevent us from using those perceptions to justify our beliefs in the existence of what we perceive. In short, whether we should look to religious experience to justify religious beliefs remains to be carefully explored further.

STUDY QUESTIONS

1. What are the five types of religious experience suggested by Richard Swinburne? Find an example of two of them from some religious, philosophical, or devotional literature.

2. Compare the view of religious experience as perception (Alston) with the view that religious experience is interpretation based on religious beliefs (Proudfoot). In what ways would their explanations of a particular account of religious experience be similar and different?

3. If you know people who have had a religious experience, ask them how they describe the experience. Which of the three explanations of the nature of religious experience presented in this chapter does each account best illustrate, and why?

4. Give an argument (either derived from this chapter or developed on your own) either for or against the thesis that religious experience can be used to justify religious beliefs. What view of religious experience have you presupposed? What objection might be raised against your argument?

5. If you are religious and do not use religious experience to justify your religious beliefs, to what do you appeal? Why do you think this provides better grounds for your beliefs than religious experience?

6. Compare and contrast arguments that might be given for and against the thesis that there is a common core to religious experience. Which perspective do you think is correct, and why? Might there be a common core to higher-state mystical experiences but not to other types of religious experience?

7. In what ways do the religious experiences of Asian religions like Buddhism and Hinduism differ from those of Western religions like Christianity, Islam, and Judaism? Why are they different? (For the latter question you might consider the fundamental perspectives on reality these religions hold.)

NOTES

1. Isa. 6:1–3,5 NIV.

2. Augustine, *Confessions*, trans. R. S. Pine-Coffin (New York: Penguin Books, 1961), VIII, 12.

3. *Mundaka Upanishad*, III, i, 8, in *Indian Philosophy*, ed. Sarvepalli Radhakrishnan and Charles A. Moore (Princeton: Princeton University Press, 1957), p. 54.

4. Some who treat religious experience do not make such a distinction and consequently arrive at a different typology of religious experience. See Carolyn Franks Davis *The Evidential Force of Religious Experience* (Oxford: Clarendon Press, 1989), ch. 2, who categorizes religious experience into interpretive, quasi-sensory, revelatory regenerative, numinous, and mystical experience.

5. *Digha-Nikaya* 2.71.2–17, quoted in Paul J. Griffiths, *On Being Mindless* (LaSalle, Ill: Open Court, 1986), p. 17.

6. Richard Swinburne, *The Existence of God* (Oxford: Oxford University Press, 1979), pp. 249–52. (See Michael Peterson, et al., *Philosophy of Religion: Selected Readings*, pt. 1, pp. 42–3. Hereafter we cite this book as PRSR2.)

7. Ralph Waldo Emerson, "Nature," "Essays and Addresses," in *Selected Writings of Ralph Waldo Emerson* (New York: New American Library, 1965), p. 189.

8. Exodus 3:1–4.

9. Swinburne, *The Existence of God*, p. 250.

10. Acts 10:10–16.

11. Richard Rolle, *I Sleep and My Heart Wakes*, in *Varieties of Mystic Experience*, ed. Elmer O'Brien (New York: Holt, Rinehart and Winston, 1964), p. 161.

12. E. Allison Peers, ed., *The Life of Teresa of Jesus* (Garden City, N.Y.: Image Books, 1960), p. 249. (See PRSR2e, pt. 1, p. 7.)

13. Nicholas of Cusa, *The Vision of God* (New York: Frederick Ungar, 1960), p. 78.

14. *Samyutta-Nikaya*, XXXVI, 115, in *Buddhism in Translations*, ed. Henry Clarke Warren (New York: Atheneum, 1973), p. 384.

15. Nicholas of Cusa, *The Vision of God*, p. 23.

16. Friedrich Schleiermacher, *The Christian Faith* (Edinburgh: T. & T. Clark, 1928), p. 17.

17. Rudolf Otto, *The Idea of the Holy* (London: Oxford University Press, 1958), p. 1.

18. Ibid., p. 12.

19. Ibid., p. 10.

20. Augustine, I, 1; C. S. Lewis, *Pilgrim's Regress* (Grand Rapids, Mich.: William. B. Eerdmans, 1958).

21. William James, *The Varieties of Religious Experience* (New York: New American Library, 1958), p. 329. (See PRSR2e, pt. 1, p. 19.)

22. Ibid., p. 346.

23. Ibid., p. 331. (See PRSR2e, pt. 1, p. 19.)

24. Wayne Proudfoot, *Religious Experience* (Berkeley and Los Angeles: University of California Press, 1985), pp. 87, 108.

25. Because "religious experience" can be used to refer to many different types of experience, Alston prefers "putative direct awareness of God" or "the perception of God." William Alston, *Perceiving God* (Ithaca, N.Y.: Cornell University Press, 1991), p. 35.

26. Ibid., p. 36.

27. Alston notes one should not overlook the Catholic mystical tradition that includes phenomena that parallel in significant ways the phenomena of sensory experience—touch, smell, and sight. Ibid., pp. 52–4.

28. Ibid., pp. 44–5. (See William P. Alston, "Religious Experience as Perception of God," in PRSR2e, pt. 1, p. 26.)

29. Ibid., p. 47.

30. Alston's views about the justification of religious belief are further addressed in chapter 6.

31. Proudfoot, *Religious Experience*, p. 223. (See PRSR2e, pt. 1, p. 39.)

32. Otto, *The Idea of the Holy*, p. 19.

33. Swinburne, *The Existence of God*, p. 254.

34. Michael Martin, *Atheism: A Philosophical Justification* (Philadelphia: Temple University Press, 1990), p. 166. (See PRSR2e, pt. 1, p. 52.)

35. C. B. Martin, *Religious Belief* (Ithaca, N.Y.: Cornell University Press, 1959), p. 67.

36. William Wainwright, *Mysticism: A Study of Its Nature* (Madison: University of Wisconsin Press, 1981), pp. 91–3.

37. Alston, *Perceiving God*, p. 270.

38. Wainwright, *Mysticism*, pp. 86–7.

39. Alston, *Perceiving God*, p. 211. See Wainwright, *Mysticism*, pp. 104–5.

40. Ibid., pp. 262–6.

41. Davis, *Evidential Force*, ch. 7.

42. W. T. Stace, *Mysticism and Philosophy* (New York: Macmillan, 1960), pp. 131–2. I have given the characteristics of his introvertive type. The extrovertive type differs slightly in items 1 and 2, but he considers this type to be a lower level, an "incomplete kind of experience."

43. Ibid., p. 37.

44. Ibid., p. 133.

45. Steven T. Katz, "Language, Epistemology, and Mysticism," in Steven T. Katz, ed., *Mysticism and Philosophical Analysis* (Oxford: Oxford University Press, 1978), p. 33.

46. D. T. Suzuki, *Essays in Zen Buddhism* (New York: Grove Press, 1949), pp. 205–7.

47. Katz, "Language, Epistemology, and Mysticism," p. 54.

48. Ibid., p. 51 (brackets in original text).

49. Robert K. C. Forman, "A Construction of Mystical Experience," *Faith and Philosophy* 5, no. 3 (1988): 259–65.

SUGGESTED READING

Alston, William. *Perceiving God: The Epistemology of Religious Experience.* Ithaca, N.Y.: Cornell University Press, 1991.

Davis, Caroline Franks. *The Evidential Force of Religious Experience.* Oxford: Clarendon Press, 1989.

Hardy, Alister. *The Spiritual Nature of Man: A Study of Contemporary Religious Experience.* Oxford: Clarendon Press, 1979.

James, William. *The Varieties of Religious Experience.* New York: New American Library, 1958.

Katz, Steven T., ed. *Mysticism and Philosophical Analysis.* Oxford: Oxford University Press, 1978.

Lewis, H. D. *Our Experience of God.* London: Allen and Unwin, 1959.

Otto, Rudolf. *The Idea of the Holy.* London: Oxford University Press, 1958.

Proudfoot, Wayne. *Religious Experience.* Berkeley and Los Angeles: University of California Press, 1985.

Rowe, William L. "Religious Experience and the Principle of Credulity." *International Journal for the Philosophy of Religion* 13 (1982): 85–92.

Smart, Ninian. *The Religious Experience.* London: Macmillan, 1991.

Stace, W. T. *Mysticism and Philosophy.* New York: Macmillan, 1960.

Swinburne, Richard. *The Existence of God.* London: Oxford University Press, 1979. Chap. 13.

Underhill, Evelyn. *Mysticism.* Cleveland: Meridian Books, 1955.

Wainwright, William. *Mysticism: A Study of Its Nature, Cognitive Value, and Moral Implications.* Madison: University of Wisconsin Press, 1981.

Yandell, Keith. *The Epistemology of Religious Experience.* Cambridge: Cambridge University Press, 1993.

CHAPTER 3 FAITH AND REASON: HOW ARE THEY RELATED?

November 18, 1978, marked one of the most horrifying religious tragedies of modern times. Virtually the entire population—men, women, and children—of the community of Jonestown, Guyana, perished overnight. This was not the result of natural disaster, disease, or violence inflicted by enemies. Rather, some 914 human beings died as a result of drinking Kool-Aid laced with cyanide in a collective religious ritual of "revolutionary suicide."[1]

The founder of Jonestown, Reverend Jim Jones, was a midwestern Protestant preacher whose church, the People's Temple, had moved to Redwood Valley in California. A social activist who pushed hard for racial integration, his teachings increasingly deviated from those of mainstream Christianity until he claimed to be a living god and to have raised some 43 people from the dead. Under increasing pressure and criticism, he and many of his congregation migrated to Guyana in 1977, carving the Jonestown community out of the jungle. But criticism and pressure continued, especially from disaffected former members, until the Jonestown leadership despaired of any hopeful future and the mass suicide was chosen as the way out of a desperate situation as well as the prelude to a happy reunion on "the other side."

Why did it happen? How could people do such a thing? It is impossible not to ask such questions, and yet the answers, at one level, are not hard to come by. The people of Jonestown believed in Jim Jones as the living god among them, and in his words as a divine message. That message told them the right thing to do, the only act that would maintain integrity in a hostile and threatening world, was to take their own lives and those of their children. The deed followed logically upon their beliefs and the commands of their divine leader.

But this pushes the question a step further back: how could people believe such insane things? Why didn't common sense and ordinary reasonableness show them that Jones could not possibly be what he said and that his message was not credible? But once again, the answer is not far to seek. These were people of faith, and for them, as for many believers, what faith requires is first of all that faith itself be strengthened and nurtured; doubt and questioning are the antithesis of faith and the bitter enemies of the religious life. So in asking them to use human reason to discern that Jones's message was not to be trusted, we would be asking them to negate the very faith by which they lived—and died.

CAN REASON BE TRUSTED?

The case of Jonestown is an extreme example, but the relationship between faith and reason has seldom been tranquil or peaceful; rather, conflict and controversy appear at every turn. In fact, quite a few people, many of them serious religious thinkers, have said things that suggest that faith[2] and reason are not compatible at all—that their relationship is, and must be, one of mutual rejection and hostility. The apostle Paul wrote, "See that no one makes a prey of you by philosophy and empty deceit" (Col. 2:8). The early Christian writer Tertullian (160–220) asked, "What has Athens to do with Jerusalem?" (By "Athens" he meant Greek philosophy, by "Jerusalem," the Christian church.) The implied answer is "Nothing—faith and philosophy have nothing in common; they are totally opposed." Pascal (1623–1662) wrote, "The heart has its reasons which reason does not know," and he implied that some persons might have to take steps to dull their reasoning faculties in order to be able to believe![3]

Still, it is much harder to bring about a clear-cut separation of faith from reason than these statements might indicate. Those who stress faith and attack reason often place a great deal of emphasis on *religious experience*: as the bumper sticker says, "God is not dead—I talked with Him this morning!" However, as we saw in the last chapter, religious experience is by no means a purely emotional "happening"; rather, it involves *concepts* and *beliefs* about the Being that is experienced. If we tried to separate religious experiences from such concepts and beliefs—from the *religious belief-system*, as we shall call it—then there would be no way of saying *who or what it is that is experienced*, or of explaining what sort of difference the experience ought to make to the person who has it. But such a religious belief-system needs to be understood, at least to some degree, and it is hard to see how understanding it is not going to involve the use of reason.

In fact, none of the religious thinkers mentioned at the beginning of this section totally repudiates reason. It has been argued persuasively that the apostle Paul's warnings are directed at a certain kind of reasoning, namely "worldly wisdom," which is the product of "human conceit that shuts itself up against the truth," not against the use of reason as such.[4] Even a cursory reading of his letters will show that he frequently makes use of reasoning, analysis, and arguments in the course of his religious teaching.[5] Tertullian, in spite of his diatribe against philosophy, was himself trained in philosophy and can be shown to have made use of it in his explanations of Christian doctrines. And while Pascal, like Paul, was severely critical of *a certain kind* of reasoning, one of the major projects of his life was the construction of an "apologetic" (a rational defense) for Christian faith.

The real question, then, is not whether reason has any place in religion—the answer to that question is obviously yes—but what kind of place reason does and should have.[6] But here also at least part of the answer is relatively uncontroversial. All religious communities in fact make use of reason, and in effect sanction its use, in the process of *teaching* the religion's belief-system to children and new converts, and in enabling the faithful to *understand*, so far as possible, what their faith is about. Such uses of reason really do not need to be debated. The really controversial question is this: What role (if any) should reason play in the *validation* (or invalidation) of religious belief-systems? Granted that we may have to make use of reason in understanding the faith, is it also true, in any sense, that having faith at all depends (or should depend) on *having good reasons to believe* that one's faith is *true*? That is the real core of the "problem of faith and reason," and that is the question to which the rest of this chapter is devoted.

STRONG RATIONALISM

The first answer to our question[7] to be considered is that of *strong rationalism*, the position which holds that *in order for a religious belief-system to be properly and rationally accepted, it must be possible to prove that the belief-system is true. Rationalism,* as used here, contrasts with *irrationalism* or *fideism*; in general, rationalism in this sense implies a reliance on reason, or intelligence, in deciding our beliefs and actions.[8] The word "prove," to be sure, is somewhat ambiguous; for our present purposes we understand as meaning *to show that a belief is true in a way that should be convincing to any reasonable person.* This means that the *premises,* or assumed truths, on which a proof is based must be such that any reasonable person who takes the trouble to investigate them should be able to determine that they are true (or, at least, that they probably are true). The *methods of reasoning* that are employed in a proof must also be such that any reasonable person who investigates them should be able to see that they are correct: that, assuming the premises are indeed true, the conclusions arrived at by those methods of reasoning are either guaranteed true or at least very likely to be true as well.

The central idea of strong rationalism was stated forcefully by the English mathematician W. K. Clifford (1845–1879), as follows:

> It is wrong always, everywhere, and for anyone, to believe anything upon insufficient evidence.
>
> If a man, holding a belief which he was taught in childhood or persuaded of afterwards, keeps down and pushes away any doubt which arise about it in his mind . . . and regards as impious those questions which

cannot easily be asked without disturbing it—the life of that man is one long
sin against mankind. . . .

Inquiry into the evidence of a doctrine is not to be made once for all and
then taken as finally settled. It is never lawful to stifle a doubt; for either it
can be honestly answered by means of the inquiry already made, or else it
proves that the inquiry was not complete.[9]

Why does Clifford set such high standards for our beliefs? In answering
this he emphasizes the serious consequences, for oneself and especially for
others, that may result from accepting a belief without adequate evidence:

A shipowner was about to send to sea an emigrant ship. . . . Doubts had
been suggested to him that possibly she was not seaworthy. These doubts
preyed upon his mind, and made him unhappy. . . . Before the ship sailed,
however, he succeeded in overcoming these melancholy reflections. . . . He
watched her departure with a light heart, and benevolent wishes . . . and
he got his insurance money when she went down in mid-ocean and told
no tales.

What shall we say of him? Surely this, that he was verily guilty of the
death of those men. It is admitted that he did sincerely believe in the soundness of his ship; but the sincerity of his conviction can in no wise help him,
because *he had no right to believe on such evidence as was before him.*[10]

We will all sympathize with Clifford in his condemnation of the shipowner;
he goes on to argue, as we have seen, that *any* belief held upon insufficient
evidence is reprehensible.

One objection often raised against Clifford's kind of view is that there
are many people, especially those who must work hard for a living and have
little education, who simply do not have the time or, perhaps, the ability to
do the kind of serious thinking he requires before one is entitled to have
faith. Clifford takes note of this objection and rejects it: "But, says one, 'I am
a busy man; I have no time for the long course of study which would be necessary to make me in any degree a competent judge of certain questions, or
even able to understand the nature of the arguments.' Then he should have
no time to believe."[11]

Clifford's opinion, very thinly concealed, is that *no* religious belief-
system is capable of meeting the high standards of proof that should govern
all of our believing, and so a reasonable (and moral) person must do without
religious beliefs. But not all strong rationalists, by any means, have been hostile to religion. John Locke (1632–1704) was a Christian whose standards for
proper belief were essentially the same as those later stated by Clifford; he
thought that Christianity, when properly understood and defended, could
meet those standards.[12]

Thomas Aquinas (1224–1274) differed in some of his views from Locke
and Clifford, but he agreed with Locke in holding that by careful rational
investigation it was possible to make a convincing case for the truth of Christianity.[13] A contemporary philosopher of religion whose position is very
close to strong rationalism as here defined is Richard Swinburne (b. 1934).[14]

The appeal of this perspective on faith and reason is undeniable. Which of us has not felt frustrated, even angry, at the many things people (perhaps especially religious people) claim to "know" but are unable to give any good reasons for? In view of this frustration, the desire to have "real proof" for the things we believe is very understandable. The strong rationalist doesn't make any sloppy appeals to "faith"; she offers to *prove* that her view is correct—and challenges you to do the same for your view, if you disagree with her.

All the same, there are reasons to question whether strong rationalism is the right view to take. For one thing, it can be questioned whether the kind of rational guarantee the strong rationalist insists on is even *desirable* from the standpoint of religious faith. There is a very common and widespread view among religious people that in faith one "steps out beyond" what can be proved or rationally guaranteed, and that this "stepping out," with its attendant risk and uncertainty, is an important, even essential element in faith. (Kierkegaard, discussed in the next section of the chapter, expresses this very powerfully.) Of course this idea that faith must involve risk and uncertainty could be wrong, but it is common enough among religious people that it needs to be taken seriously. If the idea is correct, then strong rationalism cannot be the right way to approach religious faith.

Another question about strong rationalism is this: Can it be made to work? That is, is it actually possible to do what the strong rationalist demands, and show that a particular religious belief-system is true in a way that should be convincing to any reasonable person? The strong rationalist (if she is religious) thinks that it is, and is prepared to show you how it can be done. Against this, though, there is the undeniable fact that, in spite of centuries of argument by strong rationalists and others, no one religious belief-system shows any signs of being proved in a way that "satisfies all reasonable people." What is the problem here?

The mere fact that not everyone is convinced by her arguments is not immediately devastating to the strong rationalist. What she will say is that her arguments are sound and *ought* to be convincing to anyone, but something has gone wrong in this particular case. Perhaps the other person simply has not studied the arguments carefully enough, or has not understood them correctly. Alternatively, someone may lack the training or even the intellectual capacity to understand some arguments that in themselves are perfectly good. (This would be true of most of us in the case of some of the advanced arguments in mathematics, for instance.) Finally, the other person may be "blinded by prejudice," so that, even if he seems a reasonable person in most everyday situations, his prejudices simply do not allow him to see the truth in religious matters.

All the same, the way the discussions of religious arguments have actually gone is not very encouraging to the strong rationalist. If her perspective is correct, one would expect that in the case of at least some religious arguments the misunderstandings and resistances would gradually be overcome, and over a period of time more and more thinkers would recognize these arguments as sound and rationally compelling. What seems actually to happen is almost the reverse: even philosophers who accept a particular argument as correct are likely, as they continue to study it, to find that it contains loopholes such that an intelligent person *could* refuse to accept the argument without being obviously unreasonable. Rather than a movement in the direction of consensus, the trend seems to be toward a recognition that *no* such arguments are convincing for all reasonable persons. It is noteworthy that the great diversity of beliefs that is so prominent a feature of contemporary society is by no means limited to uninformed or unreflective persons. On the contrary, it is found also among thoughtful, sincere, and knowledgeable individuals.

It is important to realize that this lack of universally convincing arguments applies not only to religious belief-systems, but to *all* arguments supporting "worldviews"—general, overall accounts of what reality is like. Sometimes the impression is given that if one wants to be religious one has to rely on "pure faith," but that if one's worldview is based on science one can have solid proof. This is a very serious mistake. It is true that many results in various branches of science are so firmly established that no reasonable person is likely to dissent from them. (A "flat-earther" is, after all, our favorite example of someone who sticks to his views in defiance of the evidence.) But science as a total worldview—the idea that science can tell us everything there is to know about what reality consists of—enjoys no such overwhelming support. This worldview (often termed *scientific naturalism*) is just one theory among others, and is no more capable of being "proved to all reasonable people" than are religious belief-systems. To claim that the strong support enjoyed by, say, the periodic table of the elements transfers over to scientific naturalism as a worldview is highly confused if not deliberately misleading.

Yet another problem with strong rationalism is this: Strong rationalism assumes that "reason" exists in human beings as a faculty which is "neutral" as between conflicting worldviews, and thus can be used to prove things to everyone (prejudice aside) regardless of what worldviews people are initially inclined to accept. But *is* reason really neutral in this way? It seems clear in everyday life that people's belief-systems—their worldviews—*do* have a considerable impact on which sorts of arguments they find convincing and believable. Philosophers, aware of this fact, have invested immense effort in trying to establish a totally "pure" and "presuppositionless" approach to philosophy. The attempt of Descartes (1596–1650) to begin his philosophizing from a stance of "universal doubt" is a well-known example.[15] Perhaps not quite all the returns are in on this effort, but a preponderance of contemporary philosophers seem to be convinced that the thing cannot be done—that there *is no* pure, assumption-free standpoint on which our knowledge can be based in a way that is independent of "where we are coming from."[16] But if this is correct—if the goal of totally eliminating from our belief-systems prior convictions and "prejudices" is unattainable—then the approach of strong rationalism cannot be made to work.

FIDEISM

The second kind of view we are going to examine is commonly called *fideism*[17]—"faith-ism." Fideism is defined in a number of ways by different writers, but for our purposes we will define it as the view that *religious belief-systems are not subject to rational evaluation.* To say, for instance, that we have *faith* that God exists and that he loves us is to say that we accept this in a way that does not depend on any evidence or reasoning, and that we refuse to have anything to do with trying to prove or disprove God's love for us.

Is this just a stubborn rejection of reason on the fideist's part? Not necessarily. The fideist reminds us that an argument (*any* argument) must rest on premises or assumptions of some kind. If someone will not grant any assumptions to begin with, then it is impossible to argue with such a person. (This, in effect, is what the philosophical skeptic does—which is what makes it so frustrating to argue with a skeptic!) Now, what is assumed as a premise in one argument may be established as a conclusion in another argument, but this process cannot go on forever; somewhere along the line we must come to our *fundamental assumptions,* those things we accept without proof just because they are so absolutely basic that there is nothing more basic by which they could be proved.

Now the important point that needs to be seen, according to the fideist, is this: *For a sincere religious believer, the most fundamental assumptions are found in the religious belief-system itself.* Religious faith *itself* is the foundation of one's life—it is, in the phrase of Paul Tillich (1886–1965), one's "ultimate concern." But if this is so, then the idea of testing or evaluating one's faith by some external, rational standard is a terrible mistake, which very likely reflects a lack of true faith. Thus it is sometimes said that if we test God's Word by logic, or science, we are really worshiping science or logic rather than God!

Now for some people the idea that religious faith must be accepted without any proof or evidence might seem uncomfortable, even frightening. But a true fideist sees no problem in lack of proof; rather, he revels in it. Sören Kierkegaard (1813–1855), a Danish thinker, heaps scorn on those who would seek the truth of religion in an objective, detached way through evidence and argument.[18] They forget that what is at stake here is their own existence as human beings. (It is almost comparable to selecting one's spouse on the basis of points scored in a beauty or body-building contest!) Furthermore, he points out, objective, rational inquiry is an "approximation-process" in which one comes closer and closer to the ultimate answer, but never quite reaches it; there is always one more bit of evidence to consider, one more book or article to read and evaluate. This, of course, means that the decision for or against God is put off indefinitely. But the person truly concerned about his soul realizes that "every moment is wasted in which he does not have God."[19] In fact, if we could *prove* God's existence and his love for us it would then be impossible to have *faith* in God—so even if our inquiry were successful, it would frustrate rather than facilitate the goal of coming to know God! As Kierkegaard says,

> Without risk there is no faith. Faith is precisely the contradiction between the infinite passion of the individual's inwardness and the objective uncertainty. If I am capable of grasping God objectively, I do not believe, but precisely because I cannot do this I must believe. If I wish to preserve myself in faith I must constantly be intent upon holding fast the objective uncertainty, so as to remain out upon the deep, over seventy thousand fathoms of water, still preserving my faith.[20]

But if assembling arguments and evidence in favor of belief in God is useless, how *does* one come to have faith? The answer is simple: you must *commit* yourself, you must take the "leap of faith," believing without having (or wanting) any reasons or evidence to show that your belief is true. The idea of a leap of faith can be illustrated by the following story: You are attending an outdoor party with a group of friends. After a while the party gets a bit slow, and just to keep things moving one of your friends offers you a bet: he bets you fifty dollars that you will not dive into your host's swimming pool in total darkness. (The pool is down the hill, well away from the lighted patio where the party is going on.) You are a good diver, so you accept the bet, strip down to your cutoffs, and proceed to the pool. Naturally, the whole group trails along behind; the fact that nobody can see where they are going makes it all the more fun. Finally, you reach the bottom of the diving board and begin climbing the ladder, surrounded by cries of "Do you think he'll really do it?" "Wait and see—he'll chicken out!" As you reach the top of the ladder, a horrible thought occurs to you. It is quite early in the spring, and the last time you saw the pool by daylight it had been drained for the winter. It is *very* dark, and strain as you will you cannot see whether the pool has any water in it or not. Furthermore, your host has something of a reputation as a practical joker; it just might appeal to him to let you jump into an empty pool. If you descend the ladder to check, everyone will say you copped out and you will lose the bet, and you really cannot afford to lose fifty dollars. So, you jump . . .

When religious people are introduced to Kierkegaard's idea of faith, many of them find it very attractive. It seems to be closer to their own idea, and perhaps experience, of faith than the "hard-nosed" logical approach recommended by strong rationalism. The idea that faith involves *commitment*, and *risk taking*, seems to make a great deal of sense to many religious people. The extent of Kierkegaard's influence is seen in the fact that he is the primary inspiration of the philosophical movement known as existentialism, as well as of the "neo-orthodox" theology of such men as Karl Barth (1886–1968) and Rudolph Bultmann (1884–1976).[21]

Still, there are some real problems with fideism. One problem is this: Given that faith is a leap, how does one decide *which* faith to leap for? For a person who already is committed, that may not seem to be a problem—but what about the person who is searching for a faith, and sees several alternative possibilities which seem about equally plausible: say, Roman Catholi-cism, charismatic Protestantism, and Baha'i? It would seem that a reasonable approach would be to carefully examine the alternatives and see which of them is most likely to be true, but that, of course, is precisely what the fideist says cannot be done. But surely it is essential to have *some* reasonable way in which the claims of competing belief-systems can be assessed. When people "buy into" religious belief-systems without giving careful consideration to whether the beliefs are reasonable and have a chance of being true, they sometimes accept ideas that are bizarre and even dangerous. (Jim Jones's Peoples Temple, mentioned earlier, and the Branch Davidians, led by David Koresh, are two examples of this.)

The notion that religious belief-systems represent the believer's "most fundamental" assumptions and thus cannot be tested by anything else may involve an ambiguity in the word *fundamental*. For the sincere believer, her beliefs are "fundamental" in the sense that they provide the basic, over-arching guidance for the way she lives her life; they establish her direction, her goals, and her reason for living. But it does not follow from this that these beliefs are "fundamental" in the sense of being *more evident*, and *more obviously true*, than anything else she knows or believes. In fact, we all find that there are obvious facts in everyday life—things we perceive through sight and touch and hearing—that more or less force themselves upon us in a way that has very little to do with what religious belief-systems we accept or reject. Simple truths of arithmetic, too, seem to have a self-evidence about them that is apparent to people regardless of the worldviews they embrace. Such truths as these are, in a way, "fundamental" in our knowledge ("episte-mologically fundamental," as philosophers would say), though they by no means provide the sort of "fundamental guidance" for our living that is of-fered by religious beliefs. But if so, then it may be feasible to *use* such episte-mologically fundamental beliefs in order to *test* religious belief-systems.

Nor does it seem to be true that one cannot test one's faith by rational standards without losing the faith itself. On the contrary, there are many cases in which this has actually been done. Martin Luther (1483–1546) thought that Copernican astronomy, with its view of the earth as moving through the heavens, was incompatible with faith: when the Hebrew leader Joshua wanted to prolong the daylight so his troops could complete their victory in a battle (Josh. 10:12–14), he commanded the *sun*, not the earth, to stand still—so it must have been the sun, *not* the earth, which was moving in the first place! More recently, Christians (including Kierkegaard and other modern fideists) have found that the damage to one's faith from accepting modern astronomy is entirely negligible. Furthermore, many believers have had the experience of coming to believe that some of their views concerning God involve logical contradictions. (For instance, one might conclude that one's belief in absolute divine control of everything that happens is inconsis-tent with one's belief in human free will.) In consequence of this, these be-lievers have sometimes modified their religious understanding of things, but few experience this as a "loss of faith." To the charge that testing one's faith by logic is placing logic above God, the retort might be that a really strong and sound faith involves the confidence that one's beliefs can *pass* any properly conducted test on the basis of logic and evidence.

Can't we, in fact, go even further than this, and say that in order to be taken seriously by a reasonable person a religious belief-system *must* be subjected to the tests of logical consistency and factual correctness? What would we make of a religious person who, calmly and deliberately, tells us that she is well aware that some of her beliefs are logically contradictory or conflict with well-known facts, yet this is no obstacle to her holding these beliefs? Wouldn't we conclude that either (1) she is badly confused and does not know what she is saying, or (2) she is not seriously interested in the *truth* of her beliefs, but is determined to maintain them (perhaps for the comfort they give her) *whether they are true or not?*[22] In fact, even fideists usually avoid admitting, straight out, that their beliefs are logically contradictory or in conflict with established facts. Usually they will say that their beliefs contain *apparent* contradictions, thus holding out the hope that, from a more ultimate perspective, it would be seen that there is not a real contradiction after all.[23] If challenged with conflicting facts, they will question the reliability of the "secular" sources of the "alleged facts" that conflict with their beliefs; thus, "young-earth creationists" challenge the scientific credentials of "mainstream" astronomy and geology, which support the conclusion that the universe is many billions of years old. But in refusing to admit *real* conflicts between their own views and logic or well-established facts, aren't these believers admitting, in effect, that it *is* valid to use logic and evidence to test the soundness of religious beliefs?

In fact, it is surprisingly difficult to avoid engaging in the rational evaluation of belief-systems. In conversations with religiously oriented persons, it often seems they are quite happy to use arguments as long as they think they have good arguments available; it is when they are stuck, or when the argument seems to be going against them, that appeals to "pure faith" begin to surface. Even sophisticated fideists are apt to be inconsistent here. They may not make any attempt to "prove" that their own faith is correct, but they are quite likely to begin pointing out flaws, inadequacies, and inconsistencies in other, competing religious belief-systems. In all fairness, though, it must be admitted that if such flaws pointed out in another's belief-system tend to cast doubt on that system, then similar flaws in one's own belief-system, as pointed out by others, must tend to cast doubt on whether one's own beliefs are correct. Simply ignoring such challenges leaves one open to the suspicion that one is not really interested in what is true, but only in holding on to one's present beliefs. What seems to be called for, then, is to *answer* the criticisms of one's convictions—to show that the objections to one's faith are mistaken or not serious, or can be met by a minor reformulation of one's beliefs that leaves the substance of the faith unchanged. To do this, of course, is precisely to *engage in the rational evaluation of religious belief-systems*, which is what the fideist says cannot be done!

CRITICAL RATIONALISM

Suppose we conclude, then, that both fideism and strong rationalism are mistaken. Unlike fideists, we will say that it *is* possible to rationally criticize and evaluate religious belief-systems, but in contrast with strong rationalists we will say that this evaluation cannot be expected to result in a conclusive, universally convincing *proof* that some particular system is correct.

If we accept this, then we are in effect affirming *critical rationalism*,[24] here defined as the view that *religious belief-systems can and must be rationally criticized and evaluated although conclusive proof of such a system is impossible.* Like strong rationalism, critical rationalism tells us to use our rational capabilities, to the greatest extent possible, in assessing religious beliefs. This involves developing the best arguments we can—the best "case," so to speak—for a belief-system and then comparing this with the case made for alternative systems. (Such a case for theism is developed in chapter 5.) It also involves considering the main *objections* to the belief-system in question. (A major objection to theism is discussed in chapter 7.) It may involve the consideration of rational foundations for belief that do *not* take the form of arguments (for this see chapter 6). Critical rationalism tells us to do all these things, but it warns us not to be overconfident or overoptimistic about the conclusiveness of such an investigation. This view is "critical" in two ways. It emphasizes the role of reason in criticizing, or critically evaluating, religious beliefs, as opposed to conclusively establishing such beliefs as true. Furthermore, the view is also "critical" with regard to the evaluation of reason itself; it takes a more modest and limited view of reason's capabilities in contrast with the excessively optimistic estimate of reason incorporated in strong rationalism.

Critical rationalism, as we have seen, emerges almost automatically if we reject both strong rationalism and fideism. There is, however, a further division that has not yet been considered, between two different varieties of critical rationalists. Some critical rationalists consider that, in order to be rational in their beliefs, they must be prepared to provide *reasons and arguments* in favor of the beliefs that they hold. They recognize, to be sure, that these reasons and arguments will not convince everyone, not even all "reasonable people," but having such reasons is nevertheless essential to being a reasonable religious believer. For those who believe in the theistic God, for example, a sampling of the arguments that might be given is provided in chapter 5 of this text. We may refer to such persons as *critical evidentialists*.

Others, however, see no need to offer arguments in favor of their religious beliefs. They consider that they have adequate basis for the beliefs without needing any arguments in their favor. Nevertheless, these individuals are not fideists; they do not consider their faith to be immune to rational investigation. They recognize that if reasonable objections are raised against their beliefs, they need to answer those objections, but they feel no need to give *positive reasons* in support of their beliefs. We might say that these people are willing to engage in *negative apologetics* (they will answer objections to their beliefs), but see no need for the sort of *positive apologetics* engaged in by evidentialists. Call this latter group *critical anti-evidentialists;* we shall hear much more about them in chapter 6.[25]

As we describe the way in which a critical rationalist proceeds to evaluate her beliefs, we will be thinking primarily of the critical evidentialist. However, much of what we say will apply to the critical anti-evidentialist as well, so long as we keep in mind that the anti-evidentialist sees no need to give positive reasons in favor of her beliefs.

The evaluation of beliefs will proceed somewhat differently, depending on whether we are concerned with some specific, relatively limited item of belief (such as the belief in life after death), or with the religious belief-system or worldview taken as a whole. Suppose, then, that we have selected some particular belief for investigation. This belief may be one we are ourselves inclined to accept, or one whose truth or falsity seems especially important to us—or it could even be determined by a course assignment!

Having selected a belief for study, the next step is to make sure that we *understand* the belief as accurately as possible. This involves deciding on definitions of key terms and exploring the implications of the belief—determining what other beliefs are required, if this one is accepted, and what other beliefs are excluded by it. If the belief in question is one we are not personally inclined to accept, we should pay careful attention to those who *do* accept it, so as to avoid misunderstandings resulting from our own lack of familiarity and possible prejudice. If on the contrary the belief is one we do accept, then we need to listen to the questions and criticisms of opponents so as to become aware of problems and ambiguities in the belief we may have overlooked through familiarity.

Once we are fairly sure we understand the belief to be studied, the next step is to look at *reasons* for and against accepting the belief. At best, such reasons will fall short of conclusive, universally convincing proof, but that does not mean they have no value at all. It has been pointed out by George Mavrodes that in many cases the success of reasons and arguments for a belief is "person-relative": that is to say, there are arguments that are convincing for one person, and actually enable her to come to know the truth about some subject, and yet these same arguments may fail completely for another, equally intelligent person.[26]

But why should this be so? Sometimes it may be simply that the premises of the argument are known to be true by one person but not by another. All of us know some things others are ignorant of, and vice versa, and a person cannot be expected to find an argument convincing if she does not know that its premises are true. In general, of course, knowledge and information can readily be communicated from one person to another, but not always. Sometimes the force of an argument can be appreciated only by persons having special training that is time-consuming and laborious to acquire. At other times one may have knowledge of some occurrence but be unable to convince others about this. (You may be very confident of your own recollection of a conversation at which you were present, and yet others may tell the story differently.) Sometimes the basis for one's belief may be in part a personal experience that cannot be adequately described or communicated to someone who has never had a similar experience. Last, but by no means least important, we all have preconceptions and prejudices that bias us toward seeing things in one way rather than in another.

None of this means that there is no such thing as the truth or that we should despair of ever being able to discover the truth. It is important, furthermore, to realize that while conclusive *proof* of a religious belief is difficult to achieve, conclusive *disproof* may sometimes be possible. If a belief can be shown to involve a logical contradiction, or to be in conflict with well-established facts, then a rational person will have no choice but to modify or abandon that belief. If certain views can be eliminated in this way, that narrows the range of remaining options. It may even be that, given unlimited time, patience, and good will, all of us could eventually overcome the differences caused by our diverse starting points and arrive at a consensus about the truth of things. In practice, however, such a goal is apt to prove elusive. In the absence of universal consensus there is really only one way to proceed: each of us must seek the truth on the basis of the other things he or she knows or reasonably believes to be true, using methods of reasoning that, upon careful reflection, commend themselves to us as likely to lead to the truth. We do not *create* the truth for ourselves; that way lies madness or the quagmire of relativism. But we must, each one of us, *seek* the truth for ourselves, and that is what philosophy is all about.

These considerations apply even more strongly when what is in question is not a particular item of belief but rather a religious worldview taken as a whole. Such worldviews are typically quite complex, involving claims about the nature of reality (metaphysics), the nature of knowledge and the methods of attaining it (epistemology), and the nature of goodness and of a good life (ethics). The complexity of worldviews means that the task of assessing them is also complex. We will want to consider whether the worldview is *logically consistent* or whether, on the contrary, contradictions are lurking among its essential beliefs. We will also want to know whether the worldview is *consistent with known facts,* and in assessing this we will, of course, be depending on various sources for these "facts" that we have come to regard as reliable. We need to ask about the *explanatory power* of the worldview: does it fit things into a comprehensive pattern in an illuminating way or does it leave us with a view of things possessing no coherent unity? A final question—difficult to formulate precisely, but immensely powerful in its influence—is this: to what extent does this worldview enable us to make sense of the actual living of our lives? Does it enable us to understand both our successes and our failures, and energize us to move in the direction of that which, upon reflection, we recognize as best and most worthwhile? Or does it fail, in the end, to cast any real light upon our actual living? (This was the central point of Kierkegaard's insistence that we must pay attention to *our own existence.* What is the point, he asked, of a

worldview that gives us no help here, however dazzling it may be in other
respects?)

Reflecting upon the rationality of religious worldviews along the lines
sketched out is no short or easy task, but we believe it can be a rewarding
one. Sometimes the process may result in a firmer grasp and a deeper commitment to the faith-perspective one had already accepted. At other times,
more or less serious modifications may seem to be called for. It does happen
that, as a result (at least in part) of such reflection, a person may undergo a
"conversion" to some entirely different way of seeing the world. Whatever
the specific result may be, it is to be hoped that the process will leave one
with a deeper understanding of the religious worldview(s) that are investigated, and a better appreciation of what is at stake either in accepting such a
worldview or rejecting it.[27]

We believe that critical rationalism, as outlined here, has significant
merits as an answer to the question of faith and reason. It cannot be denied,
however, that the study of religious beliefs according to the principles of critical rationalism sometimes proves to be rather frustrating. In a sense, the
critical rationalist is in a more exposed, more vulnerable position than either
the fideist or the strong rationalist. The critical rationalist is committed to the
task of rational evaluation of religious beliefs, unlike the fideist who makes
his "leap of faith" and is then able to ignore issues of rational justification.
But the critical rationalist, unlike the strong rationalist, has no assurance that
by proceeding properly she will be able to prove, conclusively, that one particular position is correct and that others are mistaken. So unlike the adherents of either of the other two views, the critical rationalist is never in the position of being able to decide, finally and for good, that the discussion
concerning the truth and validity of her religious beliefs has reached its ultimate conclusion.

Broadly speaking, the approach taken throughout this text is that of critical rationalism. If we were fideists, then many of the arguments we put forward and discuss concerning the truth or falsity of religious beliefs would
lose their point. If we were strong rationalists, the arguments might remain
but they would be used in a different way, and we would be making stronger
claims for their conclusiveness than we in fact find ourselves able to make.
Critical rationalism fits together well, furthermore, with the emphasis on the
consideration of alternative religious views which is present throughout the
text. In a sense, the critical rationalist *needs* alternative views, and the proponents of these views, more than either the fideist or the strong rationalist.
The strong rationalist *proves,* and *knows with certainty,* that her own view is
right, so her concern with other views can be limited to studying them to determine their errors, as well as looking for the best way by which their proponents can be persuaded to embrace "the truth." And the fideist, once he
has performed the "leap of faith," has very little need for alternative views—
at most, they may be of use, by way of contrast, in displaying the excellence
of the "chosen" view, which, judged by its own internal standards, will
always emerge as superior in any comparison.[28] The critical rationalist, in

contrast, has *no* absolute rational assurance that her own view is correct, so she needs the competing views both in order to assess their merits in comparison with her own, and for the sake of the penetrating criticism of her own view which is most likely to come from those who do not share it.

We have laid a good deal of stress on the continuing, open-ended nature of critical reflection as advocated by critical rationalism. It may seem that this serves to show that Kierkegaard was right after all, in saying that those who try to judge faith by objective, critical reflection will go on forever that way, and will never reach the point of *having* faith and of *being* religious. Does not this emphasis on an open-ended, never final process simply confirm what he said?

Not necessarily. A person may recognize that she cannot support her belief with evidence that will be convincing to all rational persons, and yet she herself may find the evidence for those beliefs rationally conclusive. Alternatively, she may recognize that, even from her own point of view, the evidence is less than conclusive and yet she may be deeply committed to carrying out those beliefs in her life. Kierkegaard, then, was right about at least one thing: religious faith often, perhaps always, involves a *commitment,* a "stepping out" and "entrusting ourselves" to something that goes beyond what we have conclusive proof of. (On the other hand, those who reject religion may have to come to terms with the fact that their own reasons for disbelief are less conclusive than they might wish.) Those who live the life of faith tell us that their commitment is *not* a tentative, partial, "fingers-crossed" sort of thing, carefully proportioned to the exact degree of rational evidence they may have for a particular conclusion. Some of the ancient Israelites were inclined to reason like this: "It seems pretty likely that our God, Yahweh, really is the one who is running the show, so by all means let's worship him, 'pay our dues,' make the appropriate sacrifices, and so on. Still, it is also true that Baal, the God of the Canaanites, has some pretty impressive credentials of his own. So, the smart thing to do is to hedge our bets a little—we will sacrifice to Yahweh, all right, but we will also do what we can to keep on the right side of Baal—just in case." According to the biblical text, Yahweh was not too happy about this approach to the matter—in fact, those who proceeded in this way were in deep trouble. A believer's commitment to God is supposed to be *total* commitment, even when one does not have total proof that one's belief in God is correct! Critical rationalism in no way speaks against such total commitment. Rather, it tells us that we should not pretend to greater rational certainty than is in fact available, but neither should we fail to exercise our powers of reflection and rational thought while we are making the most important decision of our lives.

It is true enough that this combination of religious commitment to "total devotion" with a mental attitude that is rational, reflective, and open to alternatives is likely to create some inner tension. But this tension is not necessarily destructive or ultimately harmful; it is rather a posture actually lived out, in a rewarding and productive way, in the lives of many reflective religious persons.[29]

STUDY QUESTIONS

1. Discuss dramatic examples in today's society of the irrational and harmful actions of persons being associated with the religious beliefs they hold. Analyze carefully the effect of religious beliefs in these cases. What other factors may be at play?

2. Which of the viewpoints on faith and reason sketched in this chapter most closely matches the approach taken by most religious persons you know? Discuss.

3. Explain strong rationalism, and discuss the reasons that make this approach plausible as a view of faith and reason.

4. Which of the objections against strong rationalism strikes you as most convincing? Discuss.

5. Explain fideism, and explain the fideist's reasons for saying that religious beliefs cannot be rationally evaluated.

6. What are some of the factors that make fideism attractive to many religious persons?

7. Have there been situations in which you, personally, have taken something like a "leap of faith"? If so, describe one of these situations.

8. Are the objections to fideism given in the text convincing or not? Discuss.

9. Is it possible to test religious beliefs by logic and evidence without ceasing to have *faith* in these beliefs? Discuss.

10. Explain critical rationalism, showing how it differs from strong rationalism and from fideism.

11. What do you see as the strong points of critical rationalism? What are its weaknesses?

12. Explain the difference between "evidentialist" and "anti-evidentialist" versions of critical rationalism.

13. Is it possible to be a critical rationalist, admitting that one's beliefs cannot be conclusively proved, without becoming "wishy-washy" in one's faith?

NOTES

1. For an account of the episode, with an interpretation of the religious worldview that lay behind the tragedy, see David Chidester, *Salvation and Suicide: An Interpretation of Jim Jones, the Peoples Temple, and Jonestown* (Indianapolis: Indiana University Press, 1988).

2. The term "faith," as used in religious contexts, is rather complex in its meaning. Faith usually involves a *cognitive* aspect; it involves *believing* that the doctrines of the religion are true. But it also is often thought of as involving, or implying, a *volitional* aspect, expressed in *commitment* to the object of faith and *obedience* to what is commanded; there may also be an *affective* aspect of *trust* or *love*. In this chapter we have in mind primarily the "belief" aspect of faith, but we in no way wish to minimize the importance of the other aspects.

3. See Blaise Pascal, *Pensées,* tr. W. F. Trotter, and *The Provincial Letters,* tr. Thomas M'Crie (New York: Random House, 1941), p. 83. (A selection is found in PRSR2e, pt. 2.)

4. See Paul W. Gooch, *Partial Knowledge: Philosophical Studies in Paul* (Notre Dame, Ind.: University of Notre Dame Press, 1987) p. 42.

5. See, for example, I Corinthians 15.

6. Note the difference between "does" and "should"—while it is clear that reason does in fact have *some* place in religion, we cannot automatically assume that the place it actually has in people's thinking about religion is the place it *should* have.

7. The three main positions discussed in this chapter result from a present-day analysis of the issues; they were not applied as self-descriptions by the historical philosophers mentioned. Some thinkers, indeed, may not be too easy to classify: many of Pascal's statements, for example, sound like fideism, yet his position as a whole seems rather to be that of "critical rationalism." Somewhat similar analyses of the alternatives on the faith-reason issue have been put forward by William J. Abraham (*An Introduction to the Philosophy of Religion* [Englewood Cliffs, N.J.: Prentice-Hall, 1985], chapters 7, 8, 9, and 10, see the selection in PRSR2e, pt. 2), and by C. Stephen Evans (*Philosophy of Religion: Thinking About Faith* [Downers Grove, Ill.: InterVarsity Press, 1985], chap. 1).

8. There is another use of "rationalism" in epistemology, in which it contrasts with *empiricism.* Rationalism in this sense is the view that the most important truths are known by "pure reason" without reliance on sense perception. That is *not* the way "rationalism" is used in this chapter.

9. William K. Clifford, "The Ethics of Belief," in *The Rationality of Belief in God,* ed. George I. Mavrodes (Englewood Cliffs, N.J.: Prentice-Hall, 1970), pp. 159–60. (Also in PRSR2e, pt. 2.)

10. Ibid., pp. 152–3.

11. Ibid., p. 160.

12. For an excellent discussion of Locke's views, see Nicholas Wolterstorff, "The Migration of the Theistic Arguments: From Natural Theology to Evidentialist Apologetics," in *Rationality, Religious Belief, and Moral Commitment,* ed. Robert Audi and William J. Wainwright (Ithaca, N.Y.: Cornell University Press, 1986), pp. 38–81.

13. An important difference is that Aquinas, unlike Clifford and Locke, did not lay on *each individual believer* (or even on each *adult* believer) the responsibility for providing rational justification for his or her beliefs. For Aquinas's views, see the article by Wolterstorff cited in the preceding note, and also Ralph McInerny, "Analogy and Foundationalism in Thomas Aquinas," in *Rationality, Religious Belief, and Moral Commitment,* (also cited in the preceding note), pp. 271–288.

14. See Richard Swinburne, *The Existence of God* (Oxford: Oxford University Press, 1979), and *Faith and Reason* (Oxford: Oxford University Press, 1981).

15. More recent philosophers who have pursued this ideal include Edmund Husserl (1859–1938) and Bertrand Russell (1872–1970).

16. Among the important philosophers who argue against the ideal of "pure, presuppositionless reason" are Ludwig Wittgenstein (1889–1951) and Hans-Georg Gadamer (b. 1900).

17. FEE-day-ism; the word is derived from the Latin word *fides,* meaning "faith."

18. Strictly speaking, these fideistic views are those of "Johannes Climacus," a pseudonym who is the ostensible author of some of Kierkegaard's books. Not all the views expressed by Kierkegaard's pseudonyms are attributable to Kierkegaard himself, so the views stated here may not fully represent Kierkegaard's own position.

19. Kierkegaard, *Concluding Unscientific Postscript*, trans. David F. Swenson and Walter Lowrie (Princeton, N.J.: Princeton University Press, 1941), pp. 178–9. (A selection is found in PRSR2e, pt. 2.)

20. Ibid., p. 182.

21. Several scholars have argued that Kierkegaard's overall position allows a larger place for the rational evaluation of faith perspectives than is suggested by the excerpts presented here. (See Marilyn Gaye Piety, "Kierkegaard on Rationality," *Faith and Philosophy*, vol. 10, no. 3 [July 1993]: 365–79; C. Stephen Evans, "The Epistemological Significance of Transformative Religious Experiences: A Kierkegaardian Exploration," *Faith and Philosophy*, vol. 8, no. 2 [April 1991]: 180–92; and Merold Westphal, *Kierkegaard's Critique of Religion and Society* [Macon, Ga.: Mercer University Press, 1987].) To the extent that this is correct, Kierkegaard may be less a "pure fideist" than is implied in the text; this would serve as a confirmation of the observation that it is difficult for a reflective person to completely avoid engaging in the rational evaluation of his beliefs.

22. It should we noted that many of us sometimes find ourselves in a position which is somewhat similar to this. That is to say, we may be aware that a set of beliefs contains or implies a contradiction, but we may have no idea *which* of the beliefs needs to be given up or modified—each of the beliefs, taken separately, seems to have strong evidence in its favor. In this case we may well decide, for the time being, to continue to accept all of the beliefs in question, since under the circumstances giving up any one of them might well leave us worse off than we were originally. This situation, however, is quite different from that of the fideist described in the text. In the situation described, we are well aware that there *is* falsehood somewhere in our beliefs; we just don't know how to identify and correct it. The fideist in the text, on the other hand, is simply unconcerned about the presence of contradictions in her belief-system.

23. For an incisive criticism of this strategy, see David Basinger, "Biblical Paradox: Does Revelation Challenge Logic?" *Journal of the Evangelical Theological Society* 30 (1987): 205–13.

24. The term "critical rationalism" is found in the writings of Karl Popper (see *The Open Society and its Enemies*, vol. 2 [Princeton: Princeton University Press, 1971], p. 231), and the meaning given to this term here is broadly consistent with Popper's use of it.

25. An excellent summary of the different typologies of approaches to the faith-reason issue, see Randall Basinger, "Faith/Reason Typologies: A Constructive Proposal," *Christian Scholar's Review* 27, no. 1 (Fall 1997): 62–73.

26. See George I. Mavrodes, *Belief in God* (New York: Random House, 1970), 17–48.

27. A good description of the process of worldview evaluation is given in William Abraham, *An Introduction to the Philosophy of Religion*, pp. 104–09. (See also the selection in PRSR2e, pt. 2.) Abraham sketches out a scenario in which, as a result of such reflection, a person adopts a particular religious perspective. Real-life examples may be found in two books recounting the "spiritual autobiographies" of contemporary philosophers: Kelly James Clark, ed., *Philosophers Who Believe: The Spiritual Journeys of Eleven Leading Thinkers* (Downers Grove, Ill.: InterVarsity, 1993), and Thomas V. Morris, ed., *God and the Philosophers: The Reconciliation of Faith and Reason* (New York: Oxford, 1994).

28. It must be said in fairness that fideists, and strong rationalists, sometimes exhibit in practice a more generous appreciation of conflicting views than these descriptions might suggest. Still, it is probably true in general that fideists and strong rationalists have *less* interest in the consideration of alternative views than do critical rationalists.

29. For an excellent depiction of this tension from the standpoint of evangelical Protestantism, see Daniel Taylor, *The Myth of Certainty* (Downers Grove, Ill.: Inter-Varsity Press, 1999). The tension is also discussed and/or illustrated in several of the essays in Morris, *God and the Philosophers.*

SUGGESTED READING

Abraham, William J. *An Introduction to the Philosophy of Religion.* Englewood Cliffs, N.J.: Prentice-Hall, 1985. Chaps. 7, 8, 9, and 10.

Evans, C. Stephen. *Philosophy of Religion: Thinking about Faith.* Downers Grove, Ill.: InterVarsity Press, 1985. Chap. 1.

Helm, Paul. *Faith and Understanding.* Grand Rapids, Mich.: William B. Eerdmans, 1997.

————, ed. *Faith and Reason.* Oxford: Oxford University Press, 1999.

Hick, John. *Faith and Knowledge.* Ithaca, N.Y.: Cornell University Press, 1957.

Mavrodes, George I. *Belief in God.* New York: Random House, 1970.

————, ed. *The Rationality of Belief in God.* Englewood Cliffs, N.J.: Prentice-Hall, 1970.

Mitchell, Basil. *The Justification of Religious Belief.* Oxford: Oxford University Press, 1981.

Pascal, Blaise. *Pensées.* Trans. W. F. Trotter, and *The Provincial Letters.* Trans. Thomas M'Crie. New York: Random House, 1941. (These two works comprise this single volume.)

Penelhum, Terence. *God and Skepticism.* Dordrecht, The Netherlands: D. Riedel, 1983.

Placher, William. *Unapologetic Theology: A Christian Voice in a Pluralistic Conversation.* Louisville, Ky.: Westminster/John Knox Press, 1989.

Swinburne, Richard. *The Existence of God.* Oxford: Oxford University Press, 1979.

————. *Faith and Reason.* Oxford: Oxford University Press, 1981.

(See also suggested readings for Chapter 6.)

CHAPTER 4   THE DIVINE
                    ATTRIBUTES:
                    WHAT IS GOD
                    LIKE?

"Throw this salt in the water, and sit with me on the morrow."
So he did. He said to him, "Well, bring me the salt that you
threw in the water last night." He looked for it, but could not
find it as it was dissolved.
"Well, taste the water on this side.—How does it taste?"
"Salty,"
"Taste it in the middle.—How does it taste?"
"Salty."
"Taste it at the other end.—How does it taste?"
"Salty."
"Take a mouthful and sit with me." So he did.
"It is always the same."
He said to him, "You cannot make out what exists in it,
yet it is there.
"It is this very fineness which ensouls all this world, it is the
true one, it is the soul. *You are that*, Shvetaketu."

—CHANDOYA UPANISHAD[1]

In this text from the sacred writings of India, Shvetaketu and his father are
probing a topic of intense interest to religious people—they are considering
the *nature of God*. The answer they arrive at, to state it all too simply, is that
God is the Being which is the inner reality of everything whatever. The salt is
imperceptible to touch or vision; nevertheless it pervades every drop of the
water. Similarly, God—or Being, or Brahman—is imperceptible to human
senses, yet nevertheless completely pervades all of reality, including the in-
quirer who raises the question concerning the nature of God: "*You are that,*
Shvetaketu."

This question concerning the nature of God will occupy us throughout the present chapter. We shall not, however, concern ourselves primarily with the specific answers found by Shvetaketu and his father, and by others in the Hindu religious tradition. Rather, we shall focus most of our attention on a view of God known as *traditional theism*;[2] this is the conception of God that has been held, with some variations, by the vast majority of thinkers in the great "theistic" religions of Judaism, Christianity, and Islam. But the view of God seen in the selection from the Upanishads, often termed *pantheism*, will not be neglected entirely; instead, it will be introduced from time to time as a contrast and an alternative to classical theism. We also, from time to time, explain and comment on another sort of conception of God that has recently become popular in some Christian and Jewish circles, a view known as *process theism*.[3]

At this point, however, a question may be occurring to the reader. What is the point, it may be asked, of inquiring about the *nature* of God when, as yet, we have not even established whether there *is* any such being as God? Would it not make more sense first to show that there *is* a God, and then to discuss his (or her, or its) attributes or characteristics?

There is certainly some point to this, but consider a counter-question: if we have no idea *what* God is, then what sense is there in asking whether God *exists* or not? Lewis Carroll wrote a marvelous poem titled "The Hunting of the Snark," but it would make little sense to ask whether there really are snarks, because Carroll never tells us clearly what sort of creature a snark is supposed to be. If we are similarly "in the dark" as to God's nature, what meaning can we attach to the question whether God exists or not?

Probably the reason why the question of God's existence seems to most of us to make reasonably clear sense is that we *do* have an idea of what God is like, and when we ask whether God exists it is *that kind* of being whose existence is being asked about. Many readers of this book, furthermore, will have a background of familiarity with the theistic religious traditions, and the conception of God's nature these readers will be presupposing is one which is at least fairly close to the traditional theism we will be studying in this chapter. Therefore it is important to become as clear as possible about that conception of God before we proceed with other matters.

The right way to understand what is going on in this chapter, then, is this: we are not meaning to assert at this point that there *really* is a being, called God, with the various characteristics discussed throughout the chapter. Rather, we are *presenting a hypothesis* concerning the nature of a being whose existence will be investigated later on. The questions we will be asking are of two kinds: First, what is the conception of God's nature held by traditional theism (and, from time to time, the conceptions held by pantheism and by process theism)? Second, is this conception one that is *coherent* and *logically consistent*? If it should develop that a certain idea of God suffers from unreconcilable internal contradictions, then with regard to *that* conception we need proceed no further: a "God" whose nature can be stated only in contradictions cannot possibly exist, and to suppose that there is such a God as that is nonsense.[4]

How will we arrive at the characteristics we attribute to God? In part, the question is one of history and tradition: the attributes considered here are some of those that *in fact* have been ascribed to God by theistic thinkers. Many such thinkers, however, would assert that there is more to it than this; they would claim that the theistic concept of God possesses an *internal unity and coherence* that goes far beyond any list of characteristics that merely happen to be ascribed to God in a certain tradition. An important source of this unity and coherence lies in the attributes considered in the next section.

PERFECT AND WORTHY OF WORSHIP

In developing our conception of God, it would be foolish to overlook the fact that, above all, *God is a being who is the object of worship.* God's "worshipability"—or, to use a word that is no longer very familiar, his "worshipfulness"—is of primary religious importance, so that a conception of God that is lacking at this point is unacceptable regardless of other merits it may possess. Whatever else may be true of God, it must at least be said that *God is worthy of worship.*

But what sort of God is required, if God is to be worthy of our worship? The attitude or activity of worship is no doubt complex and difficult to describe completely and accurately. But there can be little doubt that worship, in the full sense of the term, is supposed to involve *total devotion* of the worshiper to the one worshiped. In worship we totally dedicate ourselves to God; we place ourselves at God's disposal completely and without reservation. Any hint of "bargaining" with God, any mental reservation by which, however subtly, we "keep our options open" with respect to a possible shift of allegiance detracts severely from the complete commitment that worship properly requires of us.

If this is the case we can ask, What must be true of God in order to make such unreserved devotion appropriate—in order, that is, for God to be "worthy of worship"? It is fairly clear, to begin with, that *God must be the greatest of all beings.* How could it be reasonable, or even plausible, to offer to God such total devotion if there exist other beings equally or even more worthy of our adulation, obedience, and so on? Under such circumstances as these, the response of a reasonable person would seem to be that God might, indeed, be entitled to a measure of honor and obedience because of his superiority to all others in the immediate vicinity—but not unreserved trust and honor and obedience, not total devotion. One would give to God his due, while keeping in mind the possibility that someone else might appear to whom even more was due. God would merit respect, honor, and a degree of obedience, but not worship.

God, then, must be the greatest of all beings. But we can go farther than this. Suppose it is plain to us that, though God is *in fact* the greatest of all beings, it is entirely possible that there should have been a being *superior* to God in one or several ways. Would this not inevitably detract from the unreserved devotion which is required for worship? As a matter of fact, we are supposing, God is the greatest of all beings, and there is nothing else in existence that could supplant him in our esteem. But things could have been different; there might very well have been some other being able to rival or even excel the God whom we worship. If so, then even in the midst of our worship, would we not occasionally find ourselves with a touch of regret for the greater things which might have been?[5]

With this line of thought in mind, we are ready to appreciate the point of a definition of God offered by the great medieval Christian thinker Anselm (1033–1109). Addressing God, he said, "We believe that thou art a being than which nothing greater can be conceived."[6] He was saying, in effect, that God is so great that *no being is conceivable that would surpass God in any way.* God, in other words is the *absolutely perfect being.* Not only is there in fact no other being equal or superior to God, but there could not be any such being, for God contains in himself all possible perfection and excellence.

This conception of God, as the *absolutely perfect being,* is one that, upon reflection, many religious persons have found to be deeply satisfying. It is, as we have seen, plausibly thought to be implied by the very idea of worship,[7] and it lays the foundation for a conception of God that is very hard to challenge as inadequate.

"Perfect-being theology" (or "Anselmian" theology, as it is also called),[8] can then be seen as a "binding thread" that ties together and unifies the discussion of the various attributes ascribed to God by traditional theism.[9] Can we, indeed, go further and say (as Anselm himself seems to say) that the notion of God as the perfect being gives us all the guidance we need in setting forth the divine attributes, so that our whole conception of God can be, as it were, woven in its entirety from this single thread?

Probably not, for several reasons. For one thing, although the idea of God as the perfect being has strong intuitive appeal, it is by no means the case that different theologians, even from the same religious tradition, will always agree on which conception of God's attributes has the effect of portraying God as "more perfect" than another. For example, it seemed clear to Anselm, as to Augustine (354–430) and most other ancient and medieval theologians, that in order to be perfect God must be *impassible*—that is, God must be incapable of emotion, and in particular incapable of feeling any sorrow or suffering as a result of the afflictions of his creatures. Since suffering is negative, a harm to the being which undergoes it, a perfect being must be *incapable* of suffering. More recently, however, many theologians have rebelled against the notion of an "impassible" God, insisting that God's perfection, and in particular his attributes of love and sympathy, positively require that he be capable of suffering along with his creatures. Clearly, we have here a major disagreement, and one that will not readily be settled by further discussions about the meaning of "perfect" as applied to God.

It should also be realized that in setting forth God's attributes we cannot possibly ignore the religious and theological tradition within which any given theology operates. If, for instance, one were to offer to the Jewish religious community a conception of God radically at variance with that which is found in the Hebrew Bible and in Jewish tradition, that conception would not be warmly received no matter how plausible a case one could make for the "perfection" of God so conceived. An interesting historical example of this is the philosopher Baruch de Spinoza (1632–1677). Born a Jew, he was excommunicated from the synagogue for his "heretical" conception of God, which was in fact closer to pantheism than to traditional Jewish theism. As we have noted, intuitions about perfection may vary, and a philosopher of religion who is seeking to apply that notion would do well to pay attention to the conception of God that actual religious communities have found best to represent perfection and worshipfulness.

A further consideration that must guide our application of the notion of divine perfection is that of *logical consistency and coherence.* As was already noted, any conception of God that is supposed to represent an actual being must at least meet the requirement of logical consistency. To be sure, a set of divine attributes that are logically inconsistent could not possibly be part of the description of a perfect being, so this criterion may already be included in the very idea of "perfect-being" theology. But while this reasoning may be valid, it is also true that humans can be quite ingenious in imagining and ascribing to God seemingly marvelous characteristics that in fact are logically inconsistent. It is important, then, to carefully investigate the logical consistency of the various attributes we wish to ascribe to God.

NECESSARY AND SELF-EXISTENT

We begin with a pair of attributes that at first may seem abstract and difficult to grasp, yet are important for pointing out the fundamental difference, according to traditional theism, between God and everything else whatsoever. First, consider *self-existence.* It is a familiar thought to us that for many things—especially living creatures of all kinds—it may take energy and often effort simply for the thing to remain in existence. We live our lives "from within," and when the inner vitality needed to do this becomes weak we feel our own existence to be imperiled and insecure. But we also depend on external beings and circumstances in various ways for our existence. Other beings brought us into existence, and we depend on food, water, air, and so on to sustain us in existence. Furthermore, we are all too aware of various things that might damage or destroy our existence; in a sense, then, we are dependent on the *non*occurrence of these sorts of things for our continued life and well-being.

Now, consider the idea of a being that is dependent on other things in none of these ways. It owes nothing to any other being for its origin or sustenance, and it is entirely incapable of being threatened, harmed, or destroyed by anything else whatsoever. Such an entity would exist wholly "from within," entirely "on its own steam." It would be, in a word, self-existent.

Now we introduce two additional terms: *necessary* and *contingent*. To say something is contingent is to say that it depends on things or circumstances other than itself: contingency plans are plans for what may or may not be done, depending on other things that may or may not happen. If on the other hand a being is not contingent in any way and it will exist regardless of anything that may happen to other things or circumstances, then its existence is inevitable, inescapable. It is, in other words, a *necessary being*, a being that *depends on nothing but itself, and, given that it exists, its nonexistence, either in the past or in the future, is absolutely impossible.*

It is very clear that God, as conceived by traditional theism, is a necessary and self-existent being in the senses I have just explained. God is eternal; no other being is relevant to his coming into existence, since he never in fact came into existence, and nothing whatever can in any way threaten or endanger God's existence. It is, then, simply impossible that God should not exist. We further note that God's necessity and self-existence are essential elements in his perfection; it seems clear that God is greater if he depends on nothing outside himself than if he were so dependent.

These characteristics of necessity and self-existence fundamentally distinguish God from all other things in existence. In particular, there is nothing in the natural world, the world revealed to us by the sciences, about which it is at all plausible to say that it is necessary and self-existent. All the familiar things of everyday life—people and animals, cars and houses, trees and mountains, stars and galaxies—come into being and pass away, and are clearly contingent beings. Even the fundamental constituents of matter—the so-called "elementary particles"—are not immutable but form, disappear, and are changed into others, as attested by high-energy physics. According to the Big Bang theory (now a consensus view among cosmologists), it seems that the very matter-energy of the universe itself had an origin. So if there is anything at all other than God that is necessary and self-existent, we have no idea what it might be and no reason to suppose that anything of the sort exists at all.

There is however another, even stronger, sense in which something may be said to be "necessary." Some propositions are said to be *logically necessary*, meaning that it is logically impossible that they be false; the falsehood of such a proposition would in some way involve a contradiction. (For example, it would involve a contradiction to deny that "Every triangle has three angles"; this is a *logically necessary proposition*.) Picking up on this, we can say that a *logically necessary being* would be a being whose *existence* is logically necessary, whose *non-existence* would be contradictory and logically impossible. It should be noted that if God's existence is logically necessary it will also be necessary in the sense previously explained, but the converse does not hold; God might be self-existent, and in *that* sense necessary, without being logically necessary.

Should God be understood as a logically necessary being? This question is deeply controversial. A good many theistic philosophers and theologians—perhaps the majority—have asserted that God's existence *is* logically necessary, but many others have disagreed. On the face of it, "God exists" does not *seem* to be a logically necessary truth, and the proposition "There is no God" does not seem, at first glance, to be logically contradictory. This proposition has even been accepted as *true* by quite a few persons who are in general quite expert in the detection of contradictions. Indeed, Immanuel Kant (1724–1804) has persuaded many philosophers with his argument that *no* proposition asserting the *existence* of something can be logically necessary. (Thus, "Every triangle has three angles" is necessary, but "A triangle exists" is not necessary.)[10]

Still, it may be that none of these considerations is decisive. Kant's arguments, while impressive, have been strongly disputed, especially in recent years.[11] Furthermore, we should not be misled by simple examples into thinking that it is always easy to determine whether a given proposition is either logically necessary or self-contradictory. Mathematics, for example, contains a great many necessary propositions whose necessity (and truth) are far from obvious, and some mathematical statements have resisted even the most intensive efforts of mathematicians to determine whether they are necessarily true or not.

The question of the logical necessity of God's existence will be pursued further in the next chapter, as part of the discussion of the ontological argument for God's existence. In closing, we note the following: if on the one hand God's existence *is* logically necessary, then this will surely count as a "perfection" of God, one of the many excellences that set God apart from all lesser beings. If on the other hand God's existence is *not* logically necessary, it will also be the case that it is *impossible* that God's existence should be necessary. In that case, "necessary existence" will *not* count as a perfection; rather, it will just be another of the many logically incoherent attributes that we humans, in our confusion, have invented and ascribed to God.[12]

PERSONAL AND FREE CREATOR

We now turn to some attributes that are more familiar to ordinary religious people. To say that God is *personal* is to say at least the following things: God has *knowledge and awareness*; God *performs actions*; God is *free* in the actions he performs; and God can *enter into relationships* with persons other than himself. These requirements seem minimal, in that a God lacking in any of them would seem *not* to be fully personal; on the other hand, if God does meet these requirements then it would seem appropriate to describe God as "personal" even though there may be many respects in which God is very different from the human persons we know.[13]

From the standpoint of theism it seems evident that personality, or personhood, should be considered as a perfection of God. Many of the finest things we know—love, intelligence, creativity, and moral goodness, for example—are attributes exclusively of persons, and if God were not personal he would be debarred from possessing any of these excellences. There is also the extremely important point that for many theists worship, and the religious life generally, are conceived in terms of a *personal relationship* with God; thus if God were *not* personal their entire idea of the religious life would collapse.

God, according to traditional theism, is also the *creator* of all things other than himself. The idea of creation is important in all the theistic faiths, and it seems essential to the idea of an absolutely perfect being that, if there are beings other than God in existence, God should be their creator. God's status as creator ensures his superiority, mastery, and ownership over all the things he has created in a way that could hardly be done otherwise. God is said, furthermore, to have created "out of nothing" (Latin, *ex nihilo*). This is not to be understood as if "nothing" were the name of some sort of mysterious "stuff" out of which God created the universe. Instead, to say that creation is out of nothing means that there was no material out of which God created; rather, all things other than God exist solely because he wills them to exist and have no other basis at all for their existence. Creation out of nothing contrasts with, and is superior to, two other modes in which the production of things might be imagined. It is superior to production from pre-existing materials because in the latter case God's act of creating would be dependent upon, and probably to some extent limited by, the materials he had to work with. (There would also be the question of how to account for the existence of the materials.) It also is superior to creation *ex Deo*, "out of God's own being," because this would tend to compromise the absolute distinction between creator and creature that is the hallmark of theistic metaphysics.

The God of classical theism is not only the creator but also the *sustainer* of finite things, which is to say that created things are *totally dependent on God for their existence from moment to moment*. A dramatic but not inaccurate way of putting this is to say that, were God for a single instant to completely forget about his creation, in that instant the entire creation would collapse into nothingness.

God, furthermore, enjoys *freedom* in creating, sustaining, and governing the world. To say that God is free means that God cannot be forced, constrained, or controlled by anything outside of himself. Unlike creatures, God has no need to adjust himself to an environment; rather, all environments exist only in virtue of his creating and sustaining activity. Moreover, God has the freedom to *choose* what sort of world to create and how to dispose of that world. To be sure, given God's essential goodness, it is impossible that God should choose anything that conflicts with that goodness. But this leaves God still with a very wide range of possibilities, among which he chooses the ones he will bring about. Indeed, it has generally been held that God was perfectly *free either to create a world or to refrain from creating;* prior to creation, there were no creatures to whom the "right to exist" was owed, nor would the goodness of creation "add to" the greatness and goodness of God in such a way that creating was for him necessary and inevitable. Thus, the decision to create was itself a free and generous choice on God's part.

These attributes fundamentally distinguish the theistic God from God as conceived in pantheism. To see this, we will consider briefly an especially interesting form of pantheism, the *advaita vedanta* of the Hindu thinker

Shankara (788–820).[14] The sole ultimate reality, according to Shankara, is Brahman, which is wholly nonempirical, entirely beyond ordinary human experience, though its existence and nature can be grasped intuitively through yogic meditation. Our ordinary experience, to be sure, indicates that both the world of nature and individual human personalities exist as independent realities. Such experience, however, is to be viewed as we view dream experiences: within the dream, we cannot help but consider the objects of the dream experiences as real, but once we awaken this is seen to have been an illusion. Similarly, in our ordinary state of ignorance we cannot help regarding the objects and persons of everyday life as real, but from the higher, enlightened standpoint, all of this—including one's own personal existence!—is seen to be illusory. Indeed, this "ignorance" is the principal obstacle that needs to be overcome in order to reach true spiritual illumination.

Brahman, then, is *not* personal; rather, it is the ultimate, impersonal "true being" that is the reality behind all the illusory appearances of the world. Other versions of pantheism describe the situation somewhat differently, but for none of them is God the creator, for creation implies a distinction between God and the universe that is alien to pantheism. Furthermore, an impersonal "being" cannot *act* and therefore cannot be *free* in its actions; rather, it simply and changelessly *is*.

The God of process theism is like the God of traditional theism in being personal. But the relationship between God and the universe is considerably different. Process theism rejects both the idea of creation *ex nihilo* and the radical distinction between God and the world posited by traditional theism. Process theism's conception of God's relation to the world is best expressed by saying that the world is *God's body,* through which he lives his life as we live our lives through our bodies. This means that God and the universe are not wholly distinct from each other, as for classical theism; rather, all finite things, including human beings, are in a sense included in God's own being. Perhaps the best way of conceiving this is to imagine that each individual cell in a human body is possessed of its own consciousness and awareness, however limited, of what is happening to it and what is going on around it. Then imagine that these individual "cell-consciousnesses" are, as it were, caught up and included in the *unified* consciousness that is the "mind" of the entire body, a consciousness that both transcends and includes each one of them. In some such way as this, each of us is a "cell" in the body of God, and because of this God is able literally to *share,* in a most intimate way, in all of our experiences, our joys and our sorrows. In the words of A. N. Whitehead (1861–1947), the philosopher whose works inspired process theism, "God is the great companion—the fellow-sufferer who understands."[15]

All of this means that the relationship between God and the universe is conceived very differently in process theism than in traditional theism. In traditional theism, there is a *one-sided dependence* of the universe upon God, whereas in process theism the relationship is better described as one of *interdependence and mutuality* between God and the universe. Whitehead went so far as to say, "It is as true to say that God transcends the World, as that the

World transcends God. It is as true to say that God creates the World, as that the World creates God."[16] Since God needs his body through which to live, even as we need our bodies, it must be concluded that *God can never be without a body*—that is, without a universe. That does not necessarily mean that the present universe is, like God, without beginning and without end, though this is a possibility. But if, as scientific evidence seems to suggest, our present physical universe had a beginning in time, we may be assured that before it there was another universe, or perhaps an endless series of universes, so that God has never been without a body—without a world.

ALL-POWERFUL, ALL-KNOWING, AND PERFECTLY GOOD

God is *all-powerful*, or *omnipotent*, he is *all-knowing*, or *omniscient*, and he is *perfectly morally good*. All of these attributes are fundamental to the theistic view of God, and each of them involves difficulties in understanding and formulation.

Apparently the natural way to understand God's omnipotence is simply to say that God can do anything whatever. But this quickly runs into difficulties. Can God create a square circle, or cause it to be true that $1 + 2 = 1$? At least since the time of Thomas Aquinas (1225–1274), it has been recognized that the exercise of God's power must be limited to what is *logically possible*.[17] The expression *square circle* is one that could not possibly apply (correctly) to anything, and so the fact that God cannot make one implies no defect in God's power. Other limitations on what God can do stem from God's own nature; God cannot do things that require embodiment (such as climbing Mount Everest) or that imply limitations (such as, for instance, forgetting something). Perhaps more significant, it is generally held that God cannot do things that imply a moral fault, such as breaking one of his promises. In view of such considerations as these, we may say that God's omnipotence means that *God can perform any action the performance of which is logically consistent, and consistent with God's own nature*.[18]

Philosophers have devised a great many puzzles with which to test definitions of omnipotence; one of the most intriguing is the "paradox of the stone." Consider the following question: can God create a stone that he cannot lift? If he cannot, there is something he cannot do, and he is not omnipotent. (It is obvious that making something one is unable to lift is a logically possible thing to do—home builders, for example, do this all the time.) Suppose, on the other hand, that God *can* create a stone he cannot lift. So far, so good, but now there is another task that God cannot perform, namely, to lift the stone in question! So either way, God is not omnipotent. (So as not to cut short the reader's attempt to wrestle with this puzzle, the solution is relegated to an endnote.)[19]

The most immediately obvious way of expressing God's *omniscience* is to say that God knows everything, or, better (since only *true* propositions can be *known*), that God knows all true propositions. A difficulty arises, however, in that it seems there are propositions that are true at some times but not at others. Consider the proposition "Martha was married last Sunday." Assuming that Martha does indeed marry on a Sunday, this proposition is true for exactly one week, from midnight on the Sunday of the wedding to Sunday midnight one week later. God, presumably, *knows* this proposition for exactly as long as the proposition itself is true—though to be sure, he would know *after* the time period in question that this proposition *had been true* during that period.[20] In view of this, we can modify our definition to say that at any time God knows all the propositions which are true at that time.

But do we also need a clause, similar to the one in the definition of omnipotence, excluding true propositions which are such that it is *logically impossible* that God should know them? Are there any true propositions of this sort? One possible candidate consists of propositions about decisions God himself is going to make. It seems likely that it is not possible for anyone, including God, to be in the process of making a decision and also, while making it, already to know what the decision will be. So if God *does* make decisions (as theism says he does), there may be truths God logically cannot know while he is making those decisions. To be sure, it might be held that God does not decide things in time, but rather, in some peculiar way, before time or outside of time. But even if this is true, it does not entirely blunt the force of the point made: there would still be an "aspect" of God's life, even if not a period of time, in which he must operate without knowledge of certain true propositions. (Other candidates for true propositions that God logically cannot know will be discussed in chapter 8.)

There is one further point to be made, before we present our full definition of omniscience. We humans not only *know* things, we also *believe* things; some of the latter are true, and others are false. Now, it may be that God has *no* beliefs over and above his knowledge, and certainly he holds no false beliefs. But then our definition of omniscience needs to be crafted so as to exclude explicitly God's holding false beliefs.

With these considerations in mind, we can define God's omniscience as follows: *At any time, God knows all propositions which are true at that time and are such that God's knowing them at that time is logically possible, and God never believes anything that is false.* The most controversial element in this definition is the clause stating that God knows only what it is logically possible for him to know. But this really should not cause any difficulty: if there are no truths that are logically impossible for God to know, then the clause in question will exclude nothing from God's knowledge, but that does not mean that the definition is incorrect or inadequate.

It is a matter of consensus among theists that God is *perfectly morally good*. Whatever character traits, principles of action, and so on it may take to qualify a being as morally perfect must definitely be held to characterize God. What needs to be clarified here mainly involves two things: What is the *content* of perfect moral goodness? Furthermore, what is the *relation* between moral goodness and God?

The specific content of moral goodness—whether, for instance, love is more important as a divine attribute than holiness and justice, or the reverse, or whether they are all equally important—is something theists find it hard to agree about. One's answers to these kinds of questions are apt to depend in important ways on particular theological views about the ways in which God acts and deals with people, and so these matters are perhaps best left to be dealt with within the various theological traditions. In what follows we shall speak generally of God's "goodness," "love," "justice," and the like, without claiming to specify exactly what each of these means or how they are related to each other.[21]

With regard to the relation between goodness and God, an initial question is whether God is capable of acting contrary to moral goodness. A few philosophers have thought that, in order for God to be morally praiseworthy, he must be capable of doing evil, even though he never in fact does so.[22] The vast majority of theistic thinkers, however, have held that God is *essentially* morally perfect—that his very nature is such that it is impossible for him to act in a way that is morally wrong. This view was, in fact, anticipated in our discussion of omnipotence, when we assumed that God is *incapable* of breaking one of his promises.

Another question about the relation between goodness and God concerns the source of the standard of moral goodness. Does there exist, independently of God, a standard of goodness to which God, like all other persons, is morally obligated to conform? On the other hand, do moral good and evil owe their existence entirely to the will and command of God? Or is there some further possibility for the relation between God and the standard of moral goodness? For the time being, we defer engaging this question until chapter 14.

None of the attributes discussed in this section can properly apply to God as conceived in pantheism. The pantheistic God can, to be sure, be said to possess "all power" and "all knowledge," since whatever power and knowledge there may be are, by definition, *its* power and knowledge; it is the ultimate substance, the "inner soul," of everything that exists. But the pantheistic God possesses no *individual mind* that would enable it either to *know* or to *act* as we understand these notions. According to Spinoza, "Neither intellect nor will pertain to God's nature," and if we were to attribute intellect and will to God, they "would have nothing in common with [human intellect and will] but the name; there would be about as much correspondence between the two as there is between the Dog, the heavenly constellation, and a dog, an animal that barks."[23] Perhaps the most striking point to be made, however, is that *the God of pantheism cannot distinguish between good and evil. All* actions performed in the universe are *equally* manifestations of the power of God; the notion that some of these actions are in an ultimate sense "good" and others "evil" must in the end be dismissed as an illusion. Pantheists may be, and often are, extremely upright and scrupulous in their personal ethics, but in the ultimate perspective good and evil—or what *we call* good and evil—are transcended. This contrasts the pantheistic God very sharply with the God of theism, who is a fighting God, a God who is unambiguously *for* good and *against* evil.

There is no reason why the God of process theism need be greatly different from the God of traditional theism with respect to knowledge and goodness. The process theist's attitude toward divine power, on the other hand, is markedly different, as shown in the title of a book by Charles Hartshorne (1897–2000): *Omnipotence and Other Theological Mistakes.*[24] Why is omnipotence a mistake? Because traditional theism depicts God as having the power to impose his will unilaterally on things and persons in his creation, as exercising coercive power over them. Process theism, on the other hand, maintains that *God's power can never be coercive, but must always be persuasive.* God does not have the power to unilaterally impose his will on nature, thus, the process God performs no miracles. Furthermore, he is not able to compel human beings to do his will—rather, he "lures" them, as Whitehead said, by holding before their minds the highest and best possibilities to which they can attain by voluntarily complying with his intentions.

Traditional theists typically see this as greatly diminishing the power and greatness of God, as making God distinctly less "worthy of worship" than if he were omnipotent. The reply to this is that, because of the inherent moral superiority of persuasive over coercive power, God's greatness is enhanced, not diminished, by his inability to use coercive power. However that may be, it is clear that this stance places process theism sharply in conflict with the theological traditions of all the theistic faiths, all of which clearly portray God as capable of exercising *both* persuasive and coercive power.[25]

GOD ETERNAL—TIMELESS OR EVERLASTING?

That God is eternal is a common conviction among theists. But how is this to be understood? The most straightforward and readily understandable way to interpret God's eternity is simply to say that *God always has existed and always will exist.* God, then, exists *through time* like other persons and things, but unlike the others, his existence has neither beginning nor end. In a word, God is *everlasting*.

Some philosophers and theologians, however, have found this to be an inadequate interpretation of God's eternity. They have said, rather, that God is *timeless, outside of time altogether*. God, on this view, does *not* experience the world moment by moment as we finite persons do; rather, he experiences the world's history all at once, in a total simultaneous present. For God, they say, there is neither past, nor present, nor future; God simply *is*. All of time is present to God, all at once and changelessly, in his eternal present. Augustine put it like this:

> Nor dost Thou by time, precede time: else shouldest Thou not precede all times. But Thou precedest all things past, by the sublimity of an ever-present eternity; and surpassest all future because they are future, and when

they come, they shall be past; but Thou art the Same, and Thy years fail not. Thy years neither come nor go; whereas ours both come and go, that they all may come. Thy years stand together, because they do stand; nor are departing thrust out by coming years, for they pass not away; but ours shall all be, when they shall no more be. Thy years are one day; and Thy day is not daily, but To-day, seeing Thy To-day gives not place unto to-morrow, for neither doth it replace yesterday. Thy To-day, is Eternity. . . .[26]

The most fundamental reason why the doctrine of timelessness has appealed to many seems to be the conviction, which has its roots in Greek philosophy and especially Neoplatonism, that the *changeability* that must characterize God if he exists through time is unacceptable as an attribute of the "most real being." A recent defense of divine timelessness puts it this way:

Such radically evanescent existence [as that of temporal beings] cannot be the foundation of existence. Being, the persistent, permanent, utterly immutable actuality that seems required as the bedrock underlying the evanescence of becoming, must be characterized by genuine [i.e., timeless] duration, of which temporal duration is only the flickering image.[27]

More recently, attempts have been made to support divine timelessness by appeal to Albert Einstein's Special Theory of Relativity. A striking feature of that theory is that, under certain circumstances, the *order of events* is different depending on the standpoint (or "reference-frame") from which they are observed. Consider, then, two events in far-separated regions of our galaxy—say, the collision of a comet with a planet, and a supernova explosion.[28] For an observer on earth, the impact precedes the explosion. But for an observer on a spaceship orbiting a planet of a distant star, the explosion precedes the impact. Now suppose we ask, "Which of the two *really* precedes the other?" According to the theory of relativity, there *is no answer* to this question! Rather, the order of these events is *relative to the reference-frame* in which they are observed, and there *is no* "absolute," privileged reference-frame that can give us the "real" answer to our question.

But now let us ask: Which of the events comes first *for God?* God is everywhere (omnipresent), so it makes no sense to identify God's "point of view" with the reference-frame on Earth, or with any other particular reference-frame. This being the case, there can be no answer to the question, "Which event comes first for God?" But surely, we say, there *must* be an answer to that question; there must be a definite order in which God experiences the two events. The only way out of this dilemma, it is suggested, is to recognize that God is timeless, so that for him neither event comes before the other, though of course he knows how the events are temporally related from any one of the innumerable reference-frames within the universe.

This reasoning is flawed, however. The reason the order of events depends (in certain cases) on the reference-frame is that the transfer of information is limited by the finite speed of light. If the observers in our example could obtain information instantaneously about the comet impact and the supernova explosion, they would know absolutely which of the two precedes the other. Instantaneous communication, if it existed, would establish an absolute reference-frame. Of course, God's knowledge of what is going on in the cosmos is *not* limited by the speed of light—unlike us, he does not have to wait billions of years to learn what is going on in remote parts of the universe! Therefore, for God, though not for us, there really is an absolute reference-frame and an absolute order of events. At least, this is so if God is temporal. That question remains at issue, but no insuperable problem is posed for divine temporality by the Special Theory of Relativity.[29]

The doctrine of divine timelessness continues to be a topic of controversy among philosophers of religion. In recent years there has been a trend away from this view and toward accepting the view that God is everlasting, which is both easier to understand and apparently more in agreement with the scriptures of theistic religions, which depict God as acting in time and history.[30] Nevertheless, timelessness continues to find able defenders and advocates. The discussion of the various divine attributes earlier in this chapter has been carried on in terms of the idea of God as everlasting, since this is the more familiar and easily understood concept. But the same attributes can, with appropriate modifications, be restated as attributes of a timeless God. The issue between these rival conceptions, then, remains very much in doubt.[31]

Here, then, we bring to a conclusion our exposition of the theistic concept of God. The concept seems to be logically consistent, though in view of its complexity it is difficult to be absolutely certain about that. It is one that has fascinated and intrigued generation after generation of philosophers and theologians. But is it more than this? Is the concept one which applies to a *real being,* one who in very truth is the creator and sustainer of all things other than himself, and who enters powerfully and intimately into the world-process and especially into the lives of his worshipers? It is this question which must be addressed in the subsequent chapters.

STUDY QUESTIONS

1. Describe briefly the conception of God implied in the story of Shvetaketu and his father. How does this differ from the understanding of God you are familiar with?

2. How is the concept of God defined in the religious tradition with which you are most familiar? How (if at all) does this idea of God differ from that of traditional theism, as explained in the text?

3. Does it seem correct to you to say that only a God who is absolutely perfect could be fully worthy of worship? Discuss.

4. Explain what is meant by saying that God is a "necessary being." Does it seem to you that an adequate conception of God should include this idea? Discuss.

5. Explain what it means to say that God is the creator. Why is the idea of creation an important part of the concept of God?

6. Do we have a more adequate idea of God if we think of God as wholly distinct from the universe (classical theism), or if we think of God as including the universe within himself (process theism)?

7. Does it lessen one's appreciation of divine power to say that God cannot do things which are logically impossible, such as changing the laws of arithmetic? Is it better to say that God is able to act in ways that are cruel and deceitful, or that God is unable to do these things?

8. Is God greater and more perfect if he exercises both persuasive and coercive power (as in traditional theism), or if he exercises only persuasive power (as in process theism)?

9. Explain what it means to say that God is "outside of time." Is God greater if God is timeless in this way, or if he exists in time with us?

10. Why has the theory of relativity led some to say that God must be timeless? What is your evaluation of this argument?

NOTES

1. Eliot Deutsch and J. A B. van Buitenen, *A Source Book of Advaita Vedanta* (Honolulu: University Press of Hawaii, 1971), pp. 14–6. (For a longer selection see PRSR2e, pt. 3.)

2. A note on terminology: We shall use *traditional theism* to denote a group of views that are in the broad mainstream of the theistic traditions, in contrast with pantheism and process theism. Views within this mainstream differ from each other in a number of ways, some of them explored in this chapter and in chapter 8. Throughout these chapters, *theism* and *theistic,* when used without qualification, will refer primarily to traditional theism; some but not all of what is said about "theism" will apply also to process theism.

3. For process theism, see John B. Cobb and David Ray Griffin, *Process Theology: An Introductory Exposition* (Philadelphia: Westminster Press, 1976; see the selection in PRSR2e, pt. 3). A good exposition of the conceptions of Ultimate Reality held by the various schools of Vedanta is found in John M. Koller, *Oriental Philosophies,* 2d ed. (New York: Scribner's, 1985), pp. 82–99.

4. Some religious traditions do seem to insist on characterizing God in contradictory terms. In many cases, the best way to understand this is that the contradictory description is attempting to convey a "deeper truth" about the divine that is not expressible in literal language. Still, unless we are somehow able to grasp this deeper truth, the contradictory description is of little help. If the contradictory description is interpreted literally—for instance, if it is said to be literally true both that God is disembodied and that he has a body—then there is no way of understanding what is thereby said about God.

5. This point is not completely uncontroversial. One philosopher suggested that we might feel no such regret were we to learn that God did not know some unimportant theorem of mathematics, especially if God *could* know the theorem if he wanted to. (Presumably, he just has not taken the time to work it out.)

This may or may not be correct. But if it is correct, it seems likely that we would feel no regret because we do not, in the case described, really feel that God is significantly inferior, or lacking in excellence, as a result of not knowing that particular theorem. Suppose, on the other hand, that God is *unable* to know the theorem: "God is great at algebra, but he just can't seem to get the hang of solid geometry." Most likely this would indeed be disturbing to us, because in this case it would seem clear that God is less great than he might conceivably be.

6. *St. Anselm: Basic Writings,* tr. S. N. Deane (La Salle, Ill.: Open Court, 1962), p. 7. (See the selection in PRSR2e, pt. 4.)

7. It could be pointed out, to be sure, that people have often worshiped gods that were very much inferior to this "perfect being" conception. This is not a decisive objection, however, for two reasons: First, the religious attitudes in question may very well fall short of *worship,* in the strong sense which has been given to this word in our discussion. Second, insofar as it becomes generally recognized that a particular kind of god falls short of maximal excellence and perfection, such a god would tend to be *eliminated* as a serious object of worship—thus, for example, the decline in polytheistic worship that tends to occur in many advanced cultures.

8. For a volume exploring this theme, see Thomas V. Morris, *Anselmian Explorations: Essays in Philosophical Theology* (Notre Dame, Ind.: University of Notre Dame Press, 1987).

9. Process theists also think of God as the "absolutely perfect being," but their conclusions about what is implied by perfection are, as we shall see, somewhat different. Pantheists would probably say that God is *perfect,* but not a *perfect being,* since according to pantheism God is not *a being* at all.

10. For Kant's arguments, see Immanuel Kant, "The Ideal of Pure Reason" in *Critique of Pure Reason,* tr. N. K. Smith (New York: St. Martin's, 1965), pp. 487–507.

11. See Robert Merrihew Adams, "Has It Been Proved That All Real Existence is Contingent?" and "Divine Necessity," both in *The Virtue of Faith* (New York: Oxford, 1987); also Alvin Plantinga, *The Nature of Necessity* (New York: Oxford, 1974).

12. For additional reading on God's existence as logically necessary, see J. N. Findlay, "An Ontological Disproof of God's Existence," in *New Essays in Philosophical Theology,* ed. Antony Flew and Alasdair McIntyre (London: MacMillan, 1955); Thomas V. Morris, *Our Idea of God* (Downers Grove, Ill.: InterVarsity Press, 1991); and John Hick, "A Critique of the 'Second Argument,'" in *The Many-Faced Argument,* ed. John H. Hick and Arthur C. McGill (New York; MacMillan, 1967), pp. 341–56 (reprinted in PRSR2e, pt. 3, as "God's Necessary Existence").

13. Note that we say God is "personal," not that God is *a person.* The latter assertion would be a controversial one, accepted by some theists but not by all. According to the Christian doctrine of the Trinity, there are *three* persons in God, designated as Father, Son, and Holy Spirit; these persons are capable of personal relationships *between themselves* as well as with created persons. Jews and Moslems, on the other hand, emphatically reject the doctrine of the Trinity.

14. *Vedanta* refers to the Hindu holy books on which this system claims to be based; *advaita* means "nondual," referring to the lack of duality between Brahman and the empirical world. It should be noted that this is only one of many ways of understanding God in Hinduism, which taken as a whole permits an almost unlimited variety of conceptions of the divine. Many Hindus worship personal deities such as Vishnu and Shiva, which are sometimes said to be "aspects" of Brahman.

15. Alfred North Whitehead, *Process and Reality,* ed. David Ray Griffin and Donald W. Sherburne, Corrected ed., (New York: Free Press, 1978), p. 351.

16. Ibid., p. 348.

17. See Thomas Aquinas, "God is Omnipotent," in PRSR2e, pt. 3 (from the *Summa Theologica*).

18. It should be noted that our conception of omnipotence and other divine attributes will make an important difference to our understanding of the "problem of evil"; see chapter 7 for more on this.

19. What seems the best solution is due to George Mavrodes ("Some Puzzles Concerning Omnipotence," *Philosophical Review* 72 [1963]:221–3; reprinted in PRSR2e, pt. 3), and may be stated as follows: The question asks whether God "can create a stone that he cannot lift." Can God accomplish this task, or not? Now, in order to have before us a definite task, it is necessary to specify *who* it is that is to be incapable of lifting the stone. (A stone that the average philosophy professor cannot lift may present no challenge for Arnold Schwarzenegger!) In the present case, the person who is to be unable to lift the stone is God himself. But God is, by definition, capable of lifting a stone of any size whatever. So the task set for God is that of creating a stone so big it cannot be lifted by a being who is capable of lifting a stone of any size at all—and this, clearly, is self-contradictory, just like the task of creating a round square. But as we have already seen, omnipotence does not include the ability to do what is self-contradictory, so God's inability to create a stone that God cannot lift creates no difficulty for the claim that God is omnipotent.

20. Some philosophers have maintained that, while the *sentence* "Martha was married last Sunday" is tensed, the *proposition* expressed by that sentence is *not* tensed and does not change in truth-value over time. There seems at present, however, to be a majority view that this solution will not work and that we must accept the existence of tensed propositions.

21. It should be noted, however, that the philosopher of religion cannot well remain completely neutral concerning the nature of divine goodness; among other things, the view taken on this point will have an important effect on one's approach to the problem of evil.

22. On this point see Bruce Reichenbach, *Evil and a Good God* (New York: Fordham University Press, 1982), chap. 7.

23. *Chief Works of Benedictus de Spinoza,* vol. 2, tr. R. H. M. Elwes (New York: Dover, 1955), pp. 60–1.

24. (Albany: SUNY Press, 1984).

25. For a thorough critique of the process view of God's power, see David Basinger, *Divine Power in Process Theism: A Philosophical Critique* (Albany: SUNY Press, 1988).

26. *The Confessions of St. Augustine,* tr. Edward B. Pusey (New York: Random House, 1949), bk. 11, pp. 252–3. For another classic statement, see the selection from Boethius in PRSR2e, pt. 3.

27. Eleonore Stump and Norman Kretzmann, "Eternity," *Journal of Philosophy* 79 (1981):444–5.

28. In order for the example to work, these events must be so situated in space-time that no causal influence can pass between them.

29. For more on this and related arguments, see Brian Leftow, *Time and Eternity* (Ithaca, N.Y.: Cornell University Press, 1991); Alan G. Padgett, "Eternity and the Special Theory of Relativity," *International Philosophical Quarterly* 33, no. 2 (June 1993):219–23; and William Lane Craig, "The Elimination of Absolute Time by the Special Theory of Relativity," in *God and Time: Essays on the Divine Nature,* ed. Gregory E. Ganssle and David M. Woodruff (New York: Oxford University Press, 2002), pp. 129–52.

30. For argument in support of this view, see Nicholas Wolterstorff, "God Everlasting," in *God and the Good,* ed. C. Orlebeke and L. Smedes (Grand Rapids, Mich.: William B. Eerdmans, 1975; reprinted in PRSR2e, pt. 3).

31. The best recent presentations are found in the article "Eternity," by Stump and Kretzmann, and in Leftow, *Time and Eternity.* For additional discussion, see Jonathan Kvanvig, *The Possibility of an All-Knowing God* (New York: St. Martin's, 1986), pp. 150–71; and William Hasker, *God, Time, and Knowledge* (Ithaca, N.Y.: Cornell University Press, 1989), pp. 144–85.

SUGGESTED READING

Basinger, David. *Divine Power in Process Theism: A Philosophical Critique.* Albany: SUNY Press, 1988.

Cobb, John B., and David Ray Griffin. *Process Theology: An Introductory Exposition.* Philadelphia: Westminster Press, 1976.

Gale, Richard M. *On the Nature and Existence of God.* New York: Cambridge University Press, 1991.

Ganssle, Gregory E., and David M. Woodruff, eds. *God and Time: Essays on the Divine Nature.* New York: Oxford University Press, 2002.

Hartshorne, Charles. *Omnipotence and Other Theological Mistakes.* Albany: SUNY Press, 1984.

Kenny, Anthony. *The God of the Philosophers.* Oxford: Oxford University Press, 1979.

Koller, John M. *Oriental Philosophies.* 2nd ed. New York: Scribner's, 1985.

Leftow, Brian. *Time and Eternity.* Ithaca, N.Y.: Cornell University Press, 1989.

Morris, Thomas V. *Our Idea of God: An Introduction to Philosophical Theology.* Downers Grove, Ill.: InterVarsity Press, 1991.

Pinnock, Clark. *Most Moved Mover: A Theology of God's Openness.* Grand Rapids, Mich.: Baker, 2001.

Stump, Eleonore, and Norman Kretzmann. "Eternity." *Journal of Philosophy* 79, (1981):429–58.

Swinburne, Richard. *The Coherence of Theism.* Rev. ed. Oxford: Oxford University Press, 1993.

Wierenga, Edward R. *The Nature of God: An Inquiry into Divine Attributes.* Ithaca, N.Y.: Cornell University Press, 1989.

CHAPTER 5   # THEISTIC ARGUMENTS: IS THERE EVIDENCE FOR GOD'S EXISTENCE?

In 1961 Yuri Gagarin circled the earth in a Soviet spaceship and pronounced that God did not exist because he did not see God out his tiny window. Although most people would have been surprised had Gagarin glimpsed God, many continue to wonder whether any good evidence supports the claim that God exists. Some believe that evidence is not necessary for a rational belief in God. Others claim that evidence such as unjustified pain and suffering counts strongly against God's existence. (We pursue these two perspectives in chapters 6 and 7, respectively.) Some believe that since we have no evidence we have no reason to believe in God, while others argue that the available evidence for God's existence can be used to ground belief.

The arguments produced by the last group are frequently referred to as *theistic arguments* or *theistic proofs*. Over the centuries theistic philosophers have sharpened and refined these arguments, while nontheists have developed serious critiques of them. In this chapter we first examine the nature and function of proof, then present four different types of theistic arguments and their respective critiques, and finally look at the role of cumulative case arguments for theism and atheism.

THEISTIC ARGUMENTS AS PROOFS

Before we consider particular theistic arguments, something must be said about what they purport to show or establish. Traditionally these arguments were termed *proofs*. This language raises three questions: What is a proof? Is the theist required to produce proofs of God's existence? Should we adopt the terminology of proof in speaking about providing evidence for or against God's existence?

In chapter 3 we suggested a *person-relative view of proof.* A proof in this sense possesses three characteristics.[1] First, the argument must be *sound;* that is, the premises must be true and the conclusion must follow validly (without breaking certain formal rules of reasoning) from the premises. Second, proofs are events having to do with knowledge. But knowledge is always possessed *by* someone. Therefore, a proof is a sound argument that someone *knows* to be sound. The person for whom it is a proof must know that the premises are true and that the conclusion follows validly. Since, on this view, not every rational person must be capable of recognizing that the argument is sound for it to be a proof, an argument will function as a proof *only* to the person who knows the argument to be sound. Third, the function of proofs is to *extend our knowledge.* This suggests two things: (1) The premises must be more readily knowable than the conclusion. This is important because in a proof one wants to move from the more to the less readily knowable. (2) The person for whom it is a proof must know the truth of the premises without inferring them from the conclusion. This is important to avoid begging the question. In short, a proof is a sound argument that the person for whom it is a proof knows to be sound and whose premises that person knows as true without inferring them from the conclusion.

But if proofs are person-relative, why all the fuss over theistic proofs? In particular, is it necessary that theists have proofs of God's existence? First, we cannot require proofs for everything we know; otherwise either the conclusion we are supporting is a reason for one of the premises for that conclusion, or we have an infinite series of arguments, each supporting the premises in the logically subsequent argument. The former is unacceptable, for by inferring the premise that supports the conclusion from the conclusion we argue in a circle. The latter is unacceptable because no finite person could ever construct the requisite infinite series of arguments.

Second, despite the fact that we frequently use the term "proof"—note the colloquial response "Prove it!"—proofs play a minor role in our intellectual life. We can prove very little, and what we can prove is generally uninteresting. Hence, though theists are within proper bounds when they put forth and evaluate arguments that purport to prove God's existence, one cannot *require* that theists prove that God exists, or correlatively, that nontheists prove that God does not exist.

Some might reply that, at the very least, persons should have proofs for those claims that are both not obviously true and really important or significant. But how are we to know what is really important or significant? We might attempt to prove what is trivial while missing what is really significant. Moreover, we have no reason to think that the class of really important things belongs to the class of provable rather than nonprovable things. The fact that something is important (to us or to anyone else) fails to inform us whether it can be derived from premises less controversial than it. This important claim might at best be inductively defensible or belong to a class of basic truths for which there is no proof.

So it seems that theists do not need to prove God's existence (nor non-theists God's nonexistence). At the same time, however, it seems proper to ask theists to present grounds or evidence of some sort for their contention that God exists, since for many people such a claim is not obviously true. Though that evidence *might* consist of proofs, it need not. Inductive reasoning or immediate experience might provide a basis for rational belief.

This leads to the third question, which asks whether we should speak of "arguments" rather than "proofs." Many contemporary theists, following the example set by Richard Swinburne (b. 1934) have abandoned the deductive model of arguing for God's existence, where proofs must be formally valid, for the inductive model.[2] Whereas Swinburne doubts that deductive forms of the theistic arguments are successful, he has confidence that inductive forms do establish the probability that God exists.

Whether one can stretch the notion of "proof" to include evidence that *tends* to establish the truth of a position gets us into a debate that we will not pursue, though some dictionaries[3] allow this extension. Clearly, if we are to do justice to the classical arguments as well as to contemporary developments, both deductive and inductive arguments must be considered. Consequently, in what follows we shall adopt "argument" in place of "proof"; this accommodates theists who offer both deductive and inductive evidence for God's existence, while maintaining our emphasis on the person-relative nature of the argument.

THE ONTOLOGICAL ARGUMENT

Without doubt the most intriguing and puzzling of the theistic arguments is the ontological argument. According to the Christian theologian Anselm (1033–1109), we can form the concept or idea of a being than which none greater can be thought. We might not know whether such a being really exists, but we know that it exists as an idea in some mind. But that than which none greater can be thought cannot exist only in the mind or understanding. Suppose it were to exist only in the mind. Then it would not be the being than which none greater can be thought, for existence in reality is greater than existence only in the mind. But we assumed at the outset the concept of a being than which none greater can be thought. Hence this being, which we name God, must exist in reality as well as in the mind.[4]

We might formalize the argument as follows.

1. Persons have the idea of a greatest possible being.
2. Suppose the greatest possible being exists only as an idea in the mind.
3. Existence in reality is greater than existence only in the mind.
4. Therefore, we can conceive of a being greater than the greatest possible being, that is, a being that also exists in reality.

5. But there can be no being greater than the greatest possible being.

6. Therefore, the greatest possible being exists in reality.

Anselm does not deny that some persons can fail to see that God (the greatest possible being) exists. However, for him this is because they have not properly understood the concept of God. Once one sees that God really is the greatest possible being, God's existence is undeniable.

There seems to be something seriously wrong with an argument that, like Anselm's, moves from a premise about *ideas* in our minds to establishing that something exists in *reality*. Yet despite these suspicions, philosophers have found it difficult to discern precisely where the argument is vulnerable and to make a strong case that this point of suspicion is a vice rather than a virtue.

One who tried to expose the vulnerability of the argument was the monk Gaunilo, a contemporary of Anselm. Gaunilo suggested that the first premise of Anselm's argument is false; one cannot conceive of or really understand a greatest possible being.[5] When I think about "humans," I know what the term means because I have had experience with humans. But when I hear the words, "being than which none greater can be thought," I can understand the meaning of the individual words, but I cannot understand the being they signify, for this being is unlike any other reality.

But Anselm's point is not that we can completely comprehend God's nature, that we can know God as God knows himself. Rather, he holds that we can know enough about God to know that, at the very least, God must be the greatest possible being. Should anyone who denies God's existence reflect on what it is to be God, that person must understand that God exists.

Gaunilo also wondered whether one could use Anselm's argument structure to prove the existence of all sorts of unreal things. Suppose, he argued, I conceive of an island more excellent than any other, an island that has inestimable wealth and delights. Since what exists in reality is more excellent than what exists solely in the mind, this island exists. By this argument we could (absurdly) prove the existence of all manner of imaginary and nonexistent things. *The reductio ad absurdum* argument Anselm used, Gaunilo uses on Anselm.

Anselm never fully and adequately replied to this argument,[6] but others have. One reply is that Anselm's ontological argument applies only to things capable of being the greatest possible. It does not apply to things like islands because, as finite, no single island is capable of being the greatest possible. The properties that would make an island the greatest possible might include mineral wealth, smoothness of sand, number of palm trees, and abundance of fruits. But for any island one conceives of possessing these properties, one can think of an island with more of them. These properties have no intrinsic maximum. But without characteristics that have a maximal limit, a greatest possible island cannot exist. This does not apply to Anselm's argument, however, since the properties that apply to the greatest possible being include properties for which there are maximums: knowledge, power, and moral perfection. God can be omniscient, omnipotent, and morally perfect.

Hence, the form of Anselm's argument cannot be used, as Gaunilo suggested, to establish the existence of all sorts of nonexistent, finite things.[7]

However, some nonexistent things possessing properties with maximums might be plugged into Anselm's argument form. Consider the idea of the greatest possible thousand dollar bill. Would an argument similar to Anselm's show that this bill necessarily exists? Of course, there could be a bill greater in value—say a one million dollar bill—but that is not the point. The point is that there could not be a greater thousand dollar bill, for any bill with this property is worth its maximum. One might question whether its other properties have intrinsic maximums—for example, being unwrinkled or of uniform color—but these are irrelevant to its being a bill worth one thousand dollars, that is, a bill of a certain denomination. In this essential aspect the bill has a maximum, and, hence, using Anselm's argument form, such a bill would have to exist.[8] Perhaps Gaunilo was correct in his thesis but chose the wrong example in the island.

A different criticism of Anselm's argument focuses on premise 3. For Anselm existence is a perfection. A perfection is something that makes whatever has it better or greater. For example, to say that health is a perfection is to say that being healthy is better, all else being equal, than being not-healthy. Similarly, to say that existence is a perfection is to say that something is better or greater because it exists, all else being equal. Put another way, it is better for a thing to exist than to not exist. One has to be careful here. Anselm is not saying that it is better for *us* that things exist rather than not-exist. This is obviously false, since we would be better off without many things—typing errors, mosquitoes, cancer. Rather, Anselm's point is that it is better *for the thing itself* to really have that property.

But is existence really a perfection? Immanuel Kant (1724–1804) argued that "'Being' is obviously not a real predicate; that is, it is not a concept of something that could be added to the concept of a thing. It is merely the positing of a thing."[9] More recently, Norman Malcolm (1911–1990) put the argument this way.

> The doctrine that existence is a perfection is remarkably queer. . . . A king might desire that his next chancellor should have knowledge, wit, and resolution; but it is ludicrous to add that the king's desire is to have a chancellor who exists. Suppose that two royal counselors, A and B, were asked to draw up separately descriptions of the most perfect chancellor they could conceive, and that the descriptions they produced were identical except that A included existence in his list of attributes of a perfect chancellor and B did not. One and the same person could satisfy both descriptions. More to the point, any person who satisfied A's description would *necessarily* satisfy B's description and vice versa![10]

But contrary to Malcolm, one could argue that A and B do not produce the same description of the perfect chancellor, for a nonexistent chancellor could satisfy description B but not description A.[11] We could assume that all descriptions presuppose the existence of what is being described, but that begs the issue in question.

To inquire whether existence is a perfection is to ask whether existence is a property, for every perfection is a property. When we say, "God is good," good is a perfection and property of God. The problem is that the word "exist" functions differently from other property words. For example, it makes sense to say "Some libraries do not have good organization," but not to say "Some libraries do not exist." From an example like this it does not follow that existence is not a property, only that if it is a property it is an unusual one. But whether this unusualness is enough to vitiate Anselm's argument is unclear. Perhaps the problem has less to do with whether existence is a property than with the fact that there are different kinds of existences—in the understanding, in reality, in mythology—and that it is not clear how or on what grounds these are comparable.

CONTEMPORARY VERSIONS OF THE ONTOLOGICAL ARGUMENT

Recently, some philosophers claim to have found a second, more persuasive argument in Anselm.[12] For example, Charles Hartshorne (1897–2000) notes that while great attention has been paid to the Anselmian argument presented here, a second, more persuasive argument in Anselm's *Proslogium* has been largely ignored. A major difference between the two arguments is how existence is to be treated. Hartshorne agrees with Anselm's critics that one cannot always treat existence as a property. However, it does not follow that existence is never a property. Although existence per se is not a property, *necessary existence* is. Consequently, for any two objects, if one exists necessarily and the other not (that is, exists contingently, such that it could either exist or not exist), the first is greater than the second.

It follows, then, that if God's existence were contingent, God would exist by chance or some cause. Hence, God would not be the greatest possible being. But God, as the greatest possible being, possesses necessary existence. Therefore, God's existence is either logically necessary or logically impossible. Since God's existence is not logically impossible, it is logically necessary.[13]

To make their argument succeed, Hartshorne and others interpret the necessity of God's existence as logically necessary existence (existence the denial of which is or entails a self-contradiction). But why should one think that God (or anything, for that matter) possesses logically necessary existence? Some have thought that Anselm, in his alleged second argument, held this view of God. John Hick (b. 1922), however, argues that Anselm meant not the modern notion of logical necessity, but *ontological or factual necessity*. Such a necessary being is not dependent on any other being for its existence; having its existence from itself, it can neither come into nor pass out of existence.[14]

Modern Anselmians reply that an adequate conception of God requires logical necessity. God must be conceived as maximally perfect, exemplifying "necessarily a maximally perfect set of compossible [mutually compatible] great-making properties."[15] Because necessary existence is a great-making property, God cannot not-exist. If a maximally perfect being (God) is impossible, then such a being cannot exist. But if a maximally perfect being is possible, then by virtue of possessing the great-making property of necessary existence, a maximally perfect being (God) exists. The debated issue concerns not only the status of necessary existence as an alleged great-making property, but the very concept of God.

Michael Tooley (b. 1941) has questioned the coherence of the concept of maximal greatness that lies behind this revised ontological argument.[16] After the fashion of Gaunilo, he contends that we can construct arguments that parallel those used in the modern ontological argument for other maximal properties but that turn out to yield a contradiction. For example, one can construct an argument to show that the maximal properties of being able to dissolve anything and being insoluble exist in every possible world. But since these are contradictory properties, the argument form used to establish these maximal properties must be suspect. Since the same argument form is used by the ontological argument to establish maximal greatness, there must be something wrong with that version of the argument.

It is easy to see that, for many, the jury is still out on the ontological argument. Some believe that the argument is obviously fallacious, for one cannot argue from concepts to reality. Others believe it is sound but not necessarily convincing, since it requires, among other things, belief that God's existence is possible, and this belief has been questioned.[17]

THE COSMOLOGICAL ARGUMENT

A second argument proposed by some theists is the cosmological argument. The cosmological argument is less a specific argument than an argument form. It begins by invoking an empirical fact about the world (e.g., contingent beings exist; there is something in motion; the universe began to exist). Then it seeks for the cause or explanation of this fact. It argues that an infinite series of causal conditions cannot provide an adequate explanation. It concludes that the existence of some necessary being, first cause, or personal agent provides the explanation. Two importantly different versions of this argument can be discerned. One, advanced by Thomas Aquinas (1224–1274), Samuel Clarke (1675–1729), Frederick Copleston (1907–1994) and Richard Taylor (b. 1919),[18] considers the explanatory causal conditions in terms of their logical rather than their temporal relation to the effect, so that the first cause to which the argument concludes is not necessarily a first cause in time but a cause on which all else depends for its continued existence. The other, advanced by Arabic philosophers such as al-Kindi (c. 870) and al-Ghazali (1058–1111) and more recently defended by William Craig (b. 1945), argues for a first cause in time. Let us begin with the second version of the argument, referred to as the *kala⁻m* argument. (The term *kala⁻m* was applied to the argumentative theism employed in defense of Islamic orthodoxy beginning in the ninth century.)

THE *KALĀM* COSMOLOGICAL ARGUMENT

We can formulate the *kalām* argument as follows.

1. Everything that begins to exist has a cause of its existence.
2. The universe began to exist.
3. Therefore, the universe has a cause of its existence.[19]

Premise 1 states a version of the causal principle that lies at the root of all cosmological arguments. Craig holds that this premise is intuitively obvious; no one, he claims, seriously denies it.

However, some do deny it, arguing that the claim that something should suddenly spring out of nothing is intelligible.[20] Some base their case on recent work in quantum physics.[21] It appears that electrons can pass out of existence at one point and then come back into existence elsewhere. One cannot trace their intermediate existence or determine what causes them to come into existence at one point rather than another. Neither can one precisely determine or predict where they will reappear; the location is only statistically probable.[22]

Craig responds that appeals to quantum phenomena do not affect the *kalām* argument. He notes that since in modern physics a vacuum is not nothing but rather a state of minimal energy, electrons do not simply appear out of nothing. The phenomena in question result from vacuum fluctuations.[23]

Given our present knowledge, it is difficult to know what to say about this argument from quantum physics. Some argue that the indeterminacy phenomena of quantum physics result from the limits of our investigative equipment. We simply are unable at this time to discern the intermediate states of the electron's existence. Others argue that the very introduction of the observer into the arena so affects what is observed that it gives the appearance that there are effects without causes. But there is no way of knowing what is happening without introducing observers and the changes they bring. Still others maintain that though the causal principle operates at the supra-atomic level, the principle is inapplicable at the subatomic and hence is not universally true. The implications of indeterminacy phenomena are unclear at this point. What can be said is that any demonstration that indeterminacy is a real feature of the world would have significant negative implications for the more general causal principle that underlies the cosmological argument.

Returning to the original *kalām* argument, what can be said about premise 2? Why should we think that the universe had a beginning in time? Craig provides four arguments, two a priori and two a posteriori, to support this premise. We have space only to look briefly at one of each. One a priori argument proceeds as follows:

4. An actual infinite cannot exist.
5. A beginningless temporal series of events is an actual infinite.
6. Therefore, a beginningless temporal series of events cannot exist.

In defense of premise 4, Craig notes that an actual infinite, which is a timeless totality that neither increases nor decreases in the number of members it contains, cannot exist, for it leads to absurd consequences. For example, imagine a library with an actually infinite number of books. Suppose also that the library contains an infinite number of red books and an infinite number of black books. It follows that, since no infinite has more members than another, the library contains as many red books as its total books, as many red books as red and black books combined, and as many books as black books minus red books. But this is absurd. Hence, though an actual infinite exists in the ideal world of mathematics, it cannot exist in reality.

Craig's point is that, with respect to actual infinites, either the members of sets correspond, so that where they correspond one-to-one they are equivalent, or else they do not correspond and the whole is greater than the sum of its parts. The former leads to the absurdity that subsets are equivalent to the whole set. The latter leads to the absurdity that two sets, one a subset of the other, though both infinite, have different numbers of members.[24] In effect, since both options lead to absurdity, there cannot be an actual infinite.

But why should one think that a beginningless series is an actual rather than a potential infinite (premise 5)? Craig contends that since the past events of the beginningless series can be numbered and conceptually collected together, the series is an actual infinite. The fact that the events do not occur at the same time is irrelevant. If there were a starting point, so that events were added to or subtracted from this point, we would have a potential infinite that increased through time by adding new members. But since the beginningless past has no such starting point, the infinite is actual, not potential.

Part of the problem here concerns Craig's definition of actual and potential infinite. For Aristotle the actual finite was an infinite that existed at a particular time, whereas a potential infinite was realized over time by addition or division. Hence, the temporal series of events, as formed by successively adding new events, was a potential, not an actual, infinite.[25] For Craig, however, an actual infinite is a timeless totality that cannot be added to or reduced. Hence, they disagree over whether a time factor is involved in determining whether something is an actual infinite and, hence, whether the beginningless series of events is an actual or a potential infinite. If it is an actual infinite, Craig's argument has import.

The a posteriori argument in defense of premise 2 relies upon recent developments in astrophysics. In 1965 two scientists at Bell Laboratories discovered background radiation in the universe. This radiation appears to be the remnant of some gigantic, early explosion called the Big Bang. Two widely held but competing models of the origin of the universe are compatible with this datum.

According to the *Oscillating Universe model,* the universe goes through repetitive cycles of expansion and contraction. Following the big explosion, it expands to a certain point, where the gravitational force of matter takes over to slow and eventually end its expansion. This force pulls the universe back together, until it reaches a point of compact density (the Big Crunch), explodes, and begins to expand outward again. This process repeats indefinitely, though not necessarily in the same way. For this still to be possible, our universe must not have passed the critical threshold beyond which the gravitational force can no longer reverse its expansion.

The other model is the *Infinitely Expanding Universe*. According to it, the Big Bang occurred only once. Since then the universe expanded outward, until sometime in the future it will die a cold death (the Big Freeze).

Determining which model is correct depends, in part, upon calculations of the total amount of matter in the universe. Some hold that the density of the matter is now insufficient to halt the expansion of the universe. Having passed the critical gravitational threshold, the universe will continue to expand forever. Others maintain that the universe contains a great quantity of currently undetected, invisible or dark matter, scattered in dust clouds within or between the galaxies, so that we have not yet passed the critical threshold beyond which contraction of the universe is possible. Very recent discoveries, however, appear to have provided a more definitive answer. Focusing on supernovas, astronomers discovered that the universe is expanding not at a constant but at an accelerating rate. Some force in the universe not only counteracts gravity but pushes the universe apart ever faster. This discovery, confirming the infinite expansion hypothesis, makes collapse most unlikely.[26]

Though in an argument it is generally inappropriate to attack the conclusion, if there is reason to think that the conclusion is false and the argument valid, this indicates that one of the premises is false. Such a criticism has been raised recently against a Big Bang theistic argument. Adopting an "inflationary" theory of the origin of the universe, some argue that, contrary to the conclusion of the *kalām* argument, the universe came into existence without a cause. Originally a vacuum with no space-time dimensions, the universe "found itself in an excited vacuum state," a "ferment of quantum activity, teeming with virtual particles and full of complex interactions,"[27] which, subject to a cosmic repulsive force, resulted in an immense increase in energy. Due to this repulsive force, the universe rapidly expanded in size. But what is the origin of this increase in energy, which eventually made possible the Big Bang? The response is that the law of conservation of energy (that the total quantity of energy in the universe remains fixed despite transfer from one form to another), which now applies to our universe, did not apply to the initial expansion. Cosmic repulsion in the vacuum caused the energy to increase from zero to a huge amount. This great explosion released energy, from which all matter emerged. In effect, contrary to the ancient Parmenidean principle, out of nothing—a primeval vacuum—everything came. Consequently, since the conclusion of the *kalām* argument is false, one of the premises of the argument—in all likelihood the first—is false.

The issues in this version of the *kalām* argument are technical and speculative. This is neither a mark for nor against the argument; it merely suggests that what initially appears to be a simple argument is exceedingly complex. The final verdict on this a posteriori version of the *kalām* argument must await further developments in theoretical astrophysics.

AN ATHEISTIC ARGUMENT FROM THE BIG BANG

In a turnabout on the Big Bang argument, Quentin Smith (1952–) argues that Big Bang cosmology is actually incompatible with a belief in God. He argues that

(1) If God exists and there is an earliest state of the universe, then God created that earliest state.

(2) God is omniscient, omnipotent, and perfectly benevolent.

(3) A universe with life is better than an inanimate universe.

(4) Therefore, if God created that earliest state, then it must either contain life or eventually lead to a universe containing life. (from 1 and 3)

(5) There is an earliest state of the universe and it is the unique event of the Big Bang.

(6) The earliest state of the universe involves the life-hostile conditions of infinite temperature, infinite curvature, and infinite density.

(7) Since the Big Bang event is inherently unpredictable and lawless, there is no guarantee that it will lead to a universe with life.

(8) Therefore, there is no guarantee that the earliest state of the universe will lead to life. (5 and 7)

(9) Therefore, God could not have created that earliest state. (4 and 8)

(10) Therefore, God does not exist. (1 and 9)[28]

The problematic (and key) premise is 4. Two objections can be raised. First, why is it necessary that God create a universe with life? The reason, given in premise 3, is that a universe with life is better than one without, and God is under obligation to create the best possible world. But many theists, contending that the notion of a best possible world is incoherent, have doubted that God is under such an obligation.[29] For any world we can name another can exist which is better. Of course, God could have a reason for creating a world with life, for example, a reason related to the good God wants to bring about. But God's having a reason to create such a world does not impose a necessity on God.

Second, and more important, God could ensure a universe with life through his subsequent intervention. There is no logical necessity that this life-engendering capacity be present at the outset. Smith responds that were God to intervene, it would be "a sign of incompetent planning. . . . The rational thing to do is to create some state that *by its own lawful nature leads* to a life-producing universe."[30] But God's intervention after the initial Big Bang is not illogical. Furthermore, why must God create the universe in the most efficient way, one that excludes subsequent intervention? As Thomas Morris (b. 1952) points out,

> Efficiency is always relative to a goal or set of intentions. Before you know whether a person is efficient in what she is doing, you must know what it is she intends to be doing, what goals and values are governing the activity

she is engaged in. . . . In order to be able to derive the conclusion that if there is a God in charge of the world, he is grossly inefficient, one would have to know of all the relevant divine goals and values which would be operative in the creation and governance of a world such as ours."[31]

Indeed, Morris goes on to wonder why we need to ascribe efficiency to God at all. It is not a property required by God's perfection, such that he is deficient without it. It may be a good property to have if one has limited time or power, but presumably God lacks neither. In short, one might question whether Smith's counterargument from the Big Bang succeeds.

THE ATEMPORAL COSMOLOGICAL ARGUMENT

The atemporal type of cosmological argument does not attempt to prove the existence of a first cause in time. The universe may be eternal. Yet the universe is contingent and hence dependent on something else for its continued existence. Thus, the cause to which the argument concludes might best be termed a sustaining cause rather than a first creative cause. It is required for any contingent thing to exist at any time.

Although the argument appears with different first premises in various writers, the fundamental structure and resulting issues are basically the same.

1. A contingent being exists.
2. This contingent being has a cause or explanation of its existence.
3. The cause or explanation of its existence is something other than the contingent being itself.
4. What causes or explains the existence of this contingent being must be either other contingent beings or include a noncontingent (necessary) being.
5. Contingent beings alone cannot cause or explain the existence of a contingent being.
6. Therefore, what causes or explains the existence of this contingent being must include a noncontingent (necessary) being.
7. Therefore, a necessary being exists.

We introduced the terms *contingent being* and *necessary being* in chapter 4. We noted that a *contingent being* is one that, though it exists, might not have existed. Not being self-sufficient, it depends on something else for its existence. For example, you are a contingent being. Although you exist now, your nonexistence at this moment was possible (for example, you could have died last night). So understood, premise 1 is true.

Premise 2 invokes a version of the *principle of causation*. According to this version, every contingent being has a cause of its existence.[32] Perhaps the most common defense of this principle is that reason must hold such a principle to make reality intelligible.[33]

One might object that though the causal principle applies to descriptions of how we *know* the world, this does not mean that it describes what actually goes on in the real world. Principles of thought need not mirror the principles of reality.

Two replies are possible. First, defenders of the causal principle argue that the success with which we have applied this principle refutes the thesis that reality does not operate according to the causal principle. If we consistently used this principle but it did not apply to reality, we should have bumped up against numerous contradictions by now. Second, if we begin at this fundamental point to drive a wedge between thought and reality, the outcome can only be skepticism about what the world is really like.

Premise 3 makes the obvious claim that something cannot be a causal condition for its own existence; to do so it would have to exist already. The point here is not primarily about time, but rather a logical point: something contingent cannot account for its own existence.

Immanuel Kant objected to the conclusion (7) that a necessary being exists. When the cosmological argument concludes to the existence of a necessary being, Kant contends, it argues for the existence of a being whose existence is absolutely necessary, whose nonexistence is absolutely inconceivable. But the only being that meets this condition is the most real being, the concept of which lies at the heart of the ontological argument. Accordingly, he claims, the cosmological argument presupposes the cogency of the ontological argument. But since the ontological argument is suspect, the cosmological argument that depends on it likewise must be suspect.[34]

However, the contention that the cosmological argument depends on the ontological argument rests on a confusion. When we discussed the ontological argument, we noted that the term *necessary being* can be understood in different ways. Like some modern defenders of the ontological argument, Kant understands *necessary being* in terms of logically necessary existence, that is, logically undeniable existence. But this is not the sense in which *necessary being* is understood in the cosmological argument. Necessity is understood in the sense of ontological or factual necessity described in chapter 4. A necessary being is self-sufficient and self-sustaining: *if* it exists, it cannot not exist. That something is a necessary being leaves open the question whether it actually exists.

The critical premise of this version of the cosmological argument is premise 5. In its defense, some argue that if all the causal conditions are contingent, each of them would require a cause of its existence. The result would be that the causal conditions responsible for the effect would be infinite. But an infinite set of causal conditions cannot explain the existence of a contingent being. Two types of arguments support this last claim.

The first argument is that there cannot be an actually infinite set of anything in reality. Although in mathematics we can speak about actual infinites, mathematical actual infinites concern only the ideal world of mathematics. If actual infinites were to exist in the real world, absurdities would result. We introduced this argument previously when we considered the *kalām* cosmological argument; there we noted the absurdity that would result if, for example, an infinite number of books existed in a library. If the actual infinite cannot exist, then one cannot appeal to an actual infinite of present causal conditions to explain the existence of any given contingent being. Hence, the causal conditions must contain at least one noncontingent causal condition or being.

According to the second argument in defense of premise 5, even if an actually infinite set is possible, such a set of causal conditions cannot explain something's existence. Where each causal condition is contingent, each one itself needs an explanation for its existence. Since each being in an infinite series of contingent beings needs a reason for its existence, an infinite series of contingent beings cannot explain the existence of any contingent being. It is as if one had a chain holding up a lamp; though each link holds up the next link in the chain, the infinity of the chain does not explain why the lamp is suspended.

But why, it might be asked, do we need to explain the existence of every contingent causal condition in order to explain something's existence? Richard Swinburne terms this requirement the *completist fallacy*.[35] We can circumvent both arguments simply by providing those causal conditions that are necessary and sufficient for the thing in question to exist. An explanation is provided once we derive the existence of the contingent thing from some relevant theory plus the existence of what is necessary for its existence.[36]

Contemporary defenders of the cosmological argument probably should concede that each contingent thing exists because of the causal activity of other contingent things in the universe. However, even with this concession, the question remains why there are contingent beings at all when conceivably there could have been none. In particular, why is there a universe (as a collection of contingent things) rather than not?[37] "When the existence of each member of a collection is explained by reference to some other member *of that very same collection* then it does not follow that the collection itself has an explanation. For it is one thing for there to be an explanation of the existence of each dependent being and quite another thing for there to be an explanation of why there are dependent beings at all."[38] To say that there always have been dependent things fails to provide a sufficient reason for why any such things exist rather than not.

Bertrand Russell (1872–1970) objects that we cannot ask about the cause of the universe; it is "just there, and that's all."[39] The argument in defense of the contingency of the universe—that since everything in the universe is contingent, the universe itself must be contingent—is, he contends, fallacious.

Russell is correct in noting that general arguments of this type can commit the fallacy of composition. For example, the argument that since all the bricks in the wall are small therefore the wall is small is fallacious. Yet sometimes the totality has the same character as the parts on account of the parts—we built the wall out of bricks; therefore, it is a brick wall. The universe's contingency, it is argued, is like the second case. If all the contingent parts of the universe, including matter and energy, ceased to exist simultaneously, then the universe itself, as the totality of these parts, would cease to exist. But if it can cease to exist, it is contingent and requires an explanation for its existence.

William Rowe (b. 1931) develops a different argument to support the thesis that the universe must be contingent. He argues that it is necessary that if God exists, then it is possible that there are no dependent beings. Since it is possible that God exists, it is possible that there are no dependent beings, and hence the universe is contingent.[40]

As one can readily see, the issues surrounding the cosmological argument, in whatever form it takes, are complex. But one further question remains, namely, even if the argument succeeded, would it show, as Aquinas held, that God (understood religiously) exists? Whether the argument establishes the existence of God understood religiously depends on whether the necessary being or first cause to which the argument concludes is the God of religion. Some suggest that the universe is the necessary being, but we have seen there is reason to doubt this. Without any other reasonable candidate, it is likely that the necessary being is God. But much more would have to be said concerning its properties to establish that the necessary being is to be identified with a being who is personal, loving, good, all-knowing, and omnipotent, and who acts purposively.

THE ANALOGICAL TELEOLOGICAL ARGUMENT

Undoubtedly the most popular argument for God's existence is the teleological argument. Like the cosmological argument, it is a causal argument. But it emphasizes the order or means directed to an end (*telos*) structure found in the universe. Also like the ontological and cosmological arguments, it has a long history and reflects the prevailing scientific worldview of the time. In our discussion we leave aside the Thomistic argument constructed on an appeal to final causes and instead focus on modern conceptions of the argument—the analogical, anthropic, and intelligent design versions.

Widely found in popular religious literature, the analogical teleological argument goes back at least to the Enlightenment and is best exemplified by William Paley's (1743–1805) argument that nature is analogous to a watch. On analyzing a watch, he says, we are impressed with its intricate means-ends adaptation. All the wheels, gears, and springs are made and adjusted so that by their motion the watch keeps perfect time. Seeing this, we cannot help but conclude that the watch had an intelligent maker who fashioned it according to a design for a purpose. When we look at nature, we quickly discover the same intricate means-ends adaptation. "Every indication of contrivance, every manifestation of design, which existed in the watch, exists in the world of nature; with the difference, on the side of nature, of being greater and more, and that in degree which exceeds all computation."[41] Just consider, for example, the astounding means-ends ordering between all the parts of the eye and the end of seeing; each part is well suited to contribute to the whole, so that if merely one part functions poorly, sight is negatively affected. Since the effects—nature and the watch—are analogous, it is reasonable to conclude that nature, like the watch, has an intelligent, purposeful maker.

But will the analogy work? David Hume (1711–1776), anticipating Paley's argument, advanced three criticisms of an analogical teleological argument. First, the strength of the argument depends upon the similarity between the things held to be analogous (the analogs). The greater the similarity, the stronger the argument; the weaker the similarity, the weaker the argument. Hume argued that the two analogs are greatly disparate;[42] our world is not like watches and other humanly contrived things. Indeed, containing vegetation and animals, it is more organic than mechanical.

Second, to think that the principle governing human creation of machines—that reason is required for means-ends adaptation—governs all of nature is unreasonable. Many natural principles govern processes like reproduction and photosynthesis other than reason. Indeed, the number of natural principles may be indefinitely large. Why choose reason or mind as the ultimate governing or forming principle of the universe? Why not choose, for example, the principles involved in generation or photosynthesis or in atomic reactions as the dominant principles? Furthermore, each principle rules over its own natural domain, whether vegetation or generation or strong and weak nuclear forces. We cannot project a governing principle from one limited area to another part of nature, to the whole of the universe, or to its formation.

Third, suppose we grant that mind accounts for the order in the universe. Does not the principle of causation hold for mind and its ideas just as much as for the material world?[43] If so, this mind must have a cause for its ordering. Hence, we have an infinite regress of causes for any event, since we cannot invoke either the mental or the material to be the ultimate cause or explanation. But an infinite regress of causes yields no satisfactory explanation for the resulting order. Hence, either we deny the principle of causation (and do not require a cause for the means-ends adaptation in the material world) or we affirm the principle of causation and allow evidence showing that each area, material as well as mental, can organize itself.

Philosophers prior to the eighteenth century generally doubted that matter could organize itself. Providing such an account, however, is one of the significant contributions of Charles Darwin (1809–1882). He argued that the order in the universe results not from conscious activity but from natural selection. Individual examples of apparent purpose occur when modifications produced by random mutations either are preserved when they benefit (or at least do not harm) the individual or are discarded when they prove detrimental to survival or reproduction. But genetic mutation and natural selection are strictly natural processes; they do not require a divine mind for their operation. Evolutionary naturalism, it is held, provides a reasonable alternative for explaining particular instances of means-end order in nature, confirming Hume's suspicion that matter can organize itself.

THE ANTHROPIC TELEOLOGICAL ARGUMENT

Despite the demise of Paley's argument in the nineteenth century, the teleological argument has experienced a renaissance at the end of the twentieth and the beginning of the twenty-first centuries. Although the argument appears in numerous forms, two recent versions have occasioned significant discussion.

Some contemporary proponents of the teleological argument grant that individual examples of means-ends ordering in the organic realm can be explained by evolutionary principles. Evolution, with its auxiliary hypothesis of natural selection, provides a paradigm that enables us to account for biological processes. However, the universe manifests certain other features that are best explained by appeal to an intelligent, purposive designer. Defenders of the *Anthropic Argument* note that the inorganic world contains a vast complex of seemingly unrelated conditions, many of which have a very low antecedent probability, given what we know about the prior natural causes. That is, the occurrence of each of these conditions, by themselves, seems highly improbable. If any of the initial conditions at the universe's origin had been different from what they were, life as we know it would not exist. Most important, we as conscious beings would not be here to witness the process. For example, had "the Big Bang expanded at a different rate, life would not have evolved. *A reduction by one part in a million million* at an initial stage would have led to recollapse before temperatures could fall below ten thousand degrees. An early *increase* by one part in a million would have prevented the growth of galaxies, stars and planets."[44] Or had the gravitational force been slightly greater, all the stars would be blue giants whose life span is too short to allow intelligent life to evolve. But had it been slightly less, the universe would be devoid of many elements essential to life. Furthermore, "if the electric charge of the electron had been only slightly different, stars either would have been unable to burn hydrogen and helium, or else they would not have exploded,"[45] giving us the heavier chemical elements. Or again, "if the 'strong force,' which binds the nuclei of atoms together, were stronger, helium nuclei would dominate the universe, and no hydrogen would be left over; without hydrogen there would be no water" and no life.[46] Finally, the universe must be so big to be so old, and it must be so old to create the chemicals necessary for life to evolve. In particular, the basic element of life—carbon—could be formed only after the universe had cooled down from the Big Bang. But the time required for the evolution of the only possible basis for spontaneous generation of life required a universe so big. In short, we could not be what we are—living, knowing beings who in part comprehend the process—without the universe having these specific conditions. Yet the inorganic improbably fits into the extraordinarily narrow window of life-making possibilities. What is antecedently unlikely is necessary for the very possibility of conscious beings knowing it.

How does one best explain why these conditions have precisely the life-engendering or life-fostering values they have? On a nonteleological schema, the antecedent probability of the particular scenario occurring that resulted in carbon-based life is extremely low. Someone has calculated the odds against our universe's formation as one in $10,000,000,000^{124}$. However, on a teleological schema, viewed from our present perspective, the features of the scenario are necessary for the present state of affairs (specifically, for human observers to exist). Thus, although we can describe the development of the requisite physical events naturally, that they occurred at all and in the pattern and narrow range necessary for evolving life points to the existence of a conscious designer. Hence, it is reasonable to claim that the best explanation for there being a universe that produces conscious life is the purposive activity of a creator.

One interesting reply grants this evidence about the extraordinary conjunction of events (called the Weak Anthropic Principle) but maintains that an infinite number of universes, independent of each other so that one universe has no contact with another, actually exist. In such a scenario, the likelihood that a life-bearing universe would arise is virtually certain.[47] Accordingly, the best explanation is not the activity of a creator but the fact that this universe is the one where all these possibilities were realized. Whether this response weakens the Anthropic argument depends on whether one is willing to accept the provocative and much discussed presupposition that an infinite number of unrelated universes, inaccessible to us, exist.

Taking a different tack, Stephen Gould (1941–2002) argues that the Anthropic argument's reasoning is flawed, for though it is antecedently unlikely that any given historical event will occur, something has to happen. Think, for example, how improbable it is that you and everyone else in the world are precisely in the position you and they are in *right now*. Even if what occurred was surprising, it is not surprising that something did occur, and hence no special explanation need be given for that fact.[48] Natural explanations suffice.

But the fact that *something* must happen does not remove the necessity for giving an explanation for the extraordinariness of what actually happens. Richard Swinburne gives the example of a madman who imprisons a victim, telling him that unless a card-shuffling machine draws ten aces of hearts sequentially from ten decks, the machine will set off an explosion that will kill him. The madman then starts the machine to make the required draws, and to the amazement of the perspiring victim it draws ten successive aces of hearts. After release, the grateful victim claims that the machine was rigged, but the madman replies that the fortunate draws needed no explanation, since the machine had to select some cards and this was the only sequence of draws the victim could have observed. But "the fact that this peculiar order [of ten aces of hearts] is a necessary condition for the draw being perceived at all makes what is perceived no less extraordinary and in need of explanation."[49]

It is true that the improbability of an event does not entail that one cannot provide a natural explanation. Natural explanations are compatible with the merest possibility. But the point of the argument is that what is sought is the best possible explanation not only of the conditions themselves, but also of the fact that among all the possible conditions those that make intelligent life possible are what exist. The appeal to a conscious, purposive designer explains better than chance the life-anticipating conjunction of these extremely narrowly ranged physical conditions and natural laws.

THE INTELLIGENT DESIGN TELEOLOGICAL ARGUMENT

The most recent formulation of the teleological argument is termed the *Intelligent Design Argument*. Proponents point out that although we cannot know that something has *not* been designed (for example, whether a piece of abstract art was painted by a human or randomly by Ruby, the Phoenix Zoo elephant noted for slinging paint), we can detect design in systems that in their functions are irreducibly complex. Such systems are "single systems composed of several well-matched, interacting parts that contribute to the basic function, wherein the removal of any one of the parts causes the system to effectively cease functioning."[50] In such systems the interacting components are ordered in such a way that, not only do they each contribute to the system, but they produce a result over and above what would result from the parts acting separately. The system's overall function must involve the complete internal complexity of the system. Michael Behe (b. 1952) cites the cilium used by some cells to swim as an instance of irreducible complexity. Cilia are complex systems that will not work unless all the constituents—microtubules, special proteins called dyneins that act as miniature motors, and connectors to convey the sliding motion of the microtubules into the bending motion that propels the cell—are present and functioning properly.

Behe argues that since by definition an irreducibly complex system is nonfunctional if it lacks a functional part, such systems cannot develop gradually by slight modifications of precursor systems, as in natural selection using random mutation. If the precursor system lacked a functional part, it would be nonfunctional. Even a process where separately functioning cells symbiotically work together and eventually combine into one system cannot account for this irreducible complexity, for the process begins with already-functioning complex systems. Rather, irreducibly complex systems must arise as an integrated unit, constructed by an intelligent agent that purposefully arranged the parts. Thus, in contrast to some defenders of the Anthropic argument, proponents of Intelligent Design reject the Darwinian macro-evolutionary account of how organisms develop. At the same time, they claim to differ from Paley in admitting only irreducibly complex systems into the argument.

If we abandon Neo-Darwinianism, have we then abandoned scientific accounts of biological development for a religious nonscience? To counteract this charge, supporters of Behe's view attempt to formulate the Intelligent Design Argument more generally as a statistical research program that provides probabilistic methods for reliably determining when something is

designed. William Dembski (b. 1960) generates an algorithm (called an Explanatory Filter) that he claims can be employed in a non–question-begging
way to determine when design rather than regularity or chance best explains
an event. First one determines whether the event can be explained by regularity. An event that has a high probability of occurring (my alarm clock ringing every morning when the timer is set to 6 A.M.) is assigned to regularity
(explainable by natural laws). Otherwise one turns to chance as an explanation, as I do when I spread grass seed on my lawn and try to explain why
any particular seed germinates and survives. To eliminate chance as an explanation and conclude to design, Dembski appeals to what he terms *specified complexity.* To exhibit specified complexity the system or event both has
to be so improbable that it cannot be reasonably attributed to chance (Dembski's figure is 1 in 10^{150}, which he calculates from the number of particles in
the universe, the duration of the universe in seconds, and the number of
changes per second that a particle can experience) and has to have a pattern
that can be determined independently of what actually happened or exists.
The specified pattern should not simply be read off of or constructed on the
event. To do so would be like painting a target around the spot where the
arrow hit and saying how good a shot one is; the pattern would be merely ad
hoc and so beg the question of design.[51]

Dembski is especially interested in information that is both complex and
specified, such as that found in Behe's irreducibly complex systems. In particular, he wonders how complex specified information arose and got into
the organisms in a lifeless, abiotic universe. Once RNA sequences exist we
can understand the laws and processes involved in their combination and
recombination as they act as both blueprints and catalysts to stimulate reactions between themselves and other molecules, though even here new
information has to be infused from outside the system. But what could order
the information-neutral physical-chemical elements such as amino acids or
kaolin crystalline structures into information-bearing paired nucleotides?
These nucleotides reproduce themselves, eventually to be linked as DNA
in a double helix spiral that has coding regions where specific sequences
convey the information used in building proteins. Regularity, determined
through algorithms and natural laws, accounts for the transmission but
not the origination of information. Chance modifies the information present
as the organism develops but cannot account for the origin of information
systems that are both complex and specified by independent patterns, for
the complexity is too improbable and the specified patterns "too tight."[52]
"Factoring in the probability of attaining proper bonding and optical iso-
mers, the probability of constructing a rather short, functional protein at
random becomes so small as to be effectively zero (no more than 1 chance in
10^{125}), even given our multi-billion-year-old-universe."[53] Therefore, information originally had to be infused by an intelligent agent from outside of
natural causes.

The Intelligent Design argument has come under significant attack from
two quarters. The first addresses the attempt to provide statistical under-

pinnings for the argument. One problem is that Dembski believes that he can construct a specified pattern after the event has occurred or the irreducibly complex system exists. But such a construction, in biology as elsewhere, leads one to think that the pattern is fabricated (recall the target painted around where the arrow hit), not specified independent of the event, as Dembski's theory requires.[54]

Furthermore, on Dembski's view design is what remains as an explanation once regularity and chance are rejected as insufficient. But then, the objection goes, since no particular observations follow or are deducible from the theory, Intelligent Design theorists fail to provide an *empirically testable* hypothesis to enable us to determine whether design provides the best explanation. But theories ought to be empirically testable by empirical observations so that they can be confirmed probabilistically or falsified.[55] Dembski responds that his appeal to Intelligent Design is a properly formed hypothesis. One can establish whether a theory is acceptable through properly constructed algorithms. The debate here, in part, concerns the nature of scientific theories.

The second set of objections arises from Behe's appeal to irreducibly complex systems, which he argues cannot have developed randomly from prior systems. Kenneth Miller (b. 1948) contends that the Intelligent Design argument, couched at the level of proteins and cells, is fundamentally no different than the argument Paley presented and suffers from similar shortcomings. Miller provides cases of irreducibly complex systems that both satisfy Behe's definition and show gradual evolutionary development. For example, the five-component system that carries sound across the middle ear is irreducibly complex in Behe's sense, but the history of its formation can be traced as "two of the bones that originally formed the rear portion of the reptilian lower jaw were gradually pushed backwards and reduced in size until they migrated into the middle ear, forming the bony connections that carry vibrations into the inner ears of present-day mammals."[56] This complex system has parts with readily discernible antecedents. With respect to cilia in cells, Miller argues that "we can find scores of cilia lacking one or more of the components supposedly essential to the function of the apparatus," but which work, albeit each in its own way. "Once we have found a series of less complex, less intricate, differently organized [cilia], the contention that this is an irreducibly complex structure has been successfully refuted."[57] Miller's point is twofold: first, that what appear to be irreducibly complex systems may not be so, and, second, that the components of systems and cells may have their functions altered or adopt parts from systems with similar or quite different functions. What develops often arises from modifications of systems that that were useful but for purposes unrelated to the evolved system.

The critical questions, then, are whether irreducibly complex systems, in the way in which Behe understands them, really exist, and if they do whether his inference that they cannot develop gradually by slight modifications follows. Whereas the first appears to be an ontological claim about how things and their components function, the second—whether they can develop gradually—is really epistemic, depending on our biological knowledge at any given time. Geneticists will complain that the debate has been carried out on the level of the organism (the phenotype), whereas it really should be debated at the level of the genes responsible for the complex systems. Depending on the environment, genes can change function in different systems or take over functions of other genes. The very fact, for example, that dynein genes are involved in a variety of activities, from the cilia's motor function to platelet activation to guiding brain development, shows that changes in genes themselves can produce a variety of structures. Indeed, small changes in genes can cause significant changes in the systems, changes that are not counterproductive to components' functioning, despite the fact that the components might function differently. Even in the formation of what might seem to be irreducibly complex systems, developmental processes are at work, so that different genes are expressed or turned on at different times to bring about the complex system. Finally, talk about irreducibly complex systems overlooks the fact of genetic redundancy, so that systems can continue to function while certain genes take on other roles.

If this version of the teleological argument is to go beyond the argument developed by Paley, it will have the daunting task to show that nature really has irreducibly complex systems not evolvable through gene modification from prior structures and that design can be objectively determined. This will involve a study of the complex relations between genes and phenotype, an understanding of the developmental process of gene expression, and a historically informed account of genetic change. All of this is becoming available with the rapid deciphering of the genetic codes of organisms.

THE MORAL ARGUMENT

The final argument at which we will look is the moral argument. This argument was espoused by Immanuel Kant[58] in the context of a postulational metaphysic (wherein we postulate that something must be the case in order to make something else possible) and more recently in the popular writings of C.S. Lewis (1898–1963). Although a version of Kant's argument has found some recent qualified support,[59] we will focus on Lewis's treatment.

For Lewis, our moral discussions and moral behavior presuppose an *objective moral law*. He rejects moral relativism, according to which what a group or person thinks is right is right for them. For one thing, without an objective moral law, we have no standpoint from which to critique the moral behavior or ideologies of others. If what a person thinks is right is right for that person only, the only possible grounds for criticism would be a person's failure to act on what the person thought or believed was right. But then the moral beliefs of Adolph Hitler and Joseph Stalin would be morally equivalent to those of Jesus and the Buddha. Second, if moral relativism were true, there could not be moral progress. To progress in one's moral beliefs, one must be able to be mistaken about one's moral beliefs and one set of moral beliefs must be better than another. But both are impossible when whatever a person or a group thinks is right, is right for them. Furthermore, those who advocate ethical relativism often do so on the grounds that moral relativism promotes tolerance, advances the good of the community, or preserves the species. But this only reintroduces objective moral values, for unless some values are better than others—tolerance better than intolerance, preservation of the species better than its demise—we have no ground for praising these values. Finally, Lewis argues that those who argue from belief relativism, which is the view that different persons or societies have different moral beliefs, to ethical relativism have failed to notice that various cultures substantially agree about what is morally acceptable and what is forbidden. The differences between cultures are less matters of value than of fact. For example, what constituted murder in Aztec society, which practiced ritual killing, differs from what constitutes murder in our society, which does not practice ritual killing.

If this objective moral law is to be justified and not mere opinion, it must be grounded in or based on something. Lewis suggests two possible grounds: the factual reality of human experience (what he calls "matter") and mind. It cannot be grounded on the factual reality observed by science, for the laws of nature tell us only what things actually do, while the moral law deals with what *ought* to occur. Put another way, we ultimately cannot help but obey the laws of nature, but we have a choice about obeying the moral law. Even though we are commanded to obey it, we can refuse. The moral law must be grounded in mind, for only mind can give instructions regarding doing the right. This mind cannot be a human mind, for the moral law continues to hold despite the births and deaths of individual human persons. Hence, a power or mind must lie behind the universe, "urging me to do the right and making me feel responsible and uncomfortable when I do wrong. I think we have to assume it is more like a mind than it is like anything else we know—because after all the only other thing we know is matter and you can hardly imagine a bit of matter giving instructions."[60]

Is Lewis correct that a naturalist account of ethics cannot suffice? There are traditions of naturalistic ethics that give a rational though material basis for moral obligations. For example, Aristotle (384–322 B.C.) argued that we can ground moral judgments in the final causes of the universe. By seeing how things necessarily are, we can discern how we ought to act. The *ought* is grounded not in the *is*, but in what *necessarily is* the case, in the ideal structure that must be realized in order to maximize the self-fulfillment of the organism.

It might be replied that contemporary philosophers no longer appeal to Aristotelian ethics because they have long abandoned the notion of final causation. This is true, but the point of the objection is simply to affirm that the moral argument cannot conclude directly that the ground of the moral law *must* be mind. Of course, this means that it is incumbent on contemporary ethical naturalists to show that the moral law can be adequately grounded in something else. At this point, the discussion must turn to evaluate recent attempts to develop sophisticated naturalistic or intuitionist ethics, a subject beyond our present scope.[61]

What, then, can be said about the moral argument? Some will doubt whether it can function soundly as an independent theistic argument. All of Lewis's premises have been challenged. Some theists might respond, however, that these challenges can be answered, so that it might function as part of a cumulative case that includes other arguments for God's existence.

CUMULATIVE CASE ARGUMENTS AND GOD

We have advocated a person-relative notion of argument, in which each person must decide concerning the soundness or strength of the argument and what he or she knows about the truth of the premises. One must be careful here. The fact that arguments are person-relative does not imply that "anything goes." Since we think and work in a community, an argument that does not meet with at least some measure of acceptance by persons in the community, that only one individual or a few think to be sound or reasonable, should raise serious questions in the advocate's mind. Though acceptance by the community does not make any claim true, the community functions as a check against mere rationalization of any position.

It might be replied, correctly, that the term *community* is still vague. We function in many communities, not merely one. To which community should the theist present grounds or evidence? To the theistic community? To the nontheistic community? What kind of evaluative criteria are to be invoked? At the bare minimum, logical criteria should be accepted by all sides. But beyond this, the appropriate criteria for communal judgments are matters for ongoing discussion.[62]

One more set of objections to the arguments must be considered. Michael Martin (b. 1932), in his extensive, detailed defense of atheism, takes on each theistic argument individually, raising serious questions about both the argument and what it would show were it sound. For each argument he concludes, first, that the argument does not warrant theistic belief, and, second, should it do so, it would not support a belief in the God of Christian, Jewish, or Muslim theism.[63]

Regarding Martin's first objection, the theist could respond that generally it is a mistake to base a thesis on one argument. Just as the prosecution in a trial brings a variety of evidence to bear on the case, so that if one piece of evidence is questioned, the case does not topple, so theists should not ground their belief on any single argument or treat the arguments independently. Theistic arguments are best seen as part of a *cumulative case for theism*, where the pieces support each other in a way that enables us to make sense of the entire picture.[64] Together they may indicate that a person has good reason to believe in the existence of some sort of ultimate reality or God. The cosmological argument concludes that a necessary being exists, a being that if it exists is not dependent upon other beings for its existence. The teleological argument proposes that such a being, as responsible for the conscious-life–anticipating dimension of the universe, acts purposively and so has conscious intelligence and will. The moral argument suggests that this being has some relation to the moral law, and that it is reasonable to conceive of the moral law as somehow grounded in it and manifested in the order of its creation.

Though Martin considers the arguments for God *serially* and claims that he could rest his case on an a priori argument that the concept of God is incoherent, he does proceed to consider other reasons as well. In doing so, one could suggest that he too is constructing an elaborate *cumulative case—for atheism*. In defense of *negative* atheism, he attempts to show both that religious language is cognitively meaningless and that the theistic arguments fail to provide any reason for thinking that God exists. "Although a conclusive case cannot be made for negative atheism, if a good case can be made for supposing that belief in God should be based on reason and that all the available reasons for believing in an all-good, all-powerful, and all knowing being are inadequate, negative atheism in the narrow sense will be justified as much as it can be in relation to our present knowledge."[65] In defense of *positive* atheism he advances the case that God is the sort of entity that could and should have provided evidence for his existence. Not only is such evidence lacking; the presence of evil provides a strong argument in favor of atheism.

Our point is that when considering arguments for or against theism, the case should not rest on one piece of evidence, just as prosecutors would be foolish to rest their case on a single piece of evidence.

THE GOD OF RELIGION AND OF PHILOSOPHY

Martin's second objection raises the important question whether the necessary, purposive being to which the arguments point is to be identified with the God of religion. His contention, with which the theist might agree, is that if we are looking for the God of the Bible or the Koran to emerge from the arguments, we will be disappointed. The arguments at best yield the concept of a being that has distinctively philosophical rather than specifically religious properties. The necessary being of the arguments has not been shown to be personal, loving, worthy of worship, or concerned for our salvation. Can, then, the necessary being of the philosophers be identified with the God of religious believers?

One way theists can explore this is by what might be termed the *method of correlation*. This involves correlating the properties of the philosophical necessary being with those of the God of a particular religious tradition. Three steps are required. First, the characteristics of this necessary being must be determined. For example, it might be held to be an eternal, conscious intelligence, creatively and purposively involved in the world. Some hold that other properties, like omnipotence, omniscience, and goodness, follow from these properties. The second step is to choose a particular religious tradition and see how its Ultimate Reality is described. What properties are appropriate to it? Is it held to be a conscious, purposive being, causally related to a contingent world separate from itself? Or is it an impersonal Absolute, a being behind the illusion of this world? Third, what properties in the two lists are consistent, inconsistent, or not duplicated? Where the lists are consistent, there is reason to believe that they describe the same being. Where the lists are inconsistent (for example, the cosmological argument supports a dualist tradition, in which God is separate from the world, rather than a monistic or pantheistic tradition), further thinking on the part of both scholar and believer is required. Where the lists have unrelated properties (for example, the theistic arguments do not speak of a personal, loving, trinitarian being who cares about the creation), one might explore whether these properties are or are not consistent with the properties that do follow.

Whatever one concludes about the relation between the Ultimate Reality of the theistic arguments and the God of religion, it is important to note that what is at stake is not a conflict or correlation between two beings, but between two conceptions of God. When seen from this perspective, the work of philosophers and that of theologians can complement each other.

It is safe to say that most philosophers, nontheists and theists alike, remain skeptical about the success of the theistic arguments. At the same time, others think that arguments on both sides yield results. While some believe that a good cumulative case can be constructed for atheism, others believe that the cumulative case of natural theology provides grounds for thinking that belief in God is reasonable. For philosophers of whatever stripe, the issues raised by the arguments provide fertile ground for debate and discussion.

STUDY QUESTIONS

1. How would you argue for or against the view that one needs evidence either to believe or not believe in God? If evidence is needed, who has the burden of proof, and why?

2. If you believe in God, to what evidence do you appeal to support your belief? If you do not believe in God, what argument would you give against God's existence? Carefully evaluate the strength of the arguments you give, noting the possibly problematic premises and critical assumptions.

3. What is Anselm's ontological argument? What argument would you give to critique its central thesis that existence is a perfection, and how might a defender of the argument reply?

4. How is the contemporary version of the ontological argument similar to and different from Anselm's version? What is one of its strengths and one of its weaknesses?

5. What are the similarities and differences between the *kalām* and atemporal versions of the cosmological argument? Take one of the versions and note its critical premises, giving arguments either in support or in criticism of those premises.

6. What are the similarities and differences between the analogical, Anthropic, and Intelligent Design versions of the teleological argument? Does the teleological argument beg the question in assuming that there is order in the universe? Does the appeal to probability helpfully circumvent this objection?

7. What is Gould's argument against the inductive form of the teleological argument? What is Swinburne's reply? Which do you find more convincing, and why?

8. Attempt to lay out formally the moral argument for God's existence (as we did for the ontological and cosmological arguments). Then proceed to evaluate each of the premises for its truth.

NOTES

1. George Mavrodes, *Belief in God* (New York: Random House, 1970), chap. 2.

2. Richard Swinburne, *The Existence of God* (Oxford: Clarendon Press, 1979).

3. *Webster's New World Dictionary of the American Language* (Cleveland: World Publishing Company, 1955).

4. Anselm, *Proslogium*, in *Anselm: Monologion and Proslogion* (Indianapolis, Ind.: Hackett Publishing Company, 1995), trans. Thomas Williams, chaps. 2–4. (See PRSR2e, pt. 4, pp. 165–7.)

5. Gaunilo, "On Behalf of the Fool," in *Anselm*, p. 123. (See PRSR2e, pt. 4, pp. 167–70.)

6. Anselm, *Prologium*, p. 132.

7. Alvin Plantinga, *God, Freedom and Evil* (New York: Harper and Row, 1974), p. 91. (See PRSR2e, pt. 4, pp. 172–3.) See also Charles Hartshorne, "What Did Anselm Discover?" in *The Many Faced Argument*, ed. John Hick and Arthur C. McGill (New York: Macmillan, 1967), pp. 330–1.

8. William J. Abraham, *An Introduction to the Philosophy of Religion* (Englewood Cliffs, N.J.: Prentice-Hall, 1985), p. 27.

9. Immanuel Kant, *Critique of Pure Reason*, A598.

10. Norman Malcolm, "Anselm's Ontological Arguments," in *The Many Faced Argument*, ed. Hick and McGill, pp. 304–5.

11. Jerome Shaffer, "Existence, Predication and the Ontological Argument," *Mind* 71, no. 283 (1962):307–25; reprinted in Hick and McGill, p. 230.

12. Malcolm, "Anselm's Ontological Arguments," pp. 301–20; Hartshorne, "What Did Anselm Discover?" pp. 321–33; Plantinga, *God, Freedom and Evil*, pp. 85–112. (See PRSR2e, pt. 4, pp. 178–83.)

13. Hartshorne is careful to insist that although this argument establishes God's necessary existence, it does not establish his *actuality* or concreteness. For Hartshorne, God in his actuality has contingent properties; he is not necessarily unsurpassable, immutable, and independent. The ontological argument, then, establishes that God exists, but it does not tell us *how*; it does not give us his content.

14. John Hick, "A Critique of the 'Second Argument,'" in *The Many Faced Argument*, ed. Hick and McGill, pp. 345–6.

15. Thomas V. Morris, *Anselmian Reflections: Essays in Philosophical Theology* (Notre Dame, Ind.: Notre Dame University Press, 1987), p. 12.

16. Michael Tooley, "Plantinga's Defense of the Ontological Argument," *Mind* 90 (1981): 422–7.

17. William Rowe, *An Introduction to the Philosophy of Religion* (Belmont, Calif.: Wadsworth, 2001), chap. 3.

18. Thomas Aquinas, *Summa Theologica* I, Q.2, A. 3; *On the Truth of the Catholic Faith* I (Notre Dame, Ind.: University of Notre Dame, 1975), chap. 13 (See PRSR2e, pt. 4, pp. 184–7); Samuel Clarke, *A Demonstration of the Being and Attributes of God*, Ezio Vailati, ed. (Cambridge: Cambridge University Press, 1998), pp. 8–12; Bertrand Russell and F.C. Copleston, "A Debate on the Existence of God," in *The Existence of God*, ed. John Hick (New York: Macmillan, 1964), pp. 167–91; Richard Taylor, *Metaphysics* (Englewood Cliffs, N.J.: Prentice-Hall, 1992), pp. 99–108. (See PRSR2e, pt. 4, pp. 187–96.)

19. William Craig, *The* Kalām *Cosmological Argument* (New York: Barnes and Noble, 1979), p. 63. (See PRSR2e, pt. 4, pp. 196–8.)

20. J.L. Mackie, *The Miracle of Theism* (New York: Oxford University Press, 1982), p. 94. (See PRSR2e, pt. 4, pp. 216–7.)

21. Paul Davies, *Superforce* (New York: Simon and Schuster, 1984), p. 200. (See PRSR2e, pt. 4, p. 240.)

22. William Lane Craig and Quentin Smith, *Theism, Atheism, and Big Bang Cosmology* (New York: Oxford University Press, 1993), pp. 182, 121–3.

23. Ibid., pp. 143–44.

24. Ibid., pp. 98–9; Craig, *Theism*, pp. 66–95. (See PRSR2e, pt. 4, pp. 198–200.)

25. Aristotle, *Physics*, vol. 3, 6.

26. James Glanz, "Cosmic Motion Revealed," *Science* 282 (Dec. 18, 1998): 2156–7.

27. Davies, *Superforce*, pp. 192, 191. (See PRSR2e, pt. 4, pp. 235, 234.)

28. Craig and Smith, *Theism*, pp. 200–1. We changed Smith's numbering and numbered Smith's final two claims as 9 and 10. See p. 219.

29. Bruce Reichenbach, *Evil and a Good God* (New York: Fordham University Press, 1982), chap. 6. See Robert M. Adams (*The Virtue of Faith* [New York: Oxford University Press, 1987], chap. 4) for a different argument.

30. Craig and Smith, *Theism*, pp. 202–3.

31. Thomas V. Morris, *The Logic of God Incarnate* (Ithaca, N.Y.: Cornell University Press, 1986), pp. 77–8.

32. It is important to be clear about this principle. Some have mistakenly interpreted the causal principle to mean that *everything* has a cause of its existence. But then even the first cause (necessary being or God) must have a cause of its existence, and an infinite regress of causes is inevitable. But by definition necessary beings are self-sufficient and self-sustaining; hence it makes no sense to ask whether they have a cause of their existence. Accordingly, the causal principle invoked is more restricted; it claims only that *contingent* beings must have a cause of their existence.

33. Taylor, *Metaphysics*, p. 100. (See PRSR2e, pt. 4, p. 189–90.)

34. Immanuel Kant, *Critique of Pure Reason*, trans. Norman Kemp Smith (New York: St. Martin's Press, 1929), A606.

35. Swinburne, *Existence of God*, p. 73.

36. Keith Yandell, *Christianity and Philosophy* (Grand Rapids, Mich.: William B. Eerdmans, 1984), pp. 59–60.

37. This argument still differs from the *kalām* argument, for whereas the *kalām* argument asks for an explanation of the universe's *coming into existence*, this argument

asks for an explanation of the contingent universe's *existence* and thus is compatible with its eternal existence.

38. William Rowe, *The Cosmological Argument* (Princeton, N.J.: Princeton University Press, 1975), p. 264.

39. Russell and Copleston, "Debate on the Existence of God," p. 175.

40. Rowe, *Cosmological Argument*, p. 164.

41. William Paley, *Natural Theology* (Charlottesville, Va.: Ibis Pub., 1986), chaps. 1, 3.

42. David Hume, *Dialogues concerning Natural Religion* (Indianapolis, Ind.: Hackett, 1980), p. 16.

43. Ibid., Book 4.

44. John Leslie, "The Anthropic Principle, World Ensemble, Design," *American Philosophical Quarterly* 19, no. 2 (April 1982): 141.

45. Stephen W. Hawking, *A Brief History of Time* (New York: Bantam, 1988), p. 125. Hawking accepts one version of the anthropic principle; he does not accept the one invoked by the Anthropic teleological argument.

46. L. Stafford Betty with Bruce Cordell, "God and Modern Science: New Life for the Teleological Argument," *International Philosophical Quarterly* 27, no. 4 (December 1987): 415. (See PRSR2e, p. 221.)

47. John D. Barrow and Frank J. Tipler, *The Anthropic Cosmological Principle* (Oxford: Clarendon Press, 1986).

48. Stephen Jay Gould, *The Flamingo's Smile, Reflections in Natural History* (New York: Penguin Books, 1985), p. 183.

49. Swinburne, *Existence of God*, p. 138.

50. Michael Behe, *Darwin's Black Box* (New York: Free Press, 1996), p. 39.

51. William A. Dembski, *The Design Inference: Eliminating Chance through Small Probabilities* (Cambridge: Cambridge University Press, 1998), chaps. 1,5.

52. William A. Dembski, *Intelligent Design* (Downer's Grove, Ill.: InterVarsity Press, 1999), p. 166.

53. Stephen C. Meyer, "Word Games," in *Signs of Intelligence: Understanding Intelligent Design,* ed. William A. Dembski and James M. Kushiner (Grand Rapids, Mich.: Baker Book House, 2001), pp. 110, 115.

54. Discussion of Dembski's additional criteria for specification are technical and must be reserved for more advanced discussion. See Dembski, *The Design Inference,* ch. 5; Brandon Fitelson, Christopher Stephens, and Elliott Sober, "How Not to Detect Design," *Philosophy of Science* 66 (September 1999): 479–83.

55. Fitelson et al., "How Not to Detect Design," pp. 475, 487.

56. Kenneth R. Miller, *Finding Darwin's God* (New York: HarperCollins, 1999), p. 118.

57. Ibid., p. 143.

58. Immanuel Kant, *Critique of Practical Reason* (Indianapolis, Ind.: Bobbs-Merrill, 1956), pp. 128–36.

59. Adams, *The Virtue of Faith*, chap. 10.

60. C.S. Lewis, *Mere Christianity* (New York: Macmillan, 1943), p. 34. (See PRSR2e, pt. 4, p. 246.)

61. For Lewis's argument that no naturalistic account can provide a justification of a moral belief, see C.S. Lewis, *Miracles* (New York: Macmillan, 1960), chaps. 3, 5. For a naturalist ethic, see Peter Railton, "Moral Realism," *Philosophical Review* 95 (1986): 163–207.

62. See Alvin Plantinga, "Advice to Christian Philosophers," *Faith and Philosophy* 1, no. 2 (July 1984): 253–71, for one perspective.

63. Michael Martin, *Atheism: A Philosophical Justification* (Philadelphia: Temple University Press, 1990), pp. 97, 100, 152.

64. Basil Mitchell, *The Justification of Religious Belief* (New York: Oxford University Press, 1981), chaps. 3–5.

65. Martin, *Atheism*, p. 39.

SUGGESTED READING

Barrow, John D., and Frank J. Tipler. *The Anthropic Cosmological Principle.* Oxford: Clarendon Press, 1986.

Bertoli, F., and U. Curi. *The Conditions for the Existence of Mankind in the Universe.* Cambridge: Cambridge University Press, 1991.

Craig, William L. *The Cosmological Argument from Plato to Leibniz.* New York: Barnes and Noble, 1980.

———. *The* Kalām *Cosmological Argument.* London: Macmillan, 1979.

Craig, William Lane, and Quentin Smith. *Theism, Atheism, and Big Bang Cosmology.* New York: Oxford University Press, 1993.

Gale, Richard M. *On the Nature and Existence of God.* Cambridge: Cambridge University Press, 1991.

Hick, John, and Arthur C. McGill, eds. *The Many Faced Argument.* New York: Macmillan, 1967.

Hume, David. *Dialogues concerning Natural Religion.* Indianapolis, Ind.: Hackett, 1980.

Leslie, John, ed. *Physical Cosmology and Philosophy.* New York: Macmillan, 1990.

Lewis, C.S. *Mere Christianity.* New York: Macmillan, 1943.

Mackie, J.L. *The Miracle of Theism.* Oxford: Clarendon Press, 1982.

Martin, Michael. *Atheism: A Philosophical Justification.* Philadelphia: Temple University Press, 1990.

———. *The Case against Christianity.* Temple University Press, 1991.

Miethe, Terry L. "The Cosmological Argument: A Research Bibliography." *New Scholasticism* 52 (Spring 1978): 285–305.

Miller, Barry. *From Existence to God: A Contemporary Philosophical Argument.* London: Routledge, 1992.

Owen, H.P. *The Moral Argument for Christian Theism.* London: Allen and Unwin, 1965.

Plantinga, Alvin. *God, Freedom and Evil.* New York: Harper and Row, 1974.

———. *The Ontological Argument.* New York: Doubleday, 1965.

Polkinghorne, John. *Science and Creation.* London: SPCK, 1988.

Prevost, Robert. *Probability and Theistic Explanation.* Oxford: Clarendon Press, 1990.

Reichenbach, Bruce R. *The Cosmological Argument: A Reassessment.* Springfield, Ill.: Charles C Thomas, 1972.

Robson, John M., ed. *Origin and Evolution of the Universe: Evidence for Design?* Kingston, Ont.: McGill-Queen's University Press, 1987.

Rowe, William L. *The Cosmological Argument.* Princeton, N.J.: Princeton University Press, 1975.

Swinburne, Richard. *The Existence of God.* Oxford: Clarendon Press, 1979.

Taylor, Richard. *Metaphysics.* Englewood Cliffs, N.J.: Prentice-Hall, 1992. Chap. 7.

CHAPTER 6

KNOWING GOD WITHOUT ARGUMENTS: DOES THEISM NEED A BASIS?

The French mystic Simone Weil (1909–1943) describes her first experience of God in this fashion: "In a moment of intense physical suffering, when I was forcing myself to feel love, but without desiring to give a name to that love, I felt, without being in any way prepared for it (for I had never read the mystical writers) a presence more personal, more certain, more real than that of a human being, though inaccessible to the senses and the imagination."[1] Simone Weil's experience is all the more striking because there was so little in her background to prepare her for it. She was raised as an agnostic in a secularized Jewish home, and (as she says) had read none of the mystical authors who might have led her to anticipate such an experience. Weil, who was trained in philosophy, had studied the arguments for and against the existence of God and found the question undecidable. After her experience, however, she wrote:

> When we are eating bread, and even when we have eaten it, we know that it is real. We can nevertheless raise doubts about the reality of the bread. Philosophers raise doubts about the reality of the world of the senses. Such doubts are however purely verbal, they leave the certainty intact and actually serve only to make it more obvious to a well-balanced mind. In the same way he to whom God has revealed his reality can raise doubts about this reality without any harm. They are purely verbal doubts, a form of exercise to keep his intelligence in good health.[2]

Simone Weil's claim here is both clear and striking. On the one hand, she points out, philosophers raise questions about the "reality of the external world"; we may deal with these doubts intellectually—examine them, seek to refute them, and so on—yet all this leaves completely unshaken our certainty of the reality of the bread we have eaten. On the other hand, philosophers doubt the existence of God, and engage in debate using theistic and antitheistic arguments. This is all well and good—fine exercise for the mind, in fact—but for the person "to whom God has revealed his reality" these doubts no more disturb her certainty of his existence than do the philosopher's doubts about the reality of bread and trees and stones.

It is safe to say that most philosophers who have considered the question of God's existence would not agree with Weil about this. Such a certainty, based on experience, as she attests to would often be dismissed as "purely subjective"; such experiences, before we rely on them, need to be confirmed by *rational*, as opposed to purely emotional, considerations. We need, in other words, to look at the question of God's existence in the light of *evidence and arguments*—just such arguments, in fact, as occupied us in the previous chapter. One very natural way of looking at the matter would seem to be this: we estimate, on the one hand, the combined strength of the various arguments for God's existence, and, on the other hand, the strength of the argument from evil as well as other arguments against theism. Then, taking these two bodies of evidence together, we weigh them against each other, and the resulting balance determines whether it is reasonable to believe in God. Thus, if the problem of evil seems to be a strong argument against theism while none of the favorable arguments has much force, then it would be rational to reject belief in God, whereas if the theistic arguments are powerful and the antitheistic arguments can be refuted, belief in God is reasonable and appropriate. It might turn out that the evidence for and against God's existence is quite evenly balanced; in this case it would be appropriate to suspend judgment and neither believe nor disbelieve.

EVIDENTIALISM

This way of looking at the matter has a name; it is called *evidentialism*. It is, as has been said, a rather natural way of viewing the subject—so natural, indeed, that many philosophers have taken it for granted without question. Of course, it must be admitted that most ordinary people, including ordinary religious people, do not think this way at all. Most religious believers have never given much thought to arguments for or against the existence of God, and they may not feel that they have missed very much. Even those who have learned something about the arguments—say, in an introductory philosophy course—seldom make a really serious effort to find out how strong the arguments are or to guide their own beliefs by these arguments. They just go on believing, or disbelieving, without troubling themselves much about arguments.

Evidentialist philosophers, however, are not greatly concerned about the fact that most people do not think about God in the way evidentialism considers proper. The sad fact is, the evidentialists tell us, that most people are very far from being rational in the way in which they decide on important beliefs, especially religious beliefs. People believe for a variety of psychological, social, and emotional reasons that have very little to do with whether a belief is supported by evidence or whether it is likely to be true. Fortunately, however, there are a few individuals who do care about reason and truth, who do not want to be guided merely by their emotions, and it is these people who should be our example. They show what it means to be guided by evidence and arguments in determining our religious beliefs.

One of the most important developments in the philosophy of religion in recent years is the appearance of a group of philosophers who sharply reject evidentialism. These philosophers are not fideists in the sense defined in chapter 3; they do not think that one's ultimate beliefs are immune to rational evaluation. But they maintain that it is possible for religious beliefs to be entirely rational and fully justified *even if there is no evidence supporting these beliefs.* This view is often referred to as "Reformed epistemology," because of the similarity between it and certain ideas which have been prominent in the Reformed, or Calvinistic, branch of Protestantism.[3] But the view itself is not logically tied to this branch of Christian belief; one need not be a Calvinist, or even a Christian, to be a Reformed epistemologist. The three leading exponents of Reformed epistemology are Alvin Plantinga (b.1932), Nicholas Wolterstorff (b.1932), and William P. Alston (b.1921); we shall draw upon each of them in setting out and analyzing the position in the subsequent pages.

CRITIQUE OF EVIDENTIALISM

The first thing we need to do is to understand more precisely what is meant by *evidentialism,* so we can then see why the Reformed epistemologists object to it. Nicholas Wolterstorff presents the "evidentialist challenge" as follows:

> It was insisted, in the first place, that it would be *wrong* for a person to accept Christianity, or any other form of theism, unless it was *rational* for him to do so. And it was insisted, secondly, that it is not rational for a person to do so unless he holds his religious convictions on the basis of other beliefs of his which give to those convictions adequate evidential support. No religion is acceptable unless rational, and no religion is rational unless supported by evidence. That is the evidentialist challenge.[4]

Now, what is so objectionable about this? Unless we are content to be irrational, the requirement that we accept only rational beliefs is hard to contest, and it certainly seems reasonable that in order for religious beliefs to be rational they must be supported by evidence. We need, however, to be more precise about what it means for a belief to be *supported by evidence.* Many different views about this are possible, but many modern philosophers who are evidentialists have been committed to an epistemological perspective known as *strong foundationalism.*[5] In order to understand this perspective, we must first discuss *foundationalism,* and then go on to consider what is distinctive about *strong* foundationalism.

Foundationalists distinguish between two kinds of beliefs that we all have. There are, on the one hand, beliefs that we hold because they receive *evidential support* from other beliefs that we have; these we may term *derived beliefs.* But there are also, it seems, some beliefs that are accepted *without* being supported by still other beliefs; these are our *basic beliefs,* and they form the "basis" on which our entire structure of belief and knowledge ultimately rests.

One may, of course, accept a belief in a basic way (that is, without accepting it on the basis of other beliefs which are taken as evidence for it), when it is quite unreasonable to do so. For instance, one might believe that someone is guilty of a crime simply because one dislikes that person. But there must also, it seems, be some situations in which it is *reasonable and proper* to accept certain beliefs without other beliefs as evidence; those beliefs that it is reasonable to accept without evidence are our *properly basic beliefs.*

There is a very important question that must be answered by any foundationalist, namely, *What kinds of beliefs can be properly basic?* The answer to this question determines what the "foundations" are on which one's beliefs must be built, and thus goes a long way toward deciding what the final structure of beliefs will be like.[6]

Now we are ready for the explanation of *strong* foundationalism. What makes strong foundationalism *strong* is just its idea about the sorts of beliefs that can properly be accepted as basic. The guiding idea has been that the properly basic beliefs should be *beliefs concerning which it is impossible, or nearly impossible, to go wrong.* If the foundations are as solid as it is humanly possible to make them, then the belief-system erected on them can also be solid and secure. In order to achieve this, strong foundationalists usually require that properly basic beliefs should be of only two kinds: they must be either *self-evident* or *incorrigible. Self-evident* beliefs are seen to be true by anyone who understands them; simple truths of arithmetic, such as "1 + 2 = 3," would be examples. *Incorrigible* beliefs are those which deal with one's own, immediate experience; examples would include "I am feeling pain," "I seem to be seeing something red," and the like. It may or may not be possible to go wrong over such beliefs (that has been debated), but they would seem to be about as immune from doubt as any we can imagine. If all our other beliefs can be built on these foundations, the goal of attaining real, solid, unchallengeable knowledge seems within reach.[7] To sum up, then, we may define the strong foundationalist's position as follows: *A person is rational in accepting a given belief only if that belief is self-evident, or incorrigible, or is derived from self-evident or incorrigible beliefs using acceptable methods of logical inference.*

From Wolterstorff's talk about the "evidentialist challenge" to religious belief it might seem that evidentialists oppose religion, but this is not necessarily the case. Quite a few evidentialists—such as Descartes (1596–1650), Locke (1632–1704), and Leibniz (1646–1716)—have thought that belief in God's existence, and other typical religious beliefs, are fully capable of being defended in a way that meets the challenge. As time went on, however, more and more philosophers concluded that theism *cannot* be defended in a way that satisfies the requirements of evidentialism. If that is true, then evidentialism and religion are indeed enemies.

But just what is wrong with evidentialism and strong foundationalism (aside from their possible conflict with theism)? Actually, the answer to this is surprisingly simple: when we apply strong foundationalism to itself it *defeats itself,* or, we may say, it *self-destructs.* (The favorite philosopher's term for this is that this view is *self-referentially incoherent.*) To see what this means, consider the statement of strong foundationalism that was given earlier: *a person is rational in accepting a given belief only if that belief is self-evident, or incorrigible, or is derived from self-evident or incorrigible beliefs using acceptable methods of logical inference.* Is this statement of strong foundationalism itself self-evident? Not likely! In fact, many people have understood it and considered it carefully without thinking that it is true. Furthermore, it is not an "incorrigible" report of one's immediate experience; it is not at all like "I seem to be seeing something red." Finally, there is no reasonable way in which this statement could be *derived* from self-evident or incorrigible propositions, so as to be justified in that way. So we get the following, extremely interesting result: *If strong foundationalism is true, then no one is rational in accepting strong foundationalism.* For a strong foundationalist, this situation is downright embarrassing!

There is, however, another problem with strong foundationalism that is equally serious: *if strong foundationalism is true, then we are wrong about most of what we think we know.* This point needs some explanation. Earlier, in explaining foundationalism, we pointed out that the strong foundationalists wanted to have an *absolutely secure basis* on which the structure of our knowledge could be erected. The idea was that, by taking as foundations only beliefs that were immune to doubt, we could secure a foundation on the basis of which our other beliefs could be built up with a very high degree of confidence and certainty.

Unfortunately, this noble project has proved to be a failure again and again. Many of our ordinary beliefs—things, indeed, that we would readily say that we *know* to be true—turn out to be unsupported when tested by these standards. Consider, for instance, this question: How do you know that you have been living for longer than, say, 45 minutes? It isn't *self-evident* that you have lived longer than that; after all, you might just have been cloned by a very speedy scientist! Nor is this something you can know by an *incorrigible* report of your own experience. You may say that you *remember* having lived for many years past, but how do we know that these are real memories of what actually happened rather than, for example, memories that have been implanted directly in your brain by a scientist? Furthermore, there does not seem to be any way this belief can be *derived* from other beliefs which are self-evident or incorrigible. Nor is this the only sort of ordinary belief that cannot be justified to satisfy the strong foundationalist's standards. If you are going to take this view seriously, you might have to give up your beliefs that trees, mountains, and other physical objects really exist separate from your perception of them, and also your beliefs that other people really have experiences and feelings of their own, as opposed to being preprogrammed robots. But this, surely, shows that there must be something badly wrong with strong foundationalism.

If strong foundationalism is rejected, does this mean that evidentialism must also be given up? Not necessarily; the two views are not logically equivalent. One might accept a version of evidentialism based on a non-classical foundationalism that allows for a broader range of beliefs to be accepted as properly basic; as we shall see in the next section, Plantinga himself adopts a foundationalism of this sort. The Reformed epistemologist, however, would question whether such a liberalized foundationalism can reasonably reject the possibility of properly basic beliefs grounded on religious experience. There can also be a *coherentist* evidentialism. Coherentism rejects the foundationalist's distinction between basic and derived beliefs, and holds instead that *all* of our beliefs are justified by the way they "cohere" (fit together in a consistent, well-integrated system) with the rest of our beliefs. We cannot go into the merits of coherentism at this point. It should be noted, however, that some religious belief-systems seem to be strongly coherent, so the prospects for showing religion to be irrational based on coherentism do not seem especially bright. In general, the possibility of a version of evidentialism not based on strong foundationalism is one that should be kept in mind for further study.

So far, though, all this is merely negative. Does anything of *positive value* for religion emerge if evidentialism is rejected? For consideration of this matter, we turn to Alvin Plantinga.

PLANTINGA ON PROPERLY BASIC BELIEFS

We must not suppose that, when the Reformed epistemologists criticize strong foundationalism, they are rejecting foundationalism as such. They still accept the foundationalist's distinction between basic and derived beliefs, as well as the assumption that there must be *properly* basic beliefs from which all of our other beliefs have to be derived if they are to be rationally justified. What they reject is merely the strong foundationalist's overly restrictive criterion for what can qualify as properly basic beliefs.

But how then shall we decide what beliefs can be properly basic? Here Plantinga, following Roderick Chisholm (1916–1999), suggests that we should not begin by setting up in advance a general requirement, such as is done by strong foundationalism. Instead, we should begin from the structure of belief and knowledge that we already have, and we should assume provisionally that this structure of belief is pretty much in order—that, as Chisholm says, "we do know most, if not all, of those things that ordinary people think that they know."[8] We should take our actual beliefs as examples: Taking some belief we think to be reasonable and justified, we should ask ourselves whether we hold this belief because it is evidentially supported by other beliefs of ours, or whether it is one that is or could be reasonably held even if it were not supported by any other beliefs as evidence. If the latter is the case, we put this belief down as a *basic* belief, and indeed as a *properly basic* belief. Examples of the kinds of beliefs that might turn out, through this procedure, to be properly basic might include the following: ordinary perceptual beliefs ("That is a tree over there"), memory beliefs ("I had scrambled eggs for breakfast"), beliefs about other people's thoughts and feelings ("Mary really got angry when you said that to her"), and other kinds as well. When we have carried out the procedure with a number of examples of different kinds, we can begin to get an overall picture of the kinds of beliefs that can be properly basic—that is, of the *foundations* of our structure of belief.

So far, so good. But at this point, Plantinga has a radical suggestion to make: why should the belief that *God exists* not be part of the foundation? Why should *this* not be one of our properly basic beliefs? The theist, after all, will certainly think that this belief *is* one that she is rationally justified in holding. If she finds (as Plantinga thinks most believers in God will find) that it is *not* a belief that she holds because it is justified inferentially from other beliefs, then the procedure just described will lead her to consider it a *basic*, and indeed a *properly basic*, belief. Why not? What is wrong with this possibility? Is there any reason why "God exists" *cannot* be a properly basic belief? If it is properly basic, then there is *no need* for the theist to produce proofs or arguments for God's existence in order to be justified in believing in God.

Many philosophers have found this proposal of Plantinga's to be bold and even startling. It raises a great many issues and questions, only a few of which can be taken up here. Note, first of all, that the fact that a belief is properly basic in no way guarantees the *truth* of that belief. One who *actually holds* a particular belief in a properly basic way will think that it is true, of course, but then anyone who holds *any* belief in any way whatsoever necessarily thinks that belief is true. But it is entirely possible for a properly basic belief to be false. For example, you walk into a friend's house and, because of what you are hearing, form the belief that someone is playing the saxophone in the next room. This is a basic belief, not inferred from other beliefs of yours. (You don't say to yourself, "I am hearing something that sounds like a saxophone; usually, when I hear something that sounds like a saxophone, there is a saxophone nearby; therefore, what I am hearing is probably a saxophone." Rather, you just hear the sounds and find yourself with the belief that there is a saxophone in the next room.) Furthermore, you are quite familiar with saxophones and perfectly capable of recognizing a saxophone when you hear one. This, then, is a *properly basic belief*. Nevertheless, your belief turns out to be false: your friend is testing out his new digital stereo system with a recording of solo saxophone music, and the reproduction is so good you could not tell it from the real thing.

In the same way, it *might* be true that "God exists" is a properly basic belief for some person even if God does *not* in fact exist. That a belief is properly basic for a person does not *guarantee* that the belief is true; that is one of the important differences between the strong foundationalism criticized earlier and the more moderate foundationalism embraced by Chisholm and by the Reformed epistemologists. (The other important difference is that moderate foundationalism begins by assuming the general soundness of the structure of knowledge and beliefs we already have; it is not a procedure by

which to *replace* or *radically reform* that structure.) But that a belief is properly
basic for some person *does* guarantee that the person is *rationally justified* in
holding that belief, so if "God exists" is properly basic for you, then it is
rational for you to believe in God.

There is an objection to Plantinga's procedure here that has been stated
forcefully by Gary Gutting (b. 1942):

> How can a believer just blithely claim that it's utterly obvious that he's enti-
> tled to believe without having any reasons for his belief? What of the fact
> that there are all sorts of honest and intelligent people who've thought a
> lot about religious belief and simply don't see belief in God as properly
> basic? . . . As philosophers, we surely have to take as clear cases only those
> that would be admitted as such by just about any rational person.[9] "Isn't it
> just common sense to admit that, when there is widespread disagreement
> about a claim, with apparently competent judges on both sides, those who
> assert or deny the claim need to justify their positions?"[10]

Plantinga is well aware of this objection, and his response to it is
illuminating:

> Criteria for proper basicality . . . should be . . . argued to and tested by a
> relevant set of examples. But there is no reason to assume, in advance, that
> everyone will agree on the examples. The Christian will of course suppose
> . . . that belief in God is entirely proper and rational; if he does not accept
> this belief on the basis of other propositions, he will conclude that it is basic
> for him and quite properly so. Followers of Bertrand Russell and Madelyn
> Murray O'Hair may disagree; but how is that relevant? Must my criteria, or
> those of the Christian community, conform to their examples? Surely not.
> The Christian community is responsible to *its* set of examples, not to theirs.[11]

Plantinga is saying, then, that a theistic philosopher is fully justified in
taking "God exists" to be a properly basic belief, *even if others do not agree.* In
saying this, he is in effect giving up something that has often been thought of
as an important goal of the philosophical enterprise. Philosophers have often
assumed that if they hit upon the right *method* for approaching philosophical
problems, and applied that method carefully and correctly, then agreement
on *substantive conclusions* would be bound to result. Descartes's *Discourse on
Method* is a striking illustration of this assumption, but it can be found in
many other philosophers going back at least as far as Plato (427–347 B.C.). To
be sure, philosophers have for the most part been unsuccessful in actually
bringing about this agreement they have sought. Plantinga is saying that it
was unreasonable to expect this in the first place—that philosophers come to
their task bringing with them deeply rooted *prephilosophical commitments,*
and those commitments may prevent them from reaching agreement even if
both sides in a dispute conduct themselves correctly in terms of the standards for philosophical reasoning and argument.[12] And on the other hand, if
the theist makes the mistake of allowing the atheist to set the rules for the
discussion by determining what beliefs can be properly basic, then we
should not be surprised if the theist comes out second best. It is clear, then,

that Plantinga is thoughtful and deliberate in his rejection of a "universal rationality" that can be relied on to bring philosophers to agreement despite differences in initial beliefs. But the student of Reformed epistemology likewise needs to be aware of this, and to realize that giving up this ideal of rationality is part of the price for being a Reformed epistemologist. (In considering this point, the reader may want to review the discussion of "critical rationalism" in chapter 3, as well as the discussion of proofs as "person-relative," in chapter 5.)

This line of thought may lead to a further objection, which may be stated as follows: Doesn't this mean that just anything goes? If the theist can take "God exists" as properly basic, then why cannot anyone else who holds a belief, no matter how bizarre, specify that this belief is properly basic and thus make himself immune to criticism? So that, for instance, Linus in the *Peanuts* comic strip, who believes that the Great Pumpkin comes every Halloween to those who believe and who waits for him in a "sincere" pumpkin patch, may believe this in a properly basic way and be perfectly rational and justified in his belief. (This has become known to philosophers as the "Great Pumpkin Objection.")

Plantinga's answer to this has two parts, depending on just how the objection is taken. On the one hand, if the objector is saying that the Reformed epistemologist is bound to accept that the belief that the Great Pumpkin returns every Halloween is properly basic, then this is just wrong. Belief in the Great Pumpkin will not, of course, be among the Reformed epistemologist's "set of examples," and there is no reason whatever to suppose that the Reformed epistemologist will or should come to the conclusion that this is a properly basic belief. Plantinga admits, to be sure, that the Reformed epistemologist "is committed to supposing that there is a relevant *difference* between belief in God and belief in the Great Pumpkin if he holds that the former but not the latter is properly basic."[13] But Plantinga thinks that differences of the right sort will not be hard to find.

The objection, however, might be taken in another way, as claiming that *the Great Pumpkinite himself,* following Plantinga's procedure for determining which beliefs are properly basic, might reasonably and properly conclude that his belief in the Great Pumpkin falls into this category. Philip Quinn (b. 1940) writes: "The difficulty is . . . that this is a game any number can play. Followers of Muhammed, followers of Buddha, and even followers of the Reverend Moon can join in the fun."[14]

Plantinga's reply to this is, in effect, "Sure, but what's the problem?" He says, "Different philosophers employing this method may arrive at different conclusions: true enough, but do we know of some reasonably viable philosophical method (for reaching epistemic criteria) of which this is not true? That's just life in philosophy."[15]

This answer brings us back to the point already made: philosophers, like other people, bring with them deeply held prior commitments, and these commitments may sometimes make the reaching of substantive agreement on important philosophical questions (such as the criteria for properly basic belief) impossible. No doubt this is in some way regrettable, but (say the Reformed epistemologists) it is the way things are and there is no point in denying it.

It is possible that by this time the reader is experiencing a certain degree of frustration. Just *how is it* that the belief that God exists acquires its status as properly basic? Obviously it is not just the fact that this *is believed* that makes it properly basic, or even that it is believed *strongly*, with commitment and emotional intensity. So what is it that gives the belief this status? It would seem we are in need of an answer to this question, unless we are supposed just to take the Reformed epistemologist's word for it that this belief is properly basic.

In order to answer this question fully, the Reformed epistemologist would need to use the procedure described earlier, beginning with a set of examples and using them to develop his replacement for the discredited standard of strong foundationalism. But Plantinga, in his writings on Reformed epistemology, does not actually do this; rather, he limits himself to giving examples.[16] We can, however, learn quite a bit from looking at his examples. One important point, not stressed until now, is that generally if not always the status of a belief as properly basic is dependent on the *conditions in which that belief is held.* In the saxophone example discussed earlier you were rational to believe, in a basic way, that someone was playing the saxophone in the next room. But if on entering the house you had heard nothing at all, or only the sound of a child crying, you would *not* have been rational to believe there was someone playing the saxophone. The justification of your belief depends crucially on the *experiential conditions* under which you believe.

Now, how might this be applied to belief in God? In answering this, it is helpful to consider some examples Plantinga gives of properly basic beliefs about God. He writes,

> There is in us a disposition to believe propositions of the sort *this flower was created by God or this vast and intricate universe was created by God* when we contemplate the flower or behold the starry heavens or think about the vast reaches of the universe. . . . Upon reading the Bible, one may be impressed with a deep sense that God is speaking to him. Upon having done what I know is cheap, or wrong, or wicked, I may feel guilty in God's sight and form the belief *God disapproves of what I have done.* Upon confession and repentance I may feel forgiven, forming the belief *God forgives me for what I have done.*[17]

There are more examples, but these suffice to make the point. What Plantinga is saying, clearly, is that under certain conditions one may have an *experience* of God's majestic wisdom in creation, or of God's speaking to one through the Bible, or of God's disapproval of one's sins and his subsequent forgiveness. When one does have such an experience, it may be entirely appropriate and rational to believe, in a basic way, the kinds of propositions cited in the earlier examples.

There are a few additional points that should be noted about these examples: First, in the examples it is not, strictly speaking, the belief that *God exists* which is properly basic but rather certain other beliefs, beliefs about what God does or has done, and says or has said. But, of course, none of those other beliefs could be true if God did *not* exist, so the difference is relatively minor. Second, it is important to be clear that the beliefs in the examples are all held in a *basic* way. I do not, for example, first examine the flower, then form certain beliefs about its structure and functioning, and then go through a process of reasoning (no doubt some version of the teleological argument) and reach the conclusion, on the basis of all this, that something with the design and function of that flower must have been created by a divine being. I might do that on some other occasion, of course, but in Plantinga's example I simply look at the flower and *see* it as God's creature—or, what amounts to the same thing, I see that God created it. Finally, note that the experiences cited in the examples are not rare and dramatic occurrences, the sort of thing that might happen to Moses, Muhammed, the apostle Paul, or St. Francis of Assisi but not to ordinary men or women. Rather, they are the kinds of experiences that are had by many, perhaps by most, religious believers at some time or other, and by some rather frequently.[18]

An interesting criticism of Plantinga's view comes from Philip Quinn. Quinn agrees with Plantinga to a degree: he acknowledges that many theists possess "noninferential justification" for their beliefs, based on their religious experiences. But he believes that, for most intellectually sophisticated adults, this justification is not sufficient to render their belief in God justified overall. For such theists will be aware of certain objections to belief in God, objections such as the problem of evil and the explanations of religious experiences as "projections" of psychological needs, as given by Freud and Marx. Quinn thinks that, for most such believers, these arguments against theism will *outweigh* the justification their beliefs derive from their religious experiences. Accordingly, such believers are in need of an evidential case for God's existence—that is, some form of natural theology—if their belief in God is to be justified overall. So while belief in God *could be* properly basic, for most contemporary adult believers it *is not* properly basic.[19]

Plantinga, however, disagrees; he holds that the belief that God exists, and other beliefs about God, are rightly and reasonably held in a basic way by one who finds that she *experiences* God's presence and activities. (Remember Simone Weil's description of her experience at the beginning of this chapter!) This conclusion, if correct, is an important one, and requires the revision of a great deal of thinking in the philosophy of religion. It seems clear, furthermore, that the conclusion is one that calls for further discussion and investigation. For this, we turn to William P. Alston.

ALSTON ON PERCEIVING GOD

Already in chapter 2 we have considered Alston's argument for the similarity of religious experience to sense perception.[20] His basic thesis about the role of religious experience in religious knowledge is that "experiential awareness

of God—the 'perception of God,' as I call it—can provide epistemic justification for certain kinds of beliefs about God. I call such beliefs 'M-beliefs' ('M'
for manifestation), beliefs to the effect that God is doing something vis-à-vis
the subject—strengthening, guiding, communicating a message, etc.—or to
the effect that God has some (allegedly) perceivable property—goodness,
power, lovingness, etc."[21] Evidently this is a strong claim, one which has
sweeping implications. Alston does not claim, to be sure, that religious experience is our *only* way of knowing about God, any more than sense perception is our only way of knowing about the physical world. (Scientific reasoning, for example, carries us to conclusions about the world that go far beyond
those which would be justified by sense perception alone.) But sense perception is the *essential basis* for our knowledge about the physical world, and in a
somewhat similar way religious experience is the essential basis for our
knowledge of God. In each case, certain "basic" beliefs are justified directly
by the experience in question (in the case of God, the "M-beliefs" mentioned
by Alston), and then various reasoning processes are used in order to justify
other beliefs, those which go beyond what is "perceived."

Now it is evident that a great many religious believers do in fact have
experiences which indicate to them that God is relating to them in the sorts
of ways mentioned by Alston. Among philosophers, however, there has
been a strong inclination to think that these experiences cannot be taken at
face value. At the very least, one would need to have *independent reason* to
believe that God exists and that he might be doing some of these things before it would be reasonable to believe that the experiences are what they
seem to be. The experiences by themselves cannot bear the weight of justifying our beliefs.

Alston thinks this is wrong—that it shows arbitrariness and prejudice
against religious experience to say that it cannot stand on its own in justifying religious beliefs. Much of his discussion is directed to defending this
point, and to showing that if we accept sense perception as the basic justification for our beliefs about the physical world, then as a matter of fairness
and reasonableness we ought to accept religious experience as the justification for beliefs about God. It is important, in Alston's view, that, just as for
sense perception, there is a *socially established practice* of forming beliefs about
God on the basis of experiential awareness of God. (Indeed, as we shall see,
there are several different socially established practices of this sort.) Alston
argues that such socially established practices of belief formation (*doxastic
practices*, as he calls them) should be accepted as reliable until and unless we
have evidence of their unreliability.

It needs to be kept in mind that in saying that M-beliefs are *directly justified* by religious experience (that, in Plantinga's terminology, they are "properly basic" beliefs), Alston is not asserting that all such beliefs are *true*. For
M-beliefs as for ordinary perceptual beliefs, there can be good reasons to
conclude that "things are not as they seem." In certain circumstances it may
look to me as though water is running uphill, but other things I know about
the world keep me from accepting that as the truth. And if I tell you that (for

example) God has ordered me to kill all Presbyterians, you will rightly disbelieve my "revelation" on the ground that God would not give me any such command as that. This situation is best described by saying that experience provides a *prima facie* justification for our beliefs,[22] which is to say that such beliefs should be accepted *unless there is compelling reason to think they are false.* This is true both for perceptual beliefs and for M-beliefs.

Not surprisingly, other philosophers have challenged these claims. Some of them have argued that religious experience is so fundamentally different from sense experience that it cannot be considered as "perceptual" experience at all. Alston, however, seems to have made out a good case for regarding some kinds of religious experiences as perceptual.[23]

Even if this is so, it may seem that we have good reason to think that sense perception is more likely to be reliable than religious experience. What we perceive with our senses shows a great deal of consistency between different observers, so long as they are not impaired in some way. Also, sense experience gives us a precise and detailed knowledge of physical things in the world and enables us to make predictions about them with considerable accuracy. None of this is true of religious experience. Many people fail to have any such experiences. Among those who do have them, different people—especially people in different cultures and religions—experience God as having contradictory characteristics, and there is no readily apparent way to check out these conflicts. In particular, there is no way to make predictions which are precise enough to serve as confirmations of religious beliefs.

Alston acknowledges the truth in these complaints, yet he maintains they do not undermine religious experience as a source of justification for M-beliefs. Rather, he argues, the differences point to ways in which our situation with respect to God is different than our situation with respect to physical objects. We could not expect to have the kind of thorough, detailed knowledge of God we have of ordinary physical things; God is too great and mysterious, too far beyond us, for that to be possible. In the same way it is out of the question to suppose we should be able to predict God's actions—or to run a "controlled experiment" on God. As for the fact that many people seem not to have such experiences, it is in keeping with the teachings of the major religions that "God has decreed that a human being will be aware of His presence in any clear and unmistakable fashion only when certain special and difficult conditions are satisfied."[24] These conditions, of course, pertain to the religious life, and those who make no effort to satisfy them have no reason to complain if they do not have such experiences.

Of all these objections, it would seem that the most difficult ones for Alston to deal with are those which are based on the fact that persons in different cultures and different religious traditions conceive of God—and, apparently, experience God—in quite different ways. One of the most striking differences, though by no means the only one, is the difference between theistic religions, where God is experienced as a personal being with whom one can enter into a personal relationship, and religions such as the *advaita* form of Hinduism (discussed briefly in chapter 4) that conceive of God as an

impersonal unity and maintain that the ultimate form of religious enlightenment is to experience the fact that there simply *is no difference* between oneself and God: *"You are that*, Shvetaketu."

Alston argues that, even if we cannot resolve the conflicts between
different faiths, a person is rational to continue in the "religious doxastic
practice" she has learned in her own religious community. He also considers
several possible ways in which one might be able to conclude that one such
practice is more likely than its rivals to be correct. It does seem likely that in
doing this we will need to be involved in some kind of an appeal to evidence
and will not be able to rest content with "basic beliefs" resting directly on
religious experience.[25] Alston calls for the use of all available means to overcome this ambiguity:

> The knowledgeable and reflective Christian should be concerned . . . [and]
> should do whatever seems feasible to search for common ground on which
> to adjudicate the crucial differences between the world religions, seeking a
> way to show in a non-circular way which of the contenders is correct. What
> success will attend these efforts I do not presume to predict. Perhaps it is
> only in God's good time that a more thorough insight into the truth behind
> these divergent perspectives will be revealed to us.[26]

PLANTINGA ON WARRANT AND KNOWLEDGE

The latest phase in the development of Reformed epistemology is found in
some recent work of Alvin Plantinga; this work is consistent with the material covered earlier in the chapter but goes beyond it. In his earlier work
Plantinga was primarily concerned with *justification*—roughly, what we are
"within our rights to believe." His main question was whether believers in
God can be justified in their belief when they hold that belief in a basic way,
not on the basis of other things they believe. In his later work, Plantinga
turns his attention to *knowledge,* and his question is the following: can believers in God (specifically, Christian believers) be truly said to *know* that there is
a God (and other important religious truths)[27] when they hold these beliefs
in a basic way? Now, it is important to see that one may have a *justified* belief
and nevertheless not *know* that what is believed is true. For instance, you
might accept an account of some recent event on the testimony of a source
you have found to be generally reliable—a respected news publication, for
example—but might later find out that the report was quite mistaken. You
were *justified* in believing as you did, but you did not *know* that the account
was true, because in fact it was not true, and you cannot know something to
be true when it is actually false.

It is possible, furthermore, to believe something that is *true* and still not
know that it is true. For instance, suppose that you are such a loyal Chicago
Cubs fan (feel free to substitute the name of your own favorite team) that you
genuinely believe, at the beginning of each baseball season, that the Cubs
will be playing in the World Series. Then suppose (you have to use your

imagination here!) that some year the Cubs actually do make it to the Series. Did you really *know,* the previous April, that the Cubs would be in the series? Of course not! You might *say,* "I knew it all along!" but the truth of the matter is that this was just a lucky guess. On the other hand, when you watched the Cubs on TV as they were winning the final game of the league championship series, *then* you really did know that the Cubs would be playing in the World Series.

Plantinga gives the name *warrant* to the key ingredient in this example—the factor that was missing in the spring, when you believed, but did *not* know, that the Cubs would be in the Series, but was present in October when you did know this. Warrant, then, is what makes the difference between mere "true belief" and genuine knowledge. In order to determine whether the believer can know that there is a God, Plantinga needs to investigate the nature of warrant.

A key element in warrant, as Plantinga sees it, is the reliability of the *cognitive faculties* by which our beliefs are produced. Beliefs that are produced and sustained through sense perception, short-term memory, and careful reasoning (these are only examples) are at least good candidates for being warranted, whereas those produced by wishful thinking (such as your belief about the Cubs) are not. Furthermore, our faculties need to be functioning in *appropriate circumstances,* those that are compatible with the basic design[28] of those faculties. For example, it is possible to place persons in a situation of sensory deprivation, where they are lacking normal sensory inputs. Under those circumstances, they are very liable to hallucinations of various sorts, and their normally reliable faculties become quite unreliable. Still further, the faculties in question need to be *functioning properly,* that is, in the way they were designed to function. If my hearing is impaired, so that I hear "bells ringing in my head," then my belief, thus produced, that a bell is ringing nearby is unwarranted. (This is so even if in fact there *is* a bell ringing in the vicinity.) Finally, the faculties in question, functioning under the given circumstances, must be such that, under those circumstances, they *reliably* produce true beliefs—that is, they arrive at the truth at least the majority of the time. Putting all this together, Plantinga's formal definition of warrant is as follows: "A belief has warrant for a person *S* only if that belief is produced in *S* by cognitive faculties functioning properly (subject to no dysfunction) in a cognitive environment that is appropriate for *S's* kind of cognitive faculties, according to a design plan that is successfully aimed at truth."[29]

Now we can return to Plantinga's basic question: can belief in God be warranted, when this belief is held in a basic way? His answer to this is yes. Plantinga holds that there is a component in the cognitive equipment of each one of us a that is specifically designed to produce a belief in God, given certain "inputs" that are commonly available in our ordinary environment. Such inputs would include the sorts of situations mentioned previously— contemplating the majesty of the starry heavens, finding God speaking to us in the Bible, or feeling disgusted with ourselves because of something wrong we have done. This component in our cognitive makeup Plantinga calls, following John Calvin, the *sensus divinitatis* ("sense of divinity"). When the *sensus* does its work, and produces in us a belief in God, it is doing exactly what it is designed to do; furthermore, the *sensus* is reliable, since the belief that it regularly produces—namely, a belief that there is a God—is in fact true.[30] In view of this, it can be seen that the belief in God, produced in this way, satisfies all the conditions for being warranted. In favorable cases, where the belief is held with sufficient firmness,[31] the believer may be correctly said to *know* that there is a God.

At this point you may be inclined to ask, "Isn't Plantinga taking too much for granted? In his talk about the *sensus divinitatis*, Plantinga is *assuming* that there really is a God, who has created in us this special 'sense.' But, of course, whether or not God exists is one of the main thing Plantinga and his critics disagree about. So how can he just take that for granted?"

This complaint is correct in pointing out that Plantinga is *not* entitled, in a philosophical discussion, simply to take it for granted that there is a God. Of course, Plantinga recognizes this. Accordingly, the conclusion he draws from his discussion is not that belief in God *is* warranted and constitutes knowledge for those who hold it. Instead, his conclusion is that, *if* there is a God of the sort Christians and other theists say there is, *then* belief in God is probably warranted and can constitute knowledge. For, Plantinga argues, if there is such a God then it is very likely that belief in God arises in the way he has described (or in some way that is generally similar to it), and if so this belief will be warranted. If, on the other hand, there is no God, then God has not implanted in us the *sensus divinitatis*, and the actual sources of belief are something quite different. In this case, belief in God is probably *not* warranted.

"But," you expostulate, "*is* there a God of this sort or isn't there? That is the very thing we want to know, and now it looks as though Plantinga has given us no help at all in knowing it." In a sense, this is correct. Plantinga readily admits that he has not shown that God exists, or that Christianity is true, and he does not have available to him any arguments that are capable of convincing "all reasonable people" of these things. His purpose in writing was concerned with two other objectives. First, he wanted to answer those philosophers who argue that belief in God is irrational, unwarranted, and so on *without* undertaking to show that God does not in fact exist. (This has actually been a fairly common strategy in recent philosophy, as is shown by the "evidentialist objectors" discussed earlier in this chapter.) Against these philosophers, Plantinga has argued that one can show religious belief to be irrational and unwarranted *only* by showing that such belief is *false*; it is not possible to make an "end run" around the *really* big question. Second, Plantinga wants to reassure those believers, and potential believers, who are worried that they may be behaving irrationally if they accept belief in God without being able to support it by universally convincing reasons and arguments. Here his main conclusion is very much to the point: one's belief in God may be justified, and warranted, and may even constitute knowledge that God exists, even if one has no arguments whatever in support of this belief.

But suppose someone is genuinely undecided about the question, and has no idea whether to believe in God or to withhold belief? In such a case, Plantinga admits that good arguments for God's existence "could be useful in preparing the way for faith and in leading some people closer to it."[32] But he would also want to say that one's search for the truth in this matter should not be limited to the consideration of such arguments. Instead, one would need to engage in a personal *religious quest;* one would need to study religious (in particular, Christian) teachings, read the Scriptures, attend public worship, and do other things that might "open one up" to the spiritual influences that will play a crucial role in enabling a person to believe.

Perhaps more than any other topic in this book, Reformed epistemology is a recent arrival on the scene of philosophy of religion. It is too early for philosophical thought on this topic to have reached any stable resolution; what can confidently be said is that the topic will continue to be debated vigorously for many years to come.

STUDY QUESTIONS

1. What is your reaction to Simone Weil's experience, and her comments on it? After reading her account, are you inclined to agree that she was able to know with certainty that God exists?

2. What is evidentialism, and why does evidentialism tend to be opposed to religious belief?

3. What is foundationalism? What is a basic belief? What is a properly basic belief?

4. Explain what strong foundationalism is, and discuss the reasons that have led philosophers to embrace strong foundationalism.

5. Discuss the objections to strong foundationalism as given in the text. Do these objections strike you as convincing?

6. Explain the Reformed epistemologists' reasons for saying it can be reasonable to believe in God even if there are no good arguments for God's existence.

7. Is it reasonable to say that, just as in sensory experience we perceive physical objects, in religious experience we perceive God? Why or why not?

8. How can Reformed epistemology deal with the objection that, whereas everyone has sensory experience of physical objects, many people do not have religious experiences in which they perceive God? Does the answer to this objection strike you as satisfactory? Discuss.

9. How can Reformed epistemologists deal with the problem of the conflicting ideas of God in different religions?

10. Explain the difference between knowing something and merely having a true belief about something.

11. Explain Calvin's idea of the *sensus divinitatis.* Does it strike you as plausible that human beings possess such a "sense" of God?

12. Do you think it is possible for human beings to *know* (as opposed to merely believing) that there is (or that there is not) a God? Discuss.

13. Do you think Plantinga has made a good case that, *if* there is a God, it is possible for persons to *know* in a basic way (not based on evidence or arguments) that there is a God?

NOTES

1. Simone Weil, *Waiting for God*, tr. Emma Craufurd (New York: Harper, 1973), p. 24.

2. Ibid., p. 212.

3. This connection is brought out in Alvin Plantinga, "The Reformed Objection to Natural Theology," *Christian Scholar's Review* 11 (1982):187–98; reprinted in *Rationality in the Calvinian Tradition*, ed. Hendrik Hart, Johan Van Der Hoeven, and Nicholas Wolterstorff (Lanham, Md.: University Press of America, 1983), pp. 363–83; also reprinted in PRSR2e, pt. 6.

4. From the Introduction to *Faith and Rationality: Reason and Belief in God*, ed. Alvin Plantinga and Nicholas Wolterstorff (Notre Dame, Ind.: University of Notre Dame Press, 1983), p. 6.

5. There is some variety in the terminology used at this point; Wolterstorff and Plantinga speak of "classical foundationalism" and "modern foundationalism." Sometimes, indeed, this view is simply refered to as "foundationalism" without a qualifier, but this tends to be confusing; as we shall see, the Reformed epistemologists are themselves foundationalists of a certain kind.

6. There is also, to be sure, the question about *how* one belief may support another— what sorts of arguments are used to show this, and so on. This is an important topic, but it is also quite complex and will not be discussed further here.

7. The reader may notice a similarity between strong foundationalism and *strong rationalism*, as discussed in chapter 3; strong foundationalism is, in fact, the leading variety of strong rationalism.

8. Roderick Chisholm, *Theory of Knowledge* (Englewood Cliffs, N.J.: Prentice-Hall, 1966), p. 57.

9. "The Catholic and the Calvinist: A Dialogue on Faith and Reason," *Faith and Philosophy* 2 (1985):241. It should be noted that, because this article is in dialogue form, one cannot automatically assume that what is said by the participants reflects the author's own view. We believe, however, that this speech of "Catholic" does reflect Gutting's view on this point. (For confirmation, see the next quotation in the text.)

10. Gary Gutting, *Religious Belief and Religious Skepticism* (Notre Dame, Ind.: University of Notre Dame Press, 1982), p. 83. (*Note:* I have emended the text of this quotation, with the author's agreement; the printed version actually reads, "widespread agreement.")

11. Alvin Plantinga, "Reason and Belief in God," in *Faith and Rationality*, ed. Plantinga and Wolterstorff, p. 77.

12. The idea that philosophical and other scholarly work is deeply shaped by prior worldview commitments is one of the important ideas that "Reformed epistemology" takes from the Reformed tradition of Christian theology. This idea, of course, fits well with the approach of "critical rationalism" as discussed in chapter 3.

13. "Reason and Belief in God," ed. Plantinga and Wolterstorff, p. 78.

14. Philip Quinn, "On Finding the Foundations of Theism," *Faith and Philosophy* 2 (1985):473.

15. "The Foundations of Theism: A Reply," *Faith and Philosophy* 3 (1986):303.

16. Philip Quinn points out two problems with the way Plantinga proceeds here. (See Philip Quinn, "The Foundations of Theism Again: A Rejoinder to Plantinga," in *Rational Faith: Catholic Responses to Reformed Epistemology,* ed. Linda Zagzebski [Notre Dame, Ind.: University of Notre Dame Press, 1993], pp. 14–47.) First, not all theists agree that beliefs about God can be properly basic. (They may hold, instead, that such beliefs need to be justified by the kinds of arguments set out in chapter 5.) So it cannot be taken for granted that a theist should have such beliefs in his list of examples of properly basic beliefs. But, second, even if the theist does have beliefs about God in his initial list of examples, this does not guarantee that they will still be on the list after he has gone through the process of establishing his standard for properly basic beliefs. The initial list of examples is subject to being revised, and if some of the examples just do not "fit" with others and with the criteria that are developed, they may be dropped from the list. (Such beliefs would then either be derived beliefs, or they would not be rational beliefs at all.) Quinn concludes that Plantinga needs to actually go through the procedure he has outlined; it is not enough just to give a few examples.

It should be pointed out that in his more recent work Plantinga does undertake the task of establishing standards for properly basic beliefs (see his *Warrant and Proper Function,* New York: Oxford University Press, 1993).

17. "Reason and Belief in God," p. 80.

18. This point has led to yet another objection, which, because of its somewhat technical nature, is relegated to a note. In Plantinga's view it would be correct to say that the basic belief that (for example) "God has created this flower" is *grounded in* the experience of seeing the flower in that particular way, even though there is no *evidence* for the belief (because, as Plantinga is using "evidence," evidence must consist of *another belief* which is the basis of the belief in question).

Now, this has led Philip Quinn (among others) to make the following point: Whenever I *do in fact* hold such a belief as "God has created this flower" in a basic way, it would also be *equally possible* for me to *infer* this belief, using as one of my premises "It seems to me that God has created this flower." My belief in God as creator of the flower would be *equally justified* whether it is basic or inferred (derived). This, it seems, tends to undercut the importance of the question whether such beliefs are basic or nonbasic. As Quinn says, "Although such propositions [as "God has created this flower"] would not need to be based on the evidence of other propositions, they always could be so based. So the cautious philosopher who did so base them would be every bit as justified in believing in the existence of God as the reckless mystic who did not" ("On Finding the Foundations of Theism," p. 479).

Plantinga's reply ("The Foundations of Theism: A Reply," pp. 303–6) centers on the following point: in general, it simply *is not true* that experientially grounded basic beliefs could also be held in a nonbasic way without loss of justification. All of us, under certain circumstances, will believe in a basic way such propositions as "There is a tree here before me." Now, could one with equal justification *infer* this belief from "There seems to be a tree before me"? The answer, drawn from the history of philosophical reflection on this topic, seems to be, definitely not! For in order to do this, one would have to *justify* the inference from the "seems" statement to the "is" statement— and this amounts to solving the problem of the "proof of the external world," surely one of the hoariest, and most resistant to solution, of all philosophical problems. Yet there is no reasonable doubt (skeptics aside) that our *basic* beliefs about trees and the like are fully justified. In the same way, basic beliefs about God may be fully justified even if *arguments* designed to show God's existence are uniformly unsuccessful.

19. For this objection, see Philip Quinn, "The Foundations of Theism Again: A Rejoinder to Plantinga." For further discussion, see William Hasker, "The Foundations of Theism: Scoring the Quinn-Plantinga Debate," *Faith and Philosophy* 15, no. 1 (Janu-

ary 1998):52–67, excerpted in PRSR2e, pt. 6, as "The Case of the Intellectually Sophisticated Theist."

20. See William P. Alston, "Religious Experience as Perception of God," in PRSR2e, pt. 1.

21. William Alston, "Précis of *Perceiving God*," Symposium on Alston's *Perceiving God, Philosophy and Phenomenological Research* 54, no. 4 (December 1994):863.

22. *Prima facie* means "at first view"; *prima facie* evidence is evidence which is sufficient to establish a conclusion, unless it is rebutted by stronger contrary evidence.

23. See Richard M. Gale, "Why Alston's Mystical Doxastic Practice is Subjective"; George S. Pappas, "Perception and Mystical Experience"; and William P. Alston, "Reply to Commentators," in the Symposium on *Perceiving God*; also, William P. Alston, *Perceiving God* (Ithaca, N.Y.: Cornell University Press, 1991), chap. 1.

24. "Christian Experience and Christian Belief," in *Faith and Rationality*, ed. Plantinga and Wolterstorff, p. 129.

25. For further discussion of the need for evidence at this point, see William Hasker, "On Justifying the Christian Practice," *The New Scholasticism* 60 (spring 1986):129–44; David Basinger, "Hick's Religious Pluralism and 'Reformed Epistemology': A Middle Ground," *Faith and Philosophy* 5, no. 5 (1988):421–32 (reprinted in PRSR2e, pt. 6); and William Wainwright, "Religious Language, Religious Experience, and Religious Pluralism," in *The Rationality of Belief and the Plurality of Faith: Essays in Honor of William P. Alston*, ed. Thomas D. Senor (Ithaca, N.Y.: Cornell University Press, 1995), pp. 170–88.

26. *Perceiving God*, p. 278.

27. In order to simplify this discussion, we will consider only the belief that God exists, and not other Christian beliefs that Plantinga is concerned with. He deals with those other, specifically Christian, beliefs in a way that is similar to, but goes beyond, what he says about belief in God as such.

28. The reference to "design" here does not necessarily imply that there is, literally, a designer of our faculties (namely, God). Plantinga allows, at least for the sake of the discussion, that we can think of evolution as "designing" us and our faculties in order to secure certain benefits—though, to be sure, if a naturalistic theory of evolution is true such talk is ultimately metaphorical.

29. *Warranted Christian Belief*, p. 156.

30. The *sensus divinitatis* may not be *wholly* reliable, since the conception of God that results from its operation may sometimes contain errors. (That is to say that the *sensus* does not function perfectly on each and every occasion.) Still, the output of the *sensus* is on the whole true and trustworthy.

31. A belief that is held in a very tentative manner, on the other hand, does *not* constitute knowledge, even if all the other requirements for knowledge are met.

32. Alvin Plantinga, "The Reformed Objection Revisited," *Christian Scholar's Review* 12 (1983):58.

SUGGESTED READING

Alston, William P. "Christian Experience and Christian Belief." In *Faith and Rationality: Reason and Belief in God*. Ed. Alvin Plantinga and Nicholas Wolterstorff, pp. 103–34. Notre Dame, Ind.: University of Notre Dame Press, 1983.
———. *Perceiving God: The Epistemology of Religious Experience*. Ithaca, N.Y.: Cornell University Press, 1991.

Alston, William P., Richard M. Gale, George S. Pappas, and Robert W. Adams. *Symposium on* Perceiving God, Philosophy and Phenomenological Research 54, no. 4 (December 1994):863–99.

Gellman, Jerome I. *Experience of God and the Rationality of Theistic Belief.* Ithaca, N.Y.: Cornell University Press, 1997.

Hasker, William. "On Justifying the Christian Practice." *The New Scholasticism* 60 (spring 1986):129–44.

———. "The Foundations of Theism: Scoring the Quinn-Plantinga Debate." *Faith and Philosophy* 15, no. 1 (January 1998):52–67.

McLeod, Mark S. *Rationality and Theistic Belief: An Essay on Reformed Epistemology.* Ithaca, N.Y.: Cornell University Press, 1993.

Plantinga, Alvin. "Reason and Belief in God." In *Faith and Rationality: Reason and Belief in God,* ed. Alvin Plantinga and Nicholas Wolterstorff, pp. 16–93. Notre Dame, Ind.: University of Notre Dame Press, 1983.

———. "Replies." In *Alvin Plantinga,* ed. James E. Tomberlin and Peter Van Inwagen, pp. 390–3, Profiles, vol. 5, Dordrecht, the Netherlands: D. Riedel, 1985.

———. "Coherentism and the Evidentialist Objection to Belief in God." In *Rationality, Religious Belief, and Moral Commitment,* ed. Robert Audi and William J. Wainwright, pp. 109–38. Ithaca, N.Y.: Cornell University Press, 1986.

———. "The Foundations of Theism: A Reply." *Faith and Philosophy* 3 (1986):298–313.

———. *Warranted Christian Belief.* New York: Oxford University Press, 2000.

Quinn, Philip. "On Finding the Foundations of Theism." *Faith and Philosophy* 2 (1985):469–86.

———. "The Foundations of Theism Again: A Rejoinder to Plantinga." In *Rational Faith: Catholic Responses to Reformed Epistemology,* ed. Linda Zagzebski, pp. 14–47. Notre Dame, Ind.: University of Notre Dame Press, 1993.

Wolterstorff, Nicholas. "Can Belief in God Be Rational If It Has No Foundations?" In *Faith and Rationality: Reason and Belief in God,* ed. Alvin Plantinga and Nicholas Wolterstorff, pp. 135–86. Notre Dame, Ind.: University of Notre Dame Press, 1983.

Zagzebski, Linda, ed. *Rational Faith: Catholic Responses to Reformed Epistemology.* Notre Dame, Ind.: University of Notre Dame Press, 1993.

CHAPTER 7 THE PROBLEM OF
EVIL: THE CASE
AGAINST GOD'S
EXISTENCE

Elie Wiesel's (b. 1928) novel *Night* portrays a chilling scene of his family being unloaded from boxcars along with other Jewish prisoners at Auchwitz:

> The cherished objects we had brought with us thus far were left behind in the train, and with them, at last, our illusions.
>
> Every two yards or so an SS man held his tommy gun trained on us. Hand in hand we followed the crowd.
>
> An SS noncommissioned officer came to meet us, a truncheon in his hand. He gave the order:
>
> "Men to the left! Women to the right!"
>
> Eight words spoken quietly, indifferently, without emotion. Eight short, simple words. . . . I had not had time to think, but already I felt the pressure of my father's hand: we were alone. . . . Tzipora held Mother's hand. I saw them disappear into the distance; my mother was stroking my sister's fair hair, as though to protect her, while I walked on with my father and the other men. And I did not know that in that place, at that moment, I was parting from my mother and Tzipora forever.[1]

Wiesel's story of the pain, suffering, and death in the Nazi death camp staggers the imagination.

Evil in the world is often cited as the primary reason why many people have difficulty believing in a God who is loving and powerful, and even why some believers encounter a crisis of faith. Theologian Eugene Borowitz (1924–2000) writes of the Holocaust:

> Any God who could permit the Holocaust, who could remain silent during it, who could "hide His face" while it dragged on, was not worth believing in. There might well be a limit to how much we could understand about

Him, but Auschwitz demanded an unreasonable suspension of understanding. In the face of such great evil, God, the good and the powerful, was too inexplicable, so men said "God is dead."[2]

Whether encountered in the indescribable horror of the Holocaust, the terrorist destruction of life at the World Trade Center, unrelenting hunger in underdeveloped countries, or the desperate suffering of terminal cancer patients—the presence of evil cannot be ignored. Evil in one form or another touches us all. Some people believe that no one has the intellectual right to believe in God unless she can somehow square that belief with the existence of evil.

Although every major worldview, whether religious or secular, addresses the phenomenon of evil, the problem of evil in Western philosophy has historically revolved around Christian theism. The claims of Christian theism about the perfect moral character and lofty purposes of God lead many people to expect that the world would be quite different than it is with respect to the evil it contains. It is not surprising, then, that the problem of evil has been at the heart of countless philosophical and theological discussions about the existence of God. In fact, many thinkers believe that this is actually the most potent rational objection to theistic belief, what German theologian Hans Küng (b. 1923) has called "the rock of atheism."[3] Just as chapter 5 explored the major arguments for the existence of God, this chapter considers the problem of evil as making a significant case against the existence of God.

Most discussions of the problem do not begin with a precise or technical *definition of evil* but instead assume that a broad, commonsense notion of evil is widely understood. This supposedly avoids conducting a debate that is unwittingly biased by some prior theory of evil. After all, even though people may differ on their definitions of evil, they agree widely on what states of affairs count as being evil. In philosophical parlance, they agree on the set of instances to which the term "evil" *applies* but may disagree vigorously on what it *implies*. The class of situations to which the term *evil* applies includes, at the very least, extreme pain, the suffering of innocents, physical deformities, psychological abnormalities, character defects, injustice, and natural catastrophes. We may legitimately characterize such phenomena as "negative" or "destructive," since such characterizations are minimal and do not taint further examination of the problem.

We can readily classify evils into two broad categories: *moral evil* and *natural evil*. The category of *moral evil* contains the wrongful and hurtful acts as well as the bad character traits of free human beings: actions such as murdering, lying, stealing, and traits such as dishonesty, greed, cowardice. Persons can be held morally accountable for all of these things. The category of *natural evil* covers the physical pain and suffering that result from either impersonal forces or human actions. Included here are the terrible pain and death caused by events like floods, fires, and famines as well as suffering and loss caused by diseases like cancer, tetanus, and AIDS; defects, deformities, and disabilities like blindness, deafness, and insanity must also be listed among natural evils.

THE LOGICAL PROBLEM OF EVIL

Thoughtful nontheists have made evil the basis of a strong objection to theistic belief. Actually, they have formulated the objection in two distinct ways— the *logical problem* and the *evidential problem*. A "problem" here is simply an argument whose premises have credibility and whose conclusion is troublesome for the person considering it. Critics who advance the *logical version* of the problem allege that there is an inconsistency between certain theistic claims about God and evil. J. L. Mackie (1917–1981) writes that "here it can be shown, not that religious beliefs lack rational support, but that they are positively irrational, that the several parts of the essential theological doctrine are inconsistent with one another."[4] On the one hand, the theist affirms that

1. an omnipotent, omniscient, perfectly good God exists,

and, on the other hand, he affirms that

2. evil exists in the world.

Mackie and other critics insist that these two statements are logically inconsistent with each other, that they both cannot be true. If the two statements are indeed inconsistent, then it is irrational to believe both. If the critic is correct, then the theist has made a serious logical mistake and must relinquish at least one of the statements in the inconsistent pair.

Of course, it is not immediately obvious that a statement asserting the existence of God is inconsistent with a statement asserting the existence of evil. If there is a contradiction between them, it must be *implicit* rather than *explicit*, putting the burden on the critic to show exactly how the contradiction arises. Critics say that some additional statements—or "quasi-logical rules," as Mackie calls them—are needed to make the contradiction explicit. Some additional statements that have been suggested include the following: that an omniscient being knows how to eliminate evil, that an omnipotent being has the power to eliminate evil, that a perfectly good being will want to or will have an obligation to eliminate evil, that evil is not logically necessary, and so forth. These statements specify more fully the meaning of key terms. The critic reasons that if God has the knowledge, power, and desire to eliminate evil, and if evil is not necessary, then there should exist no evil whatsoever. For the critic, these supplementary statements complete the logic, showing the inconsistency in the theist's claim that both God exists and evil exists.

Theistic philosopher Alvin Plantinga (b. 1932) is well known for his attempt to rebut the charge of inconsistency. His *Free Will Defense* offers a way of proving the consistency of the relevant theistic claims. Since the critic alleges that it *is logically impossible* that both God and evil exist, the theistic defender must show that it is *logically possible*. In other words, the defender must show that both claims can be true, though he need not show that they are in fact true. As Plantinga indicates, the general strategy for proving consistency between any two statements whatsoever involves finding a third statement that is possibly true, consistent with the first statement, and in conjunction with the first implies the second statement. The third statement, of course, need not be true or known to be true; it need not even be plausible. The statement only needs to be *possible* because the matter of determining consistency between or among propositions has to do with whether they can all be true together, not with whether any one or all of them are in fact true. What the Free Will Defender must do therefore is to find a statement that meets these conditions.[5]

Plantinga suggests that the ideas of contemporary logicians about *possible worlds* provide a method for discovering the needed statement. A possible world is simply a total possible state of affairs, a total possible way things could have been. Plantinga's search for the third key statement begins with a description of a possible world, a brief scenario of human freedom in relation to divine omnipotence:

> A world containing creatures who are sometimes significantly free (and freely perform more good than evil actions) is more valuable, all else being equal, than a world containing no free creatures at all. Now God can create free creatures, but he cannot *cause* or *determine* them to do only what is right. For if he does so, then they are not significantly free after all; they do not do what is right *freely*. To create creatures capable of *moral good*, therefore, he must create creatures capable of moral evil; and he cannot leave these creatures *free* to perform evil and at the same time prevent them from doing so. God did in fact create significantly free creatures; but some of them went wrong in the exercise of their freedom: this is the source of moral evil. The fact that these free creatures sometimes go wrong, however, counts neither against God's omnipotence nor against his goodness; for he could have forestalled the occurrence of moral evil only by excising the possibility of moral good.[6]

The requisite statement can now be extracted from the heart of this story:

> *God is omnipotent and it was not within his power to create a world containing moral good but no moral evil.*

The claim here is that it is *possible* (or possibly true) that

> *God would create a world of free creatures who choose to do evil.*

In other words, for any world God might create, populated by whatever free creatures, it is not within God's power to bring it about that those significantly free creatures never go wrong.[7] This new statement, together with one asserting the existence of God, implies that evil exists. It can now be seen to be *possible* for God to exist and for evil to exist. Thus, the critic's charge—that it is *not possible* for God and evil to exist—is refuted.

J. L. Mackie, Antony Flew (b. 1923), and other critics raise a formidable objection to Plantinga's ploy. Arguing that it is *logically possible* that there be a world containing significantly free creatures who always do what is right and that God's omnipotence is the power to bring about any logically possible state of affairs, they conclude that God could indeed have created a world containing free creatures who always do what is right. There is surely no contradiction in the description of such a situation. If the critics are right about this, then the Free Will Defense is mistaken. As Mackie queries, "Why could [God] not have made men such that they always freely choose the good?"[8] After all, God is all-powerful.

Plantinga's reply to Mackie's objection involves sophisticated reasoning about the logic of omnipotence and freedom which is reminiscent of certain points discussed in chapter 4. Plantinga's reasoning about such matters exhibits more clearly the force of the Free Will Defense. Many thinkers, theists and nontheists, accept the standard definition of *omnipotence as the power to bring about any state of affairs the description of which is not logically self-contradictory.* This definition is quite naturally taken to mean that there are no *nonlogical* limits to what an omnipotent being can do. Hence, God has the ability to bring about any *intrinsically possible* state of affairs. Thus, he has the ability to bring about, for example, white polar bears and pieces of paper that are triangular because they are intrinsically possible; but he could not bring about married bachelors and square circles because they are intrinsically impossible.[9]

At this point, Plantinga introduces a distinction in the discussion of the logical limits on omnipotence by pointing out that there are states of affairs which are possible *in themselves* (i.e., intrinsically) but which are not possible *for God* to bring about. To establish this point he argues for a particular understanding of the logic of free will. If a person is free with respect to an action, then whether she performs or refrains from performing that action is up to her, *not* God. Although a world in which all persons always freely do what is right is certainly possible, it is not a state of affairs which was within God's power to create; all of the free creatures in that world would have to help bring it about by their own choices. The Free Will Defender insists that God cannot *determine* the actions of *free* persons.

However, Mackie and Flew counter by saying that such insistence is based on an *incompatibilist view* of freedom (the position that free will and determinism are logically incompatible), whereas they adopt a *compatibilist view* (the position that free will and determinism, either physical or divine, are logically compatible).[10] The compatibilist typically holds that a person is free in that, if a she had chosen to do otherwise than she did, she would have done otherwise; but the compatibilist holds nonetheless that the person was determined to choose in precisely the way she did. According to compatibilists, then, God could indeed have created a world containing moral good but no moral evil. In such a world, persons could have chosen, say, to perform only right actions, although all of their choices were determined.

Plantinga responds that free will is not compatible with any form of determinism, and thus that God could not create just any world he pleased. He explains that God thought it good to create a world containing significantly free creatures, beings who, like himself, are centers of creative activity. Plantinga defines very precisely the concept of *significant freedom* that functions in the Free Will Defense: "A person is free with respect to an action A at a time *t* only if no causal laws and antecedent conditions determine either that he performs A at t or that he refrains from so doing."[11] If this is an acceptable definition of freedom, then the Free Will Defense stands. Morally significant freedom is not compatible with any form of determinism. Therefore, while it is possible that there be a world containing only moral good and no moral evil, whether such a world exists is actually up to the free creatures who inhabit that world and not up to God.

The compatibilist-incompatibilist debate is an important exchange within the overall framework of the logical problem of evil. Other discussions focused, for example, on the exact statement about evil that is selected to construct the inconsistency argument. As we have seen, the most popular form of the argument involves the claim that evil exists per se. However, some critics have admitted that perhaps the *sheer existence* of evil is not inconsistent with the existence of the theistic deity but have contended that the *amount* of evil in the world might well be. They argue that God could have created a world with less evil than the actual world possesses. Plantinga responds that the Free Will Defense still applies and shows that possibly it is not within God's power to create a world containing less moral evil than the present world.

Other critics, who concede that God's existence and any amount of moral evil are compatible in a world with incompatibilist freedom, have thought that specifically *natural evil* is inconsistent with the existence of God. Although God must respect free will, they argue, he need not allow blind physical forces to harm people. Plantinga counters that possibly what we call natural evils are due to the actions of significantly free but nonhuman persons (e.g., rebellious spirits). Thus, the Free Will Defense still applies. Interestingly, some philosophers misunderstood Plantinga as claiming that there are in fact such rebellious spirits, whereas he is only claiming that their possibility is sufficient to rebut the argument that God and natural evils are inconsistent.[12] It is simply the persistent application of the logic of the Free Will Defense.

THE EVIDENTIAL PROBLEM OF EVIL

Although the logical problem of evil marks an important phase of the ongoing debate, during the 1980s discussion turned increasingly to the evidential problem. Although it was generally agreed that Plantinga, Keith Yandell (b. 1938), and other theistic philosophers had cast serious doubt on all formulations of the logical problem, many nontheistic critics were convinced that evil still presents a serious threat to theistic belief. The *evidential problem of evil* is essentially a challenge to theists to square their belief in God with the facts of evil in the world. Their allegation is not that theism is internally *inconsistent* but that it is *implausible*. Their argument rests not on a matter of logic but on the issue of whether theism provides a reasonable explanation of the facts of evil. A number of nontheistic philosophers—Edward Madden (b. 1925), Peter Hare (b. 1935), Michael Martin (b. 1932), Wesley Salmon (b. 1925), and William Rowe (b. 1931)—issued their own versions of this evidential challenge.[13]

One attempt to construct a viable statement of the argument was made by Wesley Salmon.[14] He focuses on the traditional teleological argument, which claims that the universe must have been produced by intelligent design. He draws on the resources of a *frequency (or statistical) theory of probability*, which rests on assumptions regarding prior probabilities, and claims that apparently pointless evil in the universe prevents it from being what we would antecedently expect of a being who is extremely intelligent, benevolent, and powerful. Thus, he concludes, the evidence of evil makes it *improbable* or *unlikely* that God exists. This argument is known as the *probabilistic problem of evil*. In response Plantinga argued that no extant theory of probability—*personalist, logical,* or *frequentist*—can be used to construct a formidable argument from evil.[15] Among the obstacles for such approaches are the inherent troubles in modern probability studies generally (e.g., the lack of any clear criterion for judging the probability of one statement on the basis of another), as well as the tendency of critics to let their own presuppositions affect their assignment of prior probabilities (e.g., the assessment of how antecedently likely it is that the God of theism would create a world with the evil this one contains). Nancy Cartwright (b. 1944) also responded to Salmon, saying that a statistical approach is completely inappropriate for treating metaphysical issues.[16]

Although Salmon's proposal was flawed, most nontheistic critics are convinced that a serious statement of the evidential problem of evil is within reach. This kind of nondemonstrative or broadly inductive argument shows that it is more rational, given the evidence of evil, to believe that God does not exist. For most critics, the important *evidence* is not the sheer existence of evil, since *some* evil seems subject to reasonable theistic explanation. Instead, instances of evil for which there seems to be no good explanation are taken as *prima facie* evidence. Of course, it is generally assumed that an acceptable theistic explanation shows why the evils in question are necessary to some greater good. If no such necessary connection can be identified, then it is typically assumed that the evils in question are pointless or gratuitous. We will have more to say about this later.

In this form of the evidential argument, theism is treated as a large-scale metaphysical hypothesis or explanatory theory that implies specific consequences for the way the world should be. If theism is true, then we would expect the world to turn out a certain way. Of course, complex global hypotheses seldom directly imply definite consequences unless they are augmented by additional assumptions. In the present case, the theistic hypothesis (i.e., that a certain kind of deity exists) must be supplemented by other assumptions. One of these assumptions, which theists as well as nontheists typically accept, is that *God would prevent or eliminate the existence of any pointless or meaningless evil.* William Rowe states that such a claim "seems to express a belief that accords with our basic moral principles, principles shared by both theists and nontheists."[17] Terence Penelhum writes: "It is logically inconsistent for a theist to admit the existence of a pointless evil."[18] On this basis, critics reason that, if God exists, we should expect no pointless or meaningless evil in the universe. Yet pointless or meaningless evil does appear to exist; the grounds are very impressive for believing that it does. Critics conclude, then, that theism does not adequately explain the way things are, that it is unlikely that God exists.

Rowe has provided a formulation of this argument which is now a standard in philosophical discussions:

1. There exist instances of intense suffering which an omnipotent, omniscient being could have prevented without thereby losing some greater good or permitting some evil equally bad or worse.

    (Factual premise)

2. An omnipotent, wholly good being would prevent the occurrence of any intense suffering it could, unless it could not do so without thereby losing some greater good or permitting some evil equally bad or worse.   (Theological premise)

3. There does not exist an omnipotent, omniscient, wholly good being.[19]

    (Conclusion)

In support of the factual premise, Rowe has offered the cases of Bambi and Sue: the fawn which suffered and died in a forest fire and the five-year-old girl who was horribly abused and beaten to death by her mother's drunken boyfriend.

If the logic of the evidential argument is correct, then discussion of it naturally turns to its premises. Typically, both theists and nontheists think that the key to the success of the argument centers on its factual premise: the claim that pointless evil exists. Keith Yandell, a theist, writes that "the crucial question is whether it is certain, or at least more probable than not, that there is unjustified evil, whether natural or moral."[20] Rowe agrees that whether the theist can overturn the evidential argument depends on finding "some fault with its [factual] premise."[21] Theists who try to rebut the factual premise divide into two camps: those who think we can know it to be false and those who hold that we cannot know it to be true. Of course, each of these approaches has elicited rejoinders from nontheistic critics, making the continuing debate very interesting and important.

Many theists embrace some theory or element of a theory describing what sorts of greater goods are connected to what sorts of evils (e.g., suffering builds character, provides meaningful contrast to the good, etc.). Traditionally, such a theory is called a "theodicy," which literally means a justification of the ways of God. Critics typically respond by citing difficult cases of evil to serve as counterexamples to the theodicies which are offered. Rowe asserts, "There exist instances of intense suffering which an omnipotent, omniscient being could have prevented without thereby losing some greater good or permitting some evil equally bad or worse."[22] Drawing from the fawn example, he says, "There does not appear to be any greater good such that the prevention of the fawn's suffering would require either the loss of that good or the occurrence of an evil equally bad or worse."[23] The fawn's tragic situation, then, is apparently pointless; it is unreasonable to believe that it serves any approvable purpose, and likewise in the case of the little girl.

Other theists who choose not to advance a positive theodicy against the factual premise instead call into question the epistemic grounds for holding it. For example, Stephen Wykstra (b. 1949) challenges Rowe's claim that it "does not appear" that there are goods that justify the evil in question. Wykstra contends that accepting an *appearance-claim* in a given situation is warranted only when it is reasonable to believe that, given our cognitive faculties and our use of them, the truth of the claim would be discernible by us.[24] Explaining that God's knowledge is infinitely higher than human knowledge, Wykstra concludes that it is not reasonable to think that if God has some justifying good for a given evil we would know it or that it would be apparent to us—that is, that we would have "reasonable epistemic access." God's ways are beyond the power of finite minds to comprehend. This Cognitive Limitation Defense holds that we are not justified in thinking that evils have no point simply on the basis that they do not "appear" to us to have a point.

Rowe replied that Wykstra's argument is not really deducible from restricted theism alone (the claim that an omnipotent, omniscient, omnibenevolent deity exists and created the world) but is drawn from some preferred version of expanded theism (restricted theism plus other claims from a particular religious tradition).[25] This means that Wykstra has unwittingly smuggled in additional claims about the inscrutability of divine purposes, the limitations of human cognition, and so on, and thus that his argument fails as a defense of restricted theism, which was the position originally under discussion. Rowe grants that Wykstra might succeed if he were defending a particular version of expanded theism that contained such additional claims. However, not all religious traditions (forms of expanded theism) insist on such a great chasm between divine and human knowledge; indeed, they affirm that humans have divinely created capacities to comprehend something of the personal and moral meanings of the universe, including those connected to evil and suffering.

It may seem that the discussion over the factual premise is inconclusive or that parties to the debate have reached a kind of rational stalemate. However, a stalemate—if that is the net result—works to the advantage of the nontheist. After all, it is the theist who advances certain claims about the existence and nature of God, and then encounters serious difficulties in showing how those claims make sense of some very serious evils. The nontheist is thereby warranted in urging that the evidential problem of evil greatly reduces the credibility of the theistic position. Of course, a total rational assessment of theism would have to take into account other criticisms as well as other positive supports, such as the traditional theistic arguments. However, since most nontheists think that the problem of evil is effective and that the traditional arguments are bankrupt or at least unconvincing, they claim to be justified in rejecting theism.

Seeking another way to rebut the evidential argument from evil, some theists have advocated the acceptance of its factual premise and the rejection of its theological premise.[26] They defend the factual premise on both *philosophical* and *theological* grounds. Along philosophical lines, they endorse the general reliability of our ordinary moral judgments, and they point out that we judge much evil in the world to be utterly pointless. Shifting to theological grounds, they support the factual premise by indicating that the theistic deity has created humankind with basically trustworthy rational and moral capabilities. Clearly adopting a version of expanded theism that is different from Wykstra's, they claim that it may be inconsistent for theists to urge so strongly that the human experience of gratuitous evil is regularly and systematically mistaken. While admitting that there is a cognitive distance between divine and human realms, they still maintain that the weight of the human experience has a bearing on the question of gratuity.

Theists who take this approach reject the theological premise. They do not surrender the standard divine attributes employed in that premise but do question the built-in assumption that God would not allow gratuitous or pointless evil. If these theists can convincingly argue that there is a place for pointless evils within a theistic conception of the world, then they stop the evidential argument from going through. Although the whole idea of a theistic universe in which there is genuine contingency will be more fully explored in chapter 8, we can here sketch the sort of theistic reasoning that can countenance gratuitous evil. A starting place is the acknowledgment of the full import of what it means to have free will. If the range of free choices available to creatures is to be really significant rather than trivial, then creatures must be capable of the highest goods as well as the most terrible evils. For God to limit the possibility of very serious evils is to delimit the possibilities of great goods. Thus, significant freedom involves even the ability to bring about utterly meaningless evils, a risk inherent in God's program for humanity.

This argument is not that the *actuality* of many evils is necessary to any greater goods; such goods presumably could have existed without these evils being actual. Thus, such evils may be genuinely gratuitous. But the *possibility* of these evils is indeed necessary to the preservation of significant free will. According to this line of reasoning, the critics' assumption—that God would not allow gratuitous evil—can be rejected. Evils that appear to be gratuitous or pointless count as evidence against theism only if it is assumed that the theistic deity would not allow them.

DEFENSE AND THEODICY

We have learned a lot from the discussions of the *logical* and *evidential* problems of evil. Among other things, we have been able to sharpen the distinction between two types of response, *defense* and *theodicy*. Defense aims at establishing that a given formulation of the argument from evil fails; *theodicy* offers an account or explanation of why God allows suffering and evil. Plantinga, as we know, designed the Free Will Defense to prove that the logical argument does not show theism to be inconsistent. Since the early 1980s, as the success of his efforts became widely acknowledged, philosophers increasingly explored whether some kind of *evidential argument* would still be viable. The increasing development of serious evidential arguments pre-dictably prompted many theistic responses, but the theistic respondents disagreed over whether defense or theodicy is the best strategy.

As nontheistic critics proposed different versions of an evidential argu-ment from evil, some theists followed with defensive rejoinders. In response to Salmon's probabilistic formulation, for example, Plantinga argues that theism is not improbable. In response to Rowe's widely discussed evidential formulation, Wykstra argues that the key factual premise cannot be known to be true. We can see that defensive strategies which are adapted to evidential arguments attempt to show that such arguments are unsuccessful in estab-lishing that theism is improbable, unlikely, or implausible. However, these strategies do not aspire to the more positive task of offering credible reasons to think that theism makes plausible sense of suffering and evil.

Actually, the intense interest in defense shown by some theists fits very well with the orientation of Reformed epistemology already discussed in Chapter 6. As we saw, Reformed epistemology levels trenchant criticisms against the evidentialist and strong foundationalist assumptions about how our beliefs are justified. Quite obviously, these assumptions have shaped nu-merous discussions between theists and nontheists over the centuries. Addi-tionally, Reformed epistemology supplies an alternative understanding for how beliefs are justified: under appropriate conditions, we may hold certain beliefs "basically," without argument. Thus, a person could be rationally en-titled to believe in God if her belief were basic and, when pressed, she was able to offer a successful defense against objections to that belief, such as some version of the problem of evil. This orientation largely supports the view that *theodicy is in principle unnecessary,* that the theist is not rationally obligated to provide a theodicy in the face of evil.[27]

Another motivation for pure defense is implied by Wykstra's Cognitive Limitation argument against Rowe. As Rowe noted, Wykstra's particular version of expanded theism stresses the immeasurable gap between God's infinite mind and finite human minds such that we cannot hope to know God's reasons for permitting the evils that are so evident in our world. As long as theodicy is conceived as the task of specifying God's reason for a given evil—say, an evil such as Rowe would cite—then it would seem that *theodicy is a priori impossible.*[28] Therefore, if theodicy is not even possible, then the theist is ostensibly left with playing pure defense against the different arguments from evil.

Not all commentators have agreed that the enterprise of theodicy is not viable. Clearly, traditional theists and their critics believed that theodicy was indeed appropriate, as displayed by the existence of numerous classic theod-icies and the equally numerous critiques of them. From Augustine to Leibniz to Richard Swinburne, we have received rich and subtle theodicies. On the other side of the ledger, we have rigorous criticisms by Voltaire, Hume, and Dostoevsky's Ivan that have become classic. Arguably, the two most promi-nent theodicists of recent times are John Hick and Richard Swinburne, both of whom articulate a vision of a theistic universe, including its possibilities for pain, as conducive to the creation of morally and spiritually mature persons. This kind of view has been vigorously criticized by nontheistic philosophers, such as Paul Draper.[29]

Of course, theists who see "God exists" as intimately connected to a whole web of theological claims are more prone to think that theodicy is viable. Given that "God exists" is already invested with certain understandings of the divine nature, attributes, and purposes, it already implicitly gestures in some directions theodicy might take. After all, Rowe's point against Wykstra is that Wykstra had unwittingly imported certain additional theological commitments into his understanding of the central theistic claim for which he crafted his defense. This point enlightens us to the fact that what Rowe calls restricted standard theism is not really rich and fruitful enough to generate much theodicy. After all, theism is not a living religion but an important belief component of the larger belief system of some living religions. It is reasonable to think, then, that a minimal or restricted theism could yield, at best, a minimal theodicy. Likewise, it is reasonable to think that theodicy, if it is going to have a fighting chance, and if it is going to be interesting and important, will have to draw upon the full resources of its own religious tradition (its key doctrines, scriptures, experiences of its saints, etc.). Whether a thinking believer engages in theodicy to answer the critic or simply to reflect more deeply on her own religious beliefs, these sources appear to provide a more complete background of the sources from which ideas for theodicy may be drawn. There is even room for interesting differences of emphasis among particular theistic traditions, whether Christian, Jewish, or Islamic.

Although the project of defense is relatively easy to characterize, the project of theodicy is somewhat more difficult. Issues regarding the nature, scope, and grounds of theodicy are all issues in *metatheodicy*. Theists disagree among themselves on some fine points, and nontheists have their own expectations for the burden that theodicy must shoulder. Is theodicy meant to suggest merely possible reasons for God's permission of evil or is it committed to advancing plausible explanations for evil? Does the theodicist have the burden of providing God's reasons for evil or simply of drawing out the implications of a given theological perspective? Must theodicy sketch a general theistic explanation, say, for whole classes of evils—or must it address individual cases? What role does moral theory play—or our general sense of life play—in the discussion of theodicy? These questions and others provide material for much discussion about the structure and role of theodicy.

THEMES IN THEODICY

A review of the classical and contemporary literature in theodicy reveals a number of recurring themes. These themes, which are generally thought to emerge from traditional theistic commitments, often crop up in discussions of evil among nonphilosophers as well, suggesting that they have broad and enduring appeal. We devote attention to several of these themes here because some involve worthwhile insights and others make instructive mistakes.

One approach that has some uptake among some religious believers is that evil is *punishment* for wrongdoing. For example, when the Old Testament patriarch Job experienced suffering, he was told by his "comforters" that he had sinned. They held the principle that, in a divinely ordered and just universe, God rewards the righteous (with health, wealth, and progeny) but punishes the wicked (with sickness, misfortune, and loss). Yet Job objected that he had not done anything wrong so as to deserve horrible suffering. Job was a kind of religious pioneer, pressing toward a vision of the world that is much more complex than his comforters' simplistic answer could grasp, a world in the benefits and burdens of life are not equitably distributed and certainly not based on merit. In this kind of world, a person must have purer motivation for having faith in God than merely to earn reward or avoid punishment.[30] Besides, the punishment theory, when presented as a comprehensive theodicy, flirts with sheer absurdity in cases such as the death of innocent infants or the tragic destruction of the population of an entire village.

A very interesting, but more complicated, theme aimed at explaining evil is embodied in the claim that this is the *best of all possible worlds.* In the eighteenth century, Gottfried Leibniz (1646–1716) reasoned this way: God is all-powerful and thus can create any possible universe; being perfect, God would want to create the very best possible universe; therefore, this universe, with its evils, must still be the best one possible. Interestingly, there may be other possible worlds which contain less evil, but the main thrust here is that this world contains the optimum balance of good and evil commensurate with its being the best overall. Obviously, some goods are made possible only by the presence of evil (e.g., compassion is made possible by witnessing suffering; fortitude by hardship). This means that God had to weigh the total value of all possible worlds and create the one in which the evils contributed to that world's being the very best one. Worlds with less evil as well as worlds with more evil, Leibniz argues, simply do not contain the exact entities and events connected in the exact ways that make this world the best.

Although best-of-all-possible-worlds theodicy invites long and sustained discussion, several problems immediately surface. First, the concept of a best possible world may well be logically incoherent, just as the concept of the highest possible integer is logically incoherent. There simply is no end to the system of integers. Similarly, why would we think that there is some best possible world? Second, the Leibnizian approach seems to imply that our world is not capable of improvement, an implication that runs counter to our ordinary moral judgments. The third, and perhaps most serious, problem regards the question of why a good God chose to create a world at all, given that it had to have this much suffering. Put another way, why did God create this world, if he could not create a better one? In Dostoevsky's *Brothers Karamazov,* Ivan Karamozov rehearses a list of situations involving the torture and murder of small children to his brother Alyosha, a Russian Orthodox priest. Then he asks a poignant question of Alyosha: "If you were God, would you have consented to create the present world if its creation depended upon the unexpiated tears of one tortured child crying in its stinking outhouse to 'dear, kind God'?" Alyosha is silent for a moment and then answers, "No, I wouldn't consent." The point is that a morally good being would not create this world at all.[31]

Another type of theme in theodicy is the *ultimate harmony* solution, which may be split into two distinct positions: The first is the *all is well with the world from God's perspective* orientation and the second is that *all will be well in the long run* orientation. The first approach, the *all's-well-from-God's-perspective position*, can be supported by either of two characteristics attributed to deity. One is *omniscience*, God's perfect knowledge. Since God's knowledge of the world is complete, whereas human knowledge is partial and fragmented, only divine judgment about the state of things is ultimately valid. After all, a chord heard in isolation may sound dissonant, but when heard in context it sounds harmonious. The analogy, then, is that only God sees how the totality of events constitutes a favorable arrangement, while we puny humans cannot. Unfortunately, this approach seriously frustrates all human moral judgments, since they are always made from a limited perspective. Although restricted theism does entail the superiority of divine over human knowledge, various forms of expanded theism trace out the implications of this in different ways. Some versions of Christian theism, for example, affirm that finite persons are creatures who bear God's image and can thus make reasonable, reliable moral judgments.

The other divine attribute on which an all's-well view is based is God's moral perfection. This line of thought emphasizes the notion that *God's morality is higher than human morality.* Even if we humans could see events of the world in a total context, we would not apply the same perfect moral standard as God would in appraising them. Theists who take this tack think that it defuses objections to belief in God based on what appear to be pointless, unjustified evils. In its strongest form, this position implies that God's ways are so much "higher than our ways"[32] that everything in the world is morally acceptable to God, in spite of the fact that it is not acceptable to many morally sensitive human beings. Obviously, this position once again undercuts human moral judgments by implying that they must be systematically mistaken. Nontheistic critics convincingly argue that, upon analysis, the concept of a higher divine morality becomes meaningless, since we would not know what such a morality would be, let alone how it bolsters the case of a theist trying to answer the problem of evil.

In a very frank condemnation of this theistic position, J. S. Mill (1806–1873) says that it makes God out to be a moral monster, one whose moral standards are totally incommensurate with our deepest moral convictions:

> In everyday life I know what to call right or wrong, because I can plainly see its rightness or wrongness. Now if a god requires that what I ordinarily call wrong in human behavior I must call right because he does it; or that what I ordinarily call wrong I must call right because he so calls it, even though I do not see the point of it; and if by refusing to do so, he can sentence me to hell, to hell I will gladly go.[33]

Theists who perceive the force of such criticisms and who understand their own religious tradition as affirming a connection between human and divine morality do not rely on the higher morality theme. While asserting the perfection of God's morality, they do not insist on complete discontinuity between divine and human moral standards. Indeed they see the reasonableness of our fallible human moral judgments as giving traction to the problem of evil in the first place.

The second distinct approach—the *all's-well-that-ends-well strategy*—does not claim that every evil is presently connected with greater goods. Instead this approach affirms that all evils will eventually result in greater goods, either in temporal life or in the afterlife. Although many criticisms of the all's-well-in-God's-sight position are also relevant to the all's-well-that-ends-well position, a few additional points must be made. First, while there may be (or may not be) greater future goods to which present evils are connected, it is far from clear how such future goods *justify* the present occurrence of those evils. How, for example, does the fact that an orphaned child develops strong humanitarian motives and becomes a great surgeon in an underdeveloped part of the globe justify, morally speaking, the brutal death of her parents at the hands of murderers? Or how could the promised bliss and beatitude of heaven justify the excruciating suffering of a cancer victim during earthly life? It is quite a conceptual jump from the notion of a good *outweighing* an evil to the notion of *compensating* for an evil—and a very large jump to the notion of a good *justifying* the existence of an evil. In light of such difficulties, many all-will-be-well advocates simply say that we humans, with our limited powers, do not know how future goods make up for present evils but that God's inscrutable wisdom does. At the very least, there needs to be more serious discussion of the kind of moral theory that bears upon this issue before we can make full sense of what it means for a good to compensate for an evil or for a good to justify an evil.

The preceding themes have been used to address the problem of evil generally. Nevertheless, it is helpful at this point to consider one theme that addresses specifically the problem of *natural evil*. Perhaps the most important solution to the problem of natural evil is known as the *natural law explanation*, which claims that, as part of his creative program, God brought about a natural order. A natural order is a world constituted by objects that behave according to physical laws. The operation of physical laws of all sorts, then, makes possible a host of natural benefits, such as physiological feelings of pleasure or even helpful warnings of pain. Furthermore, a generally stable and predictable natural order supports a moral order in which rational deliberation and choice can take place and in which free choices can be carried out in action. But the possibility of natural evil is inherent in a natural system. The same water that quenches our thirst can also drown us; the same neurons that transmit pleasure can also transmit intense and unbearable pain.

Critics of natural law theodicy, such as H. J. McCloskey (b. 1925), argue that God could greatly reduce or eliminate natural evils, either by miraculously intervening in the present natural system or by creating an entirely different natural system.[34] Some theists, such as Richard Swinburne (b. 1934), point out the difficulties with either demand. On the one hand, the notion of frequent divine intervention contradicts both the omni-attributes of God and the concept of a natural system.[35] After all, if God is omnipotent and omniscient, he would create a natural system in which he does not have to intervene frequently; if he is perfectly good, he would create a natural system that is good on the whole. Moreover, the very concept of a natural system implies that it is not frequently adjusted from outside the system, that it runs more or less of its own accord and would be abrogated by repeated divine intervention. On the other hand, many theists doubt that the critic can envision in sufficient subtlety and detail what a genuinely better natural system would be like.[36]

Now, a theme in theodicy tailored specifically for the problem of moral evil, one which has been expressed on the scholarly as well as the popular levels, is the theme of free will. This theme predates Plantinga's famous Free Will Defense and had actually been used as an ingredient in various traditional theodicies. As we have seen, Plantinga's defensive maneuver rests on the claim that it is possible that God created persons with free will who chose moral evil. Free Will Theodicy, by contrast, is more aggressive, affirming that it is not merely possible but true that God created significantly free beings who went wrong. Although God knew that free moral beings might willfully commit evil, God granted free will anyway because a world of free creatures with a meaningful range of choice is more valuable than a world of automatons. This scenario represents a very important element in the theistic vision of both the grandeur and the peril of being human.

Nontheistic critics suggest a number of ways in which the free will maneuver needs further justification. For one thing, they ask for reasons to accept the *incompatibilist view* of free will that figures into the explanation of evil.[37] After all, there are several *compatibilist views* of the nature of free will. Even some critics who are willing to concede the incompatibilist assumption simply argue that God could have created free human beings with stronger dispositions toward right conduct than they actually have. Surely, doing this would have reduced much of the evil brought about by the misuse of free will. Theists typically respond that God has created humans with an inclination toward the good that is as strong as it can possibly be and still remain consistent with freedom of choice. Critics challenge that such a move seems ad hoc and that there is no reason to believe that this is so. So the debate goes on.

We could identify many other responses to the problem of evil, but most of them have either marginal or no importance to restricted theism or to major forms of expanded theism: evil as an illusion, evil as an absurd element inherent in created reality, evil as caused by demonic spirits, and so on. Indeed, when such responses have been offered, critics have subjected them to rigorous analysis and rebuttal.

SOME IMPORTANT GLOBAL THEODICIES

In addition to identifying some specific themes that address the problem of evil, we can also identify broader, more comprehensive explanations that weave together various selected themes. These explanations, which we will call *global theodicies*, generally articulate a systematic vision of God's ways with the universe. Three of these theodicies have become very important in the literature on evil and deserve closer examination: *Augustinian theodicy*, *Irenaean theodicy*, and *process theodicy*.

The first view to analyze is Augustinian theodicy, which traces back to the early Christian philosopher and theologian St. Augustine (354–430 A.D.). Augustine offered a Christian and theistic interpretation of reality that brings together several strands of thought. One of Augustine's ideas was that the universe—that is, the whole of God's creation—is good. God creates only good things, and thus every created thing is good in its essence. Evil, then, is not a thing, not an entity. Metaphysically speaking, evil does not represent the positive existence of anything; rather, it is the lack of good, the *privation* of goodness.[38] Unlike God, who is eternal and unchangeable, the universe was created out of nothing (*ex nihilo*) and is thus mutable or changeable. For Augustine, this explains how its original goodness is corruptible and thus can manifest evil.[39] It is particularly the misuse of free will that allows the entry of sin or evil into human experience. Augustine understood the Christian doctrine of the Fall to specify that an originally perfect creation rebelled against God through Adam's transgression. Augustine goes on to explore how this original sin brought guilt and punishment upon the whole race, how believers will be redeemed by divine grace, and how history itself will climax in the establishment of God's kingdom.[40]

Clearly, the Augustinian-type theodicy dominated the collective imagination of Western Christendom from the fifth century A.D. onward and provides background for many of the most popular Christian answers for the problem of evil even in contemporary times. It has been the subject of a great deal of scrutiny. Critics have charged, for example, that Augustine failed to solve the paradox that evil poses in light of his own strong view of the majestic power and unquestionable sovereignty of God. Perhaps one of the most vexing questions is how, on his account, an originally good and free creature can engage in sin. If human beings once enjoyed an ideal state or "golden age" in which there was no evil, how is it that they would ever choose to do evil? It is well known that, in the end, Augustine retreated into the "mystery of finite freedom."[41]

A second, alternative approach to theodicy can be traced to Bishop Irenaeus (c. 130–c. 202 A.D.), a major thinker in early Eastern Christendom. His work reflects certain Greek influences and is distinct from the thinking of Augustine and the fathers of the Western church. John Hick (b. 1922), a modern-day proponent of *Irenaean theodicy*, explains that it involves a scenario in which Adam and the original creation were innocent and immature, possessing the privilege of becoming good by loving God and fellow creatures.

But it would be an error to think that original innocence can be equated with original perfection. Indeed, it is not clear that God can instantaneously create morally mature persons, since moral maturity almost certainly requires the experience of grappling with temptation over time, and, according to some, actual participation in evil. Hence, evil as we know it must be explained not as a decline from a state of pristine purity and goodness but rather as an inevitable stage in the gradual evolution of the human race.

Hick's rendition of the Irenaean approach is called *soul-making theodicy* because it paints a picture of God's grand scheme of helping human beings become morally and spiritually mature. On this view, a special kind of environment is required for the whole soul-making process. An environment conducive to personal growth must be one in which there are real challenges, real opportunities for the display of moral virtue, and real possibilities of expressing faith. A major component of this environment is a community of moral agents who interact in special ways and even in a natural order of impersonal objects that operates independently of our wills. Obviously, in such conditions, there is the genuine risk of evil—of failure and ruin, suffering and injustice. Interestingly, Hick even deems it important that the world appear as if there is no God, and evil certainly plays an important role in forming this appearance. For Hick, the potentially atheistic appearance of the world creates "epistemic distance" between creature and creator, thus making room for genuine faith and trust in God. Actually, this point relates to the issues of the silence of God and the religious ambiguity of life that were discussed in chapter 1.

For Irenaean theodicy, God's ultimate plan is the universal salvation of all persons, a process that extends beyond earthly existence and into life after death. For those people who, for whatever reasons, depart mortal life without having achieved the proper degree of moral maturity (or so we might say), God pursues this same objective for them in the life to come. God continues his efforts in the afterlife, providing occasions for exercising love and trust, until all persons are brought into proper relation to him. This affirmation of divine persistence completes the progressive, developmental, and eschatological (concerning the destiny of individuals and the world) orientation of Irenaean theodicy.[42]

Hick's very famous version of Irenaean theodicy contains elements of *free will, natural law,* and *character-building* explanations, as well as some themes that are distinctively Hick's. Various criticisms have been leveled against the different aspects of his view. G. Stanley Kane (b. 1938), for instance, has argued that the "epistemic distance" Hick wants to postulate between humanity and God in order to make room for faith can be maintained at much less cost.[43] Severe moral and physical evils do not seem necessary to give the appearance that God does not exist, since there surely are other ways in which God can conceal his presence.

Critics have also criticized Hick's view as lacking in empirical support for its central claim: that the world is engaged in a program of soul making. There are enough failures in temporal life alone to cast grave doubt on whether a program of soul making is under way. Surely, there are so many people whose character is ruined rather than developed that thoughtful people might question the effectiveness or even the existence of the soul-making process. Moreover, many critics wonder whether the goal of soul making, even if it did succeed in an ample number of cases, could ever justify the means used to achieve it (e.g., great hardship, suffering, catastrophe). After all, we have all heard of persons who became shining examples of humanitarian activity or of moral courage, but many of them had to fight through senseless losses of family members or had to endure severe, prolonged, and involuntary pain. In response to this last point, Hick points out that each person must ultimately decide whether he thinks the soul-making process is worth it.

Process theodicy is the third major explanation of evil we must investigate. Process philosophy, advocated in the writings of Alfred North Whitehead, modifies the classical attributes of the theistic deity and thus generates a distinctive type of theodicy that has gained serious attention among contemporary philosophers and theologians. Process thought in general is based on a view of reality as *becoming* rather than *being*, which is a reversal of the traditional approach. It is not surprising, then, that the central theme in process theodicy is the concept of change, development, evolution—both in God and in finite creatures. Creatures are conscious, ever-changing centers of experience and activity. God, for process thinkers, has two natures: his Primordial Nature and his Consequent Nature. God's Primordial Nature contains all eternal possibilities for how the creaturely world can advance; God's Consequent Nature contains the experiences and responses of creatures as they choose to actualize some of these possibilities in their lives. As God's Consequent Nature changes in response to events in the creaturely world, God may also be said to change or to be in process.

Process theodicy rests squarely on the rejection of the classical concept of divine omnipotence, which process thinkers take to be inadequate and laden with fallacies. Process philosophers and theologians deny that God has a monopoly on power or is "infinite in power," as traditional theology affirms. Finite creatures are also centers of power and thus can bring about new states of affairs as well. Process thinkers typically speak of this creaturely power in terms of "freedom," and thus their terminology is at points reminiscent of traditional discussions. The process version of freedom is rooted in the very structure of reality, with each creature having the inherent power of self-determination. Thus, we may say that God has all of the power that it is possible for a being to have but not all of the power that there is. Creatures have some power of their own, power that allows them to choose good or evil possibilities for their lives. God's power, then, can meet real resistance by creatures. According to process thinkers, divine power must be viewed as *persuasive* rather than *coercive*. God can try to lure creatures toward the good and away from evil, but he cannot force them to choose the good. The process exponent David Ray Griffin (b. 1939) states that God cannot eliminate evil because "God cannot unilaterally effect any state of affairs."[44]

Instead, God offers persons possibilities for the realization of good, adjusting his plans appropriately when they fail to live up to the divine plan and trying to lure them into fulfilling the next set of ideal possibilities, with the ultimate aim of enhancing and enriching their experience.

One intriguing theme in process theodicy is that all positive and negative experiences in the creaturely realm are ultimately conserved and reconciled in God's own conscious life. Thus, all things can be said to work out all right in so far as God "include[s] in himself a synthesis of the total universe."[45] In the Kingdom of Heaven, God brings about a kind of synthesis of all earthly experiences but does not unilaterally rectify all evils. Typically, process thinkers have not conceived of "personal immortality" or "life after death" as central to the defense of God's goodness against the problem of evil, as traditional Christian thinkers sometimes do.[46] Neither is there any final, definitive, eschatological culmination of all things. Thus, for process thinkers, the continual, ongoing synthesis of all experiences in God's own conscious life is the basic hope for the triumph of good and the redemption of the world.

Process theodicy has certainly forced classical theists to rethink and refine their fundamental concepts.[47] But classical theists, as well as some nontheists, have raised a number of serious objections to process concepts as well. For example, the process concept of divine power has come under severe criticism. The process attack on the classical concept of divine power has been said to be pure caricature, using such loaded terms as "totalitarian" and "monopolistic." This caricature sets up an oversimplified "either/or" distinction between *coercive* and *persuasive* power and anticipates the fuller discussion of such matters in chapter 8. Critics of process theodicy have suggested that there may even be a range of modes of divine power, such as "productive power," "sustaining power," or "enabling power," many of which are compatible with moral persuasion.[48] Also, there may be within the process model of power a confusion over the "possession of power" and the "ownership of power." With respect to property or things, ownership is exclusive (e.g., if one person has all of the marbles, then others have none). But with respect to power or agency, ownership is not exclusive. One person may have the power to lift the pencil from the desk, but other persons and God may also have that same power. Many classical theists have intended not a monopolistic or competitive view of divine power but only one compatible with the possession of some power on the part of finite creatures.

Another general criticism of process theodicy focuses on the concept of divine goodness, declaring that its orientation is essentially *aesthetic* rather than *moral.* If the aims of the process deity are to make creaturely experience richer and more complex, even at the cost of pain and discord, then there is the risk of violating many ordinary moral principles in the process. Both classical theists and nontheistic critics have voiced this objection. Classical theology seems to entail that God would not be morally perfect if he caused or allowed suffering in order to attain merely aesthetic aims. Process theists have replied that aesthetic value is a larger, more inclusive category than moral value, a maneuver that appears to make God's goodness unlike anything we are capable of recognizing and approving. Of course, hanging on the issue of whether God is morally good is the related question of whether he is worthy of worship.

HORRENDOUS EVILS AND THE ASSESSMENT OF THEISM

The complete list of themes as well as the comprehensive theodicies into which those themes have been incorporated is much longer than we can treat in this chapter. However, the sampling of approaches here begins to acquaint us with the wide range of moves available to theists and the corresponding countermoves open to critics. Interestingly, there is a common assumption underlying both the antitheistic arguments from evil and theistic responses: *God (who is omnipotent, omniscient, and wholly good) would not allow any evil unless it is necessary to a greater good.* Meeting this criterion, many argue, is the only thing that would provide God with a *morally sufficient reason* to permit evil. Critics claim that there exist evils that are not necessary to a greater good, and theists provide explanations about how the evils are connected to such goods.

Understandably, in the exchange that ensues, nontheistic critics who believe that they can dismantle various theistic answers are willing to claim that there are *gratuitous evils*, that is, evils which are not necessary to the existence of greater goods. Another avenue open to critics, which is seldom explored, pertains to whether a greater-good justificatory scheme is even viable. After all, such a scheme is consequentialist in essence, making the moral weight of an evil depend on some extrinsic factor. It may well be that critics should pursue the intuitions of Dostoevsky's Ivan Karamazov, who states that some actual evils are intrinsically so negative and destructive that no external goods could outweigh them.

Ivan's point prompts further reflection on the nature and aims of theodicy itself. Must theodicy provide global and generic answers about how God ensures that a world that includes evil can be good on the whole? Or should theodicy be more concrete and specific, attempting to explain how God's goodness allows no person's life to be engulfed by evil and thereby rendered not worth living? Nontheists who pursue Ivan's line of thinking here have a very formidable case. Marilyn Adams (b. 1943), a theist, states that future discussions of theodicy, if they are to be fair-minded, must migrate from the global level to the individual level. What she calls *horrendous evils* are evils that are so destructive of meaning within an individual's life that his or her life is not a great good to him or her.[49] One can see Rowe's specific example of baby Sue in this light. Whether individual lives are ultimately ruined by horrendous evils is clearly the most pressing question for nontheists to pursue as well as the most difficult question for theists to answer.

In addressing this issue, Adams indicates that theists must relinquish the shared methodological assumption that they are obligated to answer the problem of evil by referring only to goods that the nontheist also accepts. She argues that these goods will be secular, finite, and temporal, whereas the theist has in his conceptual arsenal infinite and eternal goods as well. She further argues that the metaphysical nature of God is such that God is the source of value but is not subject to the normal network of rights and obligations that so many formulations of the problem of evil assume to prevail among creatures. After all, most arguments from evil assume that God has duties, similar to those pertaining to creatures, to bring about some kind of offsetting goods for the evils cited, and, indeed, that there is no other way for God to be *good.*

Based on her particular understanding of Christian theism, Adams explores other conceptualities for how it is that God is good and how that goodness is related to individual lives whose meaning and value are threatened by horrendous evils. One claim that she advances is that the Christian doctrine of the Incarnation (of God's becoming human in the man Jesus of Nazareth) symbolizes God's intimate identification with the human condition, including suffering. This allows her to say that all suffering, no matter how terrible, is already invested with a positive aspect. Adams also claims that God, the divine personal being and consummate maker of meaning, will ultimately save every finite person. This allows her to argue that any created persons who experienced horrendous evils will be able at some point to affirm the value of their own lives.

Adams's contribution may not so much be in the details as it is in the larger shift it portends for the discussion of the problem of evil and theodicy. Fellow theists will no doubt debate the problematic nature, for Christian theism, of her universalism. While many nontheistic critics will recognize that Adams has helped clarify the most poignant version of the argument from evil, they will almost certainly press the issue of why an explanation that involves highly specific Christian doctrines should be credible to those who do not embrace Christian commitments. Of course, at this point, we encounter the question of the key trade-off in framing the dispute over evil. On the one hand, we could pursue the debate in generalities and thus maintain as much common ground as possible. This option generally involves theists arguing that God would create and sustain a certain kind of world, with the aim of pursuing certain kinds of aims, particularly with human persons. Critical rebuttals, then, typically revolve around an overall cost-benefit assessment of God's alleged approach. On the other hand, the debate could be pursued at the concrete level, a level at which theists are increasingly inclined to bring the full resources of their specific religious traditions to bear. At this stage, critics will have to decide whether their demand is for theists to give an answer that satisfies nontheistic metaphysical and moral visions or for theists to show how their own (expanded theistic) commitments generate an answer that is plausible on its own terms.

In the end, the dispute over evil is one of several considerations relevant to the rational acceptance or rejection of theistic belief. A reasoned judgment, therefore, must be made in light of all the relevant arguments for and against the existence of the God of theism. What is more, a final judgment must also take into account how well the overall theistic position fares in comparison to other worldviews, either religious or secular.

STUDY QUESTIONS

1. Why is the problem of evil so acute for Christian theism? Explore how other worldviews might encounter their own distinctive problems of evil.

2. Carefully distinguish between the two main versions of the problem of evil. What must be the strategy of the critic of theism in pressing each problem? What must be the strategy of the theist in answering?

3. Explain the difference between defense and theodicy. Rehearse some of the arguments that can be given for why theodicy is not viable and some of the arguments for why it is. What do you think?

4. Looking for a way to construe how evil counts as evidence against the existence of God, some philosophers formulated the argument from evil in probabilistic terms. Is this a promising attack on theism? Why or why not? Is there a more promising way to formulate an evidential problem of evil?

5. Explore some of the standard answers for evil as well as full-scale theodicies that have been offered by theists. Which ones to you think are most effective? Which ones are less effective or even unacceptable? Investigate some of the standard rebuttals to these theodicies which critics have offered.

6. Do you think that any feasible theistic answer to the problem of evil must rely somehow on a greater-good line of reasoning? Why or why not?

7. Explore the subtle distinction, as some theists have, between being committed to the actuality of gratuitous evil and being committed to the possibility of gratuitous evil.

8. According to Marilyn Adams, what is "horrendous evil"? Why does this concept represent an important topic for theists? For nontheists, such as William Rowe?

9. What is Adams's proposal for how theists might construct a theodicy for horrendous evils? In what ways is her proposal vulnerable to criticism?

NOTES

1. Elie Wiesel, *Night* (New York: Bantam, 1960).

2. Eugene Borowitz, *The Mask Jews Wear* (New York: Simon and Schuster, 1973), p. 99.

3. Hans Küng, *On Being a Christian*, trans. E. Quinn (Garden City, N.Y.: Doubleday, 1976), p. 432.

4. J. L. Mackie, "Evil and Omnipotence," *Mind* 64 (1955): 200.

5. Alvin Plantinga, *The Nature of Necessity* (Oxford: Clarendon Press, 1974), p. 165.

6. Plantinga, *Necessity*, pp. 166–7.

7. Plantinga's own very detailed argument delves into such concepts as "Liebniz's Lapse" and "transworld depravity." It can be read in more detail in his *God, Freedom, and Evil* (Grand Rapids: William B. Eerdmans, 1977; reprint of 1974 Harper and Row) or in very analytical detail in his *Necessity*, pt. 9.

8. J. L. Mackie, "Evil and Omnipotence," p. 209.

9. More technically, we would say: states of affairs consisting in polar bears' being white, states of affairs consisting in bachelors' being married, and so on.

10. John Mackie, "Theism and Utopia," *Philosophy* 38 (1962): 153–9; Antony Flew, "Compatibilism, Free Will and God," *Philosophy* 48 (1973): 231–44.

11. Plantinga, *Necessity,* pp. 170–1.

12. Plantinga, *God, Freedom, and Evil,* pp. 55–9.

13. Madden and Hare, *Evil and the Concept of God* (Springfield, Ill.: Charles C. Thomas, 1968); Michael Martin, *Atheism: A Philosophical Justification* (Philadelphia: Temple University Press, 1990), chap. 14; William Rowe, *Philosophy of Religion: An Introduction* (Belmont, Calif. Dickenson, 1978), pp. 86–9; Wesley Salmon, "Religion and Science: A New Look at Hume's *Dialogues,*" *Philosophical Studies,* 33 (1978): 143–76.

14. In order to bolster his frequentist or statistical argument, Salmon contends that a statement such as "an omnipotent, omniscient, perfectly good God exists" has a "very low" numerical probability (a value much lower than .5) in relation to some statement like "Evil exists." Conversely, he seeks to show that, given the existence of evil, the probability of the statement "an omnipotent, omniscient, perfectly good God does not exist" is high (definitely above .5). See Salmon, "A New Look," pp. 143–76.

15. Alvin Plantinga, "The Probabilistic Argument from Evil," *Philosophical Studies,* 35 (1979): 1–53.

16. Cartwright points out that the probabilistic argument from evil immediately faces the difficulty of specifying the appropriate reference class. Obviously, no person is directly acquainted with a whole class of universes such that we can arrive at a statistical measure of how many of them contain evil relative to how many were divinely created. Therefore, Salmon resorted to comparing the universe with other entities whose origins can actually be observed. But Cartwright contends that this move begs the question in advance by deciding to include entities into the reference class which are all brought about by mechanical production. Furthermore, Cartwright argues that frequentist techniques are wholly inappropriate for treating metaphysical issues, such as that of God's existence. If any type of inductive approach is appropriate, she holds that it would be the employment of experimental methods. She suggests, for example, that we imagine an experimental situation in which a bunch of random parts are thrown into a box and shaken together until they come out as a set of gears finally tuned to some end. Surely the probability of the initial random collection coming out in a highly ordered configuration is as near zero as can be, a conclusion completely opposite the one generated by Salmon's approach.

It would be interesting to explore Richard Swinburne's claim that frequentist techniques are appropriate to issues such as the existence of God. See Swinburne, *The Existence of God* (Oxford: Clarendon Press, 1979), pp. 5–21.

17. Rowe, *Philosophy of Religion,* p. 88.

18. Terence Penelhum, "Divine Goodness and the Problem of Evil," in *Readings in the Philosophy of Religion: An Analytic Approach,* ed. Baruch Brody (Englewood Cliffs, N.J.: Prentice-Hall, 1974), p. 226.

19. William Rowe, "The Problem of Evil and some Varieties of Atheism," *American Philosophical Quarterly* 16 (1979): 336.

20. Keith Yandell, *Basic Issues in the Philosophy of Religion* (Boston: Allyn and Bacon, 1971), pp. 62–3.

21. William Rowe, *Philosophy of Religion,* p. 88.

22. Rowe, "The Problem of Evil," p. 337.

23. Ibid., p. 338.

24. Stephen Wykstra, "The Humean Obstacle to Evidential Arguments from Suffering: On Avoiding the Evils of 'Appearance,'" *International Journal for Philosophy of Religion* 16 (1984): 85.

25. William Rowe, "Evil and the Theistic Hypothesis: A Response to Wykstra," *International Journal for the Philosophy of Religion* 16 (1984): 95–100.

26. See Michael Peterson, *Evil and the Christian God* (Grand Rapids, Mich.: Baker, 1982), chap. 4. See also William Hasker, "The Necessity of Gratuitous Evil," *Faith and Philosophy* 9, no. 1 (January 1992): 23–44. This article resulted from a paper read originally at the American Philosophical Association meeting, Cincinnati, Ohio, April 1988.

27. One can readily see why a theist who accepts Reformed epistemology would think that defense against the problem of evil is all that is rationally required. The critic advances an argument from evil against belief in God, and the theist defends against it. But the theist need not feel that he must have an argument for belief in God. Instead, he can simply take belief in God as basic.

28. Plantinga actually alludes to something like this point: "Perhaps God has a good reason [for evil], but that reason is too complicated for us to understand." Plantinga, *God, Freedom, and Evil*, p. 10.

29. Paul Draper, "Pain and Pleasure: An Evidential Problem for Theists," in *The Evidential Argument from Evil*, ed. Dan Howard-Snyder (Bloomington, Ind.: Indiana University Press, 1996), pp. 12–29.

30. For example, chapters 7 and 12 of the biblical Book of Job argue that sometimes the righteous suffer and the wicked prosper.

31. This encounter between Ivan and Alyosha constitutes one of the high points of world literature and deserves careful reading. Fyodor Dostoevsky, *The Brothers Karamazov*, trans. Constance Garnett (New York: Norton, 1976), Book Five, "Pro and Contra," chaps. 3–5. The quote from Alyosha is on p. 226.

32. Isaiah 55:8–9 KJV reads: "For my thoughts are not your thoughts, neither are your ways my ways, saith the Lord. For as the heavens are higher than the earth, so are my ways higher than your ways, and my thoughts than your thoughts." However, in light of the overall teachings of ecumenical orthodox Christianity, this passage is not best interpreted as meaning that God's purposes are radically alien to anything we could understand, or that divine moral standards are completely discontinuous with human standards.

33. John Stuart Mill, selection from *An Examination of Sir William Hamilton's Philosophy* included as an appendix in Richard Taylor, ed., *Theism,* (New York: The Liberal Arts Press, 1957), pp. 89–96.

34. H. J. McCloskey, "God and Evil," *Philosophical Quarterly* 10, no. 39 (1960): 97–114.

35. Richard Swinburne, "Natural Evil," *American Philosophical Quarterly* 15, no. 4 (October 1978): 295–301. Also see Bruce Reichenbach, *Evil and a Good God* (New York: Fordham University Press, 1982), chap. 5.

36. Reichenbach, *Evil,* chap. 4.

37. See, for example, Anthony Flew, "Divine Omnipotence and Human Freedom," in *New Essays in Philosophical Theology,* ed. A. Flew and A. MacIntyre (New York: Macmillan, 1955), pp. 144–69. Also see Flew, "Compatibilism, Free Will and God." *Philosophy* 48 (July 1973): 231–44.

38. Augustine, *Enchiridion,* i, 8, 7.

39. Augustine, *City of God,* xii, 1, 6.

40. Augustine, *Confessions, City of God, Enchiridion.*

41. Augustine, *On Free Will,* III, xvii, 49.

42. For the specific way in which John Hick works out this type of Irenaean theodicy, see his *Evil,* pts. 3 and 4.

43. G. Stanley Kane, "The Failure of Soul-Making Theodicy," *International Journal for Philosophy of Religion* 6 (1975): 1–22.

44. David Ray Griffin, *God, Power, and Evil* (Philadelphia: Westminster, 1976), p. 280.

45. Alfred North Whitehead, *Religion in the Making* (New York: Macmillan, 1926), p. 98; also see his *Process and Reality* (New York: Macmillan, 1929), pp. 524–5.

46. We should note that there have been attempts by some process philosophers to provide a process account of personal immortality, life after death. See the discussion of this in David Ray Griffin, *Evil Revisited* (Albany: SUNY Press, 1991), pp. 34–40.

47. See the full-scale discussion of process theodicy in Michael Peterson, "God and Evil in Process Theodicy," in *Process Theology*, ed. Ronald Nash (Grand Rapids, Mich.: Baker Book House, 1987), pp. 121–39.

48. Nancy Frankenberry, "Some Problems in Process Theodicy," *Religious Studies* 17 (1981): 181–4.

49. Marilyn Adams, *Horrendous Evils and the Goodness of God* (Ithaca, N.Y.: Cornell University Press, 1999).

SUGGESTED READING

Adams, Marilyn. *Horrendous Evils and the Goodness of God*. Ithaca, N.Y.: Cornell University Press.

Basinger, David. *The Case for Free Will Theism*. Downers Grove, Ill.: InterVarsity Press, 1996.

Drange, Theodore. *Nonbelief and Evil*. Buffalo, N.Y.: Prometheus Books, 1998.

Griffin, David Ray. *God, Power, and Evil: A Process Theodicy*. Philadelphia: Westminster Press, 1976.

———— *Evil Revisited: Responses and Reconsiderations*. Albany: SUNY Press, 1991.

Hasker, William. "The Necessity of Gratuitous Evil." *Faith and Philosophy* 9, no. 1 (1992): 23–44.

Howard-Snyder, Daniel. *The Evidential Argument from Evil*. Bloomington, Ind.: Indiana University Press, 1996.

Larrimore, Mark, ed. *The Problem of Evil: A Reader*. Oxford: Blackwell, 2001.

Mackie, J. L. *The Miracle of Theism*. Oxford: Clarendon Press, 1982.

Madden, Edward, and Peter Hare. *Evil and the Concept of God*. Springfield, Ill.: Charles C. Thomas, 1968.

Martin, Michael. *Atheism: A Philosophical Justification*. Philadelphia: Temple University Press, 1990.

O'Connor, David. *God and Inscrutable Evil: In Defense of Theism and Atheism*. Lanham, England: Rowman & Littlefield, 1998.

Peterson, Michael. *Evil and the Christian God*. Grand Rapids, Mich.: Baker Book House, 1982.

————. *The Problem of Evil: Selected Readings*. Notre Dame, Ind.: University of Notre Dame Press, 1992.

————. *God and Evil: An Introduction to the Issues*. Boulder, Colo.: Westview Press, 1998.

Plantinga, Alvin. *God, Freedom, and Evil*. Grand Rapids, Mich.: William B. Eerdmans, 1977.

Reichenbach, Bruce. *Evil and a Good God*. New York: Fordham University Press, 1982.

Rowe, William, ed. *God and the Problem of Evil*. Oxford: Blackwell, 2001.

Steward, Mel. *The Greater-Good Defense*. New York: St. Martin's, 1993.

Swinburne, Richard. *Providence and the Problem of Evil*. Oxford: Clarendon Press, 1998.

Tilley, Terrence. *The Evils of Theodicy*. Georgetown University Press, 1991.

CHAPTER 8 DIVINE ACTION: HOW DOES GOD RELATE TO THE WORLD?

In late May 1940, in the early days of World War II, a British and French force of over 300,000 men was encircled by German armies near Dunkirk, in northern France. The military balance heavily favored the Germans, and the situation of the Allied forces was desperate; it was expected that nearly all of them would be killed or captured. A flotilla of ships and boats (over 800 in all) was assembled, including many small commercial and private boats volunteered for the occasion. Unusually calm weather on the English Channel, together with heavy fog that inhibited dive bombing by the Luftwaffe, made possible the evacuation of the British and French forces with far fewer casualties than might have been expected. Many persons at that time, believing that the Allied cause was just and that God desired an Allied victory in the war, interpreted these events in terms of divine providence: *God had acted* in providing the unusual weather conditions that made the evacuation possible.

God's action in the world is a central component in all of the monotheistic faiths. The most crucial events for Judaism are those surrounding the Exodus: God's leading Israel out of Egypt and into the promised land through Moses' leadership. The central events of Christianity are the life, death, and resurrection of Jesus Christ. Key events for Islam include the Hegira of Mohammed from Mecca to Medina and the giving of the Koran to Mohammed by the angel Gabriel. Events such as these are of intense interest and concern to believers in these faith traditions.

These particular "acts of God" (as they are believed to be) are perhaps best approached through the scriptures and theologies of their respective faiths. But there are more general questions concerning divine action in the world that lend themselves to philosophical treatment. Note first of all that divine action becomes a serious possibility only if God is conceived as *personal*, in the sense discussed in chapter 4. An impersonal, pantheistic deity may be the power behind *everything* that happens but cannot be the doer of *particular* actions. In order to act in the world God must be *aware* of specific events and circumstances. God must also have an *interest* in such matters; God must *care* what goes on in the world. Furthermore, God must have some power to *influence or affect* the course of events: an "act of God" must be something that would not have occurred had not God been involved in the event in a special way.

To say this, however, leaves a great many questions about divine action unanswered. There are different ways in which such action may be considered, depending on several variables. The most important variables are, first of all, divine *power*: what sort of power does God exercise in the world? Second, there is human *freedom*: assuming that human beings (and perhaps some other creatures) have been gifted with *free will*, how is this freedom to be understood? Finally, there is divine *knowledge*: precisely what sort of knowledge of the world should be ascribed to God? All of these questions are intensely controversial, and in combination they lead to several different *theories of divine providence*—theories that spell out how God acts in overseeing and caring for the world he has created. These theories are discussed in subsequent sections of this chapter.

These questions about divine action are not just of theoretical interest. On the contrary, they have important implications for the religious life and for questions about which many people care deeply—that, of course, is why they are so controversial. As we set out the various views, we shall point out in particular their implications for two topics. One topic is the problem of evil, discussed in the previous chapter. One's views concerning divine action affect very directly one's response to this problem, and help to determine which of the approaches suggested in chapter 7 is most viable. Another topic, of great interest to many believers, is prayer. Prayer is universally acknowledged to be a central element in the religious life, but it also raises many questions. What is the point of praying when God already knows everything we could possibly tell him? Can we possibly suppose that our prayers can somehow induce God to do something he might otherwise not have done? What is really going on when we offer our prayers to God? These questions, and others, lend special importance to the topic of this chapter.

WHAT KIND OF POWER DOES GOD EXERCISE?

All of the major monotheistic religions have traditionally held that God is omnipotent in the sense defined in chapter 3: God can do anything that is logically possible and consistent with God's perfect nature. Power that is this extensive allows for a great many ways in which God could act so as to bring about a desired result in human history. God's *initial creation* of the world is important in setting up the many and varied possibilities for things God desires to bring about later on. God is able to *prearrange circumstances* in such a way that things subsequently come about in a "purely natural" way, yet as intended by God. God could also prearrange circumstances so as to influence a particular human being in some special way—one might, for instance, be struck by a particularly marvelous sunrise, and come thereby to see something of the greatness and beauty of God himself. God can also influence human persons directly, either overtly (a voice speaking out of a burning bush), or by dreams and visions, or secretly, without the person herself being aware of it. Omnipotence also means that God can perform miracles; he can cause things to occur in the world that are beyond the ordinary powers of the natural things the world contains. (The topic of miracles is addressed in chapter 10.) Of course, the fact that God *could* act in certain ways to bring about his purposes does not ensure that God *does in fact* act in those ways. Nevertheless, it should be clear that omnipotent power opens up a great many different ways in which God is able to bring about things he desires to have happen.

There is, however, one prominent view that does not see God as having the extensive range of powers discussed earlier. We are referring, of course, to *process theism*, which has already been introduced in chapters 4 and 7. Process theism's account of divine power is an integral part of its overall system of philosophy, which is too complex to expound here. But two ideas are especially important in this regard. First, *all* finite entities, not only human beings, are endowed with a degree of freedom.[1] The freedom is greater and more significant the "higher" and more complex the entity—freedom for a human means more than freedom for a mouse, and the freedom of a mouse is greater than that of a single-celled organism—but freedom and creativity exist at every level; there is no true determinism anywhere in nature. The second idea is this: God's role in the world is to present constantly, to every entity, the "initial aim" that represents the best that this entity, at this moment, can be and become. The initial aim represents, so to speak, God's "ideal will" for that entity at that moment. But the decision as to what that entity shall *actually* be and become—the "subjective aim," as it is called—is made by the entity itself; once having presented the initial aim, God has no further role in the decision. This kind of exercise of divine power is summed up in the phrase "God always persuades, but never coerces." It is important to notice, furthermore, that this limitation on God's power is not the result of a divine choice. It is not that God has in any way *decided* not to intervene unilaterally in earthly affairs; God *cannot* do this.

Process theists claim several advantages for their view, as compared with more traditional versions of theism. It overcomes the opposition between *natural* and *supernatural*, which has become problematic for many in the modern world. God's action, in providing the "initial aim" for each finite entity, is not an "intrusion from outside" into the natural order. Rather, that order needs and depends on God's constant "lure toward the best" in order to fulfill its own potential. Furthermore, in portraying God as leading us through sympathy and persuasion, process theism models the divine-human relationship on the best of human interpersonal relationships, rather than on relationships marked by power and domination. On the process theist account, prayer becomes primarily a spiritual exercise by which one seeks to become conformed to the divine purposes for oneself and for the world.

One cannot "move God" to do more than God would otherwise do: God is always supplying the best possible "initial aim" for each entity, and beyond that there is nothing more God can do. But if in prayer one becomes changed so that one's thoughts, desires, and purposes accord more closely with the divine will, then the "initial aim" in the subsequent stages of one's own life may be different than it would otherwise be: the closer we are to God's purposes for the world, the greater the possibilities for good that open up in our lives. It is in this sense, then, that "prayer changes things."

One of the most important advantages of process theism concerns the problem of evil. Remember that God's power is limited always to persuasion. This means that, if some person resists and rebels against the divine persuasion, there is literally nothing God can do about it. Therefore, since there is nothing more God can do to prevent evil and suffering, there is also no remaining question as to why he does *not* do more. This does not mean, however, that process theism has no problem of evil at all. God bears a considerable amount of responsibility for the *overall character* of the world, since it is his "lure" that has prompted the development of the sorts of creatures it contains—creatures capable of experiencing great joy, but also of both suffering and inflicting great sorrow. If someone were to say that, all things considered, it simply is not worth the cost for the world to contain beings with the great powers for harm and destruction that are possessed by humans, the process theist would have to acknowledge that it is God who has guided the evolutionary process in such a way that beings like us are produced.[2] But God's responsibility for *particular instances* of evil is arguably less than for competing views. (For more on this topic, see the discussion of process theodicy in chapter 7.)

In spite of these apparent benefits, process theism has been subjected to much criticism. Most of this criticism centers on the curtailment of divine power in this view, as compared with all versions of traditional theism. Granted that the exercise of "persuasive power" by God is in many situations highly beneficial, would not God be still greater, and more perfect, if God were also able to unilaterally control aspects of the world on occasion? This limitation on divine power seems clearly incompatible with the core traditions of the major theistic religions, all of which ascribe to God much more extensive powers than process theism allows for. Within traditional theism God can and will guarantee an ultimate triumph of goodness in the world. But within process theism there can be no such guarantee. God is obligated to do all that God is capable of doing, and process theists believe that infinite divine love, working persuasively over a sufficiently long time, can produce great things. There can, however, be no real assurance that things will ever be significantly better than they are at present.

WHAT KIND OF FREEDOM HAS GOD GIVEN?

The different varieties of traditional theism agree with each other, and against process theism, that God is omnipotent in the sense that has been defined in chapter 4. Furthermore, they will generally assent to the proposition that God, in creating human beings, has endowed them with freedom, or "free will." But there are importantly different ways in which this freedom can be understood. According to the *compatibilist* conception, a human action is "free" if the following requirements are met: (1) the immediate cause of the action is a desire, wish, or intention internal to the agent; (2) there is no external event or circumstance that compels the action to be performed; and (3) the agent could have acted differently, if she had chosen to. If these criteria are satisfied, the action comes, as we might say, "from within"; it cannot rightly be said that the agent is *forced* to perform it. This is "compatibilist" free will, because it holds that free will is compatible with deterministic causation, so long as the three conditions given are satisfied.

A good many philosophers and theologians, however, are not satisfied with this way of understanding free will, because they do not think this sort of freedom is sufficient to make humans morally responsible for their actions. These philosophers and theologians insist, on the contrary, that in order for an action to be truly free it must have been *really possible*, with *all the antecedent conditions remaining exactly the same*, for the agent to have chosen differently. One philosopher has expressed this *libertarian* view of free will by saying that, when a person is free with respect to performing an action, she "has it in her power to choose to perform A or choose not to perform A. *Both A and not A could actually occur*; which *will* actually occur has *not yet been determined*."[3]

Process theists affirm libertarian free will, and so do proponents of the views to be discussed later in this chapter. But there is an important strand of thought in the theistic traditions that affirms instead compatibilist free will, holding that we act "freely" whenever we are not hindered from doing what we most want, in the circumstances, to do. This is so *even if the action in question was causally determined and, in that sense, could not have been otherwise.* In view of this, these theists are able to hold both that human beings are free in most of their actions, and also that *all human actions happen as they do because they have been efficaciously decreed by God, and could not have happened in any other way.* In view of this latter affirmation, their view is termed *theological determinism*; it is sometimes also called "Calvinism," because of its association with John Calvin, the Protestant reformer.[4]

Calvinists, or theological determinists, affirm in the strongest possible terms the *sovereignty of God*: it is God alone, through his sovereign decrees, who has determined everything that has ever happened or that ever will happen. Calvinists hold that only by affirming such a strong sense of sovereignty can the majesty and greatness of God be sufficiently affirmed; any view that allows some decisions about the course of events to be made by human persons and not by God deprives God of his glory and is demeaning to him.[5] Furthermore, Calvinists insist that only if God in this way directly controls all things can we place in him the *absolute trust* that is essential to a proper religious life. Prayer, in the context of theological determinism, is best seen as an expression of *submission to the will of God.* There can be no thought that in prayer human beings could persuade God to do something he was not already planning and intending to do. After all, God made his plans long before we ever decided to pray, and those plans will be fulfilled precisely, down to the smallest detail. It may be, however, that sometimes God, desiring and intending to do a certain thing, also moves human worshipers to *ask* him, in prayer, to do that very thing—and thus, in a sense, he acts "in answer to prayer." But the true worshiper's thought, in offering her prayers, must always be "Thy will be done."

Theological determinism has some impressive support, but it has also attracted heavy criticism. It is sometimes thought that such sovereignty is incompatible with human freedom, but Calvinists rightly point out that there is no such incompatibility *if the compatibilist definition of freedom is accepted.* More significantly, opponents ask whether it does not deprive our lives of much of their significance, if in everything we do we are merely "following the script" set out in the divine decrees. Are we not, in fact, in the role of puppets being manipulated by a puppet master? Can there really be meaningful personal relationships between humans and God, when one party in the relationship exercises complete, unilateral control over the other? How can God place any real value on the love that human beings express toward him, when that love is simply the inescapable result of God's decree that those humans shall love him? Feminist theologians criticize views of this sort as interpreting God exclusively in "masculine" terms of power and authority, while ignoring the "feminine" values of relationship and nurture.

The objections, however, become most intense when the problem of evil is addressed. This problem, as we have seen, is significant for all varieties of traditional theism, but critics argue that it is especially severe for theological determinism. As one leading Calvinist has forthrightly said, this view "does not, in the final analysis, attribute certain evils to the human will and certain others to natural causes; rather, all are finally attributed to the divine reason and will."[6] But this immediately invites the question, *why* would God deliberately create a world containing so much evil and suffering, when nothing whatever prevented him from creating a world without these things? Perhaps the most hopeful strategy for a reply lies in the approach that "all is well within the world from God's perspective," discussed in the previous chapter. Such an approach holds that *each and every evil state of affairs is a necessary condition of a greater good that God could not obtain without the evil in question.* Such an assertion, however, may well be met with incredulity, given the enormity of some of the evils that actually exist. Furthermore, it may be asked, if "all is well" and *everything in this world is exactly as God wishes for it to be,* what are we to make of the *anger of God against sin* that is so strongly emphasized in the Bible as well as in the Koran? How can God be *both* completely pleased that things are going exactly as he wishes, and angry and disappointed at some of the very events he has planned and set in motion?

Clearly, these questions do not admit of easy answers. When pressed, theological determinists will often acknowledge that the relationship between God and evil is inscrutable—that we humans do not, and in fact cannot, comprehend the way such issues are resolved in the mystery of the divine will. But, they add, this in no way excuses us for denying the majesty and sovereignty of God in our misguided attempts to comprehend these mysteries in a way that is intelligible to our limited human minds.

DOES GOD KNOW WHAT WOULD HAVE HAPPENED?

The remaining views concerning divine action agree with each other in affirming both divine omnipotence and libertarian free will. This means that the proponents of these views agree that, to the extent that God grants freedom to human beings, he *cannot* unilaterally control their decision making. He can either grant humans freedom or control their decision making, but he cannot simultaneously do both, as is believed possible by theological determinists.

These views differ, however, concerning the nature of *God's knowledge*, and because of this they have different understandings of God's action in the world. Robert M. Adams (b. 1937) highlights a key issue as follows:

> "If President Kennedy had not been shot, would he have bombed North Vietnam? God only knows. Or does he? Does even he know what Kennedy would have done?"[7]

Here Adams asks us to imagine a situation in which President John F. Kennedy escaped the assassin's bullet and lived to face the difficult choices posed by the escalating war in Vietnam. Lyndon B. Johnson, Kennedy's successor, did choose to bomb North Vietnam, with fateful consequences. Would Kennedy, if he had survived, have made the same choice? Adams's real concern, however, is not about Kennedy's decision as such. Rather, he asks whether *God knows,* with respect to this decision that was never actually made, how Kennedy *would have made* it. Not how Kennedy *might* have made the decision, or what he would have been *most likely* to do, had the situation arisen, but how he *definitely would have decided.* Does God know *that*?

If your answer to this question is affirmative, you have aligned yourself with the theory of divine *middle knowledge,*[8] also termed *Molinism* for the Jesuit theologian Luis de Molina (1535–1600), who originated the theory. According to Molinism, this truth concerning Kennedy is only one of a vast array of similar propositions God knows, not just about Kennedy but about each one of us. God knows, concerning each created free person, how that person *would have chosen* in any possible situation of libertarian free choice in which that person might find herself, *even if the choice is never actually made at all.* Indeed, God knows concerning each *possible person,*[9] each person God *might have created* but did not, what *that* person would have done in any possible situation of free choice with which the person might have been confronted. These propositions have come to be known as "counterfactuals of freedom," because they describe how a given person would *freely* choose under contrary-to-fact circumstances.[10]

You may ask, what does all this knowledge God is supposed to possess have to do with anything of importance? A great deal, actually. Middle knowledge, if God indeed possesses it, makes possible a remarkable way in which God can exercise providential control over the course of events. Suppose, for instance, God is deliberating over whether or not to create you—trying to decide whether you shall be one of the inhabitants of his world or not. Will your presence in the world be on balance a good thing, or not? Clearly, the answer to this will depend in part on the *free decisions* you will make during your lifetime. These decisions, furthermore, are not wholly predictable on the basis of your genetic makeup, environmental circumstances, and the like. (Not, at least, if you are *free* in the libertarian sense of that word.) It begins to look, therefore, as though God is *taking a risk* in creating you. If you decide, in many or most cases, to act in a way that aligns with God's purposes, his decision to create you will turn out well, but if you do not act in such a way, his decision may not turn out well.

Given middle knowledge, however, this element of risk is completely eliminated. In considering whether or not to create you, God can "play over" in his mind all the possible scenarios for your future life,[11] and he will *know with certainty* what you would do in each possible situation. He does not, of course, *control* your decisions; those decisions are the decisions you would *freely choose* to make. Furthermore, God has no choice about the "counterfactuals of freedom" that are true of you; they are entirely beyond his control. But given those counterfactuals, and supposing that he does decide to create you, God can select, with full confidence, the *best* life-plan for you, the one that best suits his overall plan for the world. Of course, it really is not that simple. For your life-plan needs to interlock with all the other life-plans of people who will come into contact with you and will affect and be affected by you. Ultimately, what God must attend to is the scenario for *the entire universe;* he must decide which things and persons to create, how they are to be arranged, and so on, so as to obtain the *best overall result* from his creative endeavors. When he makes his decision, he can count on the plan's being carried out exactly as intended, *even though many elements of the plan depend on the libertarian free choices of his creatures.*

This brings us to what Molinists see as the greatest advantage of their view. Middle knowledge allows God to have a very high degree of control over what goes on in the world, even though that world contains free persons whose actions are not causally determined by God or by anything else outside themselves. As God is planning his world, the choices of creatures are not "free variables" that can make the plan turn out well or badly, depending on how the choices are made. Rather the choices are *incorporated into the plan itself,* and God can be absolutely confident that it will be carried out exactly as intended; there is no risk or uncertainty in the situation at all.[12]

Because of its embrace of libertarian freedom, Molinism can say (as Calvinism really cannot) that God does some things because they are prayed for, and refrains from doing other things because they are not prayed for. Indeed, Molinism even supports the view that God grants certain blessings because they *will be* prayed for in the future. Correspondingly, it is perfectly meaningful and sensible to "pray for something to have happened," to pray for a favorable outcome of some event that *we know has already been decided,* provided that we do not yet know *how* it has been decided. (Thus, some have speculated that we still ought to pray for the salvation of Judas Iscariot, the betrayer of Jesus.) God, through his middle knowledge, knows that a particular person *would pray* for the blessing in question if placed in certain circumstances. He also knows that those circumstances will in fact obtain, and that the prayer will in fact be offered. And because of the prayer (which has yet to be made), he decides to grant the blessing![13]

In dealing with the problem of evil, it seems plausible that Molinists will affirm the same reply we earlier attributed to Calvinists—namely, that *each and every evil state of affairs is a necessary condition of a greater good that God could not obtain without the evil in question.* After all, why would God deliberately incorporate some evil state of affairs into his world, when he could avoid it with no corresponding loss? Furthermore, this proposition seems somewhat more plausible coming from the Molinist than it did from the Calvinist. For one thing, one of the good things God wishes to preserve in his world is the libertarian freedom of his creatures, and this is a good that plays no part in the Calvinistic scheme. Furthermore, according to Molinism God does not start with a "clean slate" in planning the world, as he does with Calvinism. Instead, there are all of these counterfactuals of freedom—propositions over which God has no control, but which have a great deal to do with the outcome of any choices God might make about what sort of world to create. Perhaps God would have preferred a world in which, for instance, Osama bin Laden became an investment banker rather than an international terrorist. But given the counterfactuals that are true of bin Laden, it simply was not in God's power to place him in the situations in which he actually found himself and have his life turn out differently than it did—and so, presumably, in a great many other cases as well.

Nevertheless, the claim that "every evil leads to a greater good" can be hard to defend, as the discussion in the previous chapter has shown. When we think of some truly horrendous evil, such as the Holocaust, we are moved to ask, "What good can *possibly* have come from this, that would justify the enormous evil and suffering involved?" To be sure, it might be that the Holocaust was permitted because in its absence there would have been some still greater evil. But it seems beyond the power of our imaginations to comprehend what this even greater evil might have been. We have to keep in mind that, according to Molinism, God has *deliberately planned* each instance of evil that actually occurs—for good reason, we are told, but sometimes it is not easy to find this assurance very comforting. As Thomas Flint (b. 1954) has stated, "if Judas sins, it is because God knowingly put him in a set of circumstances in which he would sin, and knowingly refrained from putting him in a set of circumstances in which he would act virtuously."[14] A difficult thought indeed!

It should not come as a surprise, at this point, that Molinism also has been vigorously attacked. On the one hand, Calvinists and other theological determinists sharply criticize Molinism for compromising divine sovereignty by asserting that God's choice of what sort of world to create is limited by counterfactuals of freedom over which God has no control. Recently, however, the most active criticism has come from non-Molinist libertarians. They point to the problem of evil, as noted in this section, and they assert that God's involvement, on the Molinist view, in planning specific instances of evil is far too intimate for this view to be acceptable. It has also been argued that Molinism, like Calvinism, undermines the genuinely personal character of a believer's relationship with God. In knowing our counterfactuals, God knows exactly "what buttons to push" to elicit a desired result from us—indeed, God exerts over us a control that is only slightly less complete than is the case for Calvinism.[15] Can God be sincere in desiring us to avoid sin when, as Flint says, he deliberately places us in circumstances in which he knows that we will sin? Can he be sincere in urging persons to repent when he knows with certainty that they will not repent?[16]

Another important line of criticism concerns the metaphysical presuppositions of this theory. Many critics urge that the truths God is supposed to know—the true counterfactuals of freedom—simply do not exist to be known. Consider the case of Sue, a college student who decides to sleep in one morning instead of going to breakfast at the dining commons. Then ask yourself, if Sue had gone to breakfast, would she have chosen grape juice or orange juice? On the mornings she does go to breakfast, she selects each with about equal frequency. We assume that she possesses libertarian free will, so given *exactly the same circumstances*, it is entirely possible for her to select either kind of juice. We might ask, what possible fact can there be about the world that makes it the case that she would take grape juice rather than orange juice? No answer seems to be possible. Thus (the critics insist), what is true of Sue is that, if she had gone to breakfast, she *might* have taken grape juice and she *might* have taken orange juice, but it is not true either that she *would definitely* have taken grape juice or that she *would definitely* have taken orange juice.[17] Since, on this view, there is no truth about what Sue *would do*, it follows also that God *does not know* what she would do, because God knows only those things that are in fact true.

The arguments concerning the truth of counterfactuals of freedom have become extremely complex and technical, and cannot be pursued further here. Numbers of philosophers hold strong views on each side of the question, and agreement does not seem likely in the foreseeable future.

DOES GOD KNOW THE ACTUAL FUTURE?

Many theists who are libertarians hold the view that *God knows the actual future in its entirety*. This has come to be known as the theory of *simple foreknowledge*—"simple" because such foreknowledge does not involve the additional complications of middle knowledge. By the same token, this view avoids the perplexing questions discussed in the previous section concerning the existence of true counterfactuals of freedom. It holds that God's knowledge comprises all actual future events, and that he knows what free agents would *probably* do under various counterfactual scenarios, while admitting that there may be nothing that they *would definitely* do under those circumstances.

So far, perhaps, so good, but abandoning middle knowledge does not enable this view to escape from controversy. There are arguments, going far back in history, which claim to establish that complete and certain divine foreknowledge is *incompatible* with libertarian free will for human beings. Here is an example of such an argument, using as an example a certain Clarence, known to be addicted to cheese omelets. Will Clarence have a cheese omelet for breakfast tomorrow morning, or won't he? The argument proceeds as follows:

1. It is now true that Clarence will have a cheese omelet for breakfast tomorrow. (Premise)

2. It is impossible that God should at any time believe what is false, or fail to believe anything which is true. (Premise: divine omniscience)

3. God has always believed that Clarence will have a cheese omelet tomorrow. (From 1,2)

4. If God has always believed a certain thing, it is not in anyone's power to bring it about that God has not always believed that thing. (Premise: the unalterability of the past)

5. Therefore, it is not in Clarence's power to bring it about that God has not always believed that he would have a cheese omelet for breakfast. (From 3,4)

6. It is not possible for it to be true both that God has always believed that Clarence would have a cheese omelet for breakfast, and that he does not in fact have one. (From 2)

7. Therefore, it is not in Clarence's power to refrain from having a cheese omelet for breakfast tomorrow. (From 5,6) So Clarence's eating the omelet tomorrow is not an act of free choice.[18]

It will be noted that step 2 consists of a definition of divine omniscience *without* the stipulation about what it is logically possible for God to know; thus, the conclusion is that Clarence does *not* have free choice about what to eat for breakfast. If we find the conclusion unacceptable (that is, if we believe that human beings do possess libertarian free will), then one possible response would be to adopt a definition of omniscience *including* the requirement of logical possibility, such as the one adopted in chapter 4. We could then conclude that the truth about Clarence's breakfast is one of the things it is logically impossible for God to know.

Many philosophers, however, are not satisfied with such a response; they wish to maintain both that human beings are free in the libertarian sense and that God has comprehensive knowledge of what such persons will freely choose to do. In order to do this, some way must be found to avoid the conclusion of the argument given in the example about Clarence. One possible way to do this is to adopt the view discussed in chapter 4, according to which God is timeless rather than everlasting. The argument for the incompatibility of freedom and foreknowledge relies on the fact that God, in the past, *already has known* what each of us will do in the future. But if God is timelessly eternal, this is not true. It is not that God *knew,* in the past, what we would do; rather, God timelessly *knows* this, and he knows it as a present reality, for all times are present to him. As Thomas Aquinas said: "He who goes along the road does not see those who come after him; whereas he who sees the whole road from a height sees at once all those traveling on it."[19] The "height," of course, is God's eternity, from which he sees at once the whole "road" of time, which we temporal travelers come to know only bit by bit as we make our way along it. Now the fact that some action is known in the present, as it occurs, has no tendency to show that the action is not done freely. No more, then, should the fact that God in *his* present knows eternally what we do, detract from the freedom of the action.

As one might expect, the success of this solution is controversial. If Clarence is genuinely *free* in deciding about the omelet, then it must be *really possible* for him to make the opposite decision and refrain from eating the omelet. But, we are assuming, God timelessly *knows* that Clarence will eat the omelet. If nevertheless Clarence is free in eating it, the following must be true:

> It is often the case that God timelessly knows a certain thing, but it is in someone's power, right now, to bring it about that God does not timelessly know that thing.

This would seem to be a rather remarkable power for us all to have!

Many other answers to the argument have been devised, but one of the most popular is based on the distinction between *hard and soft facts.* Consider, then, the following statement:

(GWB) The 43d President of the United States was born in Texas in 1946.

This statement is undeniably true; furthermore, it concerns an event that occurred in the past, specifically in 1946. Anyone who uttered this statement in 1960 would have made a true statement. Nevertheless, up until the inauguration of President George W. Bush it was still possible for someone to make this statement false, by preventing his election and inauguration to the office. So from 1946 until 2001 the proposition (GWB) was a *soft fact* about the past—a true statement about the past such that it was still within someone's power to do something that would make the statement false. Since January of 2001, on the other hand, this has been a *hard fact* about the past; it is a true statement about the past which is such that no one, now, can have the power to make it false. But now consider:

(3) God has always believed that Clarence will have a cheese omelet tomorrow.

This fact, it is urged, is strikingly similar to the preceding fact concerning the birth of the President. Like that other fact, it is a true statement, and it is about the past. But it is also like that other fact in that, up until a certain time, it is in someone's power to do something that would make the statement false. For it is in Clarence's power to refrain from eating a cheese omelet tomorrow—and if he were to refrain, then God would not, at any time in the past, have believed that he would eat one. So it is in Clarence's power to do something such that, were he to do it, God would not have held the belief that he did hold. With regard to propositions of this sort, then,

(4) If God has always believed a certain thing, it is not in anyone's power to bring it about that God has not always believed that thing

is incorrect. It *is* in Clarence's power to do such a thing, in that (as already noted) it is in his power to do something such that, were he to do it, God would not have held the belief that he did hold. So premise (4) is false, and the argument fails to establish its conclusion.

It may occur to the reader, however, that the parallel between (GWB) and (3) breaks down at one point. In the case of (GWB), we have a proposition about a past event, to be sure, but one that is *described in terms of a future event*, namely the event of George W. Bush's becoming President. If on the other hand he had been prevented from becoming President—thus making (GWB) a false statement—this would not have involved any change at all in the actual events of the past. (At the time of his birth his mother, Barbara Bush, would not have noticed the difference at all!) But in the case of (3), what would need to be different is something that *actually occurred in the past,* namely, God's having been in a particular "state of mind," a state described by saying he believed Clarence would eat a cheese omelet. Many philosophers would argue that, in view of this difference, (3) should be classified as a *hard fact*—one which, unlike (GWB), cannot be made false at any time in the future. Others, however, maintain that, in spite of this difference, (3) remains a "soft fact" until breakfast time. The debate over this issue, like that over the counterfactuals of freedom, has become extremely complex, and cannot be pursued further here.

But suppose the simple foreknowledge theory survives this argument. There remains another consideration, one that up until now seems to be somewhat less controversial. It appears that the knowledge of the future attributed to God by simple foreknowledge is of *no use whatsoever* in God's providential governance of the world. That is to say, this knowledge does not enable God to do anything different, or better, than he is able to do given "only" comprehensive knowledge of the past and present. To see this, consider God as he is deciding, in the year 2000, what he shall do, over the next 20 years, in governing the world.[20] Suppose that, in doing this, he "looks ahead" to the world as it is in 2020. Suppose, further, that he sees something in the world of 2020 he disapproves of—something he would wish to have different. Can we suppose, then, that God takes some action in 2000 so as to avoid the undesired outcome in 2020? A little reflection shows this thought to be incoherent. For the world of 2020, as he sees it in 2000, is by hypothesis the *actual* world of 2020, and to suppose that God does something in 2000 with the result that the world he sees is *not* the actual world of 2020 is self-contradictory. The conclusion is clear: God must decide what he is going to do in 2000 *before* he "looks ahead" to see how things have come out in 2020. But this means, that God's foreknowledge *cannot be used* to decide upon his actions in governing the world. Simple foreknowledge, if it exists, is useless. (Note that a similar argument will apply to the knowledge of the future possessed by a timeless God, if God is timeless. Timeless knowledge of the future also will not enable God to do anything more in governing the world than if God knew only the past and present.)

This result does not necessarily do away with the theory of simple foreknowledge. Some may feel that it is good for God to *have* this knowledge, even if the knowledge is not of use to God in his providential governance. It may be that some plausible answer to the argument will be proposed, though none has surfaced as yet. But then, the argument itself is of relatively recent provenance; it is almost certain that more remains to be said on the topic.

WHAT IF THE FUTURE IS TRULY OPEN?

The final view to be considered, known as "open theism" or "the openness of God," rejects both middle knowledge and simple foreknowledge. In the light of the arguments that have been given, the view accepts that there are some aspects of the future that cannot be known with certainty by anyone, including God. This is not because of any deficiency in God's knowledge, but because it is the *inherent nature* of the future to be indefinite. God knows with certainty those aspects of the future that are already fixed and certain, and he knows as indefinite those aspects of the future that are, as of now, open and indefinite. (It would hardly be a perfection in God's knowledge to "know" as certain and definite something that is in fact uncertain and indefinite!)

God as conceived by open theism is both omnipotent, able to perform any action whose performance by him is logically possible, and omniscient, in that he knows everything that is inherently capable of being known. Perhaps the most striking thing about this conception, however, is the *relational* nature of God, which is able to emerge here as in none of the other views. We have seen how the heavy emphasis on control and domination in Calvinism, and to a lesser extent in Molinism, tends to undermine the *personal relationships* between God and his worshipers—relationships which, nevertheless, both of these views typically wish to affirm. Open theism is better placed to emphasize the relational and nurturing aspect of God, as urged by feminist theologians among others. Open theism sees God as having brought about a creation that is *genuinely different* from God himself, and has granted it a significant, though limited, degree of *freedom and autonomy*. This freedom and autonomy are present to some extent even in the physical creation (as seen in the indeterminacy revealed by quantum mechanics), but are most evident in the freedom bestowed on rational creatures, in particular human beings. God desires that his creatures should utilize this freedom to develop their full potential, and especially to respond to him in love and worship. Freedom, furthermore, is essential for this: love and adoration given automatically, of necessity, would be of no more value than the applause of an audience created out of electronic bits by a video animator. Because the creatures really exist and decide their lives in a degree of independence from God (though all the while depending on him for their very existence), God can be delighted or else deeply disappointed by their responses, just as he is portrayed in the scriptures of the theistic religions. Calvinism, on the other hand (and to a lesser extent Molinism) is strongly inclined to embrace the doctrine of *divine impassibility*, which means that God in the end either *does not care* what happens in his creation, or else is *completely delighted* with it regardless of the enormous amount of sin, evil, and suffering that occur.

Open theism seems to some of its adherents to grant to the practice of prayer an importance unequaled by any of the other views. This view is fully able to recognize the importance of prayer in changing the individual's orientation, enabling spiritual development, and the like. But the sense of the future as genuinely open lends a significance to *petitionary prayer*—asking God for things to happen—that the other views cannot easily match. To be sure, what is prayed for must itself be in harmony with God's purposes; it cannot be supposed that God will honor unworthy requests. But there may well be some things—religious teachings imply that there are—that God would like to bestow upon his people, but will do so only in response to their requests. In a real relationship, asking makes a difference.

Open theism is also in a favorable position, compared with other varieties of traditional theism, in dealing with the problem of evil. This view does not hold, with Calvinism, that God unilaterally controls all events and has sovereignly decreed the evils of this world because he prefers a world containing these evils to any that does not. Nor does it hold, with Molinism, that God has deliberately chosen and planned each instance of evil that occurs. According to open theism, God is genuinely grieved, angry, and disappointed at much that takes place, yet is able to overcome evil in order to fulfill his ultimate purposes. Not everything that happens is as God wishes it; God has taken a risk in creating free persons. But as Thomas Oden (b. 1931) has stated, "If Eden is Plan A, and Eden does not work out, due to the self-determining volatility, frailty, and fallibility of human freedom, then God has a Plan B and a Plan C."[21] On this view, one need not hold that each and every instance of evil leads to some "greater good"; on the contrary, there are evils that are *not* desired or approved by God, and that make the world, on balance, less good than it would be without them. Yet God is able—through "Plan B" or "Plan C," if necessary—to overcome evil and to attain his ultimate purposes. It is thus arguable that open theism is in a better position than any other version of traditional theism to respond to this important problem.

Like the other views considered, open theism has met with opposition and criticism. Theological determinists are even more harshly critical of open theism than of Molinism and simple foreknowledge because it loosens further the absolute control by God they consider to be essential. Molinists sometimes claim that the divine risk taking postulated by open theism is morally intolerable: if God could not be guaranteed the precise outcome of his creative activity, he would not have created at all. (This has the consequence, possibly unintended, that the divine creation of the universe was a bad idea unless Molinism is true!) Open theists reply that God does not take risks for their own sake, but for the sake of the very great good that is made possible through God's generous act of creation. Another criticism is that open theism cannot account for *predictive prophecy*, in which a prophet is inspired by God to announce what will take place in the future. (It should be noted that, if the argument in the previous section is correct, this objection applies also to simple foreknowledge and to divine timeless knowledge.) Open theists reply that much prophecy is conditional; God states what will happen *if* human beings act in certain ways. Other prophecy is based on existing trends and tendencies in the world, while in still other cases God announces what God himself intends to bring about in ways that do not depend on the actions of human beings.

Process theists, on the other hand, criticize open theism because it retains the traditional doctrines of divine omnipotence and creation *ex nihilo*, which they have rejected. They believe that, because of these doctrines, open theism has serious difficulties with the problem of evil.[22]

Many of the criticisms are motivated by the departure of open theism from theological tradition. That there is such a departure, with respect to comprehensive divine foreknowledge, cannot be denied; how seriously this counts against the view is itself a theological question and cannot be pursued here.[23] Sometimes it is alleged that open theism, like process theism, is unable to guarantee the fulfillment of God's plan even in the most general respects. To this charge open theists reply that the power of God on their view is *exactly the same* as that postulated by Calvinism and Molinism, and this power is sufficient for God to be able to fulfill his purposes.

It may well be that in the end the viability of open theism depends on the success of the philosophical arguments against Molinism and simple foreknowledge. If there really are true counterfactuals of freedom, and if it is logically possible for these truths, as well as truths about the contingent future, to be known, then it is plausible that a God who is perfect in knowledge would know them.[24] If on the other hand these truths do not exist and/or are unknowable, the viable options, from among those considered here, are reduced to three: process theism, theological determinism, and open theism. In that three-way contest, many theistic believers will find open theism to be the most credible and attractive position to hold.

STUDY QUESTIONS

1. Does it seem to you to be important for religious faith that God is able to act in the world? Why or why not?

2. Are you aware of any events in which it seems to you that God has acted? If so, describe.

3. Is it an advantage or a disadvantage for religion to limit God's action to the exercise of "persuasive power," as is done by process theism?

4. Explain the difference between the libertarian conception of free will and the compatibilist conception.

5. What are the advantages and disadvantages of affirming that God determines everything that occurs in the world?

6. Does it seem plausible to you that there are truths about what persons would freely choose to do in circumstances that never actually arise (the "counterfactuals of freedom," as posited by Molinism)?

7. Would the high degree of control over human actions assumed by Molinism jeopardize a genuine personal relationship between human beings and God, as is suggested in the text?

8. If it should turn out that it is logically impossible for there to be both comprehensive divine knowledge of the future and genuine free will for human beings, which is more important?

9. What is your evaluation of the argument claiming that comprehensive divine foreknowledge is incompatible with libertarian free will for human beings? Does the argument based on "hard and soft facts" provide a sufficient answer?

10. Is it more important to see God as closely related to the world (as in open theism), or to see God as having tight control over events in the world, as in Calvinism and Molinism?

NOTES

1. The "entities" in view here are those items that possess some degree of inherent unity, as opposed to mere aggregates—molecules, cells, and organisms, but not stones or bodies of water.

2. On the assumptions of process thought, God *could not* have brought into existence beings with the positive potentials of human beings, but lacking the human capacity for evil. God could, however, have refrained from guiding the development of life in such a way that creatures with human-like potential would appear.

3. David Basinger, "Middle Knowledge and Classical Christian Thought," *Religious Studies* 22 (1986): 416.

4. Historically speaking, a better name for the view might be "Augustinianism," after Augustine of Hippo, who seems to have been the first to clearly formulate such a view. Thomas Aquinas is sometimes interpreted as a theological determinist, though this is in dispute. Theological determinism is characteristic of Sunni Muslims, and of their greatest theologian, Al-Ghazali. (Shiite Muslims, on the other hand, affirm libertarian free will.)

5. They sometimes say also that the *power of God* is lessened if libertarian freedom is accepted, but this is a mistake. The difference concerns how God has chosen to *exercise* his power—in particular, what sort of freedom he has bestowed on creatures—and not the power itself, which is *precisely the same* for theological determinists and their opponents.

6. Paul Helm, *The Providence of God* (Downers Grove, Ill: InterVarsity Press, 1994), p. 198.

7. Robert M. Adams, "Middle Knowledge and the Problem of Evil," in *The Virtue of Faith and Other Essays in Philosophical Theology,* ed. R. M. Adams (New York: Oxford University Press, 1987), p. 77.

8. So termed because God's knowledge of the "counterfactuals of freedom" (see later in this chapter) which are the primary content of his "middle knowledge" is in a sense intermediate between God's "natural knowledge" of all the necessary truths, and his "free knowledge" of truths that depend on God's own actions. The counterfactuals are logically contingent, yet outside of God's control.

9. Strictly speaking, these are truths about the *uninstantiated essences* of persons, not about the persons themselves, who by hypothesis do not exist.

10. Actually, the propositions in question also cover choices that are actually made. Because of this, the more correct term for them would be "subjunctive conditionals of freedom." But "counterfactuals of freedom" is the label that has stuck.

11. It is, of course, merely a manner of speaking when we describe God as taking an extended time to make up his mind on something. For God, the whole process is instantaneous. But no harm is done, in this case, by speaking anthropomorphically.

12. How pleased God is with the result will depend on the counterfactuals he had to work with in the creation situation. Conceivably, God might have found the counterfactuals that are actually true to be quite unfavorable to his creative purposes. It might be, then, that God settled on a world that (though it was one of the best available to him) was nevertheless just barely worth creating—only a little better than no world at all. Those who actually affirm Molinism, however, seem to take a much more optimistic view of the situation.

13. An amusing (though no doubt unintended) example of this is supplied by a television commercial. A fan is watching a live football game on a special type of set. Just as the kicker is approaching the ball to attempt a crucial field goal, the viewer jumps up, hits the "hold" button, and heads out the door. At a neighborhood church, he spends a number of minutes in fervent prayer. Then he returns to his set, hits the "play" button, and raises his arms in triumph as the ball sails through the goal posts. According to Molinism, it could very well be that the kick was successful because of the fan's prayer!

14. *Divine Providence,* p. 118.

15. The *range of control* is less complete for Molinism, because the variety of responses God can elicit from us is limited by the counterfactuals of freedom. The *security of control,* on the other hand, is exactly the same—God can be absolutely certain of our responding to any situation in exactly the way he has planned for us to respond.

16. William Wainwright, a philosopher who is himself inclined to accept Molinism, nevertheless writes, "Calvinism appears to imply that God is the author of sin and that His counsels, exhortations, and commands are sometimes deceptive. I have argued that [Jonathan] Edwards is correct in thinking that Arminianism has similar implications" ("Theological Determinism and the Problem of Evil: Are Arminians Any Better Off?" *International Journal for the Philosophy of Religion,* 50, nos. 1–3 [December 2001], p. 93). It should be noted that the "Arminians" mentioned here are assumed to believe in middle knowledge.

17. According to the branch of logic that deals with counterfactual propositions, "in circumstances C, agent A *might* do X" is the contradictory of "in circumstances C, agent A *would refrain* from doing X."

18. William Hasker, *God, Time, and Knowledge,* p. 69.

19. Thomas Aquinas, *Summa Theologiae,* trans. Fathers of the English Dominican Province, 2d ed. (London: Burnes, Oates and Washbourne, 1920), I, 14, 13, reply obj. 3.

20. As before, the description of God as making decisions in a temporal framework is merely an aid to the imagination, not to be taken literally.

21. Thomas C. Oden, *The Living God, Systematic Theology: Volume One* (San Francisco: Harper, 1987), p. 306. It should be noted that Oden is not an open theist, and has been quite critical of this view of God. But on this central point he is in agreement with open theism over against its alternatives.

22. For an argument that open theism is approximately on a par with process theism in this regard, see William Hasker, "The Problem of Evil in Process Theism and Classical Free Will Theism," *Process Studies* 29, no. 2 (Fall/Winter 2000): 194–208.

23. Some orthodox Christians see this departure from tradition as a strong reason to reject the view, while others view it as a relatively minor deviation from tradition that does not pose a serious problem. Included in the latter group are philosophers such as Peter Geach, J. R. Lucas, and Richard Swinburne, and theologians such as John Polkinghorne, Walter Brueggemann, and Jürgen Moltmann.

24. If it should turn out that it is possible for God to foreknow the decision of free agents, but that (as was argued in the last section) he is unable to use that knowledge, the resulting position would in practice be little different from open theism. It seems doubtful, however, whether this is a viable position to hold.

SUGGESTED READING

Beilby, James K., and Paul Rhodes Eddy, eds. *Divine Foreknowledge: Four Views*. Downers Grove, Ill.: InterVarsity Press, 2001.

Berkouwer, G. C. *The Providence of God*. Trans. L. B. Smedes. Grand Rapids, Mich.: William B. Eerdmans, 1952.

Cobb, John B., Jr., and Clark H. Pinnock, eds. *Searching for an Adequate God: A Dialogue between Process and Free Will Theists*. Grand Rapids, Mich.: William B. Eerdmans, 2000.

Fischer, John Martin, ed. *God, Foreknowledge, and Freedom*, Stanford, Calif.: Stanford University Press, 1989.

Flint, Thomas P. *Divine Providence: The Molinist Account*. Ithaca, N.Y.: Cornell University Press, 1998.

Griffin, David Ray. *God, Freedom, and Evil: A Process Theodicy*. Philadelphia: Westminster Press, 1976.

————. *Evil Revisited: Responses and Reconsiderations*. Albany: SUNY Press, 1991.

Hasker, William. *God, Time, and Knowledge*. Ithaca, N.Y.: Cornell University Press, 1989.

Helm, Paul. *The Providence of God*. Downers Grove, Ill.: InterVarsity Press, 1994.

Molina, Luis de. *On Divine Foreknowledge: Part IV of the Concordia*. Trans. Alfred J. Freddoso. Ithaca, N.Y.: Cornell University Press, 1988.

Pinnock, Clark, Richard Rice, John Sanders, William Hasker, and David Basinger. *The Openness of God: A Biblical Alternative to the Traditional Conception of God*. Downers Grove, Ill.: InterVarsity Press, 1994.

Sanders, John. *The God Who Risks: A Theology of Providence*. Downers Grove, Ill.: InterVarsity Press, 1998.

Tiessen, Terrance. *Providence and Prayer: How Does God Work in the World?* Downers Grove, Ill.: InterVarsity Press, 2000.

Zagzebski, Linda. *The Dilemma of Freedom and Foreknowledge*. New York: Oxford University Press, 1991.

CHAPTER 9   MIRACLES: DOES
                 GOD INTERVENE
                 IN EARTHLY
                 AFFAIRS?

> Blinded and paralyzed on one side of his body, a retired French
> accountant refused to believe that nothing would help him just
> because his doctors couldn't find a cure. . . . [So he] decided to
> journey to the famous "Our Lady of Lourdes" shrine and beg
> the Lord for a miracle. . . . Within hours of bathing in the
> spring, he regained his sight and could walk without crutches.1

Dramatic healings such as those linked to the spring at Lourdes form only a
small portion of the class of events alleged to be miraculous. A person
spared in a devastating earthquake that killed everyone else directly affected, water turned into wine, a baby born of a virgin—all these events and
more have been called miracles. Moreover, miracles are typically invested
with religious significance. Specifically, the concept of miracle is normally
linked with God and his relation to the world. It should not be surprising
then that philosophers of religion have long been interested in this intriguing subject.

MIRACLES DEFINED

The term *miracle* is used in ordinary discussions to refer to a wide variety of
occurrences. Some individuals use it to describe any *unexpected event*—from
the unanticipated passing of a difficult exam, to the rediscovery of a hope-
lessly lost heirloom, to a rapid and welcomed change in a person's behavior.
Others use the term in a more restricted sense, applying it only to those very
unusual events that apparently conflict with known scientific laws—events
such as the survival of a ten thousand–foot fall by a flight attendant or the
total recovery of a person dying of cancer.

However, "miracle" is most frequently defined in a distinctively religious sense. That is, for most individuals, a miracle is not only an unusual event, but also the *result of some sort of divine activity.* For example, the contention in the opening story is not simply that the retired accountant regained his sight and the use of his legs, but that God brought these things about. It is this sense of the term that has generated the greatest volume and intensity of philosophical discussion.

What exactly does it mean to say that God has caused a certain event? Many theists hold that many if not most events are acts of God in the broad, fundamental sense that God has created the universe, established the "laws" upon which causal interaction within this universe is based, and continues to sustain such interaction by divine power.[2] In this sense, the birth of a baby or a summer thunderstorm can be said to be acts of God. Most of these theists, however, also maintain that there are some events—for example, healings—that would not have occurred in the exact manner in which they did if God had not *directly* intervened, that is, if God had not at some point and in some manner directly manipulated the natural order. Miraculous occurrences, not surprisingly, are normally considered to fall within this category of "direct acts of God."

However, opinion differs on what type(s) of direct divine activity should be labeled miraculous. Since the time of David Hume (1711–1776), it has been very popular in philosophical circles to define miracles as direct acts of God that "violate" natural laws.[3] But what exactly does it mean to say that a natural law has been violated? This question stands at the threshold of a very complex and debatable issue. However, it is possible to state what most individuals seem to have in mind when they speak of miracles as violations.

Natural laws are, for present purposes, statements that describe what will (or probably will) happen or not happen under specifiable conditions. They describe the inherent tendencies or dispositions of things in the world to act and react in certain ways. Accepted scientific laws may be viewed as specifications of some of these natural laws. Our knowledge of well-established scientific laws leads us to believe, for example, that water does not turn instantly into wine and that those who have genuinely died do not (at least in a physical sense) come back to life. But let us assume that someone actually were to turn water instantly into wine or rise from the dead. Not only would we then be required to acknowledge the occurrence of an event that our knowledge of scientific laws gives us good reason to believe will not occur, but, more importantly, we would then be required to acknowledge the occurrence of an event for which it appears no natural explanation could ever be forthcoming. Thus we would be justified in assuming that a natural law has been violated.

Many theists, however, do not believe we should limit our application of the term "miracle" to only those events for which no plausible natural explanation is (or could be) available. Consider, for example, the following story related by R. F. Holland (b. 1932). A child riding his toy motor-car strays onto an unguarded railway crossing near his house, whereupon a wheel of his car gets stuck down the side of one of the rails. At that exact moment, an express train is approaching with the signals in its favor. Also a curve in the track will make it impossible for the driver to stop his train in time to avoid any obstruction he might encounter on the crossing. Moreover, the child is so engrossed in freeing his wheel that he hears neither the train whistle nor his mother, who has just come out of the house and is trying to get his attention. The child appears to be doomed. But just before the train rounds the curve, the brakes are applied and it comes to rest a few feet from the child. The mother thanks God for the miracle, although she learns in due course that there was not necessarily anything supernatural about the manner in which the brakes came to be applied. The driver had fainted, for a reason that had nothing to do with the presence of the child on the line, and the brakes were applied automatically as his hand ceased to exert pressure on the control lever.[4]

The event sequence described in this situation includes no component for which a natural explanation is not available. Boys sometimes play on train tracks; drivers sometimes faint; and the brakes of trains have been constructed to become operative when a driver's hand releases the control lever. But another explanation presents itself in this case: that God directly intervened to cause the driver to faint at the precise moment. As many theists see it, if God did directly intervene in this instance, the event could justifiably be considered a miracle, even though a totally natural explanation would also be available. In short, to generalize, many theists do not want to limit the range of the term "miracle" to only those direct acts of God for which no natural explanation can presently be offered. They want to expand the definition to cover any event in relation to which God can be viewed as having directly manipulated the natural order, regardless of anyone's ability to construct plausible alternate causal scenarios.[5]

Moreover, even here a finer distinction is sometimes made. When we think of God directly bringing about an event, it is quite reasonable to conceive of God's manipulation of the natural order occurring *at the time* that the event takes place. For instance, if we think of God bringing it about that the driver in our scenario fainted, it is quite natural to conceive of God doing something just before the train rounds the bend. But as philosophers such as Robert Adams (b. 1937) have pointed out, there is another way to think of God's activity in this context. We can conceive of God creating "the world in such a way that it was physically predetermined from the beginning" that nature would act in the appropriate way "at precisely the time at which God foresaw" it would be needed.[6] For example, we can conceive of God creating the world in such a way that a specific individual driving a train would faint at a specific time in order to save the life of a young boy. In this case, God does not directly intervene in the sense that he directly manipulates a natural order already in place. However, he still directly intervenes in the sense that he purposely manipulates the natural order to bring about some event that would not have occurred without this intentional divine activity.[7]

When we consider the miraculous in these senses, various philosophical questions arise. One question (for violation miracles) is whether natural laws can be violated. Let us turn first to the question of whether a violation of a natural law is possible. Alistair McKinnon (1925–) offers us a popular negative response.[8] Natural laws, he tells us, are simply "shorthand descriptions of how things do, in fact, happen"—that is, shorthand descriptions of the "actual course of events." Accordingly, to claim that an occurrence is a violation of a natural law is to claim that the event in question is a "suspension of the actual course of events" and this, of course, is an impossibility. Events may well occur, he acknowledges, that seem at present to be incompatible with how we believe things normally happen. But a true counterinstance to what we now believe to be a natural law only shows the law to be inadequate. Since natural laws, by definition, describe "the actual course of events," we must in principle always be willing to expand our laws to accommodate any occurrence, no matter how unusual. We can, by definition, never have both the exception and the rule.[9]

Many, however, find this line of reasoning questionable. To maintain that a natural law accurately describes the natural order is to say only that it correctly identifies what will occur under a specific set of *natural* conditions. But to maintain that an event is a *miraculous* counterinstance to a natural law is not to maintain that some event has occurred under the exact set of *natural* conditions covered by this law and nothing more. To say that water has miraculously turned into wine, for example, is not to say that water has turned into wine under the exact set of natural conditions under which the relevant laws tell us this will not occur. It is to maintain that an additional nonnatural causal factor, namely, direct divine activity, was also present in this case. Accordingly, it is argued, unless it is assumed that supernatural activity is impossible, it cannot be assumed that a miraculous counterinstance to a natural law—a counterinstance produced in part by *divine* circumvention or modification of the natural order—is conceptually impossible.[10]

This brings us directly to the more fundamental question concerning the possibility of miracles: is it possible for God to intervene in earthly affairs? Of course, many individuals do in fact deny the existence of any type of supernatural being. Even some who affirm the existence of such a being— for example, process theists—deny that this being can unilaterally intervene in earthly affairs in the sense necessary to produce miraculous events. However, few philosophers today maintain that the existence of a supernatural being, or the ability of such a being (if it exists) to intervene, can be demonstrated to be impossible.[11]

Most philosophers are currently concerned instead with another type of question related to the miraculous: what can be known or reasonably believed? Specifically, they are interested in three related but distinct questions: Under what conditions can a person reasonably maintain that certain unusual events have actually occurred as reported? Under what conditions can a person reasonably maintain that an event could have no natural explanation? Under what conditions can a person reasonably maintain that God was directly involved in bringing about a given occurrence? Each will be considered in some detail.

MIRACLES AS HISTORICAL EVENTS

Many theists do not claim only that certain types of events could justifiably be considered miracles if they were to occur. They claim that certain events meriting the label of miraculous have actually occurred. If these events have natural explanations available, as is the case in Holland's story about the boy and the train, the accuracy of such claims can be assessed in the same way we assess any historical report. We can, for example, try to determine whether the original source was trustworthy and whether what was originally reported has been faithfully transmitted.

Yet what of those allegedly miraculous events that are incompatible with current natural laws? What, for instance, of the Christian belief that Jesus came back to life after he had been dead for three days, or that Jesus turned water into wine? Are there conditions under which a theist can (or at least could) justifiably claim that seemingly unexplainable events of this sort have actually occurred as reported?

Most philosophers currently grant that reports of *repeatable* counterinstances to current laws cannot justifiably be dismissed. That is, most grant that if a counterinstance to our current laws can be made to recur, given equivalent natural conditions, we are not in a position to dismiss reported occurrences of this event. However, few (if any) of the types of counterinstances to our current laws considered to be miraculous by theists—for example, healings and resurrections—fit into this category. They are at present not repeatable under specifiable natural conditions. Furthermore, there are a number of philosophers (most notably Antony Flew) who argue that when considering the accuracy of reports of events of this type, we ought to be *much* more skeptical.

It is clearly possible, Flew acknowledges, that nonrepeatable counterinstances to well-confirmed natural laws have occurred (or will occur). However, as Hume has rightly pointed out, the wise person proportions his or her belief to the evidence. When we consider the evidence rationally, it is not difficult to see the problem at hand. We have well-known natural laws that justifiably lead us to believe, for instance, that dead people remain dead and that water does not turn into wine. Such laws are not the product of inaccessible scientific studies or outmoded historical hearsay. Such laws can be, and are, tested and reconfirmed daily. The dead stay dead, and untreated water persists as water.

On the other hand, the alleged counterinstances to our current natural laws are supported only by *personal testimony* from the past, and such testimonial evidence will by its very nature always be weaker than the evidence for the laws they contradict. For one thing, while many people have found the laws in question to hold, only a few (and possibly biased) individuals claim that the counterinstance occurred. Whereas the evidence supporting the laws in question is objective, the testimonial reports of those who claim to have witnessed the event are quite subjective.

Accordingly, Flew concludes, we can never have better reasons for accepting the report of a nonrepeatable counterinstance to our current laws—for example, the claim that Jesus rose from the dead—than for rejecting the report as inaccurate. If such an event were repeatable—that is, if it could be produced by anyone under specifiable natural conditions—then we would need to take it seriously. But with respect to reports of nonrepeatable counterinstances, "no matter how impressive the testimony might appear, the most favorable verdict history could ever return must be the agnostic and appropriately Scottish 'not proven'."[12]

Does not this line of reasoning, though, demonstrate an arbitrary and dogmatic naturalistic prejudice? What right, it might be argued, does Flew have to assume that the laws of science have the ultimate or final voice in relation to history? How can other, nonnatural factors be ruled out automatically? For example, many theists believe that specific "miraculous" events have occurred because they are recorded in "holy writings" such as the Bible, sources whose accuracy is thought to be guaranteed by their divine origin. Moreover, the types of miracles recorded in such revelations are often thought to furnish theists with clues as to how God still works in the world today. For example, many Christians believe the Bible to teach that God sometimes intervenes in response to prayer. Thus, when such theists are told of alleged occurrences that fit divine patterns, these reports are often initially granted a reasonable degree of reliability. In short, many theists do in fact believe nonnaturalistic evidence to be quite relevant to the question at hand. How then can Flew justifiably dismiss such evidence completely?

This criticism, however, may well be misguided. Flew repeatedly emphasizes that he is, in this context, only discussing what we can conclude on the basis of the historical (natural) evidence alone. He is not attempting to rule out the possibility that the historicity of certain events could, for some people, be settled on the basis of nonnatural criteria—for example, a revelation from God. Moreover, it is not clear that Flew's decision to consider only "natural" historical criteria can in this context be considered arbitrary. He makes this decision because he is assuming that theists generally wish to use miracles to help establish or support religious belief. He rightly sees that an alleged miracle can have this apologetic value only if, among other things, the occurrence in question can be established objectively on "natural" grounds.[13]

Some theists today, of course, do not desire or even believe it is possible to certify to the satisfaction of all rational individuals that particular allegedly miraculous events have actually occurred as reported. Instead they want to hold only that they are justified in believing this for themselves. Historically, however, theists have often wanted to use miracles to support belief in God's existence, or establish that Jesus is God, or support the claim that some text is an *authentic* divine revelation. Thus, to the extent that this is still the case, it does not appear that Flew's line of reasoning can be accused of involving arbitrary, dogmatic naturalism. In this context, the question of how the actual occurrence of reported events can be authenticated in a public, objective sense remains paramount.

Even granting all this, is Flew's line of reasoning sound? No one denies that natural laws are continuously *open* to confirmation or disconfirmation and thus that we are indeed justified in using such laws to predict in general what will or will not occur under certain conditions. No one denies, for example, that we have well-established laws that justifiably lead us to believe that a withered leg does not instantly return to its normal shape and, thus, we should not expect such an occurrence. Furthermore, no one denies that reports of nonrepeatable counterinstances to well-established current laws should be viewed with a certain amount of initial skepticism. However, there are those who believe it unreasonable to assume that the evidence supporting even the most highly confirmed laws would *always* furnish a sufficient basis for dismissing reports of nonrepeatable counterinstances to them.

As some see it, to make this assumption fails to take into account, for instance, the *prima facie* reliability of our sensory belief-forming faculties. We rely on these faculties daily and, in general, they serve us quite well. In fact, the general reliability of such faculties must be presupposed by those formulating our natural laws. Thus, in those cases where we had no reason to doubt the reliability of these belief-forming faculties—for instance, if we were to observe a seeming counterinstance ourselves or if it were directly observed by a friend whose character and objectivity were beyond question—it is not clear that it would always be justifiable to decide in favor of the natural laws in question, even if such laws were very well established and the occurrence in question could not be repeated.[14]

Moreover, Richard Swinburne (b. 1934) adds, we do not have merely the assumed reliability of our belief-forming faculties and the evidence of the relevant natural laws to consider; we must also consider any relevant physical traces. For instance, in the case of an alleged healing of a withered leg, we might have relevant traces such as X-rays (or photographs) of the leg taken just before and just after the alleged occurrence. An even more compelling physical trace would be a videotape of the incident. Now, of course, X-rays, photographs, and videotapes can be altered. Thus, such physical traces could not conclusively verify that the event had actually occurred as reported. Since the traces would in this case be incompatible with well-established natural laws, caution in drawing a conclusion would indeed be justified. But we have generally accepted methods for assessing (analyzing, testing) the authenticity of X-rays, photographs, and videotapes, and if such assessment made it highly likely that they were reliable, Swinburne contends, such data would obviously stand as very strong evidence for the accuracy of the report in question.[15]

In short, to some there appears to be no strong basis for refusing automatically to acknowledge the accuracy of reports of nonrepeatable counterinstances to our current natural laws. The fact the alleged occurrence is incompatible with well-established natural laws does count strongly against the report. In addition, it is not easy to say exactly when the assumed reliability of our faculties and/or the physical evidence can justifiably be held to counterbalance or even outweigh the long-standing scientific evidence. But a decision concerning the accuracy of such reports, it is argued, must finally be made on a case-by-case basis.[16]

MIRACLES AS UNEXPLAINABLE EVENTS

As we saw earlier, not all individuals believe that a miracle must be an event for which no plausible natural explanation is available. However, since the time of Hume, the majority of philosophers have conceived of miracles as "violations" of natural laws. That is, they have assumed for the sake of discussion that miracles are events for which no totally natural explanation could be forthcoming. For such philosophers, a second important question quite naturally arises. Even in those cases where no one denies that a nonrepeatable counterinstance to our current laws has occurred, could we ever be in the position to claim justifiably that any such event is permanently unexplainable in this sense? If, for instance, we all agreed that someone has actually come back to life after being dead for three days, would we be in a position to claim justifiably that this acknowledged counterinstance to our current laws could never be explained naturally?

It might appear that a promising response is inherent in the very definition of miracle. As was stated earlier, miracles are probably best understood to be direct acts of God that would not have occurred in the exact manner they did if God had not directly manipulated the relevant natural cause-effect patterns. But this is simply another way of saying that such events do not have totally natural causal explanations. Accordingly, it might appear that any direct act of God is automatically an event that is permanently unexplainable naturally. That is, to be more specific, it might appear that the question of whether we can justifiably claim that an alleged miracle could have no adequate natural explanation actually collapses into the question of whether we can justifiably claim that an event is a direct act of God.

However, this line of reasoning is seen by some to be based on a confusion. It is true, they grant, that if an event is a direct act of God, this occurrence itself cannot have a totally natural causal explanation. But the primary purpose of natural science is not to determine what nature has in fact produced. The main objective of science, rather, is to determine what nature is capable of producing—what can occur under solely natural conditions. For instance, the primary purpose of natural science is not to determine whether natural factors alone actually caused any specific person's cancer to enter remission. The primary purpose of science is to determine whether natural factors alone could have produced an event of this type. Hence, when considering whether we could ever be in a position to maintain justifiably that an event is permanently unexplainable scientifically, the question is not whether we could ever be in a position to maintain justifiably that a specific state of affairs, itself, *was* not produced by nature alone. The question, rather, is whether we could ever be in a position to maintain justifiably that an event of this type *could* not have been produced by nature alone.[17]

If we accept this reading of the issue, what ought we to conclude? Could we ever be in a position to label an event permanently unexplainable in this sense? The most common argument denying this possibility can be stated succinctly. It might now appear that some type of event could never be explained. But it is always possible that new information (generated by further scientific investigation) will force us to revise our current set of natural laws related to any given type of occurrence. Therefore, we can never decisively state that any given type of event could never be given a natural explanation.[18]

Not all philosophers agree, however. Such philosophers are not assuming that they have complete and incontrovertible knowledge of the natural order, nor do they even assume that any specific law can ever justifiably be considered immune from revision. Their claim is weaker: even granting that we might gather significant new scientific data and greatly revise our current set of laws accordingly, if some events were to occur, we could justifiably rule that events of this type could never be given a natural explanation.

But what are the criteria by which such events are to be identified? The key, according to Swinburne, lies in our ability (or inability) to devise new scientific laws to accommodate seemingly unexplainable events. We have to some extent good evidence about the "laws of nature," and some of these laws are so highly confirmed that any modification we would suggest to account for the odd counterinstance would be so clumsy and ad hoc that it would upset the whole structure of science. For example, let us imagine that we experience the "resurrection of . . . a man whose heart has not been beating and who was dead by other currently used criteria." Or let us assume we see "water turning into wine without the assistance of special apparatus or chemical catalysts." The relevant laws in such cases are well entrenched; they cannot be modified or given up easily. Accordingly, Swinburne concludes, if events of this type were to occur, they could justifiably be considered permanently unexplainable events.[19]

Margaret Boden (b. 1936) argues in an analogous manner. She grants that observable phenomena cannot normally be dismissed as lying forever outside the range of science, but she is not convinced this would always have to be the case. She invites us to consider the logically possible case of a leper whose missing fingers reappear instantly under the most stringent fraud-detecting conditions—for instance, in the presence of doctors or TV cameras. Such an event, she argues, would conflict with so many accepted scientific facts that any attempt to revise our present scientific laws to accommodate events of this type would so weaken the predictive power of such laws that they would no longer be of practical value. Accordingly, she concludes, if such an event were actually to occur, the scientist, of necessity, would be forced to identify it as a permanently unexplainable phenomenon.[20]

Such reasoning has a *prima facie* appeal, but an obvious question arises. Swinburne and Boden freely acknowledge that the scientific enterprise *is* continually discovering new, often startling and unexpected, information about the causal relationships that exist in our universe. Also, they freely acknowledge that the annals of science record numerous instances in which supposed counterinstances to long-standing scientific laws were later demonstrated—sometimes only after significant conceptual shifts—to be consistent with such laws or revisions of them. Accordingly, is it not the height of scientific provincialism for anyone to maintain solely on the basis of the data now available that certain events could justifiably be labeled permanently unexplainable?

Swinburne and Boden obviously think not, and it is important to understand why. It is not, as mentioned before, because they believe they have some privileged understanding of the "true nature of reality." It is rather that when faced with an acknowledged counterinstance to very highly confirmed laws, they see only two basic options: to either modify the laws to accommodate the occurrence or affirm the adequacy of the laws and declare the event permanently unexplainable. They feel that in some conceivable instances, the latter would be the more reasonable choice.

But is there not another option? Let us assume that after extensive testing we cannot explain how water has turned into wine. Why must we in this case either radically modify the relevant laws or declare the event permanently unexplainable? Why cannot we simply continue to run further tests or label the occurrence a "freak event" and await the occurrence of similar events before seriously investigating further?

According to Holland, such a noncommittal posture would place the relevant laws in a state of uncertainty and would therefore weaken the strength of the scientific method.[21] But not everyone has found such a response convincing. Acknowledged counterinstances to our current laws, it is granted, do challenge the reliability of such laws. In fact, if it were true that the occurrence of acknowledged counterinstances to well-established laws required us to either modify such laws immediately or declare the counterinstances to be permanently unexplainable, the latter might well in some cases be the most reasonable choice. But only *repeatable* counterinstances, these critics maintain, actually require us to make such a decision. With respect to nonrepeatable counterinstances, this is a false dilemma. As long as a counterinstance—no matter how unusual—is not repeatable, a third alternative is always open to us: to continue to acknowledge the functional adequacy of the current laws in question while we search for new or modified laws to accommodate the unusual occurrence in question.[22]

Even if this is correct, however, little of religious significance *necessarily* follows. As stated before, although many philosophers are interested in determining whether certain types of events can justifiably be said to be violations of natural laws, it is doubtful that most theists actually share this concern. For most theists, what is of primary importance is whether, and only whether, the events in question would have occurred at the exact time and in the exact manner they did if God had not somehow acted.

MIRACLES AS ACTS OF GOD

This brings us to our final set of questions: those concerning our ability to establish that God has directly intervened in earthly affairs. For some philosophers, the most crucial of these questions continues to be the following: are there imaginable conditions under which all rational individuals would be forced to admit that God has directly intervened—that is, are there imaginable conditions under which no rational individual could remain a strict naturalist?

Some believe that an affirmative answer is required. Let us assume, Grace Jantzen (b. 1948) argues, that we have compelling evidence for believing that Jesus rose from the dead. In this case, she tells us, to attempt to revise the relevant natural law would hardly be the appropriate response, for what could be gained by making this law read, "All men are mortal except those who have an unknown quality, observed on only one occasion and hitherto accountable for only by divine intervention." "Where there is a single exception to a perfectly well-established and well-understood law, and one that is inexplicable unless one appeals to divine intervention . . . the skeptical response would be inadequate."[23]

Robert Larmer comes to a similar conclusion. Let us "suppose that one hears of a man who claims to perform miracles of healing through the power of God." Let us further suppose that we are "able to capture on film occasions when, immediately following the prayers of this man, fingers lost to leprosy were regrown to their original form and length in a matter of seconds, and occasions when eyes severely burned by acid were immediately restored to sight." Finally, let us assume "not only that this man appears to have the power to heal any kind of disease or injury, but also that no interposition of any [object or force] has any effect on his apparent ability to heal" and that "his power is apparently independent of distance, since people in distant countries have experienced dramatic healing after this man prayed for their cure." In such a case, Larmer argues, the most rational response would clearly be to acknowledge God's interventive activity. To hold out for a totally natural explanation would be uncritical, dogmatic and question-begging.[24]

Neither Jantzen or Larmer, it must be emphasized, is arguing simply that supernatural activity can justifiably be considered a plausible causal explanation when it cannot be shown that nature left to her own devices could produce the event. Their claim is stronger: that if some conceivable events were to occur, it would be most reasonable for all rational individuals to assume that God has directly intervened.

Some believe, however, that those making this claim have overlooked an important factor. There are, it is acknowledged, conceivable situations that, when considered in isolation, might make divine intervention a plausible causal hypothesis. But no actual event, and thus no causal hypothesis for it, can be considered in isolation from the rest of the relevant evidence. To assume, for example, that a remarkable healing is the result of direct divine intervention is to assume not only that God exists but also that God's existence is compatible with other relevant experiential data. It is to assume, for example, that God's existence is compatible with the evil we experience. Accordingly, if such a "healing" were to occur, the crucial question, it is argued, would not be, as Jantzen and Larmer imply, whether divine causation is the most plausible causal explanation for this event alone. The crucial question would be whether divine causation is the most plausible explanation, given all that this implies.[25]

Now let us assume that in comparing the plausibility of believing that God has healed the individual in question (and, hence, that God's existence is compatible with the amount and types of evil in the world) with the plausibility of believing that God's existence is not compatible with all that we commonly experience (and, hence, that God did not heal the individual in question), someone decides that God's nonexistence is more compelling overall. In other words, let us assume that the *prima facie* evidence for God's existence that has been generated by the "healing" in question is not of sufficient weight in the mind of a given individual to make the supernatural perspective the most plausible explanation for all the relevant data. Could Jantzen or Larmer justifiably accuse such an individual of being stubborn or intellectually dishonest or irrational? Larmer believes so. Specifically he believes that there are conceivable contexts (such as the one mentioned earlier) in which every rational person would have to acknowledge that the evidence for God's existence is so strong that it clearly outweighs any evidence against God's existence—for instance, that generated by evil.[26]

However, Larmer's contention is based on the assumption that we possess (or could in principle possess) a set of neutral, non–question-begging criteria for belief assessment in relation to which we can objectively determine the comparative strength of the evidence for and against God's existence. And many philosophers—in agreement with such diverse figures as Hume and Kierkegaard—continue to believe that no such criteria exist, that the comparative assessment of evidence for and against God's existence will, by its very nature, ultimately always be primarily a subjective, relative matter.[27]

For many theists, though, the crucial question is not whether there are imaginable conditions under which all rational individuals would have to acknowledge divine intervention. The important issue, as they see it, is whether *the theist* can (could) justifiably claim that God is, at least in part, directly responsible for certain occurrences. That is, the important question is whether there are conditions under which the theist can reasonably claim that certain events are direct acts of God.

In response, theists might assume a purely defensive posture. They might maintain that unless it can be shown that a given occurrence is not a direct act of God, they are justified in claiming that it is. Given our discussion of this approach to religious belief in chapter 6, they might be successful. However, many theists have positive reasons for maintaining that God does (or at least can) directly intervene in earthly affairs. Specifically, many theists claim that they have acquired—from written revelation, oral tradition, or personal experience—accurate information about God's general "patterns of action" in our world. They believe that when they observe (or at least if they were to observe) some specific event fitting such a pattern, they can (or at least could) justifiably label it a direct act of God.

To accept a *divine-pattern thesis* of this sort, it must be emphasized, is not to argue that God can act only in accordance with recognized patterns. Consider, for instance, the following situation. One day Jim notices a peculiar phenomenon in his garden: his vegetables continually grow from seed to full maturity in one hour and then quickly regress again to seed. Try as he will—for example, by discussing the occurrence with respected botanists— Jim can find no specific natural cause for this strange phenomenon. Moreover, although Jim is a proponent of the divine-pattern thesis, he is not aware of any divine action pattern in which this unusual phenomenon fits. Accordingly, Jim will quite likely refrain from claiming that this is a direct act of God. In doing so, he will not thereby be claiming that the occurrence is *in fact* not a direct act of God. He will be indicating only that he has at present no sufficient reason for thinking God is directly involved.

Also, theists who accept this divine-pattern thesis are not arguing that God must always intervene in a predictable manner. Consider, for example, the following scenario. John, a theist, has grown up in a home in which the Bible is accepted as literally true. He has been taught, accordingly, that if one prays to God in time of trouble, God will directly answer. In other words, John believes he has acquired "knowledge" of a specific divine behavior pattern related to petitionary prayer. One day John finds himself in a serious personal crisis. His little girl is gravely ill, and there seems little hope for her recovery. John prays to God, beseeching that he save her life. Happily, the next day the girl is inexplicably improved and later goes on to make a full recovery. If, in this case, John claims that this is a direct act of God because the "healing" fits an accepted pattern of how God interacts with the world, he would not thereby be saying that his prayer "forced" God to act. He would be claiming only that the fact that the healing fit an accepted divine action pattern was a sufficient reason to believe God had in this case chosen to intervene directly.

Moreover, in no such case are theists professing absolute certainty. They are claiming only that they are justified in believing that it is more likely than not that a given occurrence is a direct act of God.

Of course, even in light of these clarifications, an important question arises. Are the theists in question justified in assuming that the sources from which the divine action patterns are derived—revelation, tradition, or personal experience—yield accurate information? In some specific cases, such an assumption may not be reasonable. Perhaps it can be shown, for example, that specific patterns affirmed by some Christians cannot actually be supported by proper biblical interpretation or by correct knowledge of Christian tradition. Or perhaps it can be demonstrated that a specific historical source trusted by some Muslims is unreliable. However, since few philosophers today maintain that God's existence can be conclusively disproved or that the concept of divine communication with humans is self-contradictory,

it should not be surprising that few wish to argue that theists cannot rationally maintain belief in the accuracy of certain divine action patterns and thus
cannot justifiably label events that fit such patterns direct acts of God.[28]

PRACTICAL CONSIDERATIONS

Have any miracles, though, actually occurred? This question has recently
generated considerable philosophical discussion. No purported miracle has
received more attention than the resurrection of Jesus.

Those engaged in this debate—most notably Flew, Michael Martin,
Stephen Davis, Gary Habermas, and James Keller—all grant for the sake
of argument that Jesus could have died, been buried, and then come back to
life. But there is considerable difference of opinion on the strength of the historical evidence for this alleged occurrence and the relationship between this
evidence and rational belief.

Although details differ, the general "evidential" case for the resurrection of Jesus—most clearly stated by Davis and Habermas—can be summa-
rized as follows.[29]

Almost all biblical scholars (whatever their personal perspective on the
resurrection) agree (1) that Jesus of Nazareth lived, was crucified, and was
buried, (2) that his disciplés claimed soon after his death that his tomb was
empty, (3) that some claimed to have experienced (met, encountered, inter-
acted with) a live Jesus, (4) that these experiences caused his disciples to believe that Jesus had risen from the dead, and (5) that this was a key belief
within early Christianity.

Moreover, although New Testament accounts of the resurrection differ
(and even contradict each other on specific details), the biblical record uniformly claims that Jesus died, was buried, and then rose from the dead. Furthermore, there exists no good reason to believe that the disciples were
lying, since their lives were so radically changed by this belief that many
were willing to die rather than denounce their faith. Nor is there good reason to believe that the disciples were hallucinating (were simply imagining
things that were not actually occurring) since none of the usual causes for
hallucination—food or sleep deprivation, drugs, mass hysteria—appear to
have been present. Finally, there was no conclusive refutation of Jesus' resurrection by Jewish authorities (for example, they did not produce the
body), although they had the power and motivation to do so. Accordingly,
while other explanations for the historical evidence cannot be shown to be
impossible, "Jesus' literal Resurrection from the dead . . . is the best explanation for the facts."[30]

However, many nontheists (most notably Martin and Flew) and some
theists (most notably James Keller) have argued that such evidence is *far*
from compelling. Again, details differ, but the essence of their critique is the
following.[31]

First, while scholars agree that Jesus lived and that he died by crucifixion,
considerable debate surrounds the question of whether either the disciples or
the very early church actually believed that Jesus had risen from the dead and

appeared to many. Some scholars believe that the resurrection story entered the Christian tradition well after its inception, while others believe we are simply not in an evidential position to say when this story became a key component of faith.[32]

Second, there is little if any independent, objective evidence for the gospel accounts of the resurrection. Furthermore, the inconsistencies among the gospels on such issues as whether the stone had been rolled away from the entrance of the tomb before the women arrived, which women were present, who was in the tomb, what the women did after their discovery, and how the disciples reacted are not simply minor difficulties. They throw into serious doubt the historical reliability of the biblical texts.

Third, even if it is true that the disciples believed Jesus to have risen from the dead and were for this reason so radically altered that they were willing to die for their faith, this in no sense increases the probability that the resurrection actually occurred. History is replete with examples of religious zealots who gave their lives for what they believed to be the truth—for example, Islamic martyrs such as those who flew planes into the World Trade Center, kamikaze pilots, and followers of Jim Jones or David Koresh. Most people who believe in the historicity of the resurrection adamantly deny that the basic beliefs that motivated devotion in these cases are true (or are even made more probable by the zeal of their adherents).

Fourth, even if the Jewish authorities were aware of the resurrection claims and could not decisively counter the resurrection story by producing the body, this does not increase the probability that an actual resurrection took place. It is just as plausible to believe that the body had been stolen and hidden by the disciples or that the Jewish authorities were not overly concerned with the followers of Jesus at this point or that they simply did not have enough evidence for an objective refutation because there were no independent, unbiased eyewitnesses to the events in question.

Fifth, the burden of proof clearly lies with those who believe Jesus to have risen from the dead. Human experience continues to confirm in the strongest possible sense an undesirable but obvious fact: dead people stay dead. Thus, the historical evidence for any claim to the contrary must be exceedingly strong. But the relevant evidence is weak at best. Hence, there simply exists no valid historical basis for maintaining that the resurrection of Jesus is an established fact (or even a reasonable probability).

Those who believe in the historicity of the resurrection are, of course, aware of these challenges and offer counters. They claim, for instance, that the gospel accounts of the resurrection, if properly interpreted, contain no significant contradictions. The critics' contention that many sincere (but possibly misguided) individuals, in addition to the disciples, have died for what they believed to be the truth misses the point, they argue. It is the fact that the disciples were in a position to know whether Jesus came back to life that makes their perspective unique.

All involved agree, though, that this "evidential" debate clearly raises important questions about the assessment of historical data. What types of evidence are relevant when assessing the alleged occurrence of an event in the past? How strong must such evidence be to establish the actual occurrence of an event? Who is in the best position to make such determinations?

However, of equal (if not greater) philosophical significance is the current debate over the appropriate relationship between the historical evidence for the resurrection and rational belief. For some on both sides of the issue, the answer is clear. Habermas, for instance, believes the historical evidence for the resurrection of Jesus to be so strong that no sincere, knowledgeable person can rationally deny that this event actually occurred. Martin and Flew, on the other hand, believe the historical evidence to be so weak that a "rational person should disbelieve the claim that Jesus was resurrected from the dead."[33]

Davis, however, offers a middle ground, based on the currently popular distinction between simply defending one's right to hold a belief and arguing that no one can rationally disagree. As already noted, Davis believes personally that the historical evidence, considered alone, clearly supports the resurrection of Jesus. But he denies that sincere, knowledgeable individuals cannot justifiably disagree. Supernaturalists, he argues, can reasonably maintain that reality cannot be explained totally in natural terms and therefore can reasonably maintain that the historical evidence supports an actual resurrection. However, naturalists can justifiably maintain that all events are part of a natural order that is uniform, and given this assumption, disbelief in the actual resurrection of Jesus is also rational. In short, as Davis sees it, one's perspective on whether Jesus actually rose from the dead ultimately comes down to one's basic worldview—one's basic perspective on the nature of reality. Since both supernaturalism and naturalism can be held by rational people, differing rational perspectives on the historicity of the event in question must also be allowed.[34]

This leaves us, though, with another important question to consider: even if we grant that Jesus did die and then come back to life, do we have any reason to believe he was raised from the dead by God, and thus that the resurrection was indeed a miracle? Habermas and Davis represent those who believe not only that the evidence for the resurrection is very strong, but that the probability that such an event could be explained without reference to divine intervention is *very* low. In fact, Habermas seems to believe that when the evidence for the resurrection is conjoined "with the claims of Jesus"— Jesus' claim, for instance, that he was uniquely related to God or that the resurrection would verify this fact—the denial of direct divine activity in this case borders on irrationality.[35] Davis disagrees. While he doubts that someone can maintain that the resurrection occurred and yet deny divine intervention, he holds, remember, that naturalists can rationally deny the historicity of this event, in which case, of course, no explanation is needed.

Critics such as Martin go even further. They argue that even if one grants that the resurrection of Jesus occurred, one can rationally deny that it was brought about by God (is a miracle) since it is just as plausible that this unusual event was the result of natural laws not yet discovered or fully understood or that this event was simply uncaused by either natural or supernatural means.[36]

Who is correct? Or at least which perspective is the most plausible? There is at present no consensus within the general philosophical community on these explanatory issues. But most philosophers agree that serious discussion of the appropriate epistemic relationship between evidence and worldviews is absolutely essential with respect to any disputed occurrence in the past.

There is, however, one other issue surrounding any miraculous claim that clearly merits attention in this context. Let us consider again our scenario concerning John and his daughter. John believes that God can and will occasionally intervene and, thus, when his daughter becomes gravely ill, he beseeches God for assistance. When she recovers, he attributes the recovery in part to God's direct activity and thanks God for this demonstration of divine compassion.

Let us, though, now expand our story. Tom, a friend of John, is very happy about the seemingly miraculous healing of John's daughter. He too has always believed that God can intervene occasionally in earthly affairs and is pleased to think that God has actually done so in the case of John's daughter. Accordingly, when Tom encounters a number of starving children during a business trip to India, he beseeches God for help. After all, he reasons, if God can heal John's daughter, surely God can also help some of these children. Yet in spite of his fervent prayer, all the children die slow, painful deaths.

The *prima facie* moral tension here is obvious. Why did God intervene in one case but not in the other? When considering instances of seemingly unnecessary suffering, many believers, as discussed in chapter 7, emphasize the extent to which God is self-limited. God cares for everyone, it is argued. But God has created a moral context in which human freedom and the natural order that undergirds it are normally allowed to function uninhibited. In such a universe undesired evils are unavoidable. However, why then has John's daughter been healed? If God's creative agenda keeps God from directly intervening in the case of starving children in India, how can God directly intervene in the case of John's daughter without violating the structure of our moral universe? How can we think that God intervenes on behalf of some and not for others?

The basic question here is not whether God can occasionally intervene, but why such interventions do not occur in a more understandable, orderly fashion. Or, as process theist David Griffin states this point, why would a God who can unilaterally intervene not do so more frequently "in order to prevent particularly horrendous evils?"[37]

Of course, many responses are available to theists. It can be argued that while situations may look analogous from our perspective, they may not be so from God's. Or it can be argued that although situations may be analogous, God is under no moral obligation to act in ways *we think* are appropriate. God justifiably does what God wants for reasons beyond human understanding.

But for some theists the tension remains, and it is strong enough to cause them to question whether God does *in fact* intervene today. Moreover, even for those theists who have resolved this "tension" for themselves, a general point appears valid. The acknowledged frequency of undesired but unavoidable evil and the expected frequency of beneficial, direct divine intervention stand in an inverse relationship. To the extent that a theist responds to specific instances of evil by claiming that God is barred from removing them because of the nature of our moral universe, this theist has less reason to expect beneficial (miraculous) intervention in any specific situation. Moreover, to the extent that a theist resolves the tension in question by claiming that "God's ways are above our ways," the less able he is to predict when and where any such intervention might occur.

This type of tension, though, must be kept in perspective. It is true that the miraculous is a complex concept, and it is true that serious theoretical and practical questions concerning our ability to identify "miracles" do exist. But nothing argued in this chapter indicates that theists cannot in principle justifiably believe that miracles can occur, or even that miracles have actually occurred.[38]

STUDY QUESTIONS

1. How is "miracle" best defined? Specifically, as you see it, could an event be considered a miracle if a natural explanation were available?

2. Why does Flew believe we cannot acknowledge the occurrence of nonrepeatable counterinstances to well-established natural laws? Do you agree?

3. Are you sometimes skeptical when you hear reports of alleged miracles? Why? Under what conditions is such skepticism justified?

4. Swinburne and others believe that we can conceive of some events that could never be given natural explanations. Why? Do you agree? Can you conceive of some possible events that you believe could never be explained naturally if they were to occur?

5. Jantzen and Larmer believe that if some conceivable events were to occur, it would be most reasonable to acknowledge supernatural causation. Briefly outline their line of reasoning and the types of criticism to which they must respond. Can you conceive of some possible events that you believe would require supernatural explanation if they were to occur?

6. Those who believe God does miraculously intervene in earthly affairs face an obvious question: given all the pain and suffering present in the world, why does God not intervene more frequently, or at least in a more systematic manner? How might a theist respond to this question?

7. Do you think that someone who believes that miracles can occur will be less likely to search for a *natural* solution to personal and social problems?

8. Do you believe that any miracles, as you define them, have actually occurred? Why or why not?

9. Briefly outline the evidential case for and against the resurrection of Jesus. Which do you consider more convincing?

NOTES

1. *Prayers God Has Answered* (West Palm Beach, FL: Globe Communications, 1985), pp. 5–6.

2. Medieval philosophers distinguished God's "primary causation" from the "secondary causation" of creatures that the divine power upholds in existence.

3. David Hume, *Enquiries concerning the Human Understanding and concerning the Principles of Morals,* ed. L. A. Selby-Bigge, 2d ed. (Oxford: Clarendon Press, 1972), pp. 109–31.

4. R. F. Holland, "The Miraculous," *American Philosophical Quarterly* 2 (1965): 43. It is not totally clear, however, exactly what Holland himself believes this story to illustrate. Christopher Hughes, for instance, believes Holland's point to be that the mother in this case "could (rationally) continue to maintain that a miracle had taken place, even if she came to believe that no divine intervention was involved." ("Miracles, Laws of Nature and Causation," *Proceedings of the Aristotelian Society* 66 [Supplement; June 1992], pp. 188–9.)

5. See Hughes, "Miracles," pp. 179–205, for an expanded discussion of this topic.

6. Adams, Robert Merrihew. "Miracles, Laws and Natural Causation (II)," *Proceedings of the Aristotelian Society* 66 (Supplement; June 1992), p. 209.

7. Not everyone is completely comfortable with this distinction. Hughes agrees that an event can be considered miraculous even if a natural explanation is available, but he does not want to apply the label of miraculous to providential activity during the creation of the world. He narrows the application of "miracle" in this context to "an event occurring in (an up and running) nature which is directly caused by God" (p. 202).

8. Alistair McKinnon, " 'Miracle' and 'Paradox'," *American Philosophical Quarterly* 4 (October 1967): 308–14.

9. The discussion of whether Hume put forth this type of *a priori* argument against the possibility of miracles continues. See Robert Fogelin, "What Hume Actually Said about Miracles," *Hume Studies,* 16, no. 1 (April 1990): 81–6; Antony Flew, "Fogelin on Hume on Miracles," *Hume Studies* 16, no. 2 (November 1990): 141–4; Kenneth G. Ferguson, "An Intervention into the Flew/Fogelin Debate," *Hume Studies* 17, no. 2 (1991): 105–11; Joseph Elin, "Again: Hume on Miracles," *Hume Studies* 19, no. 1 (1993): 203–12.

10. See, for example, Hughes, "Miracles, Laws of Nature and Causation," or David Basinger, "Miracles as Violations," *Southern Journal of Philosophy,* 22, no. 1 (1984): 1–7. For two recent discussions of what it would mean for a natural law to be violated, see Michael Levine, "Miracles," in the *Stanford Encyclopedia of Philosophy,* 1997, http://plato.stanford.edu/entries/miracles, and Theodore M. Drange, "Science and Miracles," *Infidels Library,* 1998, wysiwyg://41/http://www.indels. org/library/modern/theodore_drange/miracles.html.

11. See chapter 3 for a fuller discussion of how philosophers currently view the status of arguments for and against God's existence.

12. Antony Flew, "Parapsychology Revisited: Laws, Miracles and Repeatability," The *Humanist* 36 (May/June 1976): 28–30.

13. Antony Flew, "Miracles," in the *Encyclopedia of Philosophy,* Vol. 5 (New York: Macmillan, 1967), p. 351.

14. Chapter 7 furnishes a more comprehensive discussion of this point.

15. Richard Swinburne, *The Concept of Miracle* (London: Macmillan, 1970), pp. 33–50.

16. J. L. Mackie is one of a number of nontheists who are sympathetic to Flew's line of reasoning but want to argue only that such considerations make the occurrence of

an allegedly miraculous event *"prima facie* unlikely on any particular occasion." See Mackie's *The Miracle of Theism* (Oxford: Clarendon Press, 1982), pp. 18–29.

17. This line of reasoning appears implicitly in Swinburne, pp. 23–32. A more explicit discussion occurs in David Basinger and Randall Basinger, *Philosophy and Miracle: The Contemporary Debate* (Lewiston, N.Y.: Edwin Mellen Press, 1986), pp. 68–71.

18. See Michael Martin, *Atheism: A Philosophical Justification* (Philadelphia: Temple University Press, 1990), chapter 9; Flew, "Miracles," pp. 348–9.

19. Swinburne, pp. 29–32.

20. Margaret Boden, "Miracles and Scientific Explanation," *Ratio* 1, no. 1 (December 1969): 137–41.

21. Holland, pp. 43–51.

22. Basinger and Basinger, pp. 59–71. For an interesting discussion of whether a scientist can accept this option, see Drange. For an interesting discussion of the general issue of miracles as unexplained events, see also Peter van Inwagen, "Of 'Of Miracles,'" in *Philosophy and Faith: A Philosophy of Religion Reader,* ed. David Shatz. (New York: McGraw Hill, 2002), pp. 402–9.

23. Grace Jantzen, "Hume on Miracles, History and Politics," *Christian Scholar's Review* 8 (1979): 325.

24. Robert Larmer, "Miracles and Criteria," *Sophia* 23, no. 1 (April 1984): 4–10.

25. See, for example, David Basinger, "Miracles and Natural Explanation," *Sophia* 26, no. 3 (October 1987): 22–6.

26. Robert Larmer, "Miracles, Evidence and Theism: A Further Apologia," *Sophia* 33, no. 1 (March, 1994): 51–7.

27. See, for instance, Alvin Plantinga, "The Probabilistic Argument from Evil" *Philosophical Studies* (January 1979): 1–53.

28. An exception would be Martin. See *Atheism* or *The Case against Christianity* (Philadelphia: Temple University Press, 1991).

29. Stephen Davis, "Is it Possible to Know that Jesus was Raised from the Dead?" *Faith and Philosophy* 1, no. 2 (1984): 147–159; "Naturalism and the Resurrection: A Reply to Habermas," *Faith and Philosophy* 2, no. 3 (1985): 303–8; "Doubting the Resurrection: A Reply to James A. Keller," *Faith and Philosophy* 7, no. 1 (1990): 99–111. Gary Habermas (with Antony Flew), *Did Jesus Rise from the Dead?* ed. Terry L. Miethe (San Francisco: Harper and Row, 1987), pp. 19–29.

30. Habermas, p. 29.

31. Martin, *The Case against Christianity;* Flew, *Did Jesus Rise from the Dead?;* James A. Keller, "Contemporary Christian Doubts about the Resurrection," *Faith and Philosophy* 5, no. 1 (January 1989): 40–60; "Response to Davis," *Faith and Philosophy* 7, no. 1 (January 1990): 112–6.

32. See, for example, Willi Marxsen, *The Resurrection of Jesus of Nazareth,* trans. Margaret Kohl (Philadelphia; Fortress Press, 1970), pp. 36–78; Hugh Anderson, *Jesus and Christian Origins* (New York: Oxford University Press, 1964), pp. 185–240; Reginald Fuller, *The Formation of the Resurrection Narratives,* rev. ed. (Philadelphia: Fortress Press, 1980), pp. 50–154.

33. Martin, *The Case against Christianity,* p. 96.

34. Davis, "Naturalism and the Resurrection." A somewhat analogous line of reasoning appears in J. Houston, *Reported Miracles* (Cambridge: Cambridge University Press, 1994), pp. 208–57.

35. Habermas, pp. 39–42.

36. Martin, *The Case against Christianity,* pp. 96–100.

37. David Griffin, in *Process Philosophy and Social Thought* ed. John B. Cobb and W. Widick Schroeder (Chicago: Center for the Scientific Study of Religion, 1981), p. 193.

38. Space considerations do not allow for the discussion of a cluster of other questions related to the involvement of humans in miraculous activity. For example, it is reasonable to hold that humans can initiate divine intervention (perhaps through prayer)? More importantly, can it be held that God sometimes intervenes (or refrains from doing so) primarily because humans have freely chosen to request (or freely chosen not to request) that he do so?

SUGGESTED READING

Adams, Robert Merrihew. "Miracles, Laws and Natural Causation (II)." *Proceedings of the Aristotelian Society* 66 (Supplement; June 1992): 207–24.

Basinger, David, and Randall Basinger. *Philosophy and Miracle: The Contemporary Debate.* Lewiston, N.Y.: Edwin Mellen Press, 1986.

Earman, John. *Hume's Abject Failure: The Argument against Miracles.* New York: Oxford University Press, 2000.

Fogelin, Robert J. "What Hume Actually Said about Miracles." *Hume Studies* 16, no. 1 (April 1990): 81–6.

Houston, J. *Reported Miracles: A Critique of Hume.* Cambridge: Cambridge University Press, 1994.

Hughes, Christopher. "Miracles, Laws and Natural Causation (I)." *Proceedings of the Aristotelian Society* 66 (Supplement; June 1992): 179–205.

Hume, David. *Enquiries concerning the Human Understanding and concerning the Principles of Morals.* ed. L. A. Selby-Bigge. 2d ed. Oxford: Clarendon Press, 1972.

Keller, James. "A Moral Argument Against Miracles." *Faith and Philosophy* 12 (1995): 54–78.

Larmer, Robert, ed. *Questions of Miracle.* Montreal: McGill-Queen's University Press, 1996.

Lewis, C. S. *Miracles.* Rev. ed. London: Collins, Fontana Books, 1960.

Martin, Michael. "Why the Resurrection Is an Impossibility." *Philo* 1 (1998): 63–73.

Mavrodes, George. "Hume and the Probability of Miracles." *International Journal for the Philosophy of Religion* 43 (1998): 167–82.

Nowell-Smith, Patrick. "Miracles—The Philosophical Approach." *The Hibbert Journal* 48 (1950): 354–60.

Otte, Richard. "Mackie's Treatment of Miracles." *International Journal for the Philosophy of Religion* 39 (1996): 151–8.

Swinburne, Richard. *The Concept of Miracle.* London: Macmillan, 1970.

———, ed. *Miracles.* New York: Macmillan, 1989.

Walker, Ian. "Miracles and Violations." *International Journal for the Philosophy of Religion* 13 (1982): 103–8.

Williams, T.C. *The Idea of the Miraculous: The Challenge of Science and Religion.* New York: St. Martin's Press, 1991.

CHAPTER 10   LIFE AFTER DEATH: ARE THERE REASONS FOR HOPE?

And the people from the margin,
Watched him floating, rising, sinking,
Till the birch-canoe seemed lifted
High into that sea of splendor,
Till it sank into the vapors
Like the new moon slowly, slowly
Sinking in the purple distance.
And they said, "Farewell forever!"
Said, "Farewell, O Hiawatha!"
And the forests, dark and lonely,
Moved through all their depths of darkness,
Sighed, "Farewell, O Hiawatha!" . . .
Thus departed Hiawatha,
Hiawatha the Beloved,
In the glory of the sunset,
In the purple mists of evening,
To the regions of the home-wind,
Of the Northwest-Wind, Keewaydin,
To the Islands of the Blessed,
To the kingdom of Ponemah,
To the land of the Hereafter!

Henry W. Longfellow, *The Song of Hiawatha*

The theme that death does not end human life sounds through all religions. The ancient Egyptians buried their mummified nobility, along with the food and valuables necessary for the long journey to the next life, in elaborate tombs decorated with statues or paintings of Osiris, god of that world. Confucians and practitioners of traditional African religions remember and appease ancestors with special ceremonies at home altars, on their graves, or at sacred sites, while Hindus and Buddhists speak of karma and reincarnation. The Koran, which uses the term "hereafter" (*al-àkhira*) 113 times, frequently discusses the resurrection and judgment. In worship, many Christians regularly recite the Apostles' Creed: "I believe in . . . the resurrection of the body and the life everlasting." In fact, the belief in life after death is so central to religion that one author contends that it is more fundamental than the belief in God, so that if God did not exist, God would have to be created in order to "function as the benevolent purveyor of man's immortality."[1]

Yet since we all die, is it reasonable to believe that we will live again after our death? Although opinion polls indicate that many people believe we will, such polls provide little help in determining the truth of the belief. Our task must be to clarify what is meant by life after death, determine its possibility, and assess purported evidence that it actually happens.

TERMINOLOGY

The first problem concerns the terminology we should use to discuss the subject. Although people frequently speak of *immortality*, we should use this term cautiously. Literally, it means "not-dying," and this appears to conflict with the fact that we all die. If immortality, understood literally, is to be possible, some part of us containing our personal identity must be able to survive physical death and corruption. Some see this continuance as non-physical (a soul that lives on for an indefinite time in another sphere of existence, with or without some sort of body); others identify it with some physical continuance.

An associated concept is *reincarnation*—after death we again take up bodily existence at some time on earth. Typically, though not always,[2] this view invokes a soul or self that survives death and can exist independently while it transmigrates from one body to another. Believers in reincarnation generally hold that transmigration occurs numerous times until we achieve final liberation.

Some religions use the term *resurrection* to refer to what happens sometime after death. According to one traditional interpretation, bodies are resurrected to be rejoined with a continuing soul. The Catholic tradition holds that unless the body reunited with the soul is the same body that died, resurrected persons cannot be the same as the deceased.[3] Other traditions hold that the resurrection body may differ in content from the present body.

Still others speak of the *re-creation* of individual persons sometime after their death.[4] There is no literal immortality, no persisting soul, but simply life after death. Human existence is gap-inclusive: we live and die, our bodies disintegrate, and in the future we are re-created to live again. The same person as the deceased is re-created, though many features (for example, appearance, physical composition, lack of certain diseases) may differ from those possessed prior to death.

Clearly, the language we use to address the topic of life after death is not philosophically neutral. *Immortality language* invokes the concept of a soul, self, or physical continuance that is both the locus of personal identity and capable of persisting through physical death. On some such scenarios one can witness one's own funeral. *Life-after-death language* accords with the truism that we all die, but in doing so (if understood literally) it rules out the identification of ourselves with a persisting soul-entity. Of course, one might take a more restricted view of death as applying solely to the body and understand life after death as life after the death of the body. Then "life after death" is compatible with viewing persons as ensouled beings, but it leads to a different understanding of death (death of the body versus death of the person).

In what follows we have to make a language choice. Since the term "life after death" seems the most neutral, we generally speak of the problem of life after death, though in some contexts the term "immortality" more accurately captures the thought.

CONCEPTS OF LIFE AFTER DEATH

Just as the language about life after death is diverse, so are people's concepts of life after death. Four bear noting.

1. According to one widely held view, we achieve our immortality in our living presence in the things or persons that continue after our death. We term this view *immortality by remembrance*. African and Chinese religions espouse forms of this view, which holds that the deceased live on through the remembrance of those who knew them.[5] This view also plays a subtle role in our own everyday experience. Craftspeople, writers, and artists put something of themselves—their ideas, beliefs, hopes, fears, and views of the world—into their work. They hope that their creations will have lasting significance so that their ideas or fame will long outlive them. Other persons gain immortality by painting on the canvas of history: holding political office, winning or losing battles, revolting against authority, committing outrageous crimes, or making great discoveries or inventions. Some obtain their immortality by improving the lives of others, while others seek to prolong their lives in their children, giving their children their own or their forebears' names.[6]

Though immorality by remembrance surely describes a kind of immortality, it is divorced from the moral and spiritual dimensions that people often associate with immortality. In religious contexts, belief in immortality and preparation for it encourage and reinforce moral action. But immortality as remembrance only advises accomplishment of the noteworthy or memorable; immoral and inhumane acts are as likely to bring remembrance as moral acts. Lee Harvey Oswald, who shot President Kennedy, is remembered by more people than is Harriet Tubman, who worked to free the slaves. Furthermore, this view fails to touch on the factual question of our own future existence. It is not insignificant that we want others to remember us, but we also want to know what will happen to *us* after we die. Is the grave or funeral pyre the end?

2. The philosophical difficulties that allegedly haunt a belief in a literal resurrection have led some to advocate a second view of life after death. For example, Rudolph Bultmann (1884–1976) concluded that "an historical fact which involves a resurrection from the dead is utterly inconceivable!"[7] Dead persons cannot be resuscitated. Resurrection, as a mythological event, must be demythologized to ascertain its *existential significance for our present life.* Resurrection language is language about power over sin and our freedom from guilt. Resurrected persons are those who live with renewed commitment to the full realization of their authentic selves.

Similarly, D. Z. Phillips (b. 1934) contends that the immortality of the soul has nothing to do with a life that extends beyond or begins after death.[8] Death is not an event that a person experiences, like drinking coffee or getting chicken pox; rather, death is the end of all that person's possibilities.[9] Accordingly, it is necessary to reinterpret immortality in terms of our present experience and life. Eternal life is not an extension of one's life but the present reality of goodness. It is not more life but the quality of our present life. Thus, when religion speaks about the eternal life of the soul, it indicates that what is important is overcoming death not in the sense that we survive death but that we die to ourselves by living unselfishly for others.

The emphasis on the quality of our present life helpfully corrects the previous view of immortality as remembrance. The doctrine of life after death should have implications for our moral living. But this view wrongly takes such implications as the doctrine's meaning and thus reduces its quantitative dimensions to the qualitative. That is, this view too leaves the factual question untouched. As we shall see, such questions as "Is death the end of our existence?" or "Should we prepare for a future life?" are not meaningless.

3. A third view, prevalent in Vedantic Hinduism and Mahayana Buddhism, is that after death those liberated from the cycle of existences experience *union with the One* or Nondual. In Vedanta, Reality ultimately is nondual, though it can be viewed diversely from the perspective either of the reality that evolves itself as this world (Brahman) or of the subject or self (*atman*). The self that I am (*atman*) transcends my senses, mind, intellect, feeling, and will; the self is pure consciousness. But my consciousness is not independent of all other consciousness; universal consciousness manifests itself in my self. Since *atman* is Brahman, individual human consciousness manifests the nondual, though in an illusory way. Because we have forgotten our essential unity or identity with the nondual and wrongly believe we are distinct from it, we are caught in the cycle of suffering. At some future time our conception of ourselves as distinct from the nondual will be recognized to be an illusion, and we will be liberated to union with it.

Here the factual question about the individual's future existence is answered, but in a way that might have little significance for the individual. Once union with the Nondual occurs, the individual no longer is aware of any uniqueness or distinct existence. It is like putting a drop of water into the ocean; the drop adds to the whole, but its identity is not preserved. Indeed, desire to preserve our identity is the root of our problems. Acceptance of this view of life after death depends on one's larger view of reality and the human predicament, that is, on whether one believes that all is one (metaphysical monism) and that the source of suffering and unhappiness is our ignorance of our identity with the One.

   4. A fourth view might be termed *personal life after death*. On this view, individual persons either continue to live subsequent to their body's death or begin to exist sometime after their own death. Two requirements must be met. First, persons after death must be the same as (identical to) and not merely similar to the deceased. Second, individuals must have sufficient reason to think they are the same person they were prior to death. That is, they must be aware of self-identity. Without this, their immortality has no more significance for *them* than would the birth of someone in Tanzania after they die. This identification can be ensured, in part, by being aware of who one is (having a first person perspective)[10] and the presence of true memories about the previous life.[11]

   We will examine in detail the view that people actually exist after their death. What we want to know is whether individual, personal life after death really does or will occur. But this question presupposes a prior one, for only if it is *possible* for persons to live subsequent to their death can they *actually* do so. In fact, almost without exception, the denial that we have life after death is grounded not on arguments against its actuality but on the contention that it is impossible.

   Several considerations govern the possibility of life after death. One consideration involves the existence of a powerful mediating agent. If living on after death is a *natural* event, if the soul can survive and in some natural way acquire another body, as Hindus believe, the existence of a separate, powerful agent is unnecessary. If living on is *not a natural* state, the existence and action of a being with the special power to bring about life after death is required. That is, if we all die, not simply in body but in self, then unless an extremely powerful God exists, we have no ground for thinking that life after death is possible. For purposes of argument, we assume that such a God exists.

   The second consideration concerns the nature of human persons. If life after death is to be possible, human persons must be the sort of beings that can live subsequent to their death. If they are not, then arguments showing that life after death is actual are moot. Thus, before discussing the question "What good reasons can be given for believing in life after death?" we must discuss the philosophically prior question "What is the nature of human persons?" with an eye toward the possibility of life after death.

PERSONAL IDENTITY AND THE SOUL

One answer to the question "What is the nature of human persons?" commences from our ordinary experience. "We cannot rid ourselves of the commonsense perspective, in which mental items are conceived as elements in the biographies of subjects. The notion of pain without a sufferer, thought without a thinker, or perception without a perceiver, remains, to the eye of intuition, stubbornly unintelligible."[12] The subject of these experiences is not the brain, body, or anything physical, but a self or I that is our personal identity.

Continuity of body or body parts like the brain is not sufficient for continuity of the person. Swinburne tells the story of the mad surgeon who informs you that he will transplant your left brain into one body and your right brain into another, and that you can now choose which body will be tortured and which made happy after the transplant. Undoubtedly you would have a distinct preference for being the person made happy, but how can you determine which transplant will be you? The fact that continuity of brain parts does not clearly establish which one is you shows that such continuity is insufficient for personal identity.[13] Our body, although a critical part of our current existence, is not something we are.

Neither can the person be identified with individual states of consciousness, categories of thought, memories, or the particular way we experience and understand the world. First, individual memories, conceptual categories, and states of consciousness can be altered or lost without loss of personal identity. We do not remember most of what occurred when we were five or ten, or even last year. We also think about things differently from the way we did a number of years ago.

Second, memory claims are not infallible. We might claim to remember certain things that never happened or happened differently from the way we remember them. Hence, we must distinguish between memory claims and true memory claims. Only the latter suffice as the criterion of personal identity. But what makes my memory claim a true memory claim? At least two factors do so: first, it must accurately report what in fact occurred; second, it must be *my* memory claim. But if only genuine memories can be used as criteria for personal identity, and if my genuine memories are memories only had by me, then it becomes impossible to hold that genuine memory claims constitute personal identity without begging the question. In sum, our mental states might be used as evidence for establishing or assigning personal identity, but they do not constitute personal identity.

Consequently, it is reasonable to think that we are an irreducible, ultimate, unanalyzable self.[14] We do not say we have a self but that we are a self. Although we recognize others through their distinctive physical characteristics and behavioral patterns, we know our own self either through some inner, intuitive self-awareness or through having experiences.[15] The currently embodied self, the subject and center of our experiences, is the agent of thinking, remembering, feeling, and understanding. In effect, we consist of two parts, the soul as essential and the body as contingent.

We might note five arguments given to defend this dualist view of the human person. The first is termed the privacy argument. We are conscious beings with individualized sets of mental experiences consisting of self-awareness, beliefs, desires, intentions, and feelings. My access to these conscious experiences is immediate, first-hand, or private. You as an "outsider" might infer from my behavior what I am thinking or feeling, but you have no direct access to my private mental life. The physical, however, is public. My body and its processes are perceptible to others in the same way they are perceptible to me. Since the public and the private are contradictory, that which is about something private cannot at the same time be about something public. Consequently, introspective reports about our selves and our mental states cannot be about something public or physical.[16]

A second line of argument focuses on human freedom.[17] It begins with the observation that we can be held morally responsible for our actions, and that moral accountability requires that we be free. The incompatibilist or libertarian view of freedom maintains that given the same causal conditions, a person can choose to do or refrain from doing a certain action. But if we are identified with our physical components, if our psychological language refers to nothing more than physiological events that occur in the brain and central nervous system, then our choices are products of and explainable in terms of prior causal conditions, and these in terms of other causal conditions that extend beyond ourselves, even prior to our own existence. If this is so, our actions are not free and we cannot be held morally accountable for our deeds. To be free moral agents we cannot be mere physical beings, part of a deterministic causal chain, but we must have a nonphysical aspect or be a nonphysical agent.

A third argument might be termed a knowledge argument. Suppose a person blind from birth learns all the physical facts about light and how it affects objects and about the neurophysiology of seeing. Once she gained her sight she would acquire additional knowledge about mental facts, such as what a particular color looks like, how one shade differs from another, and what it is to appear vivid. But mental facts about what we perceive differ from physical facts about light waves and neurophysiology. This diversity of kinds of facts requires a diversity of kinds of substances: physical and mental.[18]

A fourth argument derives from the notion of intentionality. Something has intentionality if it is about something, that is, if it is directed toward something beyond itself. "Some (perhaps all) mental states—thoughts, beliefs—have intentionality. No physical state has intentionality. Therefore, (at least) those mental states with intentionality are not physical."[19]

Finally, some dualists appeal to the alleged existence of human paranormal powers. Minds purportedly have the power to communicate with other minds where no normal communication (in terms of a physical causal chain) would be possible (telepathy), to discern physical states of affairs without being able to perceive them (clairvoyance), and to move physical objects without using physical means (psychokinesis). For example, some experiments suggest that persons can communicate telepathically with others at a distance, even when the subject is enclosed in chambers walled with lead and iron.[20] But paranormal phenomena seem incompatible with a materialistic conception of the mind, for they presuppose that the mind is capable of receiving information about the world and other minds or of producing physical effects without requiring, as brains do, intermediate physical agencies.[21]

For some philosophers, these and other strains of evidence[22] indicate that humans are some sort of nonphysical self or soul that currently exists in close, functioning conjunction with a body. Philosophers differ on the nature of this soul. One contemporary dualist adaptation of a Thomistic view[23] holds that the soul is a substance that occupies a body in some nonspatial way. It "is an individuated essence that makes the body a human body and that diffuses, informs, animates, develops, unifies and grounds the biological functions of its body. The various chemical processes and parts (e.g., DNA) involved in morphogenesis are tools, means or instrumental causes employed by the soul as it teleologically unfolds its capacities toward the formation of a mature human body that functions as it ought to function by nature."[24] Though in one sense the soul is simple, yet it is complex in that it has a variety of faculties, functions, or abilities, most notably life sustaining and mental.

A Cartesian substance view maintains that two kinds of substances, extended and unextended, exist. As an unextended, thinking substance, the soul (I, self, mind) differs from but currently relates to the body. The soul's functions are mental, including self-awareness, memory, conceiving, and emoting. Although currently occurring in close or integrative conjunction with the body, the functions of the soul can be sustained apart from it. The Cartesian view differs in part from the Thomist view by assigning life-related functions to the physical or biological.

A third view, termed emergent dualism, differs from the other two views in holding that the soul is not a divine addition to but an emergent from the physical. Indeed, many organisms, for example, those with consciousness, have souls of varying degrees of complexity. The human being, therefore, is fully connected to its evolutionary antecedents. At the same time, this view is truly dualistic, for what emerges from the physical is more than mental properties, but an individual that provides unity to human experience and can continue after the physical that gave rise to it disappears.[25]

IMMORTALITY OF THE SOUL

The implications of psychophysical dualism for life after death are obvious. If the self is identified with a nonphysical entity or substance that is currently but only contingently embodied, then, since dying is a physical process, it is possible that the soul's existence would not terminate at physical death. Death might significantly affect the quality of soul-life. The corruption of the body would end functions, such as sensation, that require mutual involvement of both the physical and nonphysical. But what is not dependent upon the physical could survive and continue. Furthermore, since the soul is the self, we have sufficient grounds for holding that life after death is personal and mental, that we survive physical death with our self-identity and self-awareness essentially intact.

What kind of existence after death does the believer in the soul envision? There are three major schemas, though each has many permutations.

The first view is that the soul at death immediately unites with a body of some sort. Some religions believe this is another physical body; others believe it is a spiritual body. In the second schema, the soul continues to exist after death but does not function until it is united with something that provides what it requires to function.[26] Some refer to this as soul sleep.[27] In the third schema, the soul continues to exist and function disembodied, either temporarily, until united with a body, or permanently. One can find this temporary disembodiment in the Roman Catholic doctrine of purgatory.

Any soul activity during a disembodied state would be of a paranormal sort. Perception would require the addition of new and different powers or the extension of currently little-used perceptual powers such as clairvoyance and telepathy; by thoughts and desires alone it would act, as in psychokinesis. H. H. Price (1899–1984) suggested that the next world is composed of souls that have mental images about which they have beliefs and desires. "There might be a set of visual images related to each other perspectively, with front views and side views and back views all fitting neatly together in the way that ordinary visual appearances do now."[28] Such a group of images might also contain tactile, taste, auditory, and olfactory images, so that a nexus of interrelated images would constitute an object. One might even have a visual image of the body one had in the prior life. This body image might form the center of one's image world, much as our body now does. The entire environment of the disembodied individual would be composed of such families of mental images and would serve as the immortal's world. Development of some such scenario would be necessary to avoid solipsism (the view that the individual self is the whole of reality).

CRITICISM OF THE SOUL CONCEPT

This view of human persons is not without its difficulties. Perhaps the most substantial problem in the context of immortality is that after death this immaterial self, if it is to continue to function in any meaningful or conscious way, would have to sustain functions such as concept formation and memory recall. This implies that unless the soul is immediately united with a body, the physical brain is not a necessary condition for these and other cognitive processes. But this runs counter to much psychological and physiological evidence that strongly indicates that mental processes are closely linked to particular areas of the brain. For one thing, certain mental abilities and the degree to which they function successfully are in part inherited. In comparing the intelligence of members of natural families, the highest IQ correlation (.86) exists between identical twins raised together and progressively diminishes, though remaining significant, for fraternal twins (.60), siblings (.47), parents and children, and grandparents and grandchildren. The farther removed the genetic relation, the lower the correlation, reaching zero in unrelated adults.[29] This indicates that heredity plays a major role in determining mental ability and function.

Second, diseases or disabilities that affect the mind (such as Down's syndrome) or susceptibility to diseases (such as some cases of Alzheimer's) are genetically based. Consider dyslexia, which not only can be inherited (since eighty percent of dyslexic persons have parents who suffer from dyslexia) but for which chromosomal regions have been identified as possible gene locations.[30]

Third, damage to the brain directly affects awareness, consciousness, memory, and conceptual ability. For example, persons whose brain hemispheres have been severed (split brain persons), when presented with an object on the left that is sensed only by the right hemisphere of the brain, cannot tell what they see, though they can point to it with their left hand. The right brain, which controls the left hand, knows the object, but the left brain, which is the main area for speech and communication, does not know of the object because no information passes through the severed corpus callosum.

Fourth, certain mental abilities are locatable in the brain. The operations of working memory are carried out in the prefrontal lobes of the cerebral cortex, which "is divided into multiple memory domains, each specialized for encoding a different kind of information, such as the location of objects, the features of objects (color, size and shape), and additionally, in humans, semantic and mathematical knowledge."[31] It is true that individual thought processes cannot yet be correlated with particular energy transfers in the brain and perhaps never will be. Yet discerning patterns of energy events or networks of functioning cells makes brain research into mental processes possible.[32]

It is true that this evidence does not irrefutably establish the falsity of dualism. Believers in the soul may maintain that the soul does not function (sleeps) while disembodied after death, or that after death immediate reincarnation or connection to some ethereal body fulfills the requirement of a causal connection to the brain for consciousness and thinking.[33] Many dualists, however, believe that that souls live and consciously function disembodied after death. Such dualists must deny the mass of psychological and physiological evidence indicating that the brain is necessary for the existence and functioning of the mind, something that is unacceptable in light of contemporary brain research.

Equally problematic is how to determine whether a persisting but disembodied soul is the same person as the deceased. If, as argued earlier, memories cannot be used a criterion to establish personal identity, then what criterion could be used to establish that the disembodied soul is that same as the deceased? If, as some think, the preceding argument is mistaken and memories can be used as a criterion of personal identity, only true memories would count. But since to determine true memories requires access to bodily events and to the connection of that soul with a particular body, bodily identity would need to supplement true memories as a criterion of identity.[34] But no body is present in disembodied existence. Finally, the dualist may suggest that identity is provided for by continuity of a soul substance. But since a substance "stands under" properties and is itself propertyless, it brings no additional content to be used to establish identity. The dualist, it seems, must resort to the position that "personal identity is unanalyzable and primitive; it cannot be broken down into a more basic something else that could be taken to constitute personal identity."[35]

THE SELF AS A PSYCHOPHYSICAL UNITY

Many contemporary philosophers reject the existence of nonphysical souls or minds as incompatible with our knowledge of humans as physical beings. Personal identity is located in our mind-body (psychophysical) unity. One contemporary view, called the *Identity Theory*, holds that human beings are nothing more than physical organisms. This should not be taken to imply that mental or psychical states such as perceiving, conceptualizing, or re-membering are not real. It does mean that insofar as a statement about a mental state reports an event, that event is a brain process, brain state, or process within the central nervous system.[36]

One can think of parallel cases. Lightning can be reported by using either the physicist's language about an electrical discharge occurring at a particular place or the ordinary observer's language of a bright flash of light, jaggedly etched across the stormy sky. Although the two use noninterchangeable language systems, both genuinely report one and the same physical event.[37]

The major problem facing the Identity Theory concerns the nature of this cross-category identity. Defenders of the view claim that mental and brain states are neither merely causally related nor simply constantly corre-lated; they are strictly identical. According to Leibniz's principle of identity, two things are identical if and only if every property of one is also a property of the other. But the properties of mental states and brain states differ, not the least in that the former are nonspatial and private, whereas the latter are spa-tial and public. One might respond that Leibniz's principle does not apply to cross-category identities. In particular, one cannot expect total identity of properties where the application of the property to one category would be meaningless (as would be the case in applying spatial predicates to mental states). But, then, what criteria do two things with different category-sets of properties have to meet to be identical? In the case of the mind and body, al-though we have mental events and brain events occurring simultaneously, something more is needed to show that they are identical rather than merely causally related.

A second view is termed eliminative materialism; its contention is that mental phenomena should be reduced to the neurophysical, so that the cor-rect account of human mental capacities is provided by neuroscience. Recent reductionists such as Douglas Hofstadter (b. 1945) have argued that the self is "an active, self-updating collection of structures organized to 'mirror' the world as it evolves."[38] These high-level structures are composed of lower-level active patterns, and these of still lower patterns, until we reach the low-est level, which consists of nothing more than neural firings. Taken individually, these neural firings are random and meaningless, but statistical regularity reveals patterns that encode the information necessary for the organism to respond interactively to other patterns of symbols in its environment. When the patterns of firings are interpreted at the highest levels, we give them meaning, and these meaning-assigned patterns become alternative ways of explaining who we are.

Hofstadter gives the analogy of an ant colony. A colony has different levels: the colony itself, groups of different ants such as the workers, teams of ants, and the individual ants themselves. We assign meanings to the higher levels (for example, the workers remove a fly carcass) and hold that these higher levels encode information for the colony. But these higher-level patterns of behavior are ultimately the mere products of the random motions of individual, unintelligent ants.

We thus exist as programmable machines, potentially replicable by sophisticated (though yet undeveloped) computers. But computer hardware is interchangeable. One kind of hardware can be made to emulate a different kind if it is fed the proper software. Thus, ultimately, it is the patterns—the software—that matter. The precise nature of the hardware is insignificant except as it is able to cause or recognize these patterns.

One problem for such reductionist accounts is the evidence of top-down causation. Mental events seem to be genuine causes of events at adjacent but lower physiological or neurological levels. One can see this where mental activity is deficient. For instance, persons suffering from agnosia receive visual stimuli but are unable to recognize what they see (for example, a face), even though they can recognize it through data conveyed through other senses.

There are other, less reductionistic but materialist models of the person, some that allow for top-down causation. John Searle (b. 1932) argues that mental phenomena are properties that emerge from physiological micro-elements and hence are as real as any other properties. Indeed, as emergent mental properties, they are a kind of physical property, namely, a biological property, that can bring about effects though "intentional causation," where the "cause both represents and brings about the effect."[39] Other materialists provide a supervenience account that holds that mental properties supervene on physical properties; that is, mental properties work through physical properties.[40] Still others advocate a constitution view, according to which persons are constituted by but not identical with their bodies.[41] We cannot pursue this variety of materialist views of the person; our interest lies in their implications for the possibility of life after death.

RE-CREATION AND SPATIO-TEMPORAL CONTINUITY

Most materialists hold that spatio-temporal continuity is necessary for personal identity. Since human persons are not mere assemblages of components but physical beings whose components have a particular causal history, more than mere persistence is necessary to establish personal identity; a persistence where what exists before is causally related in relevant ways to what exists after is required. Hence, if we are to experience life after death, something physical, identified with our self, must causally continue. Since it appears that nothing comparable to a self continues after the body dies, the prospects for life after death on a materialist position appear dim.

Despite these appearances, theistic materialists have developed several scenarios to show that life after death is possible. Peter van Inwagen (b. 1942) argues if the causal chain that connects our components is broken, divine re-assembly cannot re-create the person. The reassembled being results from a divine miracle, not natural processes, and would no longer be human. Hence, since spatiotemporal continuity of the causally related features that make for life is necessary for personal identity, some sort of causal, material continuity must hold between my present material composition and my future composition for the human person as a material organism to exist in the future. He suggests that at the moment of death God preserves the essential matter that is the human person, to be used later to re-form that person. What exactly this matter is van Inwagen leaves undeveloped. He refers to it as the "naked kernel," the seed that continues to exist until God "clothes it in a festal garment of new flesh."[42] Elsewhere he refers to it as "the 'core person'—the brain and central nervous system—or even some special part of it."[43]

But how can this core person/matter be preserved through decay or cremation? Van Inwagen responds that it is possible that we only *seem* to die, for example, to decay or be burned. At the last moment before death God snatches away and preserves our core matter, substituting something that looks like it. To pull off this switch, God must deceive—and, one might say, do an excellent job of it, since no physician or embalmer has yet caught on about the true status of the deceased's remains.

To avoid this deception, Kevin Corcoran (b. 1964) modifies this scenario, suggesting that God, at the very last instant of an earthly life, causes the simple elements (not divisible into parts) that compose the body to fission (split into two) into spatially segregated sets of causally related simples. One set becomes the corpse, while the other continues to exist in some other sphere.[44]

But which set is the real person: the corpse (such that the person really did die) or the fission-person in another space (such that the person really did not die)? There seems little reason to think that one of these rather than the other is the person, since the respective composition of the two is the same. However, if there is little reason to choose one rather than the other, how can persons conclude that they have survived their death rather than died? Perhaps then neither is the person, for on the traditional view of identity, if both the deceased and the continuer can be the person, neither are.

Corcoran's response is that the person is the *closest continuer*. Since the deceased did not continue, there is only one continuer, which is the person. But then the continuer is contingently but not necessarily the person, for it is possible that the corpse really survived for a period of time before dying. Corcoran responds that having what becomes the corpse live for a time and then die would not be a possible scenario, for God is a loving being who cannot let people suffer demise. Since God as omnipotent cannot do the impossible or what is contrary to God's nature, it is impossible for the deceased to have been that person.

This reply assumes, first, that God cannot decide regarding the annihilation of persons. But traditionally, God is free (though perhaps morally constrained) to dispose of his creation as he wills.[45] Second, this view assumes that annihilation is incompatible with God's love. But many hold that annihilation (rather than, for example, consignment to hell) is compatible with God's love.

A third materialist scenario rejects the requirement of spatiotemporal continuity and instead holds that since we are physiological organisms that at base are composed of coded matter, God could physically re-create and program us with all the physical and psychical characteristics we possessed before we died. Specifically, since consciousness is a brain process or emergent biological property of brains, our brain could be re-created and programmed to have neural components and structures identical to those we had when we died so that we would have substantially the same memories, ideas, perspectives, and personality traits as we had before we died.

This is possible even on the radical reductionistic view of persons. If we are only programs that are to some extent independent of specific hardware, an omnipotent and omniscient being could re-create us simply by programming our unique software program into hardware of some relevant sort. The precise nature of the hardware may be insignificant, so long as it can boot up, run, and carry out the functions and commands of the relevant programs. We would thus be gap-inclusive persons: we would exist, cease to exist at death, and again exist at the time of re-creation.

But would re-created persons be the same as the deceased? After all, as gap-inclusive they are neither spatially nor temporally continuous with the deceased. Yet why should we think that spatiotemporal continuity is necessary for personal identity? It is true that we often consider spatiotemporal continuity necessary for identity. If a fire destroyed Van Gogh's *The Reapers* and then a skilled copyist precisely re-created it, we would hesitate to affirm that the re-creation is an authentic Van Gogh or to pay millions for the exact replica. But the reason spatiotemporal continuity is important in *The Reapers* is that the identity of the painting *as a Van Gogh* involves more than the particular distribution of paint on canvas. It is a Van Gogh because it was painted by Van Gogh. Were it destroyed by fire and repainted by the skilled copyist, though the content would be identical, it would no longer be a painting Van Gogh created. Spatiotemporal continuity is essential to the painting's identity in order to make it a Van Gogh, that is, to preserve the special causal sense captured in the identification of the painting as a Van Gogh.

But is spatiotemporal continuity necessary for the painting to have its identity as *The Reapers*? If one considers the painting insofar as it is *The Reapers* (where its origins are not part of its identity conditions), then one would look to the properties of the painting to determine that it is *The Reapers* rather than Caillebotte's *The Floor Scrapers*. That is, we might identify an object by its unique set of essential characteristics, which may or may not include its origins.

Critics respond that it is not merely the possession of unique, essential characteristics, but the possession of them connectedly over time and space that is necessary for something's identity. Yet we make interesting exceptions to the spatiotemporal continuity criterion of identity. We do not require continuity for abstract objects, such as wars, plays, pieces of music, or even this chapter that, if erased on disk and then identically recopied, would be the same chapter. But what about concrete objects like ourselves? Consider an expensive necklace, whose diamonds have been removed and dispersed over the years. A jeweler, wishing to reassemble the same necklace, collects all the diamonds and restrings them (even with a different string) in the same order (or even in a different order if the necklace is not defined by the order of its diamonds). Would it not be appropriate to say that he has reassembled the same necklace, even though the components lack continuous connectivity?

But, someone might object, at least the diamonds continued to exist. Then consider the way persons *as characters* function in plays. Hamlet has identity through the acts of a play; we experience no logical difficulty considering him *in the play itself* as a gap-inclusive person whose existence is punctuated by intermissions between acts. (Of course, the actor has spatiotemporal continuity between scenes or acts, but one clearly can distinguish between the actor and Hamlet.) It might be objected that the content of the acts, which may contain references to experiences offstage, requires we assume that the character has a life between acts. But one could write a play in which the character expressly has no experiences between the acts. As persons in the context of plays have identity despite being gap-inclusive, so people in real life may be gap-inclusive, with the re-creating assistance of God. Just as the character in Act I may not know that she is gap-inclusive, so we too may not know that human persons are gap-inclusive.

Our discussion of spatiotemporal continuity introduces a second objection, namely, that the deceased and the re-created cannot be identical. The objection is based on the contention that it is logically possible for God to create more than one person who looks the same, makes identical memory claims, or has an identical personality to the deceased. On this multiple replica scenario, where we have two claimants, James and John, both claiming to be re-creations of Peter, we have no grounds for deciding which is really Peter.[46] If we have no grounds, then, since according to the principle of identity both persons cannot be Peter, neither is Peter. The fact that someone looks identical to Peter and makes memory claims about performing Peter's actions at a previous time does not compel us to assert that that person really is Peter and did those actions.

One reply is that God can do only what is logically possible. But since it is logically impossible that two or more numerically distinct individuals be identical to each other and to the person who died, God cannot re-create two individuals identical to the deceased. Hence, the multiple replica scenario fails: though we might not be able to discern whether it was James or John who was identical with the deceased Peter, God cannot make both identical with him. At least one is only similar to him.

But, the objector might respond, how would someone know which person was similar to and which was identical with the deceased? One response is that while it is true that we cannot deduce identity from memories, a person cannot have *true* memories about experiences undergone by a particular person and still not be that person. Identity appears to be deducible from true memories. Hence, although we may not be able to discern whether James or John is identical with the deceased Peter, both cannot be identical with him, given that only one can make true memory claims.

But since memories may be uncheckable, appeal to true memories may not suffice to establish identity in any given case. Lynne Baker (b. 1944), using her Constitution View of the person, suggests an appeal to a first-person perspective. She distinguishes between the conditions necessary to be an organism and those necessary for being a person. A human person is a person because it has a first-person perspective. But having a first-person perspective is not necessary for being a bodied being; all sorts of animals are bodied beings lacking this perspective. Persons, then, are not identical to but constituted by their body, and the sameness of persons between times is the sameness of their first-person perspective, not the sameness of the body.[47] Whereas the relation between me and my first-person perspective is necessary, the relation between me and a body is contingent though essential (to exist I must be embodied in some form). Given this view, suppose that God made one hundred replicas of my body. Although these replicas have identically constituted bodies, they cannot have my first-person perspective, that which makes a person me. Although others might not be able to distinguish me from the replicas, I know who I am in virtue of my first-person perspective.

A distinct advantage of this view is that it "allows that a person's resurrection body may be nonidentical with her earthly biological body."[48] Since I am not identical with but constituted by my body, it is possible for my first-person perspective to be in or from a different body, just as it was possible that Michangelo carved his masterpiece *David* out of a different piece of marble or even wood. The particular marble he used was contingent, though *David* could not have existed without some sculpted medium. The advantage, then, is that this view can accommodate those who maintain a psychological criterion of identity of some sort and who deny that spatiotemporal continuity is a necessary condition for personal identity.

Baker contends that although sameness of first-person perspective is the criterion for sameness of person over time, there is no criterion for sameness of first-person perspective.[49] We have reached a basic experience. An interesting feature of this discussion is that we have returned to fundamentally the same response that some dualists give to the personal identity problem: the soul or re-created person is identical to the deceased because of this basic awareness of the self.

The conclusion of all this is that both perspectives on the human person—that we are souled beings or that we are psychophysical unities or even mere programs—appear to allow, in one version or another, for the possibility of life after death. One cannot reject life after death on the grounds that it is contradictory. At the same time, both views face serious challenges: the one whether we have adequate grounds for thinking that disembodied souls can exist as cognitively active persons, the other whether spatiotemporal continuity is necessary for all cases of personal identity.

A POSTERIORI ARGUMENTS FOR LIFE AFTER DEATH

If one grants that life after death is possible, a second question arises: is there any reason to think that people actually live after death? Defenders of life after death propose two sorts of arguments: a priori philosophical arguments and a posteriori arguments from particular kinds of experience. We first look at a posteriori arguments, then turn to a priori arguments. Three types of a posteriori arguments seem attractive to some who think about these issues.

1. The first notes particular experiences of some persons who either almost died or who died but were resuscitated (depending on one's definition of death). Lying near death in a hospital room, many people report hearing caregivers pronounce them either dying or dead. They then find themselves leaving or out of their body, witnessing from a different perspective (often from above their body) their immediate surroundings and the health care personnel working to resuscitate their body. They possess a new body, variously described as an amorphous cloud or a spiritual body, shaped like their physical body, incapable of interacting with the physical environment of their original body. Subsequently they experience passing through a dark place, often described as a tunnel, until they come to a different realm. Here they meet other persons, known or unknown to them, who though not physically embodied are often recognizable, with whom they communicate in some telepathic way. They often also encounter a being of light, exuding love and compassion, who helps them recall (as if by an instantaneous videotape) and evaluate their past. Despite their strong desire to stay and enjoy this peaceful, happy experience, they either want to or are told to return to their physical bodies.[50]

No doubt people have such *near-death experiences.* The problem is how to understand or explain them. Some believe that they are hallucinations, brought on by physiological conditions in the body. "A change in blood pressure in the inner ear can evoke a sense of rising, hovering, floating in space." Such a change can occur when the blood flow through the body is checked, as with cardiac arrest. Likewise, the experience of visualizing one's body "as if from the outside becomes more common when a person is subject to serious emotional stress" (as happens in near-death experiences) or is taking powerful drugs (as sometimes happens with dying persons).[51]

However, others respond that the reports do not mirror the patterns created by stress- or drug-induced conditions.[52] One study of dying patients concludes that the presence of pain medication or stress has no appreciable affect on the frequency of near-death experiences.[53] Furthermore, descriptions of the immediate circumstances surrounding their physical body given by persons having near-death experiences have an amazing accuracy, not characterized by what one would expect in a drug-induced account. Sometimes the persons describe what is going on in the room or in nearby rooms that they could not observe from their patient-bed. Paul Badham (b. 1942) cites a case of a patient accurately reporting two coins on the top of a high cupboard in the room.

At the same time, experiments—for example, where secret numbers have been placed in a surgical unit near the ceiling, in a position that only could be viewed from above—have failed to yield consistently positive results. People who reported having near-death experiences in such places have been unable to provide the secret numbers.

Perhaps these after-death experiences can be explained by appealing to psychological or physical factors. Christians, for example, have a penchant for interpreting the being of light as Jesus, Hindus as the death god Yama or other Hindu deities. The descriptions sometimes convey imagery distinctive to certain religions—for example, gates of pearl. This suggests that these experiences may be individual projections, colored by the persons' religious backgrounds and beliefs and occasioned by the traumatic experience through which they are going.

Yet the descriptions can vary significantly from standard religious expectations. Raymond Moody (b. 1944) writes, "I have not heard a single reference to a heaven or a hell anything like the customary picture to which we are exposed in this society. Indeed, many persons have stressed how unlike their experiences were to what they had been led to expect in the course of their religious training."[54]

Part of the puzzle of these cases is the difficulty experienced in recounting the kind of body possessed. It is invisible, weightless (floating), and able to move through physical objects, yet it has perceptual powers and can hear (though more so in terms of thought-transfer than having auditory experiences). This suggests that this world and the people in it are "embodied" in a way that makes them recognizable and locatable from a particular perspective, yet possessing only a partial, one-way relationship to our present world—aware of the physical environment yet unable to influence it. However one interprets this new body, two of the elements we deemed necessary for personal immortality are present: awareness of one's own identity and recollection of one's past.

2. The second a posteriori argument comes from psychical events such as apparitions of or *mediumistic communication with deceased persons.* The dead really appearing or mediums really communicating with deceased persons would provide evidence that people survive death.

Appeal to mediums working through séances often is discounted, not only because of the possible and proven cases of fraud, but because what they recount of the deceased often can be accounted for more easily by appealing either to role playing by various parts of the medium's conscious or unconscious personality or to telepathic communication from those present and seeking information about the deceased. The sitters' expectations, perhaps in some way communicated to the alleged medium, are met.

However, some cases are more difficult to explain in this fashion. In some instances deceased persons allegedly have communicated with or appeared to the living and conveyed to them information that was verifiable but previously unknown. C. D. Broad (1887–1971) recounts the case of a North Carolina farmer who appeared four years after his death to inform a surviving son about the location of his lost will.[55] R. W. K. Paterson reports a series of interesting cases where the information communicated was independently checked. In one case, the wife, deceased in 1970, of a Reverend David Kennedy reportedly communicated through several mediums about such common events as waking him to remind him to preach in a service, locate clean collars, and comment on his voting.[56]

A puzzling feature of most of these cases is that the communicants give no indication that their life has continued on in any meaningful way in the afterlife.[57] They give no detailed indication of their new surroundings, occupations, or interests; what is said consists of information about the past or vague generalizations ascribable to the medium's beliefs about the afterlife. Indeed, when visualized, the apparitions are seen in the clothes or situations surrounding their death or past life.

3. A third a posteriori argument commences from the claim that *certain persons actually have come back to life*. In Christianity, the belief that Jesus was resurrected from the dead is coupled with the theological assertion that this event both foretokens and makes possible our resurrection. The Apostle Paul's argument is this: If Christ was raised from the dead, we will be raised from the dead. Christ was raised. Therefore we will be raised.[58]

The soundness of this argument depends on the truth of both premises. Since the first premise is theological, knowledge of its truth depends on accepting other claims, including that God exists, that he can reveal his promises and purposes, that he is trustworthy to keep them and powerful enough to implement them, and that he actually revealed this to Paul. The orthodox Christian theist presumably would have little problem with any of these presuppositions. The truth of the second premise depends on whether the claim that Jesus was resurrected is historically true. Christians often introduce claims about witnesses to the living Jesus, the empty tomb, and the rise and success of Christianity as evidence that it really occurred.[59]

Each of these a posteriori arguments depends upon claims persons make about experiences they have had. To evaluate the claims means that we must consider the criteria that we ordinarily invoke to evaluate the testimony or report made by other persons. The difficulty, generally, is not that people have had the experiences that they claim to have had but how to understand and interpret those experiences. This brings us back to the larger worldview that each of us brings to our experience and to the reports from others. To the shaping of this worldview this book is addressed.

A PRIORI ARGUMENTS FOR LIFE AFTER DEATH

Supplementing these a posteriori arguments from particular experiences are numerous a priori arguments that commence from ideas rather than experience. Let us note three of them.

1. The first argument was developed by Thomas Aquinas (1224–1274).[60] He argued that *we are made for an ultimate end,* which is happiness. But happiness cannot be achieved in this life, for our individual fortune is fickle, our body and will weak, and our knowledge imperfect. But since God cannot have made us in vain, we must be able to achieve the end for which we were made, and this requires that we continue to live after death.

But why should one think that we cannot achieve happiness in this life? Aristotle (384–322 B.C.) suggests that happiness is not a momentary feeling of pleasure, but a state in which persons manifest virtues throughout their lifetime.[61] If we engage in the activity of reason or contemplation, we can attain it. We need not lose happiness simply because of momentary adversity.

Aquinas, however, understands happiness differently. Human happiness must relate to the ultimate end for which we were made, which is God. Since our knowledge of God by faith is an act of the will, not the intellect, our present knowledge of God by natural reason can be erroneous and uncertain. Hence, knowledge or contemplation of God, in which lies our ultimate happiness, is not (except momentarily) attainable in this life. To fully experience this beatific vision, we must live subsequent to our death.[62]

Aquinas's argument rests on the very interesting (and debatable) thesis that we would have been made in vain if we cannot achieve our ultimate end. But is God's creation of us compromised if we fail to achieve our ultimate end, no matter what other ends we realize? If we achieve limited fulfillment of human potential or a partially realized life of happiness, or if we come to know God in our own limited way and actualize our intellectual capacity through contemplation of what truth can be known and live a virtuous life, participating in the grace of God, we seem to have no grounds for the claim that we have lived in vain. On the other hand, if part of our end is fulfilled in contemplative communion with God, it would seem reasonable to think that God would not let us fail to achieve this highest end for which we are made. Clearly, this argument comes laden with theological as well as philosophical presuppositions.

2. A second a priori proof, using basically the same argumentative structure as the first, commences from moral premises. In general, the *moral argument* asserts that since finite human existence is insufficient either to achieve the moral ideal or to provide an adequate basis on which to recommend the performance of good rather than evil, humans must be immortal. Immanuel Kant (1724–1804) advances the former contention.[63] The moral law tells us that we must strive to achieve the highest good. But unless we can realize this highest good, we cannot be commanded to attain it. But this highest good—the perfect alignment of our individual wills with the moral law, so that we act solely out of respect for the moral law (what Kant calls holiness) and not out of inclination—is not achievable in this life. Hence, if the moral law is to have any bite, if we are to be obligated to live under it, we must be able to live past death, at least to the point at which we can become holy. Life after death is a postulate of the moral law.

But why, one might ponder, must we be able to realize completely the highest good in order to be commanded rationally to pursue it? Often goals are ideals toward which a person strives, which may, at best, be only partially realizable. I have the ideal to be truthful and am commanded morally to speak the truth, although I have no illusions about attaining perfect truthfulness. The command to attain perfection "is merely a rhetorical way of saying: 'Never be contented with your present level of moral achievement.'"[64]

In Kant's defense it might be argued that there is a difference between commanding that we *strive* to attain a goal and commanding that we *attain* it. The moral law commands the latter, not the former. Yet perhaps we have argued backwards. Instead of arguing from the moral obligation to what can be, perhaps we should argue from what is attainable (we can do) to what we ought to do. If we cannot achieve it, we are under no obligation to do so.[65]

3. A third argument, advanced by Plato (428–347 B.C.), applies to the dualist conception of the human person. Plato argued that the *soul is immortal because it is imperishable*, it is imperishable because it is indestructible, and it is indestructible because it is simple (not divisible into parts).[66] But why cannot the soul perish in other ways, for example, by simply being annihilated? There seems to be no reason why what is simple cannot be annihilated. On the other hand, since annihilation would require the activity of some outside agent, Plato's argument, if sound, would suggest that in itself the soul lives on and does not die with the disintegration of the physical body.

PROSPECTS

What conclusions can be drawn from our discussion? First, we have seen that there is considerable debate over how best to understand the human person. The conclusion the investigator draws depends not only on the particular evidence marshaled but also on how it fits into one's larger philosophical schema. We have considered arguments that life after death is possible on different perspectives on the human person, though problems persist. If one adopts the view that the soul is the real person, then it is possible that the soul persists through death, since physical death does not necessarily mean the end of the soul. If one adopts a materialistic view of the person, then the possibility of life after death depends upon the existence of a powerful, omniscient being who is capable of re-creating, in some fashion, persons to be essentially the same as the deceased. If one denies the existence of God or that God has such powers, or if spatiotemporal continuity is necessary for identity, then life after death for the anthropological materialist seems less likely, if not impossible.

What about its actuality? Here the evidence is far from clear. The a posteriori arguments depend upon claims that might have other plausible explanations. The a priori arguments rest on claims concerning, for example, the appropriate goal of human action or what the moral law requires. In both cases readers must evaluate the claims and judiciously decide which explanation best accounts for the data.

Often those who find arguments for immortality unconvincing have already adopted a nontheistic worldview, whereas those who find them convincing have adopted a particular theistic worldview in which these claims not only make sense but contribute in an important way to a present, meaningful existence in which encounter with God and the desire to realize their end in God play an essential role and in which the afterlife simply provides for a higher realization of these possibilities. This is not a defect, but a recognition that any view of the world should have a coherence of structure and meaning.

STUDY QUESTIONS

1. Do you believe in life after death? What arguments or evidence do you give to support your answer?

2. What presuppositions about human persons do those who talk literally about human immortality make? How might these presuppositions differ from those held by someone who speaks simply about life after death? Why do you think that language matters when we speak about important topics?

3. We noted four different views of life after death. In what ways are they similar and different? What are the strengths and weaknesses of each position?

4. What evidence do you think best supports the view that we are nonphysical selves? Note a strength and weakness of this evidence.

5. Describe the materialist conception of human persons. Describe the strengths and weakness of this view. What are the implications of this view for the possibility of life after death?

6. In what ways would the afterlife differ for the believer in a soul from that described by the materialist? What problems (for example, population, human fulfillment, time consciousness) might result from humans living after their death?

7. Which arguments, if any, presented in this chapter for the actuality of life after death do you think are the strongest? Why do you think so? Note a crucial premise of one of the arguments and evaluate its truth.

NOTES

1. Corliss Lamont, *The Illusion of Immortality* (New York: Philosophical Library, 1965), p. 7.

2. According to the Theravada Buddhist doctrine of *anatta*, there is no persisting self substance to transmigrate. See David Kalupahana, *Buddhist Philosophy* (Honolulu: University of Hawaii, 1976), pp. 38–42.

3. Thomas Aquinas, *Summa Theologica,* Part III Supplement, Q. 79, A.2. Paul Badham quotes a 1976 Catholic catechism for adults approved in Ireland and the United States, which states that each person will one day rise again "as the same person he was, in the same flesh made living by the same spirit." Paul Badham and Linda Badham, *Immortality or Extinction?* (N.J.: Barnes and Noble, 1982), p. 5.

4. John Hick, *Death and Eternal Life* (New York: Harper and Row, 1976), chap. 15; Bruce R. Reichenbach, *Is Man the Phoenix? A Study of Immortality* (Grand Rapids, Mich.: William B. Eerdmans, 1978), chap. 5.

5. "After his death his words remain established. This is what the ancient saying means. I have heard that the best course is to establish virtue, the next best is to establish achievement, and still the next best is to establish words. When these are not abandoned with time, it may be called immortality." *Tso chuan,* in *A Source Book in Chinese Philosophy,* ed. Wing-Tsit Chan (Princeton, N.J.: Princeton University Press, 1963), p. 13. For its place in African religions, see J.S. Mbiti, *African Religions and Philosophy* (New York: Doubleday, 1970), pp. 32–3.

6. George Santayana, *Reason in Religion* (New York: Collier, 1962), pp. 174–8.

7. Rudolph Bultmann, in *Kerygma and Myth,* ed. Hans Werner Bartsch (New York: Harper and Row, 1953), p. 39.

8. D.Z. Phillips, *Death and Immortality* (London: Macmillan, 1970), pp. 41–55.

9. Ludwig Wittgenstein, *Tractatus Logico-Philosophicus,* 6.4311.

10. Lynne Rudder Baker, *Persons and Bodies: A Constitution View* (Cambridge: Cambridge University Press, 2000), chap. 3.

11. A problem relating to the second of these conditions dogs those who advocate reincarnation. Alleged reincarnates are born with their unique genetic code inherited from their parents and go on to develop their own physical characteristics, personality, memories, and categories of understanding. They begin life as infants who have no recollection of former lives, and few ever remember them. One might hypothesize the continuity of a spiritual soul, but without memories, awareness of self-identity, and consciousness of continuity or consistency of experience with the past, one cannot discern whether the person is a reincarnated person or a new individual. Reincarnationists, however, point to exceptional cases where children appear to remember past existences and exhibit features (e.g., being able to speak certain languages) that seem to require previous existence.

12. John Foster, "A Brief Defense of the Cartesian View," in *Soul, Body and Survival,* ed. Kevin Corcoran (Ithaca, N.Y.: Cornell University Press, 2001), p. 17.

13. Richard Swinburne, *The Evolution of the Soul* (Oxford: Oxford University Press, 1986), p. 149.

14. Richard Swinburne, *The Coherence of Theism* (Oxford: Oxford University Press, 1977), p. 119.

15. H.D. Lewis, *The Self and Immortality* (New York: Seabury, 1973), p. 45.

16. J.P. Moreland and Scott B. Rae, *Body and Soul* (Downers Grove, Ill: InterVarsity Press, 2000), pp. 159–60.

17. Swinburne, *Evolution of the Soul,* chap. 13; William Hasker, *The Emergent Self* (Ithaca, N.Y.: Cornell University Press, 1999), chap. 4; Moreland and Rae, *Body and Soul,* chap. 4.

18. Moreland and Rae, *Body and Soul,* pp. 160–3.

19. Ibid., p. 164.

20. L.L. Vasiliev, *Experiments in Mental Suggestion* (Church Crookham: Institute for the Study of Mental Images, 1963).

21. Hick, *Death and Eternal Life,* p. 121; Badham and Badham, *Immortality,* pp. 90–2.

22. Other arguments can be found in Hasker, *Emergent Self,* pp. 122–46, and Charles Taliaferro, *Consciousness and the Mind of God* (Cambridge: Cambridge University Press, 1994), chap. 3.

23. The degree to which Thomas Aquinas was a dualist is debated. For him, humans are a unity, the soul being the substantial form of the body. At the same time, he argued that the soul is immaterial and incorruptible, capable of existing apart from the body. For a careful restatement of Aquinas, see Eleanor Stump, "Non-Cartesian Substance Dualism and Materialism without Reductionism," *Faith and Philosophy* 12 (October 1995), 505–31.

24. Moreland and Rae, *Body and Soul,* p. 202.

25. Hasker, *Emergent Self,* chap. 7.

26. Swinburne, *The Evolution of the Soul,* chap. 10.

27. Oscar Cullmann, *The Immortality of the Soul or Resurrection of the Dead?* (London: Epworth Press, 1958), pp. 51–3.

28. H.H. Price, "Survival and the Idea of 'Another World,' " *Proceedings of the Society for Psychical Research* vol. 50, pt. 182 (January 1953). (See PRSR2e, pt. 9, pp. 447–57.)

29. V. Elving Anderson, "A Genetic View of Human Nature," in *Whatever Happened to the Soul,* ed. Warren S. Brown, Nancey Murphy, and H. Newton Malony (Minneapolis, Minn.: Augsburg Fortress, 1998), p. 58.

30. Ibid., p. 60.

31. Patricia S. Goldman-Rakic, "Working Memory and the Mind," *Scientific American* (September 1992), 115.

32. Malcolm Jeeves, *Brain, Mind, and Behavior* (Minneapolis, Minn.: Augsburg Fortress, 2000), pp. 79–81.

33. Swinburne, *Evolution of the Soul,* chap. 15. (See PRSR2e, pt. 9, pp. 457–68.)

34. Terence Penelhum, *Survival and Disembodied Existence* (London: Routledge and Kegan Paul, 1970), chaps. 5 and 6.

35. Moreland and Rae, *Body and Soul,* p. 180.

36. J.J.C. Smart, "Sensations and Brain Processes," *Philosophical Review* 68 (1959); reprint C.V. Borst, ed., *The Mind/Brain Identity Theory* (New York: Macmillan, 1970), chap. 8, p. 56.

37. U.T. Place, "Is Consciousness a Brain Process?" *British Journal of Psychology* vol. 47 (1956); reprinted in Borst, *Mind/Brain Identity,* p. 47.

38. Douglas R. Hofstadter and Daniel C. Dennett, *The Mind's I* (New York: Basic Books, 1981), p. 192.

39. John Searle, *Minds, Brains and Science* (Cambridge: Harvard University Press, 1984), p. 61.

40. Jaegwon Kim, *Supervenience and Mind: Selected Philosophical Essays* (Cambridge: Cambridge University Press, 1986).

41. Baker, *Persons and Bodies.*

42. Peter van Inwagen, "Dualism and Materialism: Athens and Jerusalem?" *Faith and Philosophy* 12 (October 1995): 486.

43. Peter van Inwagen, "The Possibility of Resurrection," in *Immortality,* ed. Paul Edwards (New York: Macmillan, 1992), p. 246.

44. Kevin Corcoran, "Physical Person and Postmortem Survival without Temporal Gaps," in *Soul, Body, and Survival,* ed. Kevin Corcoran (Ithaca, N.Y.: Cornell University Press, 2000), pp. 210–7.

45. Stephen T. Davis, "Physicalism and Resurrection," in Corcoran, *Soul, Body, and Survival,* p. 238.

46. B.A.O. Williams, "Personal Identity and Individuation," *Proceedings of the Aristotelian Society* 57 (1956–1957): 239.

47. Lynne Rudder Baker, "Material Persons and the Doctrine of Resurrection," *Faith and Philosophy* 18 (April 2001): 160.

48. Ibid., p. 164.

49. William Hasker argues that a first-person perspective criterion is not a criterion at all. To have a first-person perspective is to see things from the perspective of a particular person. I see things the way I do because of who I am as a distinct person. But then "to say that P_1 and P_2 have the same first-person perspective is just to say that P_1 and P_2 are the same person, and the criterion [of a first-person perspective] reduces to a tautology." William Hasker, "The Constitution View of Persons: A Critique," unpublished paper, p. 16.

50. See Raymond A. Moody, Jr., *Life after Life* (New York: Bantam, 1976).

51. Badham and Badham, *Immortality or Extinction?* p. 73.

52. R.W.K. Paterson, *Philosophy and the Belief in Life after Death* (London: Macmillan, 1995), pp. 145–9.

53. K. Osis and E. Haraldsson, *At the Hour of Death* (New York: Avon, 1977), pp. 186–7.

54. Moody, *Life after Life*, p. 140.

55. C.D. Broad, *Lectures on Psychical Research* (London: Routledge and Kegan Paul, 1962), pp. 137–9.

56. Paterson, *Philosophy*, pp. 161–72.

57. Hick, *Death and Eternal Life*, p. 140.

58. I Corinthians 15:12–23.

59. For an extended argument to this effect, see Frank Morison, *Who Moved the Stone?* (London: Faber and Faber, 1930). We have briefly dealt with this in Chapter 9.

60. Aquinas, *Summa Theologica*, Supplement to part II, Q.79, A.2.

61. Aristotle, *Nicomachean Ethics* (Indianapolis, Ind.: Bobbs-Merrill, 1962), Bk. I, chaps. 7–10.

62. Thomas Aquinas, *Summa Contra Gentiles*, III, chap. 35.

63. Immanuel Kant, *Critique of Practical Reason* (Indianapolis, Ind.: Bobbs-Merrill, 1956), Bk. II, chap. 2.

64. C.D. Broad, *Five Types of Ethical Theory* (London: Routledge and Kegan Paul, 1930), p. 140.

65. Paterson, *Philosophy*, p. 111.

66. Plato, *Phaedo*, 100b–107a. See René Descartes, "Synopsis," *Meditations on First Philosophy*.

SUGGESTED READING

Badham, Paul. *Christian Beliefs about Immortality*. London: Macmillan, 1976.
———, and Linda Badham. *Immortality or Extinction?* N.J.: Barnes and Noble, 1982.
Baker, Lynne Rudder Baker. *Persons and Bodies: A Constitution View*. Cambridge: Cambridge University Press, 2000.
Blackmore, Susan. *Dying to Live: Near-Death Experiences*. Buffalo, N.Y.: Prometheus Press, 1993.
Cooper, John. *Body, Soul, and Life Everlasting*. Grand Rapids, Mich.: William B. Eerdmans, 1989.

Corcoran, Kevin. *Soul, Body and Survival.* Ithaca, N.Y.: Cornell University Press, 2001.

Davis, Stephen T., ed. *Death and Afterlife.* London: Macmillan, 1989.

Edwards, Paul. *Immortality.* New York: Macmillan, 1992.

———. *Reincarnation.* Amherst, N.Y.: Prometheus Press, 1996.

Hasker, William. *The Emergent Self.* Ithaca, N.Y.: Cornell University Press, 1999.

Hick, John. *Death and Eternal Life.* New York: Harper and Row, 1976.

Kvanvig, Jonathan L. *The Problem of Hell.* New York: Oxford University Press, 1993.

Lewis, H.D. *Persons and Life after Death.* London: Macmillan, 1978.

———. *The Self and Immortality.* New York: Seabury, 1973.

Paterson, R.W.K. *Philosophy and the Belief in Life after Death.* London: Macmillan, 1995.

Penelhum, Terence. *Survival and Disembodied Existence.* London: Routledge and Kegan Paul, 1970.

Perry, John. *Personal Identity and Immortality.* Indianapolis, Ind.: Hackett, 1979.

Reichenbach, Bruce R. *Is Man the Phoenix? A Study of Immortality.* Grand Rapids, Mich.: William B. Eerdmans, 1978.

Swinburne, Richard. *The Evolution of the Soul.* Oxford: Oxford University Press, 1986.

Taliaferro, Charles. *Consciousness and the Mind of God.* Cambridge: Cambridge University Press, 1994.

Tipler, Frank. *The Physics of Immortality.* New York: Doubleday, 1994.

Walls, Jerry L. *Hell: The Logic of Damnation.* Notre Dame, Ind.: University of Notre Dame Press, 1992.

CHAPTER 11   RELIGIOUS
LANGUAGE:
HOW CAN
WE SPEAK
MEANINGFULLY
OF GOD?

A fascinating science fiction story portrays a high lama who purchases a Mark V Automatic Sequence Computer to install in his monastery in Tibet. However, the lama requests that the computer be modified to print out letters and not numbers. The curious purpose of all this, as he expresses it, is to accelerate the completion of a list of all the names of God that his monks are compiling. A task that would have taken another fifteen centuries will now take only a hundred days. By systematically combining sequences of letters in a special alphabet, the computer will eventually list all of the real names of God. It is not long until the computer is installed in the lamasery in the mountains of Tibet. George and Chuck, the two engineers sent to oversee its operation, are about to go stir-crazy watching the monks tirelessly pasting long strips of names into books.

When Chuck is finally able to inform the high lama that the machine is on its last cycle, he receives such an enthusiastic response that he inquires further into the religious significance of the all the activity. "Well," says the lama, "they believe that when they have listed all his names—and they reckon that there are about nine billion of them—God's purpose will be achieved. The human race will have finished what it was created to do, and there won't be any point in carrying on." Chuck later relays this incredible story to George: "When the list's completed, God steps in and simply winds things up . . . bingo!" At the thought that the end of the project will be the end of the world, George gives a nervous little laugh. Thinking the matter over, the two Americans realize if the world does not end when the project is finished, it may mean trouble for them at the hands of hundreds of angry monks whose lifework has been spoiled by a computer. They make plans to leave "Project Shangri-La," as they call it, before the computer finishes its last long series of names. On the evening of the last day, Chuck and George say good-bye to the monks and ride the tough mountain ponies down the winding road from the lamasery toward the old DC-3 that is waiting for them at the end of the runway. They descend the mountain in the cold, perfectly clear Himalayan night, ablaze with the now familiar stars:

. . . George glanced at his watch.

"Should be there in an hour," he called back over his shoulder to Chuck. Then he added in an afterthought: "Wonder if the computer's finished its run. It was due about now."

Chuck didn't reply, so George swung round in his saddle. He could just see Chuck's face, a white oval turned toward the sky.

"Look," whispered Chuck, and George lifted his eyes to heaven. (There is always a last time for everything.)

Overhead, without any fuss, the stars were going out.[1]

HUMAN LANGUAGE AND THE INFINITE

The story reminds us of the universal preoccupation with language about God—from animistic religions which hold that naming the divine gives magical power to the intellectual who ponders how human words can appropriately apply to deity. In the last hundred years or so, philosophers have become particularly concerned with the nature and role of language in general and have developed a number of different theories about religious language in particular.

There are two major reasons why philosophers pay close attention to religious language. The first is that they are interested in questions of *meaning* and thus in how words about God derive their meaning. For example, the language that the Judeo-Christian tradition employs to talk about God is drawn from ordinary discourse, from the language we use daily to speak of creaturely phenomena. However, the Judeo-Christian tradition teaches that the Creator is not the creature, that God is "high and lifted up," indeed, that God is "transcendent." Most great religions involve some kind of teaching about the transcendence of the divine. How, then, can language about the finite realm be used about God? We know what we mean when we speak, for instance, of ordinary rocks and ordinary eyes. But what can it mean to speak of God as being a "rock" or as having "eyes," since rocks and eyes are mere creaturely realities?

The second reason for the intense interest philosophers have shown in religious language is that they seek to analyze and evaluate *beliefs.* Beliefs, of course, are expressed in the form of *statements* or *propositions.* As a prelude to further philosophical scrutiny of religious beliefs, it is crucial to understand the language in which they are couched. Of course, much religious language is not used to make direct assertions of belief but is instead used for a variety of distinctively religious purposes, such as prayer, liturgy, and admonition. Yet philosophers know that other religious uses of language rest upon or assume certain prior beliefs. Worshiping God, for instance, assumes that there is such a being as God and that he is worthy of our adoration and devotion; petitioning God presupposes that God actually hears and responds to prayer; and so forth. When the precise beliefs behind these and other religious activities are made explicit, we have a set of *theological statements,* truth-claims about God and his relationship to the world. Therefore, once we grasp the meaning of theological terms and, in turn, of the theological statements in which they appear, we can ask questions about what rational grounds one could have for accepting or rejecting those statements. Other chapters in this book use religious language in order to discuss such matters as the attributes of the theistic deity or whether there is rational justification for certain theological claims, whereas this chapter looks at the structure, meaning, and impact of theological discourse itself.

THE CLASSICAL THEORY OF ANALOGY

The great medieval thinkers were well aware of the problem of using creaturely language to speak of God. They did not question whether religious language has any meaning but realized the difficult problem of accounting for its meaning. To solve the problem, Thomas Aquinas (c. 1224–1274) developed what is now known as the classic theory of "analogy" or "analogical predication." The theory has been standard fare in discussions of religious language throughout the intervening centuries and has remained attractive to many.

A predicate term in a sentence attaches some property, relation, or activity to the subject term. Thus, predicates define or characterize the subject in particular ways. Typical examples of the sorts of statements employed in both academic theology and popular religion are not difficult to find. Let us consider some examples drawn from Jewish and Christian traditions:

> God created the heavens and the earth.
> God brought the Israelites out of Egypt.
> Yahweh spoke to the prophets.
> God is just.

Aquinas held that when a word—for example, "just"—is applied both to a created being and to God, it is not being used *univocally* (i.e., with exactly the same meaning) in the two instances. Yet neither is the word being used *equivocally* (i.e., with two completely different meanings), as when "hot" is used to apply to pepper corns and race cars. There is a connection between divine justice and human justice, a similarity between a certain quality in God and a certain quality in persons. As Aquinas indicates, this allows the word to be used *analogically.*[2] It is the similarity within difference and difference within similarity that allows the analogical use of the same term in two different contexts.

James Ross (b. 1927) believes that the traditional analogy theory provides a helpful middle way between the univocal and the equivocal uses of terms when speaking of God and thus avoids *anthropomorphism* and *agnosticism*, respectively. *Anthropomorphism* is the view that God differs from creatures merely in degree and thus that no alteration of meaning in our terms is necessary to speak of him. *Agnosticism* is the view that God is so different from us that we cannot say anything intelligible about him at all. The promise of the analogy theory is that we can actually express truths about God in human language while never having to suppose that he has anything precisely in common with creatures.

Ross admits, however, that the theory of analogy is a very complicated matter that has already received volumes of commentary. Drawing from various passages in Aquinas, we can discern a sophisticated theory of analogy, which Ross attempts to augment and systematically present in terms of modern semantic analysis. Ross, like Aquinas, takes it to be obvious that ordinary terms already have meaning when used appropriately in religious contexts and hence offers the theory of analogy as a positive account of how meaning is transferred from ordinary contexts to religious ones. Such transfers of meaning plainly occur in a multitude of common situations in which we are already familiar with the objects and qualities involved, making analogy part of the structure of ordinary discourse that must be explained by an overall theory of language. Consider the multitude of ordinary cases in which we say things such as "Susan's anger is volcanic" or "The fox is very clever." The peculiarity of a theory of religious language is that it must describe the transfer of meaning from contexts where terms are used to speak of the familiar, observable realities of the creaturely realm to contexts where those terms speak of God and spiritual realities.

In neither ordinary contexts nor religious contexts can we simply employ just any analogy we choose. There are constraints built into our language on how a term can be used analogously. Aquinas and other Scholastic philosophers stated these constraints in terms of rules for analogy, with the rule called the *analogy of proper proportionality* considered to be the basis of the meaning of religious language. This rule states that God and creatures have qualities and engage in activities in proportion to their respective modes of being—infinite and finite, respectively. Thus, we can say both "God is wise" and "Socrates is wise" but make an adjustment for the shift in meaning between the two sentential contexts. The shift is proportional to the two modes of being to which the predicate term "wise" is related.

In the two statements "God is wise" and "Socrates is wise," Socrates is said to stand in a certain relationship to some state called "being wise" in a way similar to that in which God stands to his state called "being wise." The term "being wise" is employed with respect to God and to Socrates because we recognize the similarity in the ways in which they are wise. Thus, the use of the predicate term "being wise" is not equivocal. Yet the reason that the term "being wise" is not univocal in the two statements rests on the difference between the two modes of being that are exemplified by a human and by God. Socrates is wise in the manner in which a human person is wise, in a way appropriate to his distinct creaturely mode of being, which is finite. God, too, is wise in a way appropriate to his mode of being, which is infinite.

This sort of shift in meaning occurs in many contexts. The statements "Lassie is faithful" and "John is faithful," for example, exhibit a shift in the type of faithfulness. Although the relationship of faithfulness here is similar between the two cases, it is not exactly the same relationship because the mode of being possessed by Lassie is different from that possessed by John. But there is a perceivable likeness in patterns of behavior that allows us to use the same term for both animal and human. The same rule of proper proportionality holds in many other contexts.

Frederick Ferré (b. 1932) maintains, as do other critics of the analogy of proper proportionality, that the theory is completely unable to provide any substantive knowledge of God. In our example, it is given that God's nature, as we shall say, is "infinite" and that one of his attributes is "wisdom." Then the formula of the analogy becomes something like the following:

$$\frac{\text{God's wisdom}}{\text{God's infinite nature}} = \frac{\text{Socrates' wisdom}}{\text{Socrates' finite nature}}$$

However, Ferré contends that the theory "cannot move a step toward explaining the 'givens' of its own formulation, nor can it explain the possibility of the independent, nonanalogical knowledge on which they depend."[3] This kind of analogy has not one but two unknowns, God's wisdom and God's infinite nature. Ferré maintains that we just cannot have any positive knowledge of these matters.

Ross points out that Ferré's criticism distorts the theory by interpreting it on a simplistic mathematical model. The purpose of Aquinas, Ross argues, was to make the meaningfulness of religious language obvious and clear from its similarity to the way we talk in everyday life, with all of its nuances and degrees of connotation, and not to stipulate an exact mathematical relationship between uses of terms. Ross contends that Ferré's mathematical modeling of the theory confuses Aquinas's use of analogy as a *theory of meaning* with a *theory of inference* in which analogy is used to lead to some knowledge about God, a pattern of argument that Aquinas never used. According to Ross, Aquinas simply did not intend this theory of meaning to be an avenue of arriving at information about God.[4] Hence, Ross defends the doctrine of analogy as an explanation of how predicates applied to God have meaning, not as a method of spelling out the concrete character of God's attributes. Ross does believe that, equipped with this theory of meaning, we can presumably understand what assertions about God mean and thereby avoid fatal equivocation when we do construct arguments about God.

The theory of analogy merits much further discussion.[5] Questions must be faced, say, about whether the notion of "similarity" can be given any clear definition. Interesting questions arise over how the important medieval doctrine of "divine simplicity" (which claims that there is no distinction between

God and his attributes such as there is between creatures and their attributes) affects the way analogy is construed. But the fact remains that religious language has historically been believed to be meaningful and that the theory of analogy has traditionally been accepted by many as an account of its meaning. It is only in the contemporary period that wholesale challenges to the meaningfulness of religious language have been waged.

VERIFICATION AND FALSIFICATION ISSUES

Traditionally, philosophers of religion had never seriously doubted that it is possible to speak meaningfully of God. Early in this century, however, a group of philosophers known as the *logical positivists* strongly questioned this confidence. They developed a theory that ties the meaning of language to empirical observation. Taking science to be the best representation of careful language, logical positivists constructed a standard or criterion by which we could judge those statements that are cognitively meaningful and those that are not. Their standard came to be known as the *verifiability principle* and was applied to all statements that were not analytically (definitionally) true.[6] The principle can be stated as follows: *A statement is a genuine factual assertion if, and only if, there could be empirically observable states of affairs that would show it to be either true or false.*

A. J. Ayer (1919–1989) expressed the principle in this way:

> The criterion which we use to test the genuineness of apparent statements of fact is the criterion of verifiability. We say that a sentence is factually significant to any given person, if, and only if, he knows how to verify the proposition which it purports to express—that is, if he knows what observations would lead him, under certain conditions, to accept the proposition as being true, or reject it as being false.[7]

Ayer and other positivists thought that theological language failed to meet the empirical standard of verifiability and thus had no cognitive meaning.[8] For them, language has *cognitive* meaning only if it speaks of matters in which it is in principle possible to give empirical evidence, matters about which questions of truth and falsity make sense. Such language, then, has *factual* or *informative* significance and thus can be properly understood.

Positivists and their intellectual followers thought that the verifiability principle handled scientific language as well as much of our ordinary talk. Likewise, traditional attacks on theism, using the same language, are equally meaningless. For positivistic critics, then, theistic claims as well as antitheistic claims are not false but meaningless.

Interestingly, the verification principle of meaning eventually came under severe pressure. One well-known problem was that the verification principle of cognitive meaningfulness failed to meet the very empirical standards of meaning that it articulates.[9] After all, no observational experiences could possibly verify this statement of the verification principle: *A statement is a genuine factual assertion if, and only if, there could be empirically observable states of affairs which would show it to be either true or false.* (Here the verification principle of meaning encounters the problem of self-referential incoherence as shown in the discussion of strong foundationalism presented in chapter 6.) Another, somewhat ironic difficulty was that the verification principle of meaning did not make completely good sense of science. The history and the practice of science are replete with cases in which scientists advanced and pondered claims—ones that they took to be perfectly meaningful—for which they were unable at the time to specify exact verification conditions. The debate between the wave and the corpuscular theories of light just begins the list of such cases. In the end, positivism failed to describe correctly the conditions under which scientific statement are meaningful—and failed to do the same for numerous other kinds of statements as well (e.g., ethical statements).

Although some religious thinkers celebrated the demise of the verification principle, many in the philosophical community—positivists and others—still believed that our statements must be linked to empirical observation. Granting that verificationist methods could supply the positive meaning for statements, they began to explore the prospects for *falsification.* They developed the requirement that if anyone purports to be asserting a factual claim, he should be able to identify the conditions under which it would be false. In this vein, a very interesting challenge to theistic claims emerged.

Anthony Flew (b. 1923) confronted theists with a "falsification principle." He embeds the challenge in a very powerful story patterned after an article by John Wisdom[10] (1904–1993):

> Once upon a time two explorers came upon a clearing in the jungle. In the clearing were growing many flowers and many weeds. One explorer says, "Some gardener must tend this plot." The other disagrees, "There is no gardener." So they pitch their tents and set a watch. No gardener is ever seen. "But perhaps he is an invisible gardener." So they set up a barbed-wire fence. They electrify it. They patrol with bloodhounds. (For they remember how H. G. Wells's *The Invisible Man* could be both smelt and touched though he could not be seen.) But no shrieks ever suggest that some intruder has received a shock. No movements of the wire ever betray an invisible climber. The bloodhounds never give cry. Yet still the Believer is not convinced. "But there is a gardener, invisible, intangible, insensible to electric shocks, a gardener who has no scent and makes no sound, a gardener who comes secretly to look after the garden which he loves." At last the Skeptic despairs, "But what remains of your original assertion? Just how does what you call an invisible, intangible, eternally elusive gardener differ from an imaginary gardener or even from no gardener at all?"[11]

Flew contends that religious believers allow nothing to count against their claims, continually modifying and qualifying them in order to prevent them from being falsified.

Flew's reasoning is straightforward. When the believer states that "God loves us as a father loves his children," we would expect divine help in times of serious trouble or disease. Yet God seems distant, absent. So the believer makes some qualification—"God's love is not like human love" or "It is an inscrutable love"—making misfortune and suffering compatible with the original theological pronouncement. In response to this maneuvering, Flew puts forth the central question: "'What would have to occur or to have occurred to constitute for you a disproof of the love of, or of the existence of, God?'"[12] The point is that if there is no state of affairs that would count against the original theological statement, then it is not really a genuine assertion at all. It says nothing, neither affirming nor denying that anything is actually the case. Flew contends that religious believers kill their own claims by a thousand qualifications.

The falsificationist critique of religious language prompted spirited discussion about whether religious claims have factual significance. No doubt, for many critics, the only kind of cognitive significance is factual significance. Philosophers who agreed that the falsification principle defines the issue essentially divided into two camps: those who thought that theological language is nonfalsifiable and those who thought that it could be shown to be falsifiable.

R. M. Hare (b. 1919) and Basil Mitchell (b. 1917) were among the many philosophers who argued that religious utterances are not falsifiable for most believers and thus were not direct statements of fact. In an effort to distinguish religious assertions from factual assertions, Hare calls the former "bliks" (a term which he coined.)[13] He says that the religious believer just has a "blik" that God exists and that a certain religious way of life is correct, and nothing can change that confidence. Hare even tells a parable about a lunatic who had a "blik" that all Oxford professors were out to kill him and who could not be dissuaded from his belief by appeal to numerous inoffensive and even friendly encounters with Oxford professors. Hare indicates that all persons have "bliks" that are not held at the level of factual claims and thus cannot be overturned by contrary facts. Although Hare's terminology tends to trivialize religious assertions, his deeper point is that they express deeply held interpretive beliefs or assumptions about the world that cannot be readily overturned by empirical observation. We might think of other important claims—such as claims about human free will or the existence of other minds—as sharing this characteristic.

Basil Mitchell also maintains that religious assertions are not straightforwardly falsifiable. Mitchell tells a story about a member of a resistance movement who meets a stranger who impresses him very much: "The Stranger tells the partisan that he himself is on the side of the resistance—indeed that he is in command of it, and urges the partisan to have faith in him no matter what happens. The partisan is utterly convinced at that meeting of the Stranger's sincerity and constancy and undertakes to trust him."[14] Although the two never meet intimately again, and the partisan sees the Stranger capturing his comrades, the young partisan remains convinced by the stranger's words. Mitchell uses this story to point out the role of trust and commitment in keeping various circumstances from conclusively falsifying a belief.[15]

By contrast, John Hick (b. 1922) attempts to provide specific verification and falsification conditions for establishing the factual significance of religious claims. Hick tells a parable of two travelers walking along a road, one believing that the road leads to a Celestial City and the other believing that it leads nowhere. During the journey together, both men encounter that it leads nowhere. During the journey together, both men encounter moments of refreshment and delight as well as periods of hardship and danger. One interprets the good times as previews of heavenly bliss and the bad times as obstacles to make him worthy; the other considers the journey to be aimless rambling. During the journey, the issue between the two travelers is not an experimental one; it cannot be decided by empirical observation. "And yet when they do turn the last corner it will be apparent that one of them has been right all of the time and the other wrong. It is at this point that verification and falsification become relevant. Although the issue between the two has not been experimental, it has nevertheless from the start been a real issue."[16] Hick indicates what verifying experiences might be, such as social existence in the Kingdom of God and perhaps a strong sense of the presence of God. The absence of such experiences, then, would constitute a falsification.

Hick takes the whole concern of verification and falsification to be that the factual significance of statements derives from their being connected to the relevant actual or possible observational experiences. He then provides a scenario in which religious statements can be seen to be factually significant, not by virtue of experiences that are available in temporal life but by virtue of possible experiences in the afterlife. Of course, if there is no afterlife, then there will be no verification of religious claims. Technically, Hick may have satisfied the pure logic of a verification/falsification type challenge, but one wonders what benefit it is to us presently to suppose that actual verification or falsification is located in the afterlife, which is something we cannot now experience.

While no longer at center stage in discussions of religious language, the entire verification/falsification issue presents us with a number of valuable lessons. For one, the whole concept of a *fact* needs serious review, particularly with respect to religion. Many religious believers rightly understand that there is a factual dimension to religious language that neither verificational nor falsificational analysis can properly understand. Indeed, key theological statements entail definite cosmological assertions that, while more complicated and less accessible than assertions about the physical realm, nonetheless purport to be large-scale truths about the way things are. The statement "God is always with his children," for example, when interpreted in context, entails the factual claim that "an invisible, eternal, omnipresent, omniscient spirit exists and somehow communes with and guides those who place their trust in him." After having rejected positivism, it remains to be seen how we can best account for the factual significance of such statements. A second lesson to be learned is that we must not confuse questions of *meaning* with questions of *truth*, as the positivists did. Settling the problem of how our statements have meaning cannot be made to depend on solving the quite different problem of how we can come to know their truth.

THE FUNCTIONS OF RELIGIOUS DISCOURSE

Some thinkers, holding that questions of factual significance are either peripheral or irrelevant, thought that allowing positivism to set the framework for discussing religious language was simply wrongheaded. For them, regardless of how we account for the factual significance of religious discourse, it has other important kinds of significance. Many of these philosophers turned their attention to what Frederick Ferré calls "functional analysis."[17] Following Ludwig Wittgenstein's (1889–1951) admonition to "look and see" the multifaceted aspects of language, they identified several important functions: *imperative* ("Bring me the glass"), *performative* ("I now pronounce you husband and wife"), and *interrogative* ("What time is it?"). It would be inappropriate to apply the verification principle to such statements, and yet they function perfectly well in our human linguistic commerce.

New and intriguing theories about the various functions of religious language or, better, of ordinary language used in religious contexts were pioneered. Rather than stipulate conditions of meaning that relate language to an external reality (as the positivists had tried to connect statements to observable states of affairs), functional analysts tried to understand the functioning of religious language at work. They sought to learn what kinds of tasks it performs. They came to see language as a complex social phenomenon that is adaptable to the ever-changing purposes of human beings. Religious language was seen, therefore, as serving certain unique human purposes. Although functional analysts who studied religious language differed among themselves on *the* basic function of religious language, a brief inspection of a couple noteworthy studies is enlightening.

An early leader in this approach, R. B. Braithwaite (1900–1990) declared that religious utterances function essentially as *moral* statements. One distinctive feature of religious language is that it involves stories that picture and reinforce a moral way of life—such as the tale of the Good Samaritan or the various narratives of Jesus' compassion for people. While these religious stories may appear to be direct assertions of fact, they actually serve to express the intentions of the one uttering them to live morally. For Braithwaite, it is not necessary that the stories be true or even that they be believed to be true for them to fulfill their primary purpose. He takes the connection between the stories and a moral way of life to be "a psychological and causal one," on the basis of the fact that most people find it naturally easier to act in a certain way if they associate their actions with certain stories.[18]

Braithwaite's analysis accents one important use of religious language to express moral intentions and reinforce moral behavior. However, critics of this theory of the function of religious language say that it transforms it into the language of morality embellished by stories—a reductionist error comparable to the positivistic mistake of trying to reduce religious statements to empirical facts.[19] Donald Hudson (1940–) has called this kind of mistake a violation of the "depth grammar" of religion, arguing that religious discourse has its own unique character and function.[20] The philosopher's task, then, is to clarify how religious language works, to expose its exact role in human affairs.

The later writings of Ludwig Wittgenstein provided some philosophers with a new way to analyze religious language. Wittgenstein suggested that language is a complex human phenomenon consisting of many "language-games." The language-games metaphor points to identifiable linguistic behaviors employed by human beings in order to accomplish certain purposes: "Giving orders . . . Describing the appearance of an object . . . Speculating about an event . . . Forming and testing a hypothesis . . . Presenting the results of an experiment in tables and diagrams . . . Making up a story; and reading it . . . Play-acting . . . Singing catches . . . Guessing riddles . . . Making a joke; telling it . . . Solving a problem in practical arithmetic . . . Asking, thanking, cursing, greeting, praying."[22] Followers of Wittgenstein began to speak of the language of science, the language of romance and love—the different linguistic activities or language-games occupy a definite region on the overall map of human language. Each language-game has rules or social understandings for how words function within its sphere. The word "solid," for example, means one thing when one is speaking of solid bodies in physics and something related to but distinct from this first meaning when one is speaking of a person's having a solid character in the area of ethics. These rules for language-games, of course, are not written in any book but are followed somewhat unconsciously by members of the linguistic communities involved. The rules, then, are there for philosophers to uncover.

In locating the language of Christianity on the linguistic map, and still extending the thought of Wittgenstein, Paul van Buren (b. 1924) says it is far from the "clear, rule-governed center" where misunderstanding seldom occurs. Religious language is "at the edges of language." He identifies *puns, poetry,* and *paradox* as linguistic activities that have a strong kinship with the language of Christianity. That bond is their common attempt to say more than we can normally say with our language, to stretch the use of words beyond their usual employment, almost to the point of lapsing into nonsense. Consider how a pun stretches "language ("A door is not a door when it is ajar)" or how poetic speech attempts to go beyond or normal linguistic frontiers ("Your eyes outshine the stars in heaven").

Our modern, materialistic Western culture, according to van Buren, pressures us to live linguistically within the safe, central parts of our language—science, economics, history, and common sense. But to live in the central regions of language is to forfeit a certain richness of experience, to forgo a certain way of being in the world. For van Buren, then, the vital role played by religious language is that of expressing a certain aspect of our humanity. Christians, as he indicates, refuse to be confined to the mundane center of language and seek to say more than can be said in ordinary or scientific talk. An example of Christian "edge-talk" is the utterance "God raised Jesus from the dead," which is misunderstood if taken as a statement of historical fact. It is actually a statement of faith that tries to press language to its limits in talking about Jesus and his ongoing influence; it performs an entirely different function for believers than it does for historians.[23] Talk of a God who is "personal, but not a person" and of a "spiritual body" just begins the list of examples of Christian edge-talk.

Those who engage in *functional analysis* have helped reveal a host of different employments of religious language. In a list that proceeds much like Wittgenstein's, they have shown us that language in religion is used in a variety of ways: to pray and petition, to sing praises, to comfort, to exhort, to affirm commitment, and so forth. Yet van Buren, along with all other functional analysts, runs the risk of falling into a certain form of *fideism*, the view that faith is immune to external critique.[24] Since religious language has its own unique character and function, it is not subject to the sorts of questions and linguistic procedures that occur in other linguistic territories. Perhaps we could call this position *linguistic fideism.*

It would be wholly inappropriate, according to van Buren, to ask, for example, whether the word "God" names someone or some thing—to ask whether some object bears the name or whether it refers to something real. Such questions are appropriate, say, to the physical sciences or to other factually oriented linguistic activities where the technique of naming objects is involved. But religion cannot ask whether its most fundamental term—the term "God," which constitutes and governs its whole field of discourse—can play by the rules of other fields in which naming and referring are key techniques.[25] Focusing exclusively on the *function* of religious language within a religious community neglects its informative dimension. It seems as though functional analysts have surrendered to the positivist charge that religious language is cognitively meaningless and have looked elsewhere to find some other way in which it can be meaningful—*functionally* meaningful.

Van Buren and other Wittgensteinian thinkers have rightly called our attention to the intimate connection of language to all areas of human life; they have forced us to recognize that much of our humanity is indeed bound up with being linguistic creatures. However, only by assuming that science and ordinary talk are central linguistic practices—a capitulation to the positivists—can van Buren justify placing religion at the "edges" of language. A more adequate interpretation may well perceive that religious language has its own inherent standards of precision and sayability, just as science does, without having to relinquish matters of precision or factual communication to science.

Moreover, it appears that van Buren fails to see the complex fabric of religious language as involving metaphysical, ethical, and historical statements that are intended by religious believers to be just that—metaphysical or ethical or historical assertions. By reducing religious language to the activity of expressing a distinct perspective on the world, van Buren still leaves unresolved the more fundamental question of whether our language can be used to say anything about that Ultimate Reality that believers take to be God. Traditional thinkers, such as Aquinas, would say that van Buren's approach (like that of Braithwaite and other functional analysts) fails to take seriously what ordinary religious believers take themselves to be saying. Believers regularly take themselves to be asserting the factual truth of certain theological teachings and narratives, or at least to be engaging in liturgies and other religious behaviors that assume such factual truths.

RELIGIOUS LANGUAGE AS SYMBOLIC

Many philosophers became dissatisfied with functional analysis just as they had with verificational analysis. Verificational analysis denied cognitive meaning to religious discourse, and functional analysis sought to find uses for it that were basically noncognitive. Most contemporary philosophers now admit that religious language has legitimate cognitive meaning, but many of them believe that its meaning cannot be *literal*. That it is impossible to speak literally of God has become a fundamental assumption of contemporary theologians as well. Both philosophers and theologians fear lapsing into the *anthropomorphism* involved in talking about God as we would talk about creatures. Not satisfied with the traditional analogical theory for avoiding anthropomorphism, more recent thinkers have developed a plethora of nonliteral interpretations: some speak of theological "models," some of "stories," others of "metaphor," and still others of "parable" as the essential mode of religious discourse.[26]

The theologian Paul Tillich is well known for his position that talk of God is *symbolic*. Tillich recognizes, as do many others, that statements such as "Yahweh spoke to the prophets" and "The Lord is my Shepherd" are not commonly considered to be capable of literal interpretation. After all, God does not really "speak" by expelling air across physical vocal chords, nor is he a "shepherd" as we typically understand it. Of course, there are many cases of broadly symbolic speech in ordinary language. We speak of the "mouth of a river" or of "Christine's character being solid." In ordinary discourse, such symbolic or metaphorical talk can be cashed out literally. We can explain for instance, that the river has a "mouth" in that it has an opening out of which things flow or that Christine's character is "solid" in that it is dependable and will hold up under pressure.

All such sentences are *predications*—sentences that attach properties, relationships, and activities to a subject. Why does Tillich agree that the ordinary symbolic statements can be given literal interpretation while insisting that theological statements cannot be? According to Tillich, when God is the subject of predication, all properties, relationships, and activities ascribed to him must be symbolic because God is *transcendent, infinite, not limited by the structure of creaturely existence*. Tillich refers to God as "wholly other"[27] to emphasize that he is radically unlike anything else we know. He says that God is not *a* being at all but "the Ground of Being."[28] Accordingly, attempts to talk literally of God must be banned, for they treat God as a particular, discrete being among other beings. That is, such talk incorrectly supposes that

God is a being of a certain kind, has certain properties, and performs certain actions—a supposition that violates God's ultimacy. For Tillich, God is "beyond" all of that. It is utterly impossible, on Tillich's view, to specify literally *what* it is that symbolic statements are asserting about God. Nothing can ever be asserted of God in the strict sense, since God cannot be described in terms of the predicates in our language. Thus, one can never claim with respect to some property or attribute that God possesses it and that this claim is true if, and only if, God actually possesses it. Questions of literal truth and falsity are quite beside the point.

While Tillich does not think that the religious symbol can be cashed out literally, he thinks it can be an avenue of revelation, a means of focusing on one's "ultimate concern," an occasion for encountering God. Tillich explains that both "signs" and "symbols" point beyond themselves to something else. The typical sign (e.g., the red light at the intersection of two streets) does not point to itself but to the necessity of cars stopping. Symbols also point to something beyond themselves. Tillich explains:

> The difference, which is a fundamental difference between them, is that signs do not participate in any way in the reality and power of that to which they point. Symbols, although they are not the same as that which they symbolize, participate in its meaning and power. The difference between symbol and sign is the participation in the symbolized reality which characterizes the symbols, and the nonparticipation in the "pointed-to" reality which characterizes a sign. For example, letters of the alphabet as they are written, and "A" or an "R" do not participate in the sound to which they point; on the other hand, the flag participates in the power of the king or the nation for which it stands and which it symbolizes.[29]

Every symbol, for Tillich, opens up a level of reality for which nonsymbolic language is inadequate. For example, artistic symbols—poetry, visual art, and music—open up levels of reality that can be opened up in no other way.

In opening up the deepest level of reality, religious symbols actually open up the deepest dimension of experience in the human soul. Born out of the collective consciousness among social groups or traditions, religious symbols participate in the dimension of Ultimate Reality, which is the dimension of the Holy. Yet the Holy transcends every concrete symbol of the Holy. Throughout the history of religion, a rich diversity of material in time and space has become at some time or other a symbol of the Holy. According to Tillich, the key to understanding the otherwise confusing history of religion is to see religions as employing symbols that rest on the ultimate ground of being (e.g., a lotus blossom, a star, a cross). The incredible power and tenacity of religious symbols is explained by the fact that they impress upon the human mind a relationship to its own ultimate ground and meaning.

Tillich's position, then, on theological language is that it directs us to something through which the Ultimate Reality can be experienced. For Tillich, Christians speak symbolically when they say something like "God sent his Son into the world to save it." Tillich maintains that taking this statement literally would be absurd. But we can still come under the power of the symbol. We know, for instance, what it is to send or move something from one place to another, to cause a change. We know that talk of a son implies a father and can draw upon rich, positive images of a loving father-son relationship. We know that a basic meaning of the word "world" is "all people" and so may envision God's love being extended to all people through his son. All of this and more sensitizes us to the power of the symbol.

Tillich's view of the symbolic nature of religious language is a classic one in modern discussions. The view is both important and interesting, but one wonders if it can be consistently held. Tillich himself claims to "interpret" the meanings of religious (and particularly Christian) symbols to us. What can this be but an attempt to give theological talk a more determinate propositional content? Others who officially endorse a symbolic view also talk of "drawing implications" (both theoretical and practical) from symbols. But the notion that symbols about God have "implications" smuggles in all sorts of logical relations appropriate to literal speech. The strong tendency to move toward some form of literal talk about God, then, even among the pan-symbolists, makes one wonder whether it is possible to avoid speaking of God in some kind of literal fashion! The rub comes both in avoiding dangerous pitfalls in our religious language that nonliteral theories were meant to avoid and in developing a positive account of how we can actually speak of God. Feminist thinkers also reject strict literalism while offering their own distinctive view.

FEMINISM AND MASCULINE GOD-TALK

According to feminist theologians, we can no longer rely on a symbolic analysis of religious language because we no longer have a sacramental understanding of the world which it assumes. The disunity, materialism, and skepticism of our age prevent us from viewing ordinary things as continuous with sacred things such that the former can properly signify the latter. Nonetheless, religious language, unfortunately, retains most of its traditional expressions, which become literalized and absolutized apart from their original context.

The central point in the feminist critique of traditional Western religious language is the expression "God the father." In historically patriarchal societies, the paternal image has been identified as the exclusive way of understanding the divine and has dominated to the exclusion of other finite images of the divine. Feminists point out that "patriarchy" has become a "model" for interpreting our world and ordering our activities. A model, according to philosophers of science, is a grid, screen, or filter which helps us organize our thoughts about the less familiar in terms of the more familiar. The patriarchal model, then, tells us not only about the nature of God but also about our relations to the divine and with one another. Thus, "patriarchy" is not just a set of interconnected images of the deity in Western religion as masculine—king, father, husband, lord, master—but is the very Western way of life, affecting patterns of governance at national, ecclesiastical, business, and family levels.

Feminist theologians warn that the twin dangers of the patriarchal model to religion are idolatry and irrelevance. To counter idolatry of the paternal image, feminist religious thinkers caution that we not be overconfident in how much our words can say about the divine. They remind us, for example, that the *apophatic tradition* in religion holds that God can only be named by what he is *not*. These reminders form an important thread in religious literature: God's self-disclosure to Moses as the One who could not be named ("I am who I am"); Augustine's reminder that God is in a significant sense inexpressible; Anselm's definition of God as "that than which none greater can be conceived;" and Simone Weil's statement that there is nothing that resembles what she can conceive when she says the word "God."[30] Truly devout religious thought maintains a healthy awareness of the gap between the infinite and finite terms we use for it. On the point at issue, feminist theologians insist that God is not really a physical being, not male, and not more masculine than feminine. Hence, we are not warranted in literalizing masculine images of the divine.

The other problem of the patriarchal model is that of irrelevance not only to large numbers women but also to ethnic minorities and residents of the third world. According to feminist thinkers, this is a widespread phenomenon in which experiences of nonmale, nonwhite, and non-Western people do not resonate with the world depicted by the prevailing patriarchal model. A hierarchical world of white male power and privilege in every sphere, supported at a deep level by monotheistic religion, is oppressive to those lower in the hierarchy. Mary Daly (b. 1933) says that, over several millennia, the world's religions have proved to be an exercise in misogyny, rendering women invisible and powerless.

The work of Rosemary Ruether (b. 1936) can clearly be seen as at attempt to regain the relevance of religion to women. She argues that historic monotheism, originating among the ancient Hebrews and expressed in Judaism, Christianity, and Islam, is a radical departure from earlier religious consciousness in the Ancient Near East. "Male monotheism," writes Ruether, "becomes the vehicle of a psychocultural revolution of the male ruling class in its relationship to surrounding reality."[31] This hierarchy became sacralized as though it were a cosmic principle essential to monotheism: that maleness is the best symbol of deity. Ruether points out, however, that the much older, polytheistic religions that were supplanted by monotheism actually envisioned a realm of paired gods and goddesses within a matrix of one physical-spiritual reality, thus validating both masculine and feminine images for the divine. To correct the male monopoly on God-language, then, she recommends using inclusive language for God that draws on the images and experiences of both genders.

Ruether and other feminist theologians point out that there are historical precedents for using inclusive language for God, both inside and outside the Christian tradition. In addition to the obvious masculine references, the Bible contains a range of feminine images. In the book of Isaiah, we find: "Now, like a woman in childbirth, I cry out, I gasp and pant." Clearly, here the efforts of God to redeem Israel are likened to those of a woman in labor.

Julian of Norwich, a fourteenth-century Roman Catholic thinker, writes, "As truly as God is our Father, so truly is God our Mother."[32] John Calvin is another example who claims that God manifested himself as both Father and Mother to the Jews.[33] Feminist theologians also cite additional feminine images for God outside the Christian tradition. Religions of the Ancient Near East provide ready examples in which positive qualities are attributed to a feminine deity, the Goddess figure, and the feminine aspect of the divine is neither subordinated nor devalued. God/ess, for Ruether, must be named by female as well as male metaphors. Denise Carmody (b. 1935) indicates that more restricted focus on the Goddess figure, typified in the female deities of both Eastern and tribal religious systems, has given rise to what she calls "thealogy" (the study of feminine divinity).[34]

Understanding that the feminist program in religion requires a careful theory of religious language, Sallie McFague (b. 1933) emphasizes the incredible power of *metaphor*. Rather than risk continuing male-dominated theories of analogy or linguistic symbolism that have tended to support maleness as directly participating in the divine, she offers a program for "metaphorical theology." After all, to speak of God, she argues, is to speak metaphorically. A metaphor, of course, is a figure of speech in which one thing is spoken of as if it were another; it is seeing one thing *as* another. Thinking metaphorically means spotting a thread of similarity between two dissimilar objects or events and using the better known one as a way of speaking about the lesser known. Metaphorical theology, then, seeks do several things: understand how various root metaphors drive models in religion; criticize literalized models (including masculine talk of God); chart relationships among metaphors, models, and concepts; and investigate possibilities for transformative, revolutionary models. Unlike symbolic speech, which refers to sacred objects, metaphorical speech employs ordinary terms about ordinary things and thus connects with our contemporary sensibility.

In her later work, *Models of God,* McFague argues that God is so far beyond us that we really do not know the divine nature. Therefore, we humans essentially project our language for God out of our human experience. Strictly speaking, the distance between infinite and finite puts all talk of God, not just masculine language, in a hypothetical mode: it is "as if" God is like this, but maybe God is not. She particularly recommends that the metaphors "Mother" and "Friend" become models for God, as "Father" has traditionally been.[35] The recommended feminist models are intended to stress properties of divine immanence over transcendence, nurture over authority, and relationship over control.[36]

Feminist proposals for religious language have predictably spurred much debate. Traditional Christian theists, for example, have argued that classical theology has never identified God ontologically as being male and has always affirmed that God is infinite personal spirit. Feminists counter by pointing out that much of the problem has been that patriarchal societies have validated exclusively masculine metaphors for the divine and thus reinforced and sacralized patriarchal social structures. Another point of discussion pertains to whether the feminist approach to religious language entails too great a degree of agnosticism about our knowledge of God. In order to dislodge masculine talk of God from its privileged position, feminists emphasize the metaphysical gap between human and divine. But their emphasis is so strong that feminists frequently conclude that we really can know nothing of God's intrinsic nature, or at least nothing that is not mediated through a selected metaphor. According to critics of the feminist position, this relativizes the issue, making it about the selection of a human metaphor for God, which becomes a kind of self-projection or group-projection. Related to this matter is the feminist claim that women experience the divine differently from the way men do—in effect, that there are gender-specific ways of knowing. They then draw the obvious conclusion that women should chose metaphors for God that reflect their own distinctive experience as females. Of course, the criticism that patriarchical models do not relate to non-White and non-Western peoples, by logical extension, supports the broader conclusion that there are ethnic-specific ways of knowing as well. Feminist literature on religious language does indeed tend to embrace this position, affirming the need to appreciate a wide variety of images for the divine. Certainly, the claim that there are gender-specific and ethnic-specific ways of knowing that may well be incommensurable needs further evaluation as an epistemological position, but that discussion ventures beyond the present study. What continues to be controversial is the nature of literal speech such that we can gauge the possibility of speaking literally of God.

CAN TALK OF GOD BE LITERAL?

In opposition to those thinkers who insist that talk of God must be nonliteral, William Alston (b. 1921) offers a sophisticated theory of how it can be literal. He makes an initial distinction between the form of our language and the reality it addresses.[37] Alston admits that human language is defective for speaking about God because its *subject-predicate structure* assumes a distinction between an object and its *properties*, whereas it is maintained in classical philosophy that God's essence has no distinctions. Thus, when a predicate term (e.g., "love") attributes a property to some subject term (e.g., "Mother Teresa"), the subject-predicate structure of the sentence assumes a distinction between Mother Teresa and her love. However, we have to use the same subject-predicate language to speak of God and God's love, although there is no parallel distinction. Alston states therefore that our conceptual grid, reflected in our language, cannot fully capture the divine reality.[38]

Alston claims, however, that the limitations of our subject-predicate language do not necessarily preclude the literal application of all predicate terms to God. The possibility still remains that our human terms are not defective for speaking of God. That is, there can be a genuine reality that is the intended target of our terms. We typically apply concepts such as love or knowledge or power or action in a literal fashion to human beings.

Human beings possess creaturely characteristics—finitude, temporality, embodiment. But Alston contends that the concepts of love, knowledge, power, action, and the like do not necessarily involve creaturely conditions. Thus, he believes that there is a core of meaning for these concepts that can be literally attributed to God.

Alston focuses on a particular category of predicate terms,[39] what he calls *personalistic predicates:*

> Personalistic predicates are those that, as a group, apply to a being only if that being is a "personal agent"—an agent that carries out intentions, plans, or purposes in its actions, that acts in the light of knowledge or belief; a being whose actions express attitudes and are guided by standards and principles; a being capable of communicating with other such agents and entering into other forms of personal relations with them.[40]

Various personalistic predicates that might be applied to God include "commands," "loves," and "guides."

The key question here is not whether we can form subject-predicate sentences with a subject-term used to refer to God and make literal use of a personalistic predicate term so as to claim that it is true of the subject. Obviously, both technical theology as well as ordinary religious discourse contain numerous such sentences. "God loves us," "Yahweh is righteous," and "Allah is merciful" merely begin the list. The real issue is whether any such truth-claim can be successful. In other words, it is whether any personalistic predicate term, used literally, can be *true of* God, or *truly applied* to God, or just *literally true* of God.

Nonliteralists insist that personalistic predicates cannot literally apply to God because of God's radical "otherness." Alston recognizes that there are different respects in which God has been thought to differ from creatures, and he arranges them on a scale of increasingly radical "otherness":

A. Incorporeality.
B. Infinity. This can be divided into
    B1. The unlimited realization of each perfection.
    B2. The exemplification of all perfections, everything it is better to be than not to be.
C. Timelessness.
D. Absolute simplicity.
E. Not *a* being. (God is rather "Being-Itself.")[41]

Different thinkers on the subject of "divine otherness" emphasize different items on the list, with those favoring the range of items near the bottom of the list representing the more extreme versions of "otherness." It would be a very rewarding project to work through each item and determine whether the type of "otherness" indicated conceptually prohibits the literal application of intrinsic, personalistic predicates to God.

Alston selects the first item on the list for inspection, the concept of God's incorporeality. His aim is to show that the concept of *incorporeality,* or of an *incorporeal being,* is not incompatible with *personalistic predicates.* If he can show that personalistic terms can be literally true of an incorporeal being, he will not thereby have proved that they are literally true of God. But he will have shown that the concept of God's incorporeality does not rule them out. There may be other divine attributes (e.g., infinity or timelessness) that inhibit us from thinking literally of God as a personal agent, but settling those issues would be part of a much larger and more comprehensive undertaking.

Alston divides *personalistic predicates* (P-predicates) into two categories: *mental predicates* (M-predicates) and *action predicates* (A-predicates). *Mental predicates* have to do with cognitions, feelings, emotions, attitudes, wants, thoughts, fantasies, and other internal psychological states, events, and processes. *Action predicates,* on the other hand, have to do, broadly speaking, with what an agent does. Philosophers have different views of the meaning of mental predicates and the meaning of action predicates.

On the matter of *mental predicates,* philosophers are divided over whether they are properly defined in terms of their behavioral manifestations. According to the *Private Paradigm* view, the meaning of an M-predicate is not defined through behavioral manifestations but is known through inner experience or introspection. This is true regardless of the fact that certain inner states (e.g., feeling depressed) regularly tend to manifest themselves in certain behavioral ways (e.g., droopy appearance and lack of vigor). Proponents of the Private Paradigm view contend that associated behaviors are not necessary to the concept of an inner state, since, in the presence of other inner states, one may not exhibit those behaviors. One could imagine, for example, that, given sufficiently high motivation not to appear droopy (e.g., wanting to do well on a job interview), one could appear more energized, even though one is feeling depressed. It seems rather unproblematic, according to Alston, to conceive of an incorporeal being having mental states on the Private Paradigm view, since this view does not require that inner states be connected to bodily behaviors.

Opposing the Private paradigm view is the *Logical Connection* view, which asserts that there is a logical (conceptual) connection between a mental state and its overt manifestations. Alston agrees that an M-predicate is applicable to a subject S only if A-predicates are applicable to it. God, on this view, can literally know, purpose, and will only if God can literally perform overt actions. Interestingly, this thesis mirrors the fundamental place of divine agency in Judeo-Christian theology. However, many who advocate Logical Connectionism assume that a being is capable of overt action only if it is capable of bodily movements and, conversely, that a nonbodily being is not capable of performing overt actions. Concepts of such M-predicates as "making," "commanding," or "forgiving" would, then, necessarily include the concept of bodily movements of the maker, commander, forgiver.

This discussion leads to the matter of *action predicates.* Since the concept of God is one of an incorporeal or nonbodily being, many thinkers conclude that the concept excludes the capability of overt actions. But Alston charges that it is question begging to assume that our concept of overt action requires specifications of bodily movements by corporeal beings. He sets out to show that the concept of action does not conceptually require bodily movements and thus to remove an obstacle to thinking of an incorporeal being as performing overt actions.

Alston refers to the well-known discussion in twentieth-century philosophy of a *basic action*. A *basic action* is one that is performed *not* by or in (simultaneously) performing some other action. A *nonbasic action* is one that is performed by or in (simultaneously) performing some other action. For example, signing my name on a check (a nonbasic action) is performed by moving my hand in a certain way (for present purposes, a basic action). If we were to analyze many examples like this, Alston thinks that we would conclude that our concepts of many particular human basic actions do indeed involve specification of bodily movements. Obviously, these particular kinds of basic actions cannot apply literally to an incorporeal being. Likewise, if we were to inspect numerous examples of human nonbasic actions, we would also conclude that they require bodily movements but are often not specific in regard to particular types of bodily movements. Making a soufflé, for instance, involves causing a soufflé to come into existence, but the range of bodily movements used to do this is quite open. A person can stir the ingredients with his right hand or with his left. Thus, it may well be that human beings may not bring about such consequences except by moving their bodies.

It does not follow, however, from the fact that bodily movement is involved in all of the kinds of human actions (both basic and nonbasic) with which we are acquainted that the concept of bodily movement is built into the concept of human action concepts. Even if we were to grant that all human A-concepts do contain a bodily movement requirement, all that follows is that no *human* A-concepts are literally applicable to an incorporeal being such as God. It does not follow that *no* A-concepts whatsoever are applicable. Why should we suppose that the action concepts that apply to human beings exhaust all the action concepts that there are? This opens up the question of whether we can form A-concepts that, first of all, are distinctively *action* concepts, and, second, do not require any bodily movements of the agent.

To address this point, Alston narrows his discussion to *intentional* actions, that is, those the agent *means* to perform. It is clear that bodily movement alone does not constitute an action, since many bodily movements are not intentional (e.g., automatic jerks, twitches, reflexes). So, what makes an action an *action*? Alston believes that only two theories have a chance at giving an adequate answer to this question: *psychological causation* and *agent causation*. He crafts an argument to the effect that neither of these two theories contains any inherent restrictions on incorporeal action.

The *psychological causation* theory asserts that the psychological background (e.g., motives, beliefs, attitudes, intentions) gives rise to a "bodily movement" and makes it an *action* rather than a "mere" movement. Since there is no conceptual obstacle to thinking of an incorporeal being as having intentions, we are left with a question about bodily movements. In the case of an incorporeal being, something would have to substitute for the bodily movement component of basic action. Alston suggests that it is just a fact about human beings that only bodily movements are under direct voluntary control; it is not a conceptual restraint on basic action per se. It is logically possible that there could be agents, corporeal or otherwise, such that things other than their bodies are under their direct voluntary control. Some agents might be such that they could bring a soufflé into being without doing something else (i.e., it would be a basic action for them). So, it appears that any change whatsoever—and not just bodily movements—can be the core of a basic action. Precisely what changes are within the repertoire of a given incorporeal agent depends on the nature of that agent. Alston's conclusion, then, is that the *psychological causation* theory poses no conceptual roadblock to ascribing action predicates to an incorporeal being. In the case of God, the way is open to conceive of his "creating light," "parting the sea of reeds," or "making a soufflé" as the performance of basic actions, actions that are under God's direct voluntary control and do not have to be brought about by his first doing something else.

The second theory, *agent causation,* is actually less problematic than the first. According to this view, a "bodily movement" is an *action* if and only if it is caused in a certain special way and not by some other event or state; it is simply caused by the *agent.* Thus, in performing a basic action, one "directly" brings about a bodily movement—not by doing something "else" to bring it about. One simply exploits one's basic capacity to perform a basic action. Given that the concept of agent causation is not restricted to corporeal substances or committed to the agent's possessing a particular kind of internal structure or mechanism, it presents no conceptual bar to attributing A-predicates to God.

Overall, then, Alston considers his case to be successful. He claims not to have proved that intrinsic predicates can be literally predicated of God but to have shown that there is no conceptual impossibility in applying mental predicates and action predicates to an incorporeal being.[42] In showing this much, he has at least established that the prospects for speaking literally about God are not dim as often thought.[43] If Alston is right, then he has gone a considerable way toward showing that theistic thinkers are not asserting and discussing propositions about God that are obviously absurd or extraneous. By the same token, he has helped show that classical critiques and denials of theistic beliefs are not beside the point.

STUDY QUESTIONS

1. Discuss various reasons for philosophical interest in religious language. Must one have a philosophical theory of religious language before using it?

2. What is the theory of analogy for explaining the meaning of religious language? What strengths is this theory supposed to have? What weaknesses have been pointed out?

3. Can you state the verifiability principle of meaning that was advanced by the logical positivists? Why was it supposed to be a boon for philosophy? What impact did it have on religious language? What sorts of responses ensued?

4. What could it mean to criticize the verifiability principle by saying that it confuses issues of meaning and truth?

5. Is verification or falsification a totally logical and objective process—in which case it is the same for all people? Or does it have a psychological aspect that takes into account the mental states of individual people—in which case it can differ from person to person?

6. What exactly is the difference between saying that a religious statement is meaningless and saying it is false?

7. Try to state in your own words the basic idea of functional analysis. How is it that the functional analysis of religious language generally ignores matters of truth and falsity?

8. Explore the various functions that language in general seems to fulfill within a linguistic community. Explore the functions that religious language seems to perform. Can any one function be identified as "basic"?

9. Make a case, as Paul Tillich would, for all talk of God being symbolic. Evaluate.

10. Explain the feminist case against masculine language for the divine. Discuss feminist proposals for how we should speak of the divine.

11. What strategy does William Alston use for showing that we can speak literally of God? Do you think he is successful? Why, or why not?

12. Explore the question of whether Alston has shown how we can avoid anthropomorphism and speak univocally of God.

NOTES

1. From Arthur Clarke, "The Nine Billion Names of God," in his collection of short stories titled *The Nine Billion Names of God* (New York: Harcourt, Brace, and World, 1967).

2. Aquinas, *Summa Theologica*, I, Q. 13, A. 5; also see *Summa Contra Gentiles*, bk. 1, chaps. 28–34.

3. Frederick Ferré, "Analogy in Theology," in the *Encyclopedia of Philosophy*, vol. 1 (New York: Macmillan, 1967), pp. 94–5.

4. Accepting the rebuttal that analogy theory is distorted if it is mathematically modeled, a counter might still be made: that while the analogy theory is, admittedly, a theory of meaning, there are *two* unknowns, not one, on the God side of the equation. Suffice it here to say that a sophisticated version of analogy theory seeks to account for the fact that the mode of God's being (which we here call "infinite"), as well as the intrinsic character of his attributes, is not really an object of full conceptual knowledge. As Ross says, the infinity of God is only approximated "when we say that God is infinitely wise, infinitely good, infinitely intelligent, etc." We can say *that* God is wise, for instance, but do not understand *how* he is wise. Such matters slip through our finite conceptual net, so to speak. See James F. Ross, *Philosophical Theology*, (Indianapolis, Ind.: Bobbs-Merrill, 1969), p. 56.

5. For an excellent treatment, see James F. Ross, "Analogy as a Rule of Meaning for Religious Language," *International Philosophical Quarterly* 1, no. 30 (September 1961): 468–502.

6. Most formulations of the verifiability principle included the condition that the statements in question are not analytic, that is, that their truth or falsity is not simply a function of their logical structure rather than a function of their relationship to possible empirical facts.

7. A. J. Ayer, *Language, Truth and Logic* (New York: Dover, 1952), p. 35.

8. As it also turned out, neither metaphysics nor ethics fared well under the positivist criterion of meaning.

9. Actually, this point leads to an interesting debate over first-order statements and second-order rules for meaning. Defenders of the verifiability criterion held that it is just that, a criterion, and therefore that it did not have to meet its own standard of meaning. In other words, it was a second-order rule that was to be applied to a first-order language. Critics held that it should have to meet its own standard of meaning and, since it is not meaningful according to its own standard, it is self-defeating.

10. John Wisdom, *Logic and Language,* vol. 1 (Oxford: Blackwell, 1951), chap. 10.

11. Anthony Flew, "Theology and Falsification," in *New Essays in Philosophical Theology,* ed. Antony Flew and Alasdair MacIntyre (New York: Macmillan, 1955), p. 96.

12. Ibid, p. 99.

13. R. M. Hare, "Theology and Falsification," in Flew and MacIntyre, eds., *New Essays,* pp. 99–103.

14. Basil Mitchell, "Theology and Falsification," in Flew and MacIntyre, eds., *New Essays,* p. 103.

15. Ibid, p. 104.

16. John Hick, "Theology and Verification," *Theology Today* 17 (1960): 260–1. Hick develops his case further in his *Faith and Knowledge,* 2d ed. (New York: Macmillan, 1966), chap 8.

17. Frederick Ferré, *Language, Logic and God* (New York: Harper, 1961), p. 58.

18. R. B. Braithwaite, "An Empiricist's View of the Nature of Religious Belief," in *The Existence of God,* ed. John Hick (New York: Macmillan, 1964), pp. 229–52.

19. Other mistakes: First, it initially assumes an inadequate theory of moral language in which statements of objective norms ("Murder is wrong") translate into expressions of subjective intentions ("I intend never to murder anyone"). Hence, whatever course of action one intends to follow becomes *moral*—a result that blatantly conflicts with our common moral experience! Second, Braithwaite mixes religious stories of quite diverse logical types, some intended as historical statements about the life of Jesus, others as parabolic, and so forth. Thus, Braithwaite overlooks numerous subtle differences in the uses of Christian stories. Third, he totally ignores what religious believers themselves understand as the function and meaning of their various assertions and stories.

20. W. Donald Hudson, *Ludwig Wittgenstein* (Richmond, Va: John Knox Press, 1968), p. 62.

21. Paul van Buren, *The Edges of Language* (New York: Macmillan, 1972).

22. Ludwig Wittgenstein, *Philosophical Investigations,* trans G. E. M. Anscombe (New York: Macmillan, 1953), §23 (p. 11ᵉ).

23. Van Buren, *Edges of Language,* p. 157.

24. See chapter 3 of this book for a fuller discussion of fideism.

25. Van Buren, *Edges of Language,* pp. 134, 137. "The word 'God' marks the point at which the religious man has come up against the final limit of what he can say about the object of his concern" (p. 135).

26. On models, see Ian T. Ramsey, "Talking about God," *Myth and Symbol*, ed. F.W. Dillistone (London: SPCK, 1966), pp. 76–97, and James Kellenberger, *Religious Discovery, Faith, and Knowledge* (Englewood Cliffs, N. J.: Prentice-Hall, 1972), chap. 3; on story, Alasdair MacIntyre, "The Logical Status of Religious Belief," *Metaphysical Beliefs*, 2d ed. (London: SCM Press, 1970), pp. 158–201; and Ian Crombie, "The Possibility of Theological Statements," in *Faith and Logic*, ed. B. Mitchell (London: George Allen and Unwin, 1957), p. 60; on metaphor, see Paul Ricoeur, "Biblical Hermeneutics," in *Semeia* 4, ed. J. D. Crossan (Missoula, Mont.: Scholars Press, 1975); on parable, Ronald Hepburn, *Christianity and Paradox* (London: C. A. Watts, 1958), pp. 192–204.

27. Among the thinkers who take this kind of approach are Paul Tillich, Karl Barth, John Macquarrie, Emile Bruner, and Rudolph Otto.

28. This theme runs through Tillich, *Systematic Theology* (Chicago: University of Chicago Press, 1951–1963) and *The Dynamics of Faith* (New York: Harper and Row, 1957).

29. Paul Tillich, "The Nature of Religious Language," *Christian Scholar* 38, no. 3 (1955): 189–97. (This piece is reprinted in PRSR2e, pt. 7, 357–65.)

30. Exodus 3; Augustine, *The Confessions*; Anselm "Proslogium"; Weil, "Waiting for God."

31. Ruether, in PRSR2e, p. 386.

32. Julian of Norwich, *Showings*, trans. Edmund Colledge, OSA, and James Walsh, SJ (New York: Paulist Press, 1978), p. 295.

33. John Calvin, *Commentary on the Book of the Prophet Isaiah*, trans. William Pringle, 4 vols. (Grand Rapids, Mich.: William B. Eerdmans, 1948), 3:326–37.

34. Denise Lardner Carmody, *Feminism and Christianity: A Two-Way Reflection* (Nashville: Abingdon, 1982), p. 23.

35. Sallie McFague, *Metaphorical Theology: Models of God in Religious Language* (Philadelphia: Fortress Press, 1982).

36. McFague, p. 21.

37. Alston also has employed more classically medieval language to make the same point. Medieval thinkers spoke of the distinction between the *mode of signification* (the form of our language) and the *perfection signified* (the reality about which we speak). Here "perfection" is synonymous with "property" or "attribute." See William Alston, "Being-Itself and Talk about God," *Center Journal* 3, no. 3 (Summer 1984): 21.

38. The point here, for Alston, is that we can know *that* God loves but we cannot comprehend *how* God loves.

39. Alston states that even proponents of nonliteral talk could presumably be led to agree that *negative predicates* and *extrinsic predicates* are literally true of God. Such *negative predicates* as "immutable" or "not identical with Jimmy Carter" are literally true of God, but presumably no opponent of literal religious language means to deny this. Moreover, various *extrinsic predicates* surely seem to be true of God, such as "thought of now by me." So he restricts the point at issue to this: whether *intrinsic predicates* can truly apply to God, particularly what he calls *personalistic predicates*.

40. William Alston, "Can We Speak Literally of God?" in *Is God GOD?* ed. Axel D. Steuer and James W. McClendon Jr. (Nashville: Abingdon Press, 1981), pp. 144–77. (Reprinted in PRSR2e, pt. 7, pp. 367–8.)

41. William Alston, "Functionalism and Theological Language," *American Philosophical Quarterly* 22 (July 1985): 221. Reprinted in William Alston, *Divine Nature and Human Language: Essays in Philosophical Theology* (Ithaca, N.Y.: Cornell University Press, 1989), p. 64.

42. Referring to the Thomistic project in religious language, some would see Alston as having shown the way to talk univocally of both finite and infinite beings. The anthropomorphism that Aquinas feared can be avoided by defining terms in ways that do not invoke finite or corporeal elements. Such terms as "know" (entertains a consistent set of justified true beliefs), "desires" (a strong feeling concerning goals to be achieved, in line with intentions), "creates" (brings into being), and "good" (morally responsible, virtuous in character, disposed to do the right) can be applied univocally to creatures and to God.

43. The total body of Alston's work on religious language deserves to be read in its larger context. An excellent resource is his *Divine Nature and Human Language: Essays in Philosophical Theology* (Ithaca, N.Y.: Cornell University Press, 1989).

SUGGESTED READING

Alston, William P. *Divine Nature and Human Language.* Ithaca, N.Y.: Cornell University Press, 1989.

Ayer, A. J. *Language, Truth and Logic.* New York: Dover, 1952.

Cooper, John. *Our Father in Heaven: Christian Faith and Inclusive Language for God.* Grand Rapids, Mich.: Baker, 1998.

Daly, Mary. *Beyond God the Father: Toward a Philosophy of Women's Liberation.* Boston: Beacon Press, 1973.

Diamond, Malcolm, and Thomas V. Lizenbury Jr., eds. *The Logic of God.* Indianapolis, Ind.: Bobbs-Merrill, 1975.

Ferré, Frederick. *Language, Logic and God.* New York: Harper and Row, 1969.

Gilkey, Langdon. *Naming the Whirlwind.* Indianapolis, Ind.: Bobbs-Merrill, 1969.

Gilson, Etienne. *Linguistics and Philosophy.* Notre Dame, Ind.: University of Notre Dame Press, 1988.

High, Dallas, ed. *New Essays in Religion Language.* New York: Oxford University Press, 1969.

Kimel, Alvin, ed. *Speaking the Christian God: The Holy Trinity and the Challenge of Feminism.* Grand Rapids, Mich.: William B. Eerdmans, 1992.

Mascall, E. L. *Existence and Analogy.* New York: Longmans, Green, 1949.

———. *Words and Images.* New York: Ronald Press, 1957.

McFague, Sallie. *Metaphorical Theology: Models of God in Religious Language.* Philadelphia: Fortress Press, 1982.

———. *Models of God: Theology for an Ecological, Nuclear Age.* Philadelphia: Fortress, 1988.

Mitchell, Basil. *Faith and Logic.* London: Allen and Unwin, 1957.

Mollenkott, Virginia. *The Divine Feminine: The Biblical Imagery of God as Female.* New York: Crossroad, 1983.

Ramsey, Ian. *Religious Language.* London: SCM Press, 1957.

———, ed. *Words about God: The Philosophy of Religion.* New York: Harper and Row, 1971.

Ruether, Rosemary. *Sexism and God-Talk: Toward a Feminist Theology.* Boston: Beacon Press, 1983.

Soskice, Janet. "Religious Language." In the *Blackwell Companion to Philosophy of Religion.* Oxford: Blackwell, 1997.

CHAPTER 12   RELIGION AND SCIENCE: COMPATIBLE OR INCOMPATIBLE?

In 1616 the Holy Office of the Roman Catholic Church condemned the view that the earth moves around the sun as false science and contrary to biblical teaching:

> It has . . . come to the knowledge of the said Congregation that the Pythagorean doctrine—which is false and altogether opposed to the Holy Scripture—of the motion of the Earth, and the immobility of the Sun, which is also taught by Nicolaus Copernicus in *The Revolutions of the Planets* . . . is now being spread abroad and accepted by many. . . .[1]

Copernicus's work was placed on the list of censored books.

At the same time, the Church wanted Galileo (1564–1642) to abandon the Copernican position that he had been advocating in both written and public discussions. But Galileo, courageous as he was brilliant, continued to defend the Copernican position. His writings on planetary motion, sunspots, comets, and other natural phenomena clearly supported the heliocentric theory. In 1633, at the age of sixty-nine and in poor health, Galileo was summoned to appear before the Grand Inquisitor in Rome. He was found guilty of teaching falsehood, forced to recant, and placed under house arrest for the remaining eight years of his life.[2]

Historians of science know that the Church was actually willing to allow Galileo to discuss the heliocentric theory as a hypothesis, but it did not want him to claim that the theory truly depicted the behavior of the sun and planets. Wanting to protect its unique right to make pronouncements about reality, the Church offered Galileo and other progressive scientists the opportunity to say that the heliocentric theory is a mathematical fiction—just one of several possible calculational schemes that could account for observed heavenly phenomena.

When he wrote the preface to Copernicus's *Revolutions*, Andreas Osiander (1498–1552) tried to make that work more palatable to the scientific community and to church theologians. He maintained that the heliocentric hypothesis is simply a convenient device for predicting planetary motion and not a true account of the causes of planetary motion. Osiander thought that he could defuse the controversy by sharply separating the domains of science and theology: science formulates mathematical fictions, but theology describes reality. The key, however, lies in precisely how the difference is defined. Galileo did not accept Osiander's option of denying to science the task of describing reality and discovering the hidden causes of observable events. Galileo believed that the heliocentric theory genuinely described reality, and thus he remained in direct conflict with the Church's geocentric view.

The Galileo affair bristles with many complex issues: the abuses of authority by institutionalized religion, the unfair lobbying activities of Ptolemaic scientists, the theological procedure by which scientific facts were derived from Holy Scripture, the emerging tension within science between the old deductive and the new inductive methods, and Galileo's own lack of diplomacy in propagating his views. Yet the most pervasive and most significant issue revolves around the operative notions of science and religion that led to conflict between them. The Galileo affair made painfully clear the need to understand the respective natures of these two powerful and important human activities. Adopting a thoughtful position on the relationship between science and religion is a prelude to approaching a multitude of specific problems that arise at their interface.

In seeking such a position, we need to understand the role of philosophy. Many people do not realize that almost all areas of intellectual investigation emerged from philosophy. Early in Western culture, study of the motions of the planets, the nature of music, the forms of government, the composition of Ultimate Reality, and much more came under the general canopy of *philosophy*, the "love of wisdom." Gradually, as the specific objects and methods of each inquiry became more clearly defined, new disciplines were born. Ultimately, many fields of study were spawned, each capable of conducting its official investigation independent of philosophy. The constellation of different disciplines that now exists—the array of natural sciences, the various social sciences, mathematics, and so forth—has emerged through a slow process of differentiation.

The present exploration, then, deals with three disciplines: *theology*, (which is the systematic articulation of religious beliefs), *natural science* (which is the empirical study of the order of nature), and *philosophy* (which, for our purposes, is the attempt to understand the most general characteristics of reality and knowledge). The attempt to define, distinguish, and interrelate the activities of theology and natural science is a philosophical undertaking. Two broad philosophical concerns are particularly relevant to this task: *metaphysical questions* (dealing with reality) and *epistemological questions* (dealing with knowledge) are crucial to differentiating the various models. As we look at the philosophical assumptions of both theology and natural science, we will see that they may be differentiated according to how their respective *aims, objects,* and *methods* are conceived.

Ian Barbour (b. 1923) has identified four basic models for understanding the relationship of religion and science: *conflict, independence, dialogue,* and *integration.* Let us consider each of these models in turn. We confine our discussion of science to the broad domain of the natural science.

DO RELIGION AND SCIENCE CONFLICT?

The Galileo affair has long been taken as symbolic of an inherent and irresolvable conflict between religion and science. Of course, other important issues have been taken as representing the conflict as well. For example, the now familiar debate over creation and evolution has been a heated controversy for more than a hundred years, pitting a view of humanity as a complex product of nature against a view of humanity as a creation of a personal deity.[3] Other examples are abundant. Relativity theory in physics drastically reinterprets concepts of space, time, and causality and thus challenges all religious perspectives that relate God to the world.[4] Technological advances in computers and artificial intelligence seem to endanger the unique status of *Homo sapiens.*[5] The decoding of the DNA molecule threatens to put "the secret of life" into the hands of scientists.[6]

In the contemporary period, two dramatically opposed schools of thought, *scientific materialism* and *biblical literalism,* agree on one key point: that religion and science are in total *conflict.* Let us sketch the basic position of each of these schools and learn why they agree on this point. *Scientific materialism* makes the epistemological assumption that the empirical method of science is the only reliable procedure for obtaining knowledge and the metaphysical assumption that physical stuff (i.e., matter and energy) is the Ultimate Reality basis of the universe. Auxiliary assumptions that complete the view of scientific materialism include the claims that only the entities studied by science are real and that only science can reveal what is real. After all, science allegedly works from publicly observable, reproducible data that are taken to confirm and disconfirm its theories. Hence, science is said to be properly objective. Religious beliefs, by contrast, are not as readily connected to such data as scientific theories and thus are said to be subjective, parochial, and uncritical.

Perhaps no intellectual movement exemplifies our general characterization of scientific materialism more than *logical positivism,* a movement whose heyday ranges from about the 1920s to the 1940s. Logical positivists, such as A. J. Ayer (1910–1989), who was discussed in chapter 11, took the strong epistemological line that the only statements that have meaning are those that are verifiable or falsifiable by empirical experience. Since religion, metaphysics, and even ethics address nonempirical or nonsensory realities, the positivists charged that these disciplines consist of pseudostatements with no cognitive meaning. For example, religion speaks of God, an entity that cannot be observed. Metaphysics speaks of being in general, which is an abstraction that cannot be observed. Ethics speaks of values, things of which we can have no sensory experience. The logical positivists denied reality to such unobservables and thus denied cognitive meaning to statements about them. The positivists claimed that, at best, terms for unobservable entities should be viewed as expressing our own subjective, psychological states and not as referring to objective realities.

Ironically, logical positivism itself eventually collapsed as philosophers began to realize that sensory input does not even provide an indubitable starting point for science. Philosophers of science became increasingly aware that the interaction of theory and observation is much more subtle and complex than the positivists ever imagined, thus threatening their pristine version of objectivity. Since the positivists could not account for cognitive significance in scientific statements, the intellectual community became disillusioned by their claim to have a standard of meaning for all statements in other areas, such as religion and ethics.

Outside professional philosophy, there are other representatives of scientific materialism and its attendant conviction that religion and science conflict. In popular culture, Carl Sagan (1934–1996) has been a spokesperson for scientific materialism. In his book *Cosmos,* later made into a series for educational television, he states: "The Cosmos is all that is or ever was or ever will be."[7] Sagan believes that the universe is eternal, that it is fundamentally physical, and that science is the only way to gain reliable knowledge about it. He has been openly critical of traditional ideas of God as being too mystical and subjective and as ultimately threatening to the scientific method.

At the other end of the spectrum from scientific materialism is *biblical literalism.* Biblical literalism is something of an anomaly in the history of Christian thought, which contains a variety of views on the relation of scripture and science. For example, St. Augustine (354–430) maintained that when some particular passage of the Bible appears to conflict with established scientific thought, that passage should probably be interpreted metaphorically.[8] Other medieval philosophers and theologians acknowledged that the Bible includes a rich diversity of literary forms and reveals truth at many levels. The Anglican tradition continues this approach to scripture and is open to figurative as well as literal interpretations, depending on the genre of literature and the context of scriptural text in question. Pope John Paul II (b. 1920), representing a stance quite different from the one the Church took toward the Galileo controversy, has said that we now have "a more accurate appreciation of the methods proper to the different orders of knowledge,"[9] clearly giving place to both religious and scientific knowledge.

By contrast, particularly during the late nineteenth and early twentieth centuries in America, a literalistic mode of interpretation became the hallmark of certain American Protestant denominations or at least of large constituencies within those denominations. Biblical literalism—often referred to as "Protestant fundamentalism" or just "fundamentalism"—can be seen as a reaction to the rise of evolutionary biology in the area of science as well as to "higher criticism"[10] in the study of scriptural texts. Fundamentalists, whose numbers seem to be strong and growing, insist that scripture is "inerrant" and should be interpreted literally. Of course, they have a certain view of what it means to interpret scripture literally. The most prominent instance of how fundamentalism employs this approach is no doubt its ongoing crusade against the scientific theory of evolution. Their so-called literal interpretation of the book of Genesis results in the belief that God created the universe in six days, each twenty-four hours long, and instantaneously created humanity at the end of the sixth day. This belief is in direct conflict with the scientific theses that the species *Homo sapiens* evolved over millions of years—and the fundamentalists are interested in no compromises.

The Scopes "monkey trial" of 1925 was a sensational clash between the forces involved in this issue.[11] In the trial, William Jennings Bryan argued that teachers should not be permitted to present biological evolution in the public schools because it is clearly contrary to scripture. Here we have religionists making factual pronouncements of a scientific nature on the basis of their reading of the Bible. Although Bryan won the decision in the trial, it was later overturned on a technicality, and evolutionary theory was permitted in the schools. However, fundamentalist opposition has continued to the present day.

In the last few decades, fundamentalists have developed a new argument known as "scientific creationism." Creation scientists try to validate their creationist position by scientific means. Instead of basing belief in the instantaneous creation of the first human beings on a literal reading of the Bible alone, they claim that they have scientific evidence for such beliefs. "True science," they argue, correlates with a literally interpreted biblical account of creation.[12] Creation scientists typically label evolutionary theory "false science" and demand equal time for "creationist theory" in the schools. In 1981, for example, a fundamentalist group succeeded in getting an Arkansas court to rule in favor of equal time for the teaching of "creationist theory," supported by whatever scientific facts seemed to confirm it and without reference to God or the Bible. We should note that the U.S. District Court overturned the Arkansas law one year later on grounds that it favored a particular religious view and thus violated the constitutional separation of church and state. It also pronounced creation science bogus science. We should also note that quite a few people who testified against the Arkansas bill were religious leaders and theologians, many of whom argued that the fundamentalists' literalistic approach to the Bible and their co-opting of science for sectarian purposes was dangerous to our intellectual and religious freedom.

Regardless of our personal feelings on these issues, a more fundamental lesson that we may learn concerns the way in which competition and conflict between religion and science are made possible. Conflict is certainly possible when religion and science are conceived in ways that closely equate their *aims, objects,* and *methods.* When the aims of theology include providing an explanation for natural objects and events that would stand on the same footing as any proposed scientific explanation, then conflict is almost inevitable. Likewise, when the proper *objects* of theological investigation include the same natural or physical phenomena that science studies, the stage is set for direct competition. Finally, when the *method* of theology is put on a par with that of science—or at least when it is not sufficiently distinguished from the method of science—then the path is open for severe competition between the two disciplines.

One clear moral emerges from the prolonged debate over evolution and creation: when the objects, aims, and methods of religion and science are not sufficiently differentiated, the stage is set for competition and conflict. We might venture a few generalizations about the history of the issue. When disciplinary or intellectual boundaries are persistently blurred, we eventually find some theologians meddling in the affairs of science, even wanting to overturn its findings for religious rather than scientific reasons. On the other side, we find some scientists and other scientifically informed persons who try to use the results of modern science to confirm philosophical naturalism and thus to discredit religion altogether. What we might hope for is a better understanding of the nature of religion and science than either side possesses in a conflict model.

ARE RELIGION AND SCIENCE INDEPENDENT?

Instead of treating religion and science as if they are in direct conflict, some thinkers and movements have treated them as if they are totally *independent*, with each area having its own very different *aims, objects,* and *methods.* Generally, this independence model produces the attitude that each field—religion and science—should stick to its own business. The image of religion and science as sealed off from one another in airtight compartments is appropriate here. Conflict, quite obviously, is thereby avoided.

In the medieval period, the separation of religion and science was supported by a kind of broad dualistic thinking that has both metaphysical and epistemological components. Metaphysically, the medieval mind saw reality as divided into two realms, supernature and nature. God is a supernatural reality, and the human soul and other objects of theology were associated primarily with this realm as well. The physical universe, on the other hand, comprised the mundane realm of nature. The general medieval posture, epistemologically speaking, was that the realm of supernature could be fully known only by revelation, whereas the realm of nature is known by the techniques appropriate to human rational investigation. Thus, both the *objects* and the *methods* of theology and science are greatly different. Obviously, the medieval tradition of *natural theology* (whose arguments we studied in chapter 5) afforded some middle ground, maintaining that the existence and a few metaphysical attributes of God could be inferred from the existence and design of nature. There was a strong conviction that the spiritual realm permeates the material realm, giving ordinary life profound significance.

In modern times, several intellectual movements, each in its own way, have advocated the strict independence of religion and science: *Protestant neo-orthodoxy, existentialism,* and *linguistic analysis.* The Protestant theologian

Karl Barth (1886–1968), perhaps the most celebrated spokesperson for *neo-orthodoxy,* tried to recapture for Christianity its emphasis on the centrality of Christ and the primacy of special "revelation" for knowing God.[13] For Barth, theology deals with God's self-revelation in Christ and therefore offers a source of religious knowledge that lies beyond our human noetic powers, our abilities to know. In fact, according to Barth, sin has so blinded human reason to the knowledge of God that it is absolutely necessary for God to bridge the gap and reveal himself to us.[14] Furthermore, the aim of religion is to effect personal encounter with God. Barth conceives of science, on the other hand, as the ongoing human search for knowledge of the natural world, employing as it does observation, experiment, rational inference, and the like. Its fundamental aim is to gain understanding about the patterns of the empirical world.

Existentialism, which influenced neo-orthodox theology, also advocated a sharp distinction between the domains of religion and science. Neo-orthodoxy sharply distinguished the transcendent realm from the finite human realm in order to support the separation of religion and science. However, the dominant distinction in the existentialist categorization of religion and science was between the realm of personal selfhood and the realm of impersonal objects. Common to all versions of existentialism is the conviction that we can understand the meaning of human existence only by being personally involved in freely making decisions. It is through commitment, being authentic, and shouldering our humanity responsibly that we work out the meaning of our own lives—not through detached speculation.

Although *atheistic existentialists,* such as Nietzsche (1844–1900) and Sartre (1905–1980) believed that we could achieve meaning without reference to God, *religious existentialists* insisted that we need to orient ourselves toward God to experience the full significance of personal life. For these existentialists, religion involves the subjective and inward orientation of one's personhood, whereas science involves the study and manipulation of objects. Once again, then, we have a strict differentiation between the *subject matter* of religion and science; the former deals with the realm of uniquely personal existence, whereas the latter deals with the realm of objects and their operations. The *methods* of knowledge are subjective and objective, respectively. The *aim* of religion is to provide an avenue of personal meaning and significance, whereas the aim of the scientific enterprise is to explain, predict, and control the behaviors of impersonal things in our physical environment. The noted Jewish theologian Martin Buber (1878–1965) poignantly makes this distinction, stating that the relation between a person and a material object is an I-It relationship but that the religious believer's relation to God is an I-Thou relationship. It is through relationship with God that one finds complete human fulfillment: "As a Person God gives personal life, he makes us as persons become capable of meeting with him and with one another."[15]

Linguistic analysis is another philosophical movement that envisions religion and science as totally compartmentalized human endeavors. Although positivistic philosophers restricted language to the statement of empirical facts and were fascinated by the prospect of building an ideal language on that basis, ordinary language philosophers were fascinated by the rich variety of functions that human language performs. Ordinary language philosophers are less inclined to assign reality to the respective *objects* of religion and science but are instead interested in analyzing the uses of these different stretches of language and the different human contexts in which they occur. Taking their cue particularly from the work of the later Wittgenstein, exponents of this approach said that religion and science are two distinct but equally legitimate "language games," each with its own vocabulary, categories, and logic. According to linguistic philosophers, the uses of language in religious contexts differ greatly from the uses of scientific language. For them, the aim of religious language (considered in depth in chapter 11) is to support and recommend a certain way of life. The method by which it does this is to use language that is effective in eliciting a certain set of attitudes and encouraging allegiance to a particular moral point of view. On the other hand, the aims served by scientific language are essentially those of explanation, prediction, and technological manipulation of observable phenomena. This language must be extremely precise and highly empirical. Thus, for ordinary language philosophy, theology and science are treated as markedly separate linguistic activities, having intrinsically different *aims* and *methods* woven inextricably into their respective languages, with no possibility of interaction or conflict.[16]

IS DIALOGUE POSSIBLE?

One may wonder whether it is possible to move beyond the independence thesis to some conception of how religion and science can interact. Can they engage in dialogue in any fashion? Ian Barbour envisions two avenues along which these two distinct fields can have meaningful dialogue. The first avenue relates to the discussion of what might be called *boundary questions;* the second revolves around consideration of *methodological parallels* between the two fields.

Let us proceed by talking about the *boundaries of science* along two different lines: the *presuppositions* required at the foundations of science and the questions raised at the *limits* of certain scientific theories, that by their nature, cannot be answered by further scientific investigation. Each of these approaches to the matter of boundaries offers interesting possibilities for dialogue between theology and science.

It is common among philosophers of science to say that science rests on certain *presuppositions*, beliefs that science cannot establish but that shape the whole enterprise. These presuppositions, taken together, provide a kind of sketch of the fundamental characteristics of the world in which science takes itself to operate, giving rise to more specific commitments about its *aims*, *objects*, and *methods*. For example, many thinkers take science to rest on the presupposition that physical nature is in a significant sense real, leading to a

belief that the objects of science are empirically real entities. Another important presupposition is that nature is intelligible, that is, accessible to mind.
Still another presupposition is that the world's order is contingent and not
necessary, which entails that its order must be known through inductive and
empirical methods. One last presupposition of science is that nature is, in an
important sense, good—that it has value and worth. This presupposition supports the aim of understanding nature and entering into commerce with it.

Such presuppositions may seem rather unremarkable and almost too
obvious to be interesting, but they have not always been so widely accepted.
In fact, their acceptance in modern times has a long and interesting history. It
is customary to speak of modern science as being indebted to classical Greek
thought, insofar as the latter's confidence in the rational structure of nature
provides one of the early driving forces for science. However, a deeper look
into the Greek worldview raises enormous doubts about whether it could
ever have evolved in the direction of modern science. Plato and Aristotle
both believed that the true nature of things is found in their "form," not in
their "matter." Thus, the objects of science, for them are the essential (nonempirical) forms of things. In this vein, ancient Greek science assumed we
could know the properties of a thing by logically deducing them from a definition of its essence—and without having to study it empirically! This is
hardly the method that modern science follows.

The Judeo-Christian *doctrine of creation*, which was formulated centuries
later and which eventually influenced pioneer thinkers, actually allowed
modern science, with its careful empirical techniques and inductive reasoning, to be born. The doctrine teaches that God freely chose to bring the world
into existence, which makes its operations contingent and thus amenable to
inductive and empirical methods. Since God is good, his creation is also
good and worthy of study. E. L. Mascall (b. 1905) explains that the doctrine
of creation supplied a philosophy of nature that overthrew the Greek perspective and gave solid support to modern science:

> A world which is created by the Christian God will be both contingent and
> orderly. It will embody regularities and patterns, since its Maker is rational,
> but the particular regularities and patterns which it will embody cannot be
> predicted *a priori*, since he is free; they can be discovered only by examina-
> tion. The world, as Christian theism conceives, it is thus an ideal field for the
> application of scientific method, with its twin techniques of observation and
> experiment.[17]

These and other implications of the doctrine were not all seen at once but
came to be understood after centuries of reflection by Christian thinkers. As
further implications were drawn, Christian philosophers realized that they
were committed to the rich and suggestive affirmations that matter is real
and intelligible per se and that appropriate methods had to be developed for
studying it. Thus, the conceptual seeds for modern science were planted by
theological insights.[18] Science began to break away from the Greek conception and to flourish anew in the early modern period. This is one of the many
lessons of the Galileo affair.

Another kind of *boundary issue* arises when we realize that some of the crowning theories of science take us to the limits of science's ability to explain. The more general and comprehensive scientific theories actually raise additional questions that science cannot answer by its own methods. These questions are essentially metaphysical, thus opening the door for dialogue between science and theology. In pushing back to the earliest history of the cosmos, astronomers and theoretical physicists, for example, ask questions about the initial conditions that existed. The physicist Stephen Hawking (b. 1942) once proposed that everything in the universe expanded from an initial infinitesimal point in which not even the most elemental laws of physics operated.[19] Since this is as far back as science can extend its impulse for explanation, it has reached a limit or boundary. At this level of inquiry, a profound question arises: how did the fundamental laws of physics first come into existence, if there was once a punctiliar time when they did not exist? Since science cannot answer such a question, some would say that the door is open for theology to say something about God as the creative ground of the existence and structure of the universe. By its own distinct methods, theology can help make sense of the contingency and general order that science discovers in the universe. It thereby offers a different perspective on the same range of objects.

Various thinkers envision different ways for theology to interact with the boundary questions of science. The philosopher of science Ernan McMullin (b. 1924), for example, distinguishes the statements and methods of theology from those of science and envisions those two enterprises as functioning on different levels of explanation. McMullin declares that, on its own level, a scientific account of the universe is in principle complete. For him, there is no need to think that the relation of theology to science is that of filling in the gaps—that is, of deriving arguments for the existence of God on the basis of incomplete explanations in science. Besides, as science advances, such gaps are eventually closed, thus preempting that role for theology. McMullin stresses, instead, that the aim of theology is to provide ultimate explanations, and its methods are oriented toward constructing them. The Christian doctrine of creation does not, he contends, explain the mechanics of how the universe began but affirms its absolute dependence on God. Interpreted in this fashion, the doctrine of creation is "consonant" with modern scientific cosmology, giving an explanation of the universe that is not incompatible with but is complementary to scientific explanation. Thus, theology—like science, history, literature, and other disciplines—contributes to a coherent worldview.[20]

David Tracy (b. 1939) proposes that religion can enter into genuine dialogue at the boundaries of science in a somewhat different manner. On the one hand, theology can contribute insight on the ethical issues pertaining to the uses of science (e.g., the use of atomic theory to build weapons of mass destruction). Tracy also believes that theology can shed light on the presuppositions required for the possibility of science (e.g., that the world requires a rational ground that can be understood from classic religious texts and the structures of human experience).[21] This is the impact religion can have on science: answering its boundary questions. On the other hand, science can

also contribute information to theology. Tracy contends that theological doctrines are culturally conditioned and limited and that enlightened theological method takes into account new scientific advances. The way evolutionary
ideas have affected modern consciousness, for example, raises the question
of reformulation of the doctrine of creation.

As we indicated earlier, another avenue for dialogue between religion
and science pertains to the *methodological parallels* between the two fields.
Although *positivists,* neo-*orthodox theologians,* and *existentialist thinkers* characterized science as *objective* and religion as *subjective,* that dichotomy came
under increasing pressure from studies showing that religion is more objective than originally thought and that science is subjective in important respects. Such studies opened the way for thinkers to seek parallels between
the methods of religion and the methods of science, rather than to concen-
trate on the stark differences between them. For present purposes, let us look
at four factors that can be cited to make a case for the methodological parallel
between science and religion: *communal paradigms, research programs, observer
participation,* and *the role of models.*

In the past several decades, such philosophers as Norwood Russell Hanson (1924–1967),[22] Stephen Toulmin (b. 1922),[23] and Thomas Kuhn (b. 1922)[24]
have persuasively argued that science is not as pristine and objective as previously thought. These authors represent a growing trend in philosophy of
science that emphasized the fact that scientific data are in a certain sense
theory-laden, that theories arise as much from the free and creative scientific
imagination as they do from an analysis of evidence, and that the acceptance
of theories is as much a function of the historical community of scientists as it
is a calculation based strictly on the evidence. We might say that this new era
in the philosophy of science stresses the theme of "personal involvement"—
and it has done this in a rich variety of ways.

Probably no contemporary philosopher of science has had broader impact than Thomas Kuhn. Kuhn argued that the method of science is not totally objective in testing theories by clear-cut criteria that refer to theory-free
data because both theories and data are dependent on the prevailing *paradigms* of the scientific community. Although Kuhn uses the term "paradigm"
in slightly different ways throughout his work, the following statement of
Kuhn's is enlightening:

> On the one hand, [the term "paradigm"] stands for the entire constellation
> of beliefs, values, techniques, and so on shared by the members of a given
> community. On the other, it denotes one sort of element in that constellation,
> the concrete puzzle-solutions which, employed as models or examples, can
> replace explicit rules as a basis for the solution of the remaining puzzles of
> normal science.[25]

"Normal science" simply means the collective efforts of the scientific community to solve the research problems they face according to the prevailing
paradigm. The paradigm contains examples of puzzles already solved and
helps decide what could count as an adequate solution of other puzzles. An

established paradigm is resistant to simple falsification by a few negative instances and can often be preserved by considering these instances to be anomalies or by articulating ad hoc hypotheses.

Kuhn's idea of a *scientific revolution* is highly suggestive of parallels with religion. Normal science, which is typically conservative and controlled by tradition, enters crisis when the prevailing paradigm encounters increasing difficulty solving some important puzzles. At some point, an alternative paradigm starts seeming attractive to the community of researchers by virtue of its ability to account for existing data while handling new data in a more satisfactory way. When such conditions are present, science typically undergoes a major *paradigm shift*, which is a "scientific revolution." Likewise, when the prevailing theological paradigm—or way of looking at the world and explaining and responding to important life situations—comes under pressure and a new paradigm seems to have much promise to a significant number of the religious community, then a *theological revolution* is almost inevitably brewing. One could interpret, say, the Protestant Reformation's break from Roman Catholicism or the modern rejection and reformulation of traditional Christian doctrines by feminist theologians in this light. We could also see the emergence of Mahayana Buddhism from Theravada Buddhism, for example, as a major paradigm shift.

All of this highlights the tremendously social nature of paradigms. Although debates continue about the exact degree of subjectivity in science, Kuhn's provocative analysis inspired some thinkers to suggest that religious traditions can also be viewed as communities that share a common paradigm. The data for religious communities are religious experience, historical events, and sacred texts—all interpreted and given significance within an overarching paradigm. Challenges to religious belief, like challenges to a scientific theory under the approved paradigm, can be deflected by calling them anomalies or by proposing ad hoc hypotheses. This actually explains the tendency of religious believers to maintain their beliefs even in light of seemingly contrary evidence—and scientists, as Kuhn has shown us, often do the same thing. That is just the way paradigms operate within the communities that embrace them.

In seeking ever more adequate ways to expose methodological parallels between science and religion, some have thought that the Kuhnian-type radical paradigm shift is too extreme. Nancey Murphy (b. 1951) maintains that the idea of a *research program* provides a better conception of methodological parallels.[26] Imre Lakatos (b. 1937) advanced the idea that a community of scientists engages in ongoing projects and endeavors that preserve at their heart a core theory that is surrounded by auxiliary hypotheses. The role of the auxiliary hypotheses is to protect the core theory. Thus, they are subject to modification and even rejection and replacement in order to keep data from overturning the core theory. The idea of a research program explains the tendency of scientists to cling to their main theory in light of seemingly adverse data while at the same time accounting for their ability to make appropriate theoretical adjustments.

Murphy thinks that it is very fruitful to interpret the task of theology as a research program as well. The core of the theological research program should contain the theologian's judgment about how to sum up the essential minimum of the relevant community's faith—perhaps revolving around the trinitarian nature of God, God's holiness, and God's revelation in Jesus. The next step is to develop auxiliary hypotheses to be explained by the core and whose future modification could help protect the core. The third step, if theology is to be genuinely parallel to science, is for the theologian to seek data that help confirm the core theory and the auxiliary hypotheses. The data describe a range of religious experiences (e.g., humiliation, love, meekness, spiritual appetite, communal support).

One might describe Murphy as wanting to look for parallels between religion and science primarily by making theology more objective, whereas followers of Kuhn do it by making science more subjective. But the question arises: why would we want to adapt a scientific method to theology (or, perhaps, adapt theology to a scientific method, depending on one's perspective)? The point of Lakatos's method is to provide an objective decision procedure for choosing between competing conceptual schemes or research programs. Those large-scale theories that generate new, confirmable data are progressive; those that fail to do so are degenerative. Obviously, theology faces a diversity of theoretical positions—Christian and non-Christian—that vie for acceptance. How do we decide among them? Murphy would answer that the respective religious research programs should project novel and important facts about human experience that can be objectively verified. Confirmation of the empirical claims that follow from these research programs would provide support for the research programs. Conversely, should the empirical claims be disconfirmed or encounter serious anomalies, the research program would seem to be degenerate rather than progressive. This would mean, at the very least, that some auxiliary hypotheses would need reevaluation so as to make the research program progressive again or, at the very most, that the program should be abandoned. Much more needs to be discussed before arriving at a final assessment of Murphy's proposal. However, we may say at this point that she envisions a positive relation between the *methods* of theology and science, a relation that reflects the fact that both can exhibit critical objectivity that makes for intersubjective testing.

Instead of arguing that religion is like science, philosopher of science Holmes Rolston (b. 1932) argues that science is like religion in an important respect. He explains that the role of personal involvement is coming to be recognized in science and that it is somewhat parallel to the nature of personal involvement in religion. While the methods of both religion and science call for personal involvement, Rolston admits that the distinct aim of personal involvement in religion is the reformation and reorientation of the person.[27] In modern times, the emergence of both relativity physics and quantum physics has supplied interesting case studies for those looking for parallels with religion. While the relationship between relativity and quantum theories may be debated, they both forced a reconsideration of the status of the observer in science. Traditional conceptions envision the observer in science separate from the object of observation. However, in developing an adequate quantum theory, Werner Heisenberg (1901–1976) and others asserted that the very act of observation itself influences the outcome of the observation, that the observer is somehow involved with the data. The Heisenberg Uncertainty Principle states that the more precisely we determine the location of an electron, the less precisely we can determine its velocity, and vice versa. This is because light must be used, say, to determine position, but even one quantum of light alters the velocity of the electron.[28] Relativity theory also assumes personal involvement when it asserts that the most fundamental measurements—such as mass, velocity, and length of an object—depend on the frame of reference of the observer.[29] For example, a moving object appears much shorter in the direction of motion, although it is the other objects that appear compressed when viewed from the moving object itself. All of this accents the intimate tie between—indeed, the inseparability of—the observer and the observed, the seeker and reality.[30]

As we can see, exciting advances made in both science and the philosophy of science put pressure on the old dichotomy between science as totally objective and religion as deeply subjective by showing the personal and communal features of the scientific enterprise. However, the dichotomy also came under pressure from some writers who insisted that religion should not be typecast as utterly subjective. We can, for example, interpret religion as having its own data for public consideration, much as science does. Its data include religious experience, rituals, and scriptural texts. Furthermore, theology can approach its distinct explanatory task with a premium placed on the conceptual criteria of coherence, comprehensiveness, and fruitfulness, which are criteria also employed in the scientific evaluation of empirical theories.

Still another factor that helps reveal methodological parallels between theology and science is the use of models in each discipline. As Ian Barbour shows in *Myths, Models, and Paradigms,* religion employs metaphors and models much as science employs them to help imagine what is not directly observable.[31] A *model,* for present purposes, is an imaginative mental construct invented to account for observed phenomena. According to Barbour,

> A model is usually an imagined mechanism or process, which is postulated by analogy with familiar mechanisms or processes. . . . [I]ts chief use is to help one understand the world, not simply to make predictions. . . . Like a mathematical model, it is a symbolic representation of a physical system, but it differs in its intent to represent the underlying structure of the world. It is used to develop a theory which in some sense explains the phenomena.[32]

Clear instances of models in practiced religion as well as professional theology are not difficult to find.

The feminist theologian Sallie McFague (b. 1933) discusses some of the prominent models in the Christian community, models that arise from human experience and help us understand certain aspects of the divine. She analyzes three personal models: *God as Mother* (representing nurture and care), *God as Lover* (representing the divine passion toward humanity), and *God as Friend* (representing a reciprocal bond between God and the believer).[33] Again, such studies of religion help show that it has more structure and is more objective than common stereotypes allow and, furthermore, that its structure and objectivity are parallel to elements detected in the scientific quest.

ATTEMPTS AT INTEGRATION

Some thinkers hold that religion and science are capable of a more intimate and organic relationship than a *dialogue model* admits. They contend that some sort of *integration* between the two fields is not only possible but necessary if we are to achieve a unified and comprehensive understanding of reality. Barbour identifies three different versions of integration between the content of theology and the content of science: *natural theology, theology of nature,* and *systematic synthesis.*

Traditional natural theology reasons from the existence of the cosmos itself and from evidence of design in nature to the existence of God. As we saw in chapter 5, natural theologians construct arguments based on human reason rather than on sacred revelation or religious experience. Perhaps the most widely popular piece of natural theology is the teleological argument in its various forms.[34] In contemporary times, the *Weak* Anthropic Principle, based on a wealth of new scientific findings, is often employed to make the argument.[35] Thus, new theories and findings in science sometimes provide fresh grist for the mill in natural theology. While the *aims* and *methods* of natural theology differ from those of empirical science, there is a sense in which they are interested in giving their respective explanations of the same *objects.* This means that natural theology may be seen as one form of integration between the content of science and the content of theology.

A different kind of integration of religion and science is attempted by those thinkers interested in articulating a *theology of nature.* Unlike natural theology, a theology of nature does not start from science and move to an accepted religious tradition, with its distinctive religious experiences and scriptural texts. A theology of nature uses the content of science to tutor, reformulate, and reinterpret traditional theological doctrines, rather than to argue for the existence of God. Within the Christian intellectual community, for example, the doctrines of creation, providence, and human nature are affected in fascinating and important ways by the most current theories propounded in the sciences. Arthur Peacocke (b. 1922) understands that science now characterizes nature as dynamic and evolutionary, with a long history of emergent novelty brought about by the interplay of chance and law. Explaining the new scientific picture of things theologically, he says that "the natural causal creative nexus of events is itself God's creative action."[36] Many see Peacocke's approach as opening the door for a closer relationship between religion and science than seems possible in natural theology because the *objects* of science (even characterized in a general way) are interpreted as mediating God's presence and activity in the world.

A third version of integration, quite distinct from *natural theology* and the *theology of nature,* is *systematic synthesis.* This is the attempt to synthesize key religious themes with basic scientific insights under the canopy of a *comprehensive metaphysical system,* a unified worldview. The process philosophy of Alfred North Whitehead (1861–1947) is probably the most important and most influential modern example of this. We might characterize Whitehead as integrating religion and science by showing how their respective *aims* coalesce in a larger and more comprehensive aim, how each field has important insight into the nature of the *objects* that populate reality, and how the fruits of their *methods* have taught us new universal themes for understanding the universe. In short, Whitehead enlists both religion and science in the service of an overarching metaphysical vision.

Whitehead rejects the medieval view as well as the Newtonian view of nature. On the medieval view, nature embodies a fixed, unchanging, hierarchical order and operates teleologically (directed toward rational ends). All substances that make up reality, for medieval thinkers, involve a dualism of spirit and matter. Spirit is eternal and our link with the life of God, whereas matter is transitory and imperfect. The Newtonian view envisions nature as involving the continual rearrangement of unchanging components of the universe. Atomism (the belief that reality operates by strict causal necessity) are hallmarks of the Newtonian picture of nature.

Whitehead acknowledges that the new concepts of nature picture it as evolutionary and dynamic, with new and novel forms emerging through time. Concepts of determinism are replaced by concepts of chance, randomness, and even chaos, allowing nature to be characterized by openness as well as structure. Furthermore, nature is understood as relational, ecological, and interdependent. Reality has come to be seen as constituted by events and relationships, rather than by separate substances and their operations. According to Whitehead, a holistic conception of reality invalidates virtually all forms of dualism. Dualistic views of human nature are replaced by evolutionary views that acknowledge the special capacities of our species while maintaining that it is the product of and interdependent with other creatures in the natural order. Thus, the medieval view of nature as a kingdom and the Newtonian view of nature as a machine have been replaced by the view of nature as a community.

The genius of Whitehead's philosophy is that it presents a systematic metaphysical interpretation of reality that is consistent with the evolutionary view of nature held by twentieth-century science. Central to Whitehead's metaphysics is the priority of *becoming* over *being,* of *transition* and *activity* over *permanence* and *persistence.* All entities, which Whitehead calls "actual occasions," are centers of conscious experience, each exerting influence on all other occasions, making reality interdependent, ecological. The great hierarchy of nature represents a spectrum of the organization and integration of experience: an entity such as an *electron* (which quantum physics tells us has a transitory and indeterminate existence) exhibits a relatively low level of integration; a *cell* has a considerably higher level of integration; and so on up the chain of plants and animals. A *human being* exhibits a very high level of integration in which all of the lower levels are incorporated. These key ideas led Whitehead to dub his view "the philosophy of organism."[37] In discussing process responses to evil in chapter 7, we learned that each entity is interconnected with the whole of reality and yet retains its own individuality and power of self-determination.

Whitehead connects ideas inspired by contemporary science with theological ideas in a very sophisticated way. For Whitehead, God (in his Primordial Nature) is the ultimate ground of order in the world, offering all logical possibilities for how events can turn out. God selects certain "initial subjective aims" and imparts them to entities in the world, seeking to actualize the possibilities he envisions. However, God (in his Consequent Nature) is influenced by events in the world as he responds and adjusts to actual outcomes, always seeking to lure things toward his ideal aims for them. In his Consequent Nature, God conserves all of the valuable experiences and achievements of the creaturely world, thus leading to a process version of immortality. Between God and the world there is interdependence and reciprocity. Whitehead's God is not in monarchical control of the universe conceived as his kingdom; rather he "persuades" and "influences" events at a very deep level.

INSIGHTS

How one conceives of the *aims, objects,* and *methods* of these two important areas of human endeavor determines whether one embraces a model of their relationship as one of *conflict, independence, dialogue,* or *integration.* Key thinkers are increasingly moving away from conceptions of the aims, objects, and methods of religion and science that lead either to outright conflict or to utter independence. There is increasing interest in the intellectual arena in some form of dialogue or integration. This shift seems correctly rooted in a fundamental intuition that the different areas of human experience should fit together somehow, in meaningful dialogue or even in an all-encompassing vision of everything. We can rest assured that scholarly interest in this endeavor is so high that there will be no shortage of creative new proposals in the foreseeable future.

STUDY QUESTIONS

1. Try to characterize the four different views presented here regarding the relationship of religion and science. Explore the basis presented for each view.

2. The relation of religion and science is very complex. On one level, it is a philosophical issue; on another level, it is a political or institutional one. Explore what this statement might mean. Use the Galileo affair and the creation-evolution debate as starting points.

3. For centuries, theological inquiry has been conducted with an awareness of the contribution of Newton to our scientific understanding of the world. Do some reading about relativity theory in physics, and then engage in your own speculation about how it might affect the way theology is done in our time. Do the same for quantum mechanics.

4. Are there significant differences between the natural and the social sciences? Begin to think about this by trying to identify the *methods, aims,* and *objects* of the social sciences and distinguishing them from those of the natural sciences.

5. This chapter discusses the relationship between theology and natural science. How do you think a discussion of the relationship between theology and social science might proceed?

6. Explore the idea that science as we know it necessitates that we make certain assumptions about the structure of reality. What do you think of the suggestion that the assumptions found within the Judeo-Christian worldview are more conducive to science than those found in other major religious worldviews? Other nonreligious worldviews?

7. Select one school of thought that tends to see religion and science as completely independent or compartmentalized. Construct an argument for the merits of the position. Then construct an argument against the position.

8. Many forms of theism assert that God created a world order that operates according to general physical laws. Explore the suggestion that some of those natural laws are contained in the theory of biological evolution. Explore.

9. What might be the difference between a model of the relationship between religion and science that posits inherent conflict between them and a dialogue or integration model that still might allow for potential conflicts?

NOTES

1. *Opere,* XIX, 323. Quoted in Jerome Langford, *Galileo, Science and the Church* (New York: Desclee Company, 1966), pp. 97–98.

2. Ibid., chap. 6.

3. Although there were evolutionary-type works in geology and some other sciences that predated Darwin's work, it is fair to say that the heated debate as we know it started with Darwin's work. Charles Darwin, *The Descent of Man and Selection in Relation to Sex* (New York: A. L. Burtt, 1874) and *The Origin of Species by Means of Natural Selection* (Chicago: Encyclopedia Britannica, 1955).

4. Albert Einstein, *On the Method of Theoretical Physics,* delivered as the Herbert Spencer Lecture at Oxford, June 10, 1933, and *Relativity, the Special and the General Theory: A Popular Exposition,* trans. R. W. Lawson, 15th ed. (London: Methuen, 1954). See also Hans Reichenbach, *The Philosophy of Space and Time,* trans. M. Reichenbach and J. Freund (New York: Dover, 1957).

5. A seminal work in this area was A. M. Turing, "Computing Machinery and Intelligence," *Mind* 59 (1960), reprinted in Alan R. Anderson, ed., *Minds and Machines* (Englewood Cliffs, N. J.: Prentice-Hall, 1964), pp. 4–30. Among recent treatments of the issues, see D. Hofstadter and D. Dennet, *The Mind's I* (New York: Basic Books, 1981).

6. A seminal work in this area is J. D. Watson and F. H. C. Crick, "A Structure for Deoxyribose Nucleic Acid," *Nature* 171 (1953): 737.

7. Carl Sagan, *Cosmos* (New York: Random House, 1980), p. 4.

8. Ernan McMullin, "How Should Cosmology Relate to Theology?" in *The Sciences and Theology in the Twentieth Century*, ed. Arthur Peacocke (Notre Dame, Ind.: University of Notre Dame Press, 1981), p. 21.

9. *Origins: NC Documentary Service* 13 (1983): 50–1.

10. For an explanation of higher criticism, see William Neil, "The Criticism and Theological Use of the Bible, 1700–1950," pp. 283–93, and Alan Richardson, "The Rise of Modern Biblical Scholarship and Recent Discussion of the Authority of the Bible," pp. 294–338, both in *The Cambridge History of the Bible: The West from the Reformation to the Present Day*, ed. S. L. Greenslade (Cambridge: Cambridge University Press, 1963).

11. See Roland Frye, *Is God a Creationist? The Religious Case against Creation-Science* (New York: Scribners, 1983), for a set of articles discussing the ensuing controversy and making a case against creationism. Also see David B. Wilson, ed., *Did the Devil Make Darwin Do It? Modern Perspectives on the Creation-Evolution Controversy* (Ames: Iowa State University Press, 1983).

12. See, for example, Henry Morris, *The Twilight of Evolution* (Grand Rapids, Mich.: Baker Book House, 1963), and Henry Morris, ed., *Scientific Creationism* (San Diego, Calif.: Institute for Creation Research).

13. Thomas Torrance has developed further some of the major points in the neo-orthodox perspective. See his *Theological Science* (Oxford: Oxford University Press, 1969), p. 281.

14. Barth provides a manageable introduction to his thought in *Dogmatics in Outline* (London: SCM Press, 1949).

15. Martin Buber, *I and Thou*, trans. R. G. Smith (Edinburgh: T. & T. Clark, 1937), p. 136.

16. A helpful summary is given in Frederick Ferré, *Language, Logic and God* (New York: Harper and Brothers, 1961).

17. E. L. Mascall, *Christian Theology and Natural Science* (New York: Ronald Press, 1956), p. 132. Also see M. B. Foster, "The Christian Doctrine of Creation and the Rise of Modern Natural Science," *Mind* 43 (1934): 446–68.

18. It would be of great theoretical interest to explore the assumptions for science that nonreligious traditions offer and then see how they compare with those offered by the Judeo-Christian worldview. Although the naturalist tradition did not, as a matter of historical fact, give birth to science, we still might ponder whether, as a matter of logic, it could have been so. We might also exercise our theoretical interests by exploring conceptions of nature in non-Christian religions that could have given rise to modern science as we know it.

19. Stephen Hawking, *A Brief History of Time* (New York: Bantam Books, 1988), chap. 8.

20. See Ernan McMullin, "How Should Cosmology Relate to Theology?" in *The Sciences and Theology in the Twentieth Century*, ed. Arthur Peacocke (Notre Dame, Ind.: University of Notre Dame Press, 1981), p. 52.

21. David Tracy, *Blessed Rage for Order* (New York: Seabury, 1975) and *Plurality and Ambiguity* (San Francisco: Harper and Row, 1987).

22. Norwood Russell Hanson, *Patterns of Discovery* (Cambridge: Cambridge University Press, 1958).

23. Stephen Toulmin, *Foresight and Understanding* (Bloomington: Indiana University Press, 1961).

24. Thomas Kuhn, *The Structure of Scientific Revolutions* (Chicago: University of Chicago Press, 1970).

25. Ibid., p. 175.

26. Nancey Murphy, "Revisionist Philosophy of Science and Theological Method" (Paper delivered at the Pacific Coast Theological Society, Spring 1983); see also *Theology in the Age of Probable Reasoning* (Ithaca, N.Y.: Cornell University Press, 1990). (See Murphy's piece reprinted in PRSR2e, pt. 10, pp. 513–31.)

27. Holmes Rolston III, *Science and Religion: A Critical Survey* (New York: Random House, 1987), pp. 12.

28. Norwood Russell Hanson, "The Philosophical Implications of Quantum Mechanics," in the *Encyclopedia of Philosophy*, vol. 7, ed. Paul Edwards (New York: Macmillan, 1967), p. 44. Also see Hawking, *A Brief History of Time.*

29. For a popular rendition of relativity, see Lincoln Barnett, *The Universe and Dr. Einstein* (New York: New American Library, 1952); also see Paul Davies, *Other Worlds* (London: Abacus, 1982).

30. Some adherents of Eastern religions have gone so far as to say that this discovered inseparability is nothing less than a reflection of our participation of the individual in the Absolute. Subsequent discussions of such a suggestion would have to distinguish whether the relation between the knower and the known is essentially epistemological (having to do with the nature and scope of our experimental methods) or ontological (having to do with the nature of things). See Fritjof Capra, *The Tao of Physics* (New York: Bantam Books, 1977).

31. Ian Barbour, *Myths, Models, and Paradigms: A Complete Study in Science and Religion* (New York: Harper and Row, 1974), pp. 41–51.

32. Ibid., p. 30.

33. Sallie McFague, *Metaphorical Theology: Models of God in Religious Language* (Philadelphia: Fortress Press, 1982).

34. David Hume threads this line of argument throughout his *Dialogues concerning Natural Religion* (Indianapolis, Ind.: Hackett, 1980). (See pt. 10 of the *Dialogues* reprinted in PRSR2e, pt. 5, pp. 255–62.)

35. L. Stafford Betty and Bruce Cordell, "The Anthropic Teleological Argument," *International Philosophical Quarterly* 27, no. 4 (1987): 409–35. (Reprinted in PRSR2e, pt. 4, pp. 218–30.)

36. Arthur Peacocke, *Intimations of Reality* (Notre Dame, Ind.: University of Notre Dame Press, 1984), p. 63. See also his *Creation and the World of Science* (Oxford: Clarendon Press, 1979).

37. The classic source of process philosophy is, of course, Alfred North Whitehead, *Process and Reality* (Cambridge: Cambridge University Press, 1929).

SUGGESTED READING

Barbour, Ian G. *Religion in an Age of Science: The Gifford Lectures.* Vol. 1. San Francisco: Harper and Row, 1990.
————. *Ethics in an Age of Technology: The Gifford Lectures.* Vol. 2. San Francisco: Harper and Row, 1993.
————. *When Science Meets Religion: Enemies, Strangers, or Partners?* San Francisco: Harper Collins, 2000.
Brooke, John Hedley. *Science and Religion.* Cambridge: Cambridge University Press, 1991.
Davies, Paul. *God and the New Physics.* New York: Simon and Schuster, 1983.
Dawkins, Richard. *The Blind Watchmaker.* New York: W. W. Norton, 1986.
Dillenberger, John. *Protestant Thought and Natural Science.* New York: Doubleday, 1960.

Gould, Stephen Jay. *Ever Since Darwin*. New York: W. W. Norton, 1977.

Hawking Stephen. *A Brief History of Time*. New York: Bantam, 1988.

Mascall, E. L. *Christian Theology and Natural Science*. London: Oxford University Press, 1979.

Murphy, Nancey. *Theology in the Age of Scientific Reasoning*. Ithaca, N.Y.: Cornell University Press, 1990.

Nebelsick, Harold. *Theology and Science in Mutual Modification*. New York: Oxford University Press, 1981.

O'Connor, Daniel, and Francis Oakley, eds. *Creation: The Impact of an Idea*. New York: Scribner's, 1969.

Peacocke, Arthur. *Imitations of Reality: Critical Realism in Science and Religion*. Notre Dame, Ind.: University of Notre Dame Press, 1984.

———. *Theology for a Scientific Age*. Oxford: Blackwell, 1990.

Peters, Ted, ed. *Toward a Theology of Nature*. Louisville, Ky.: Westminster/John Knox Press, 1993.

Polkinghorner, John. *The Way the World Is: The Christian Perspective of a Scientist*. London: Triangle Press, 1983.

———. *One World*. Princeton, N.J.: Princeton University Press, 1987.

———. *Reason and Reality: The Relationship between Science and Theology*. Philadelphia: Trinity Press International, 1991.

———. *Serious Talk: Science and Religion in Dialogue*. Valley Forge, Pa.: Trinity Press International, 1995.

Rae, Murray, et al. *Science and Theology*. Grand Rapids, Mich.: William B. Eerdmans, 1994.

Ratzsch, Del. *Philosophy of Science: The Natural Sciences in Humans Perspective*. Downers Grove, Ill.: InterVarsity Press, 1986.

Rolston, Holmes, III. *Science and Religion: A Critical Examination*. Philadelphia: Temple University Press, 1986.

———. *Genes, Genesis, and God: Values and Their Origins in Natural and Human History*. Cambridge: Cambridge University Press, 1999.

Wilson, E. O. *Consilience: The Unity of Knowledge*. New York: Knopf, 1998.

CHAPTER 13

RELIGIOUS DIVERSITY: HOW CAN WE UNDERSTAND DIFFERENCES AMONG RELIGIONS?

A Zen Buddhist gives the following description of his religious experience and beliefs:

> Reached a white heat today. . . . Monitors whacked me time and again . . . their energetic stick wielding is no long an annoyance but a spur. . . .
>
> At next dokusan [the roshi or Zen master] again asked for Mu.[1] Quickly raised my hand as though to smack him. Didn't intend to really hit him, but the roshi, taking no chances, ducked. . . . How exhilarating these unpremeditated movements—clean and free. . . .
>
> . . . Didn't intend to tell Roshi of my insight, but as soon as I came before him he demanded: "What happened last night?" . . . [H]e began quizzing me: "Where do you see Mu? . . . How old is Mu? . . .
>
> Threw myself into Mu for another nine hours with such utter absorption that I completely vanished. . . . I didn't eat breakfast, Mu did. I didn't sweep and wash the floors after breakfast, Mu did. I didn't eat lunch, Mu ate. . . .
>
> Hawklike, the roshi scrutinized me as I entered his room, walked toward him, prostrated myself, and sat before him with my mind alert and exhilarated. . . .
>
> "The universe is One," he began, each word tearing into my mind like a bullet. "The moon of Truth—." All at once the roshi, the room, every single thing disappeared in a dazzling stream of illumination and I felt myself bathed in a delicious, unspeakable delight. . . . For a fleeting eternity I was alone—I alone was. . . .

"I have it! I know! There is nothing, absolutely nothing. I am everything and everything is nothing!" I exclaimed more to myself than to the roshi, and got up and walked out. . . .[2]

The religious beliefs and practices expressed by this Zen Buddhist seem worlds apart from those associated with Western religions. Yet he takes these beliefs as true and this way of religious life as fulfilling. But if his beliefs differ in significant ways from others' religious beliefs, can all these beliefs be true? If so, what are the implications of this for understanding what ultimate Reality is like? If not, how do we decide which are true and which not? In short, how are we to understand and interpret diverse religious claims?

RELIGIOUS DIVERSITY

In our complex world, we cannot affirm conscientiously one particular religious perspective and merely ignore the others. Modern communications, tourism, educational exchange, immigration, and international business have produced a cultural integration that hails as one hallmark of the new millennium. Diversity and plurality are its bywords. Yet contact among diverse religions is not a new phenomenon. The major religions never existed in complete isolation from other religions; their origins and development intertwine. Judaism developed its unique particularism amid numerous Semitic religions; Christianity grew out of Judaism; Islam developed later in contact with both. Hinduism amalgamated the thought and practices of Aryan invaders with the Dravidic religion indigenous to India. Buddhism arose in reaction to Hindu ascetic culture and developed in China through interaction with both Confucianism and Taoism. And what is true of the major religions applies even more to the sects or religions that grew out of them: Baha'i out of Islam; Mormonism, Christian Science, and Unitarianism from Christianity; Unificationism out of Korean Protestantism, Neo-Confucianism, and Buddhism; Sikhism out of Hinduism and Islam.

From a purely historical point of view, then, one should not think of religions in isolationist terms. Some even argue that we could construct not only an integrated history of the individual religions, but perhaps also a generic history of religious faith and practice.[3] Such an account would look very different from that found in standard religion texts, which devote distinct chapters to individual religions, their history, personages, beliefs, and practices. It would be a history that elicits how the actual beliefs and practices of one religion influenced those of other faiths. It might contain, for example, a tale about a wealthy prince who renounces his worldly power and goes off to live in ascetic poverty, a story that originates in Hinduism or Jainism, is passed down through Buddhism, Manicheism, and Islam, and finally is Christianized to play a role in the Christian religious experience of Tolstoy. Or it might trace a religious practice like the use of prayer beads from Buddhism through Islam to Catholicism.[4]

Neither can we ignore the similarities in the practices, rituals, and beliefs of the various religions. Many religious ceremonies use candles and incense and include offerings of various sorts to the gods; Hindus and Christians eat a divine meal; Muslims, Hindus, Jains, and Sikhs remove footwear before entering places of worship. As for beliefs, Judaism, Christianity, and Islam are monotheistic; most religions believe in spiritual beings influencing human affairs; avatars (physical incarnations of deity) play an important role in Christianity and Hinduism; the Golden Rule is prominent in Confucianism and Christianity.

But notable differences exist as well. Theravada Buddhism is nontheistic; Vedantic Hindus believe that Ultimate Reality (termed *Brahman* or *nondual Absolute*) lacks any distinctions. Orthodox Christianity is trinitarian and Hinduism polytheistic, whereas Islam and Judaism are strictly monotheistic. We could go on, but a detailed study of comparative religions lies beyond the scope of our book. Our point is simply that the various religions make similar and different truth-claims, and this raises the fundamental question of this chapter: how should advocates of one religion confess the truths of their religion and approach the truth-claims of another religion?

Our question is often misunderstood. We are not asking how an advocate of one religion should approach an advocate of another religion, but how one should approach *what* another person advocates. On the one hand, to ask how we should approach the truth-claims found in other religions is an epistemological question about what beliefs it is rational to hold and an ontological question about what really exists. Answers to these questions require that we consider the truth-claims of the various religions. The questioner seeks to understand sympathetically other persons' religious claims, to interpret what they mean and what significance they have for believers' lives, and to evaluate critically their alleged truth. On the other hand, to ask how we should approach other persons is a moral question. Advocates of other religions should be treated, at the very least, as the ethics of our religion demand persons should be treated. Often words like tolerance, understanding, caring, and compassion dominate such discussions.

It is sometimes forgotten that evaluating persons' truth-claims and morally relating to persons are separate issues. Thus, some suggest that unless we adopt the relativist claim that whatever persons think is correct is correct for them and renounce any belief that religious truths can be evaluated intersubjectively and interculturally, we are being intolerant of persons from different religions. They then trot out the blemishes of religion—jihads, crusades, terrorism, inquisitions, and pogroms.

We should not ignore the wrongs that believers have done in the name of their religion; they were and are deplorable—whether committed in Amritsar, Beirut, Belfast, Jerusalem, Kashmir, Kosovo, or New York City. But we should not mistakenly infer that statements about how we should treat those with whom we disagree follow directly from epistemological claims about the truths or falsehoods they hold. Nor should it imply anything about the legitimacy of disagreement. Tolerance of and openness to others does not mean that we must agree with what they believe or think. Otherwise, the rational discussion in our book about disagreements would be morally intolerable.

EXCLUSIVISM

Philosophical approaches to religious diversity can be classified under three broad headings: exclusivism, pluralism, and inclusivism.[5] For the *exclusivist*, salvation, liberation, human fulfillment, or whatever else one considers as the ultimate goal of the religion, is found solely in or through one particular religion. Although other religions contain truths, one religion is exclusively effective by alone providing the way of salvation or liberation. Adherents of other religions, although sincere in their piety and upright in their moral conduct, cannot attain salvation through their religions. To be saved, they must be told about and acknowledge the unique way. The unique salvific structure specified by this religion is both *ontologically necessary* (the objective conditions for salvation must really be in place) and *epistemically necessary* (those seeking salvation must know about the conditions) for salvation. Beliefs of this sort help explain religious evangelistic fervor and missionary zeal.

Exclusivists who have thought carefully about their view defend it on the grounds that religions make incompatible truth-claims. But incompatible truth-claims cannot both be true. Hence, where they contradict, at least one claim must be false. This might be termed doctrinal exclusivism: the doctrines of one religion are mostly true while contradictory claims in other religions are mostly false. Since religious doctrines frequently connect with salvation, if one religion's doctrines about salvation are mostly correct, those that contradict it are incorrect.

One example of a Christian exclusivist is the Protestant theologian Karl Barth (1886–1968), who contrasts religion with revelation. Religion stands opposed to faith as the defiant, arrogant, human endeavor pitted against the revelation of God. Religion is our impossible and sinful attempt to understand God from our viewpoint and overcome by our own efforts our estrangement from him. Religion is impossible because only God can accomplish reconciliation; religion is sinful because it replaces God with something we have made and hence is idolatry.[6] Salvation comes only through the true revelation of God, in which he shows and gives himself to us. Since attempts to save ourselves are doomed to failure, it is critical that we discover the locus of the divine salvific initiative. Once we discover where God has truly revealed his unique purposes, it would be folly to go elsewhere for salvation.

Barth does not deny that other religions contain truths, high moral ideals, and aesthetic values, or that their adherents are moral or sincere. Indeed, Barth denies that Christianity is the true religion in the sense that it is the climax or fulfillment of all human religion. However, because of the uniqueness of Jesus Christ, Christianity is the *locus* of true religion. In the event of Jesus Christ, God uniquely provides and reveals the means for our reconciliation with God. Revelation not only destroys religion; it creates true religion. Thus, even Christians must realize the inadequacy of their own religion when viewed outside of grace and revelation.

Exclusivism is not a distinctly Christian phenomenon; most religions at heart are exclusivistic. For example, Muslims hold that the revelations of other prophets were incomplete and mixed with untruths. Muhammed is the true and final prophet of God, whose "teachings are absolutely perfect; . . . the only source for anyone to know about God and His system of life is Muhammad (peace be on him)."[7] Through him God uniquely has spoken. Only in the Koran are God's words unmixed with human words; only here are God's words addressed not to a particular people but to all humankind, and only the Koran contains everything needed for right living. "It is because of these special features of the Koran that all people of the world have been directed to believe in it. They have been told to give up all other books and follow it alone."[8] Christians are heretics who believe only partial truths, and polytheists are infidels.

CRITIQUE OF EXCLUSIVISM

Many find it difficult to believe that the faithful of other religions are doomed because they have not heard the gospel of a given religion and sought salvation in the prescribed manner. People who live morally upright or profoundly righteous lives devoted to God and to others abound in all religions. They are living evidence that their religion can deliver on its promise to transform humans. Have they failed on the ground that they do not acknowledge a particular religious mediator, follow someone's teachings or practices, or conceive of God in a particular manner? It is unjust for God to condemn a person who has never heard or is unable to understand what is necessary for salvation.

In reply, it should be noted that not all exclusivists are committed to God's condemnation of people who in this life never encountered the true religion. Some exclusivists believe that a loving and just God will provide opportunities for persons to hear and understand the message of salvation after their death, so that ultimately all will have an equal opportunity for salvation.[9] Salvation depends not on the availability of or exposure to the message but on a person's knowledgeable acceptance.[10] Only after providing this opportunity will God impose judgment on those who continue to disbelieve the truth.

Others object to exclusivism on the grounds that a God who truly desires that all persons come to know, love, and worship him would not narrowly bind his revelation solely to a particular time, way, person, community, or culture. Just as advertisers tailor their message to different audiences, so an infinite God can speak in diverse ways to different cultures, adapting his message to that culture's motifs and thought patterns. Diverse revelations would contain different characteristics and thoughts because they are expressed in diverse cultural dresses. Thus, religion need not pit human creative reason against divine revelation but might embody diverse perceptions of the divine revelation or salvific truth. Barth presupposes that there is only one revelation; hence, he can contrast all religion with that revelation. But this presupposition might be questioned, given both an infinite God capable of communicating in different forms and through individuals who claim either to have received divine revelations or to be that revelation.

EXCLUSIVISM AND JUSTIFIED BELIEF

In the face of these objections, the critical question is whether exclusivists can be justified in holding that their position is the only true position, or whether exclusivism is a sign of arrogance. First, the fact that *many* people hold a specific belief does not mean that their belief is correct. For example, that many people in certain societies entertain racist views does not entail that racism is a correct view. Religious diversity among cultures only shows that our environment (birthplace, parents, upbringing, and community) strongly influences what we believe, not that those beliefs are justified or true. What gives the thoughtful exclusivist pause, then, is not the existence of diverse opinions, but that seemingly sincere persons who have carefully considered their own faith and that of others and believe their view to be justified advocate different religious perspectives.

Second, it is important to note that mere diversity of religious beliefs poses no problem for the exclusivist. Disagreement among people does not mean that those who disagree, whatever their side, are unjustified in holding their views. The disputants may have good reasons for thinking their view is correct and that of their opponents incorrect. Indeed, this is often the case when we disagree with other persons and attempt to show they are mistaken; we believe we are correct (even though we may be mistaken) and would be foolish to advocate persuasively a view that we do not think is correct. Further, the disputants may even agree that their opponents are justified in holding their own position and still believe that the others' views are incorrect, for having justified views does not entail that those views are true. That someone is justified in believing that a food is poisonous does not mean that it really is poisonous.

Alvin Plantinga further argues that it is perfectly justifiable for believers to maintain their exclusivist beliefs in the face of religious diversity. Believers may hold that their beliefs are true and that beliefs incompatible with theirs are false because their beliefs are warranted, perhaps by evidential reasoning, but also because the beliefs are properly basic (see chapter 6). Properly basic beliefs are formed in such a way that the believer is justified in taking them to be true and in believing that contrary beliefs held by others were not formed under proper epistemic conditions. It is not that believers do not have to defend their beliefs against criticism; they do. Rather, we cannot employ a neutral set of criteria to adjudicate which religious claims are true. Hence, in the face of the contrary beliefs held by others, it is not *prima facie* obvious that believers ought to abandon beliefs they take as justified.

To the objection that this is arrogant, Plantinga replies that all competing views are in the same boat. Just as the believer "thinks that there is an important epistemic difference: . . . that somehow the other person has *made a mistake,* or *has a blind spot,* or hasn't been wholly attentive," so those who object to the exclusivist position also hold that the exclusivist has made a mistake or has a blind spot.[11] If the charge of arrogance holds against the exclusivist, it also holds against those who maintain that exclusivists are mistaken and unjustified in their view.

In short, Plantinga concludes, the appeal to religious diversity does not so much defeat exclusivism as undercut it. It might reduce the believer's level of confidence or degree of belief, but it need not do so. The exlusivist can still justifiably claim that since one's beliefs have been formed by properly functioning faculties, one is truly warranted in holding them and has no good reason to abandon them.[12]

Paul Griffiths (b. 1947) argues that religious doctrines serve five functions.[13] They provide rules that govern the life and conduct of the religious community; they express truths that denominate bounds of orthodoxy, stating what beliefs are or are not acceptable in the community; they shape the spiritual experiences and religious practices of the community; they are instruments to bring members into the religious community by education and evangelism; and they express truths that explicate what is required for salvation. Griffith suggests that this analysis of religious doctrine points to the fact that religious communities cannot easily abandon or water down their beliefs without sacrificing key elements of their community life. Their unique beliefs serve vital functions in creating and sustaining their community.

PLURALISM

In light of the concerns expressed earlier, some abandon exclusivist claims and acknowledge that, although different religions manifest different responses to the divine Reality, each can successfully facilitate salvation, liberation, or self-fulfillment. As Hinduism affirms, many coequal routes lead to liberation or salvation. "In whatever way men approach Me, I am gracious to them; men everywhere . . . follow My path."[14] Some internal checks and balances may govern religious claims, but these are satisfied when the religious tradition has produced profound scriptures, impressive intellectual systems, new visions of human existence, and saintly lives. This second position, called pluralism, has been adopted by John Hick (b. 1922), among others.

Several questions arise. First, Hick admits that some religions have fundamentally differing and incompatible views of Ultimate Reality. For some, it is nondual, apersonal, beyond everything and nothing, transcending the illusory world in which we live and think. For others, the Real is personal, the creator God immanently involved in human affairs. Since these conceptions of the Real seem irreconcilable, all these diverse religious conceptions of God cannot be true. How, then, does the pluralist address the exclusivist argument regarding incompatible truth-claims?

In response, Hick invokes a distinction, adopted from Immanuel Kant, between the Real itself (the noumena) and the Real humanly and culturally perceived and experienced (the phenomena). When religious persons speak about the noumenal Ultimate Reality, they can describe only how it appears to them. Their characterization depends upon the interpretative concepts they use to understand and structure their world and give meaning to their existence. Thus, those who hold that the Real is nondual and indescribable employ one set of interpretative concepts, metaphors, and images; those who see the Real as personal use another set. This is why the Real can be described in diverse ways.

Hick employs the familiar story of the blind men and the elephant.

> An elephant was brought to a group of blind men who had never encountered such an animal before. One felt a leg and reported that an elephant is a great living pillar. Another felt the trunk and reported that an elephant is a great snake. Another felt a tusk and reported that an elephant is like a sharp plough-share. And so on. . . . Of course they were all true, but each referring only to one aspect of the total reality and all expressed in very imperfect analogies.[15]

We cannot tell which is correct because we possess no ultimate perspective from which to view the blind men feeling the elephant. In seeking the Real we are all blind, trapped by our individual and cultural concepts.

It is not that one set of concepts or structures is true and another false. For Hick, statements about the Ultimate Reality are metaphors validated by their efficacy in bringing about salvation or personal transformation; religious traditions preserve them because many people find them meaningful. Hick believes that those who hold that religious concepts are projections of human characteristics on the divine are partially correct. The presence of anthropomorphic projections should not be used to debunk religion, for they register our conscious attempts to relate our conceptual framework to Ultimate Reality and to respond to its activity in our lives. But ascribing our religious concepts *totally* to projection is incorrect; religious concepts arise out of religious experience and thus express the ways in which we experience, conceive of, and respond to Ultimate Reality. He warns about projecting from our limited understanding a definitive, descriptive characterization of Ultimate Reality.

Second, what can pluralists say to exclusivists like Barth, who claim that Jesus Christ is the unique revelation of God and the unique means through which salvation is attained? Hick's response is to deny the orthodox view of the Incarnation, that Jesus really was divine.[16] God's spirit can work in all persons, transforming them so that they fully manifest God. The Incarnation is a myth describing God's activity in human lives. For Hick, a myth is a statement that, though "not literally true, nevertheless tends to evoke an appropriate dispositional attitude to" what the myth is about.[17] In the myth of the Incarnation Christians see someone (Jesus) who more fully realized the openness to being transformed to an Ultimate Reality–centered life. But this description also can be true of other great religious founders and saints.

The center of religion, for Hick, is not theological doctrine but personal transformation.[18] Hence, he cautions that religious doctrines, such as the Incarnation, should not be unduly emphasized. Neither should they be considered as true or false in the way in which we consider scientific beliefs to be true or false. Religious dogmas and historical claims are attempts to answer personal questions about human existence and experience of the divine.[19] Consequently, they are true insofar as they succeed in changing our attitudes and life-patterns. Hence, although doctrines of the various religions might seem to contradict, when properly viewed as life-expressing truths they often do not. They simply express the diverse ways people from different cultures react to the Ultimate Reality they encounter. In this way Hick counters the exclusivists' premise that incompatible truth-claims cannot both be true.

In other words, Hick is less concerned with theological truths (understood as propositions) than with the existential or life-changing aspects of religion, less concerned with dogma than with religious experience. Religion is significant because it transforms human existence from self-centeredness to Reality–centeredness. Exactly what one believes is not all that important; it is a mythic projection of one's own experiences, culture, and conceptual categories onto Ultimate Reality. For Hick, therefore, exclusivists' attempts to convert or sweep all people into one religion's kingdom fail to capture the essence of religion. What matters is that the Real so affects us that we are transformed.

CRITIQUE OF PLURALISM

Pluralism is attractive; it accords well with our attempt to accept other persons without being judgmental. Yet this appeal sometimes involves the confusion between epistemological and ethical considerations noted earlier in this chapter. As we argued there, it is a mistake to affirm that being judgmental about truth-claims or beliefs necessitates maltreating persons who hold differing beliefs and that being tolerant implies not rationally assessing but merely accepting the diverse truth-claims. Hence, we need to consider more carefully the strengths and weaknesses of the pluralist position.

What, then, is at issue in this debate? The answer is, in part, the nature of religion. For many pluralists, the significant aspect of religion is its power to transform the individual, to move someone from concern with self to being Reality–centered. This being the case, religious beliefs and practices are important means to personal and social transformation but are not intrinsically or ultimately significant. Thus, two people can disagree about a certain belief or practice, and it makes no ultimate difference. Hick writes, "I hold that someone who differs from me about, for example, whether Jesus had a human father is probably (though not certainly) mistaken; but in holding this I am also conscious that he/she might nevertheless be closer to the divine Reality than I. This awareness is important because it has the

effect of de-emphasizing such differences of historical judgment. They can
never be more than penultimately important."[20]

But is this a fully adequate view of religion? Do not religions make truth-
claims about the Ultimate Reality? Pluralists differ among themselves on this
question. For some, truth is not to be understood propositionally, as if propositions are true or false apart from the time, perspective, and individual who
believes them.[21] Rather, truth must be seen humanly, in terms of what propositions and beliefs mean to individual persons, and this is both a historical and
an existential matter. Truth is how reality appears to us at a particular time and
place, in a particular historical perspective. Religious orientations "can be
seen as less or more true in the sense of enabling those who looked at life and
the universe through their patterns to perceive smaller or larger, less important or more important, areas of reality, to formulate and to ponder less or
more significant issues, to act less or more truly, less or more truly to be."[22] The
problem with this claim about truth is that this very general claim cannot be
called true, for it is subject to the same restrictions this view imposes on other
truth-claims, namely, that truth is not propositional and is relative to a particular time and place. One could, of course, restrict this view of truth to religious
truth-claims, but such a move would be arbitrary and question begging.

Other pluralists hold that religious adherents make truth-claims, but
only about Ultimate Reality understood phenomenally (as it appears to
them). Consequently, religious claims do not contradict each other. For example, the claims that something appears to me to be blue and to you not to
be blue do not contradict. They would contradict only if we both claimed
that the object itself was the color each of us perceived it to be. Similarly,
on this view, religious adherents speak about what they have encountered
from their cultural-religious perspective, not from some external, objective, all-encompassing point of view. Hence, their claims cannot be really
contradictory.

Furthermore, the language and concepts we use to approach the Real
are not subject to the type of scientific verification that characterizes our
ordinary experience. They are "linguistic pictures or maps of the universe,
whose function is to enable us to find salvation/liberation. . . . They accordingly test themselves by their success or failure in fulfilling this
soteriological function."[23] What Ultimate Reality really is like can be verified
only eschatologically, if at all.[24]

Hick agrees that we can engage in rational scrutiny of religious systems.
The criterion to be used to distinguish authentic from inauthentic manifestations of the Real is "soteriological alignment." By this he means that
an authentic religion fosters transformation of human existence from self-
centeredness to Reality–centeredness, demonstrated by the saintly lives
of the religion's followers and by the religion's role in spiritual and politico-
economic liberation.[25]

Some will find this is too broad. Under this criterion Hick allows not
only traditional religions but also the great secular movements as well to
count as authentic manifestations of Ultimate Reality. For example, he notes

that the book on post-Maoist reform in China and on Communism is still open, for these have been at least partially successful in transforming society.[26] His position might also be viewed as too narrow, for while the great religions produce saints, their success has been limited. Even the world religions have produced their share of individuals who have shown their dark side in the name of the very religion they espouse. Criteria in addition to the saintly lives of the adherents must be used to distinguish authentic from inauthentic manifestations of Ultimate Reality.

One also might object that the pluralists' contention—that truth-claims are both historically and culturally subjective and only about the phenomena —leads inevitably to skepticism about Ultimate Reality. Unless we can speak about the Ultimate Reality, not only cannot we know anything about the real elephant (using Hick's analogy), we cannot even assert that there is an elephant.

Hick responds that although we cannot prove that Ultimate Reality must exist, we must trust the basic veridicality of our religious experience and thought. To preserve this against the claim that religious experience results merely from human projections, we must *postulate* that there is a noumenal Real.

Yet why conclude that religious experience is not a human projection, if there is no way that one can understand or say anything true about the Real in itself? Unless we can speak about Reality, what have we postulated? For any of the blind men to have postulated that what he really felt was an elephant, he must have known what an elephant was. Even Hick cannot completely resist saying something about Ultimate Reality. For him it is "rich in content," the "One without a second," for there cannot be a plurality of ultimates. Furthermore, the Real "produces . . . the phenomenal world of ours"; it is the "ground or source" of the phenomenal divine attributes, of religious experience, and of love and justice, consciousness and bliss; it has a presence and impact on the phenomena. These suggest, at minimum, that causal predicates apply to Ultimate Reality. Insofar as it fosters or hinders salvific transformation,[27] Ultimate Reality must have some consciousness of and concern for human beings.

Indeed, unless pluralists can ascribe goodness, love, and justice to Ultimate Reality, their objection to exclusivism, noted earlier, namely, that a God with these properties would not limit his revelation and salvific work to a particular culture or religion, fails. This criticism of exclusivism's consistency presupposes knowledge of the appropriate predicates of Ultimate Reality.

In short, it is well and good for pluralists to say that Ultimate Reality that meets us, but what is Ultimate Reality? The very willingness of some pluralists to admit atheistic Marxism and naturalistic humanism into the camp of religions alongside and on equal footing with theism[28] suggests the seriousness of the problem. Jews, Muslims, and Christians maintain that there really is a God, the encounter with whom brings meaning to our lives; naturalists hold that we can find meaningful existence apart from affirming or encountering the divine; Satanists deify evil and power. But the rational claims of these belief systems are very different. In the first, meaning comes from an encounter with a good, personal God; in the second meaning is self-created; in the third, it is evil that gives power and meaning.

Pluralists such as Hick face a dilemma. If we have no clear concept of God, if we are left with nothing to be said about God or Ultimate Reality in itself, our religious belief becomes indistinguishable from agnosticism. If we can speak about God, then we can employ some consistent set of predicates to describe the God's properties. Hence, we have a content about which we can make claims and are not completely blind. We can, in principle, evaluate which of the blind men's claims, if any, are correct.[29]

In short, it seems that a pluralist view such as Hick's is accepted, not only at the extremely high price of skepticism, but in disregard of what believers think they are doing. In making fundamental dogmas into myths, "it rules out people's most precious beliefs in things normative. It asks Muslims, in effect, to deny that the Koran is central to God's purposes. It asks Jews to deny that God spoke definitively through Moses. It asks Christians to deny that Jesus is the Incarnation of God in history."[30] It also prevents believers from addressing certain problems facing their faith. For example, Hick's own soul-building theodicy, which we discussed in chapter 7 as an approach to the problem of pain and suffering, he now treats as a true myth that cannot apply to the transcendent Real and hence cannot be used to justify its goodness, power, or justice.[31]

PLURALISM AS A PLURALITY OF SALVATIONS

The theologian S. Mark Heim argues that most pluralists, including Hick, are really inclusivists in disguise, for although they recognize a plurality of approaches to salvation, they in effect advocate only one salvation brought about by Ultimate Reality. They make "salvation the universal, cross-cultural constant in interpreting religious traditions." But in doing so they abandon their religious pluralism by forcing on the world's religions one way of salvation, that advocated by the pluralists themselves, namely, the 'transformation from self-centeredness to Reality-centeredness."[32] Further, they betray their pluralism when they deny that diverse religions have real differences.

Seeking to distance himself from Hick's version of pluralism, Heim argues that a true pluralist holds that the religious traditions really are distinct in ways that should be acknowledged and valued. Since the specifics of a religious tradition can have significant truth-value, they are not to be sacrificed for the good of some overarching concept of salvation. Rather, the distinctive teachings of each religion inform outsiders about what that community considers important relative to its distinctive view of attaining salvation.

Each religion, then, has its own salvation that may be similar to or different from that found in other religions. But in terms of the internal coherence of the religion, it is the fulfillment or culmination of a distinctive approach. In this sense, each religion is properly exclusivist. Indeed, recognition of this exclusivism—that each religion offers "distinctive truth or insight available in any one or several of them that is not available elsewhere" is necessary for proper appreciation of other religions.[33] Attempts to syncretize religions or assimilate them into some metareligion fail to do justice to their uniqueness and distinctive salvations.

The salvations advocated by different religions have both this-world and other-world (eschatological) dimensions. Heim especially emphasizes the former, remaining somewhat agnostic about the latter. Although in this life the ways religions recommend achieving salvation often lead to fulfillment, the fulfillments found in the different religions are not different visions of the same salvation, but express alternative conceptions. Since each religion leads to a salvation that fulfills its distinctive vision, achieving religious fulfillment requires the distinctive path described by each religion.

This means that each religion can have its own validity when it delivers on the salvific promises it makes. We have no ultimate viewpoint from which to assess religions and their claims. Each person argues from his or her own evaluative orientation. Believers are justified in privileging their own viewpoint; indeed, we can do nothing else, for if we do not think that our own viewpoint is true, we have no reason for holding it. But from the claim that we preference our own view it does not follow that an objective viewpoint exists from which we can assess other religions and their claims. There is no specially sighted person who can accurately describe the elephant.

Heim adopts a version of "orientational pluralism," according to which reality is not multifaceted; only one reality exists. In trying to know this reality, people adopt different orientations that may be incompatible with each other in the sense that the same person cannot consistently hold several perspectives. Each view may be consistent with, follow from, and be advocated with justification from a particular perspective. At the same time, although believers may think that people holding a different religious perspective are justified in their belief, they need not think that the conclusions the other religions arrive at are true. That is, a person may be justified in holding a religion or viewpoint but still be mistaken.

That each religion can argue its correctness not only allows for diversity of religious beliefs but also applauds these diversities as constituting the real distinctness of the religions. Without real belief differences, we would have little reason for dialogue. Instead of covering up real differences or making them subservient to some metareligion, a plurality of beliefs is encouraged, for by these different beliefs people are really bettered or fulfilled.

One might legitimately wonder, however, how there can be a plurality of fulfillments when the various traditions are not consistent. Heim's response is that though there may be many salvations or fulfillments, it does not follow that all the details the diverse religions provide about these salvations are true. The key point is that since salvations can be many, the fact that one person experiences liberation (e.g., Nirvana) as the result of self-renunciation does not contradict the claim that another person experiences personal immortality by belief in Christ or attains social harmony as the result of instituting the Confucian virtues. Different people can obtain different salvations in differing ways. For Heim the determination of the final or eschatological salvation is irrelevant to the fact that religions can provide diverse salvations here and now. Heim thus wants to have both the subjective fulfillment provided by the diverse religions in their practices and the possibility of objective, future salvations.

Heim's analysis is insightful when religion is viewed as addressing multiple ways of fulfillment. He correctly helps us beyond the subjective transformation of Hick's pluralism to see that maybe there are diverse though perhaps mutually incompatible ways of attaining human fulfillment. But his analysis will work only if there really are diverse human predicaments for the diverse salvations to address. Whereas Heim can be agnostic about an ultimate salvation, suggesting rather that the penultimate human salvations suffice to legitimate the various religions that espouse them, he cannot be agnostic about an ultimate human predicament. For should there be an ultimate human predicament, addressing the penultimate predicaments may leave that fundamental predicament untouched, so that the salvations offered may provide little more than penultimate or Band-Aid solutions to subordinate problems. The claim that some ultimate human predicament needs to be addressed and that one religion or another successfully addresses this predicament brings us to the inclusivist viewpoint.

INCLUSIVISM

If we acknowledge that different religions offer life-transforming experiences and that God may reveal himself or graciously act in various ways in diverse places, while at the same time we affirm that religious claims are either true or false, we may adopt what is termed religious *inclusivism.* On the one hand, in common with exclusivism, inclusivists hold that there is one absolute provision for salvation truly made known in only one religion. Salvation is available only because special conditions revealed in one true religion are met. On the other hand, in common with pluralists, inclusivists hold that God can be encountered and his grace manifested in various ways through diverse religions. All can experience salvation, regardless of whether they have heard and acknowledged the basic tenets of the one true religion. Inclusivism thus extends beyond exclusivism because, though it makes exclusivistic claims for the absolute truth of one religion and what it accomplishes, it allows that adherents of other religions can be saved because the conditions specified by the true religion have occurred. Put in philosophical language, a particular salvific event may be ontologically necessary for salvation (salvation cannot occur without it) but not epistemologically necessary (one need not know about it to be saved or liberated).

The Catholic theologian Karl Rahner (1904–1984) argued that persons can be saved only because a particular salvific event has occurred. Christianity is an absolute religion and cannot recognize any other religion as providing *the* way of salvation. It not only tells us of God's unique Word, incarnate in Jesus who died on the cross for all persons, but provides the social context in which Jesus Christ comes to persons. However, God is love and desires that everyone be saved. To accomplish this salvation, God applies the results of Jesus' atoning death and resurrection to everyone, even to those who have never heard of Jesus and his death or have never acknowledged his lordship. In this way God makes it possible for everyone, even those not within the context of historical Christianity, to be transformed and reconciled to God.

One might think of an analogous scenario. In a particular town a large number of poor people owe debts they cannot pay from their meager resources. But unless they pay, their creditors will foreclose on their property. Learning of their plight, a rich woman in another town deposits a large amount of money in their town bank, with the stipulation that it be used to satisfy the debts of the poor. Since the poor cannot remove their debts without these resources, the benefactor's funds are objectively necessary for relieving their plight. However, their liberation does not depend on their knowledge of her identity or of the way she provided for their financial relief. The very application of her resources pays their debts and transforms their lives.

Rahner notes that although Christianity began historically with Jesus of Nazareth, it had a prehistory. The New Testament claims that in pre-Christian times many Israelites and followers of other religions were saved subjectively by their faith and objectively by the still-future obedience of Christ. Some, like Melchizedek, were even priests of non-Israelite religions. The appearance of Jesus is the point at which Christianity faced the Jewish people, requiring those who heard the gospel to take a position on it. That is, when Christianity became a historical factor in first century Palestine, it became realistic to claim that salvation depended upon some response to the proclaimed gospel. But Christianity is not a real historical factor for many cultures, where people have never heard a proclamation of the Christian gospel. Hence, since people in these cultures remain in a position comparable to those of the pre-Christian era, we can apply what is said about the pre-Christian Jewish and non-Jewish righteous to them. Since God desires that everyone be saved, it is reasonable to think that God applies the same grace he applied to those of the pre-Christian era to individuals today who have never heard about Jesus. The Spirit of God is at work in the lives of people who worship in other religions, though they do not recognize God's activity in Christian terms. Rahner terms these persons *anonymous Christians* because, although they lack an explicit Christian faith, they consciously or unconsciously seek and worship God.[34]

Yet if Christianity is the true religion, whereas others contain various admixtures of falsity, should non-Christians then practice their own religion? Rahner holds that religious faith is not solely an internal matter; a social form is necessary for salvation. This form is always culturally embodied in the religion (including practices and beliefs) that person embraces. Since different religions embody different degrees of truth, they have different degrees of lawfulness, that is, ability to facilitate a right relationship with God. But just as the theological impurity of pre-Christian Judaism did not prevent its adherents from encountering God in and through their religion, so the theological impurity of contemporary religions does not prevent their adherents from finding God. Indeed, these religions can be the mediators of supernatural grace. It is not an all-or-nothing matter; supernatural grace can be manifested in various degrees in all religions. It is only that the New Testament delineates the definitive difference between right and wrong and the unique, salvific revelation of God in Jesus Christ, and it is only through a relationship with God in Jesus Christ that the fullness of God can be known and experienced.

Advocates of inclusivism in other religions may well invoke a similar point of view. Just as the Christian might speak of Christianity as the only true religion and of persons whose lives manifest the grace of God as anonymous Christians, so Muslims may speak of the absolute truth of Islam and of Christians or Jews as anonymous Muslims. Jews may see others as anonymous Jews, while Buddhists view others as anonymous Buddhists. Each could hold that though one particular religion is the absolute or true religion, other religions as well contain significant truths. These religions perceive dimly, partly, and perspectivally the truths found in clearer form in the one true religion. Since not all religious doctrines or practices in all religions are true, cross-religious criticism is in order. This, then, can provide an authentic basis for interreligious dialogue, where the differences are appreciated and worthy of rational discussion and debate.

CRITIQUE OF INCLUSIVISM

If persons can achieve salvation without knowing anything at all about a specific religious tradition, why then should one try to convert them? Why not simply encourage them to continue to live according to what they know and believe so that they can lead transformed lives in the light of their own religion? Rahner holds that bringing members of other religions to the knowledge of the true basis of their faith is a stage of development in their Christianity. "The reflex self-realization of a previously anonymous Christianity is demanded (1) by the incarnational and social structure of grace and of Christianity, and (2) because the individual who grasps Christianity in a clearer, purer and more effective way, has, other things being equal, a still greater chance of salvation than someone who is merely an anonymous Christian."[35] Other inclusivists might reply that it does matter that persons know the true basis of their salvation because, since liberation comes through knowledge, truth matters. Hence, religions have an obligation to enlighten others as to the objective basis of their transformation. In any case, the exclusivist content of inclusivism provides a basis for justifying proselytizing.

Others have questioned the confidence that Rahner has in the lawfulness of other religions. The Christian theologian Clark Pinnock (b. 1937), for example, sees that religion at times is "dark, deceptive, and cruel. It harbors ugliness, pride, error, hypocrisy," and other characteristics that do not lead to salvation. He notes the dark side found in Aztec sacrifices, Haitian voodoo, the Hindu deities Kali and Shiva, as well as the caste system of India that "sanctions pious neglect of the poor."[36] Yet, although religions as social phenomena might be idolatrous, God is at work in lives of individuals outside the Christian faith. He suggests two criteria for discovering where God is present in persons: they fear God and pursue righteousness in their behavior.

An even more serious objection is that if many religions believe that they are the one true religion, how does one decide which religion makes the correct claims? Some feel it is simply a matter of determining the locus of unique divine revelation. Rahner and Barth are certain that God has come in Jesus Christ; Muslims hold that Muhammed gave us Allah's mature revelation; Buddhists assert that the Buddha showed the path to enlightenment. But this simply pushes the problem back. How do we adjudicate claims to divine revelation? Some have suggested that we can do this by evaluating the life of the claim maker. But are we able to know enough about the individual religious founders to make comparisons that could establish the spiritual or moral superiority of one over the other? Is the moral life of Jesus superior to that of the Buddha? Others have appealed to the character of the tradition that grew out of the work of the founder; yet this is risky, for the history of each religion is replete with events that both credit and discredit the teachings of the religion.

A different way of assessing religions appeals to criteria by which we can evaluate the religious systems themselves. To this approach let us turn.

CRITERIA FOR ASSESSING RELIGIONS

One conclusion we might draw from the discussion to this point is that we must take seriously the contention that religions make specific truth-claims about Reality. Some say God exists; others not. Some assert that many gods exist; others only one God. Some declare that God becomes incarnate; others not. Some claim that Jesus is the God incarnate; others that it is Krishna. Some claim that Christ is actually present in the bread and wine of Holy Communion; others that the elements are symbolic only. Some accept Ali, Muhammed's son-in-law, as the first Imam and rightful successor of the Prophet; others do not. Some believe we should pray facing Mecca; others face the Wailing Wall. We could go on presenting contrasts. The point, however, is that we have good reason to think that religious believers are making truth-claims and that these must be given their due place.

If believers are making truth-claims about reality, then specific beliefs are subject to rational evaluation. Sometimes we can use the canons of logic, human experience, and perhaps trained intuition to establish probabilistically that some beliefs are true and others false. In fact, much of what has already transpired in this book is directed toward evaluating religious claims on these grounds. However, as we have seen, rationally evaluating individual religious beliefs is a daunting task.

But probably we want to go beyond evaluating individual religious beliefs, for many religious beliefs (e.g., Christ is present in the bread and wine of Holy Communion) are meaningful only in the context of a broader set of religious claims held by a specific religious tradition. We want not only to evaluate individual beliefs but also to be able to make comparative evaluations of religions themselves. In deciding whether to be a Muslim, Hindu, Sikh, Jew, Christian, or whatever, we want to know whether that particular religious system is true or more true than any other. This is an even more difficult task than evaluating individual religious beliefs, for religious systems contain many propositions, some of which are true and others false. Thus, one has to weigh not only individual statements but also whole systems of statements, according to some non–question-begging criteria.

In the face of philosophers who are skeptical that a set of external, religiously neutral, non–question-beginning criteria can be found, Keith Yandell (b. 1938) suggests the following.

1. The propositions essential to that religion must be consistent with each other.

2. Knowing that the religious system is true must be compatible with its being true. If the truth of the system entails that we cannot know it is true—for example, if, like Madhyamika Buddhism, it claims that all views are false—that is reason to suspect its truth.

3. The truth of a religious system must becompatible with what must exist for it to be true. For example, the claim that Ultimate Reality has no distinctions is incompatible with the claim that religious statements that affirm this are true and not false.

4. If the only reason for offering the religious system is that it promises to provide a solution to a problem, and it fails to do so, there is no reason to accept the system. For example, if a religious system were introduced to resolve the problem of pain and suffering, but clearly did not accomplish this, there would be no reason to advocate that religious system.

5. Essential truths of the system should not contradict well-established data, for example, in the sciences or psychology.

6. Ad-hoc hypotheses to avoid evidence contrary to the religious system count against that religious system.

7. A system should be able to account for and explain broad reaches of human experience.[37]

To Yandell's criteria one might add

8. It should satisfy some basic moral and aesthetic intuitions and provoke and inspire persons to live more morally responsive and responsible lives.

This list is carefully enunciated and evocative, but one might wonder whether the criteria are non–question-begging. For example, it might be suggested that all world religions claim to satisfy criterion seven, but what additional criteria can be employed to determine that the explanation presented by any given tradition is adequate? Further reflection on the criteria in this list is warranted.

This brings up one final issue. Although we have spoken of religions as systems that at least make propositional truth-claims, it is mistaken to view religious systems as consisting of impersonal, objective statements of religious beliefs uniformly accepted by all advocates of that religion. Religious systems are complex bodies that have grown and developed historically. What a Christian or Hindu believes today differs (for some, remarkably) from what first-century Christians or eighth-century Hindus held. This is not to say that contemporary believers are not Christians or Hindus, but they are Christians or Hindus not only because they embrace certain beliefs but also because they participate in a historical tradition that is Christian or Hindu. The tradition is not pristine; we cannot get back to the original founders and believe exactly what they believed and practice as they did. The tradition is cumulative and dynamic, social and personal. Hence, any description of that religion contains an important subjective dimension.

Religions are embodied historically in cultures, making it difficult to isolate distinctively religious beliefs from cultural ones (for example, is monogamy a Christian religious or a Western cultural prescription? Is Hinduism isolable from the caste system?). Religions are embodied in individual believers, and no two believers hold exactly the same beliefs. Thus, in assessing religions we must not speak about the totality of the assertions made by religious advocates but rather about what might be held to be essential to a specific religion. Yet even here difficulties emerge, for what must a person believe to be a Christian, Muslim, or Hindu? The diversity within each tradition bears witness to the difficulty of discerning a particular creedal essence.

The claim that each religion is a strand in the religious history of the world is intriguing. Yet even if there are generic religious concepts such as faith and God, not every claim about these concepts is true. Suppose humans have participated throughout history in a universal religion in the same way as they have participated in a universal science. In science, not every avowed scientific belief is true nor every practice sanctioned; alchemy, for instance, was wrong-headed. Yet each scientist grapples with reality, seeking to understand how it operates and to discern what causal explanations best suffice. Similarly, if God operates in the world, encountering humans, it becomes a task of all humans, no matter what their religious tradition, to understand that God and appropriate this belief in their life. That some religious beliefs are true and some false, that some practices are propitious and some not, must be accepted as a consequence of human finite understanding.

STUDY QUESTIONS

1. Make a list of some of the differences between various religions you know about. Are these differences significant or not? Defend your view, noting in particular the criteria you used to decide significance.

2. What is religious exclusivism? What critique might be given of exclusivism? How might the exclusivist respond to each of the objections?

3. How does the story of the blind men and the elephant help us understand religious pluralism? How might this analogy be turned into a criticism of pluralism?

Would the story and its point change significantly if the men were not blind but partially sighted? Explain.

4. Why does Hick think personal transformation is more important than religious beliefs? What do you see as the proper relation between personal transformation and religious beliefs? Do beliefs matter? Defend your view.

5. Develop two criticisms of Hick's religious pluralism. How would Hick respond to each of these criticisms?

6. In what ways does Heim's pluralism differ from the traditional pluralism of Hick? What advantage does Heim propose that his view has?

7. How is religious inclusivism similar to and different from both exclusivism and pluralism? How does Rahner defend his view?

8. Develop two criticisms that might be given of inclusivism. How would the inclusivist reply to each?

9. Compare pluralism with inclusivism on the question whether religions make truth-claims about reality. What dilemma does Hick face on this issue? How might Hick respond to that dilemma?

10. Use the criteria suggested by Yandell to evaluate your own or another religious tradition. Are the criteria clear enough to be applied, and do they successfully discriminate among religions? Justify your answer.

NOTES

1. *Mu* is part of an ancient Zen *koan* or saying. Literally it means "not, not having, or having nothing."

2. Philip Kapleau, ed., *The Three Pillars of Zen* (Garden City, N.Y.: Anchor Press, 1980), pp. 237–9.

3. This is a central theme in Wilfred Cantwell Smith, *Towards a World Theology* (Philadelphia: Westminster, 1981).

4. Both are described in more detail in Smith, *World Theology,* pp. 6–13.

5. Alan Race, *Christians and Religious Pluralism: Patterns in the Christian Theology of Religions* (Maryknoll, N.Y.: Orbis Books, 1982).

6. Karl Barth, *Church Dogmatics* I, 2 (Edinburgh: T. & T. Clark, 1956), p. 303.

7. A. A. Maududi, *Towards Understanding Islam* (Pakistan: n.p., n.d.), p. 60.

8. Ibid., p. 81.

9. Jerry L. Walls, *Hell: The Logic of Damnation* (Notre Dame, Ind.: University of Notre Dame Press, 1992), ch. 4. Not all exclusivists are comfortable with postmortem evangelization. See Ronald H. Nash, *Is Jesus the Only Savior?* (Grand Rapids, Mich.: Zondervan, 1994), pp. 150–8.

10. It might be noted that this view begins to narrow the gap between exclusivism and inclusivism, as discussed later.

11. Alvin Plantinga, "Pluralism: A Defense of Religious Exclusivism," in *The Philosophical Challenge of Religious Diversity,* ed. Philip L. Quinn and Kevin Meeker (New York: Oxford University Press, 2000), p. 182.

12. What might need defense is Plantinga's claim that the proper functioning of our knowing faculties is a sign that our beliefs are true. Perhaps our beliefs are simply consistent with the culture or community in which we live and thus enable us to function properly in that context. Plantinga's views about basic beliefs and proper function have been presented in chapter 6, and we refer the reader there for further discussion. See David Basinger, *Religious Diversity: A Philosophical Assessment* (Aldershot, England: Ashgate, 2001), p. 62.

13. Paul J. Griffiths, "The Uniqueness of Religious Doctrines," in *Christian Uniqueness Reconsidered: The Myth of a Pluralistic Theology of Religions*, ed. Gavin D'Costa (Maryknoll, N.Y.: Orbis Books, 1990), 157–70. (See PRSR2e, pt. 11, 539–48.)

14. *Bhagavad-Gita*, trans. Eliot Deutsch (New York: Holt, Rinehart and Winston, 1968), IV, 11.

15. John Hick, *God and the Universe of Faiths* (London: Macmillan, 1977), p. 140. (See PRSR2e, pp. 565–6.)

16. John Hick, ed., *Problems of Religious Pluralism* (New York: St. Martin's Press, 1985), p. 35; also John Hick, ed., *The Myth of God Incarnate* (London: SCM, 1977). (See PRSR2e, p. 564.)

17. John Hick, *An Interpretation of Religion* (New Haven, CT: Yale, 1989), p. 348.

18. Hick, *An Interpretation*, chap. 3.

19. The reader should contrast Hick's vision of the function of religious dogmas with Paul Griffiths's view, noted earlier in this chapter.

20. Hick, *Problems*, p. 89.

21. Smith, *World Theology*, p. 190.

22. Ibid., p. 94.

23. Hick, *Problems*, p. 80.

24. Whether Hick can consistently hold this is problematic, since there is reason to think that the same epistemological difficulties that plague our present awareness would still apply. This is exacerbated for Hick when one considers the variety of views of the afterlife, some of which, such as metaphysical Absolutism, where the individual unites with the nondual, would not allow for any individual verification. Eschatological verification would seem to be a remnant of Hick's earlier days as a Christian theist.

25. Hick, *An Interpretation*, pp. 248, 300–1.

26. Ibid., p. 308.

27. Ibid., pp. 243, 247, 249, 350.

28. Smith, *World Theology*, chap. 7.

29. Peter Byrne, "John Hick's Philosophy of World Religions," *Scottish Journal of Theology* 35, no. 4 (1982): 297.

30. Clark Pinnock, *A Wideness in God's Mercy* (Grand Rapids, Mich.: Zondervan, 1992), p. 70.

31. Hick, *An Interpretation*, pp. 359–60.

32. S. Mark Heim, *Salvations: Truth and Difference in Religion* (Maryknoll, N.Y.: Orbis Books, 1995), p. 129.

33. Ibid., p. 227.

34. Some have objected to this terminology, in that it is either patronizing or that it "tends to obscure the difference that Jesus makes when he is known through faith in the Gospel." Pinnock, *A Wideness*, p. 105.

35. Karl Rahner, "Christian and the Non-Christian Religions," in *Christianity and Other Religions* ed. John Hick and Brian Hebblethwaite (Glasgow: Collins, 1980), pp. 76–7. (See PRSR2e, pt. 11, p. 558.)

36. Pinnock, *A Wideness,* pp. 90–1.

37. Keith E. Yandell, "Religious Experience and Rational Appraisal," *Religious Studies* 8 (June 1974): 185–6.

SUGGESTED READING

Barnes, Michael. *Religions in Conversation.* London: SPCK, 1989.

Basinger, David. *Religious Diversity: A Philosophical Assessment.* Aldershot, England: Ashgate, 2001.

D'Costa, Gavin. *Theology and Religious Pluralism: The Challenge of Other Religions.* Oxford: Blackwell, 1986.

———, ed. *Christian Uniqueness Reconsidered: The Myth of a Pluralistic Theology of Religions.* Maryknoll, N.Y.: Orbis Books, 1990.

Griffiths, Paul. *An Apology for Apologetics: A Study in the Logic of Interreligious Dialogue.* Maryknoll, N.Y.: Orbis Books, 1991.

———. *The Problems of Religious Diversity.* Oxford: Blackwell, 2001.

Heim, S. Mark. *Salvations: Truth and Difference in Religion.* Maryknoll, N.Y.: Orbis Books, 1995.

Hick, John. *Christianity and Other Religions.* Glasgow: Collins, 1980.

———, ed. *Problems of Religious Pluralism.* New York: St. Martin's Press, 1985.

———. *An Interpretation of Religion.* New Haven, Conn.: Yale, 1989.

Hick, John, and Brian Hebblethwaite, eds. *God and the Universe of Faiths.* London: Macmillan, 1977.

Knitter, Paul. *No Other Name? A Critical Survey of Christian Attitudes toward World Religions.* Maryknoll, N.Y.: Orbis, 1985.

Nash, Ronald. *Is Jesus the Only Savior?* Grand Rapids, Mich.: Zondervan, 1994.

Pinnock, Clark H. *A Wideness in God's Mercy.* Grand Rapids, Mich.: Zondervan, 1992.

Quinn, Philip L., and Kevin Meeker, eds. *The Philosophical Challenge of Religious Diversity.* New York: Oxford University Press, 2000.

Rice, Alan. *Christians and Religious Pluralism.* Maryknoll, N.Y.: Orbis Books, 1982.

Sanders, John. *No Other Name! A Biblical, Historical, and Theological Investigation into the Destiny of the Unevangelized.* Grand Rapids, Mich.: William B. Eerdmans, 1992.

Smith, Wilfred Cantwell. *Towards a World Theology.* Philadelphia: Westminster Press, 1981.

CHAPTER 14   RELIGIOUS ETHICS: THE RELATION OF GOD TO MORALITY

> While my own view is that the balance of considerations
> supports permitting the practice of [active voluntary
> euthanasia] . . . there is reason to expect that legalization
> of voluntary active euthanasia might soon be followed by
> strong pressure to legalize some nonvoluntary euthanasia of
> incompetent patients unable to express their own wishes.
>
> DAN BROCK, HASTINGS CENTER REPORT (MARCH–APRIL 1992)

What are we talking about when we discuss ethics? As we shall see, this is a very complex question. But a basic distinction may help us get started. Let us assume that we want to engage in an ethical discussion about the right of terminally ill patients in severe or unbearable pain to end their lives. Some of the issues we might consider would be primarily *descriptive*. That is, they would relate to what *actually* is the case. How many individuals experiencing what they believe to be severe or unbearable pain attempt to end their lives? Does public opinion currently support some forms of active euthanasia? Would some who are terminally ill feel obligated to end their lives if it were allowed? What abuses are possible?

Other issues, however, would be primarily *prescriptive (normative)*; that is, they would center on what we *should* believe or how we *ought to* behave. Should any individual who is thinking clearly have the legal right to end her life when it no longer seems worth living? Should only terminally ill individuals have this right? Should anyone have the right to make such a decision for a mentally incompetent individual? Ought we ever allow physicians to assist people in ending their lives?

Philosophers certainly do not deny that *descriptive ethics* is important. They realize that we cannot, for example, create proper public policies if we do not know what people actually believe and how they live or do not consider the possible consequences of any change in policy. Most philosophers, though, feel such considerations lie primarily in the domain of the anthropologist, sociologist, or political scientist. On the other hand, philosophers continue to be very interested in *normative ethics.* That is, they continue to be interested in the question of what people ought or ought not believe or how they ought or ought not act. Specifically, philosophers continue to be very interested in questions of the following type: What is the origin of the normative ethical principles we affirm? Under what conditions can such principles be rationally affirmed? Which set of normative ethical principles (hereafter simply referred to as *ethical principles*) is the correct one?

THE SOURCE OF RELIGIOUS ETHICAL TRUTH

There is no standard order in which ethical issues such as those mentioned earlier are discussed. However, in the area of religious ethics a rather natural progression arises. All of us affirm ethical principles related to almost every aspect of our lives. That is, we believe we have some understanding of how we, our family and friends, and even those with whom we will never have any direct contact *ought* to behave. But what is the origin of the ethical principles we believe to be true? At one level an answer is readily available. We initially acquired the vast majority of these principles in the same fashion as we first acquired what we believe to be true about U.S. Presidents or proper nutrition or types of automobiles: from some respected authority. For instance, most of us initially believed it was wrong to disobey our parents or engage in certain forms of sexual behavior because of what our parents, teachers, and religious leaders told us.

What, however, is the *ultimate* origin of the ethical principles we hold to be true? Are they solely the product of human thought? Were they "created" by God? Do such principles originate in some source independent of both? Or are there multiple sources?

All of these options have their proponents. Even among theists, a wide variety of opinion exists. However, the vast majority of theists continue to claim that the basic ethical principles they affirm in some sense have their origin in God, as opposed to human thought or some source totally independent of both.

What exactly does it mean, though, to say that ethical principles originate in God? One interpretation is the seemingly paradoxical contention that, although the basic ethical principles we affirm are not totally independent of God, they are *not* a divine creation. To draw an analogy with the laws of logic may help. Consider the law of noncontradiction—the contention that something cannot be both what it is and what it is not at the same time. Few theists have thought this law to be totally independent of God, or something that God discovered. But it is also true that few theists hold that this law was created by God, or that it somehow came into existence as the result of divine decree. It is, rather, normally thought to be an eternal truth that has always existed in the mind of God. For example, according to this line of reasoning, the fact that humans cannot be both alive and not alive in the same sense at the same time is not true because God decreed that it should be so. Rather, the nature of reality (what it is to be alive or not to be alive) simply makes such a state of affairs an impossibility. What God did was decide whether humans would actually come into existence and, thus, whether the logical truth in question would actually apply to the world as it is.

Some have suggested that basic ethical principles might reasonably be viewed the same way. Let us consider, for instance, the widely accepted moral belief that it is wrong to inflict pain unnecessarily. We should not, we are told, view this ethical principle as independent of God in the sense that it is a principle with which God came in contact and then determined should guide all divine and human behavior. Of course, if God had not created beings capable of experiencing pleasure and pain, this specific "truth" would have no relevance for our world. But this moral belief did not come into existence as the result of some divine decree, and God cannot do away with it at will. Rather, the fact that inflicting unnecessary pain is wrong is simply *inherent* in the very concept of any being who can experience such pain. Hence, much like the laws of logic, this principle is best viewed as having always existed in God's mind.[1]

Moreover, proponents of this "autonomy thesis," as it is often called, deny that viewing the origin of our ethical principles in this manner is a threat to theism. Louis Pojman, for instance, argues that "if there is an inherent logic to goodness that precludes God's inventing right and wrong, why should that bother religious people? It is widely recognized that God's omnipotence isn't threatened by the fact that the laws of logic exist independently of him. Why should the fact that there is a logic to ethics threaten the notion of God's sovereignty or omnipotence?"[2]

Many theists, however, have not liked the idea of anything in *any* sense being independent of God or limiting divine activity. Thus, they have wanted to argue that the basic ethical principles they believe to be true have their origin *solely* in God in a stronger sense. One popular way in which this has been envisioned—by individuals often labeled divine command theorists—is to maintain that ethical principles find their inception in God's commands.[3]

To claim that this is so, it is important to point out, is not to hold that the commands themselves are seen as the *origin* of these ethical principles. God is not envisioned as mindlessly "uttering" statements that somehow magically become the basis for ethical standards the moment they leave "God's lips." God's commands are seen as an expression of God's will.[4] Just as a parent's command for a child to go to bed is best interpreted as an expression of what the parent wants the child to do, so too are God's commands best seen as an expression of how God wants us to live.

However, even given this clarification, a well-known challenge remains. If the ethical principles by which we are to live originate in the commands that express God's will, then it appears that we would be justified in doing anything God commanded. It appears, for instance, that even if God commanded us to kill innocent people routinely, or arbitrarily and capriciously commanded us to treat small children kindly one day but torture them the next, our obedience would be justified (indeed required) simply because God has said this should be done. Surely, argues the critic, this is unacceptable. Surely a rational theist would not affirm a theory about the origin of correct ethical principles that had *this* implication.[5]

One popular response has been developed by ethicist Robert Adams (b. 1937).[6] He wants to tie the origin of ethical truth to the will of God but denies that the "believer is committed to doing the will of God just because it is the will of God." That is, Adams denies that the theist would always be required to do what God commanded solely because God commanded it. He grants, for instance, that it would not be wrong for the theist to refrain from practicing cruelty, even *if* God commanded cruelty. This is so, we are told, because God's commands can be viewed as worthy of obedience "only if certain conditions are assumed—namely, only if it is assumed that God has the character which [we] believe Him to have, of loving His human creatures."[7] Otherwise it would not be wrong to disobey him. Stated in more positive terms, Adams's response is that if we assume that God is a personal agent who loves human creatures—an assumption Adams believes we can justifiably make—then we need not fear that those commands originating in the will of God will obligate us to act in a capricious, unloving manner.[8]

Others have elaborated more fully on the important connection between God's commands and character. It is certainly true, they acknowledge, that God has the ability to command us to kill innocent people. God obviously can formulate the relevant concepts and could communicate the divine intentions to us. However, the divine moral will expressed by God's commands does not exist in a vacuum, nor is it dependent on some autonomous moral standard that has existed eternally in God's mind. God's will, rather, is an aspect of God's nature—that is, it is an expression of the type of being God really is. Once we understand the type of being God really is, it is argued, the criticism in question loses its force.

First, God is the all-knowing creator of everything. Thus God knows exactly how all aspects of the divine creation function best. God knows, for example, exactly what will satisfy us individually and what will help us to live together harmoniously. Second, God does not just happen to be caring and loving most, or even all, of the time. God could not be unloving because God's essential nature is never changing. God necessarily wills our individual and corporate fulfillment. Accordingly, it is concluded, God's commands could not be arbitrary and capricious in the way the critic envisions. God, for instance, could not command us to kill innocent children "just for the fun of it" since this would be inconsistent with God's nature.[9]

But could God not have been a different type of being, one who believed that lying, cheating, or killing innocent children was an intrinsically meritorious action? A powerful, supernatural being who held such beliefs could conceivably exist, theists respond. However, the God we worship is not such a being. In fact, the vast majority claim, he could not have been such a being.

Thus, the criticism in question simply fails to apply, and, accordingly, it remains perfectly reasonable to maintain that God's nature is the ultimate origin of the ethical principles we believe to be true.[10]

THE AUTHORITATIVE BASIS OF RELIGIOUS ETHICAL TRUTH

Even given that God's nature is the origin of ethical principles, a significant question remains: what gives the ethical principles that originate in God their authority? Why ought the theist obey what God communicates? As Alasdair MacIntyre (1929–) has phrased this question, "What conditions must be satisfied for it to be rational for someone to treat God's [ethical] beliefs as authoritative?"[11]

In reality, some theists may follow God's commands primarily out of fear, others out of love or the belief that it will generate the best consequences, and still others primarily because their culture has ingrained this desire or duty in them. However, as MacIntyre and others rightly point out, theists could not justifiably view the ethical principles originating in God as the ultimate ethical standard if they did not think that God were *perfectly good.*

What basis, though, do theists have for maintaining that God is good? Religious critic Kai Nielsen (b. 1925) contends that there are only two possible avenues of response.[12] One option, we are told, is for theists to claim that God's goodness is a factual or evidential matter. That is, they might claim that God is good because God has, for example, given them a purpose for living or healed a loved one or offered guidance in times of need.

However, this will not do, Nielsen is quick to point out. We can claim that an individual possesses a certain characteristic only if we already have some understanding of the characteristic in question. For instance (to cite an example not found in Nielsen's writings) we can claim that a new acquaintance is friendly *only if* we already understand what it means for someone to be friendly. In a similar fashion (to return to Nielsen's argument) we can claim that God is good by appealing to the actions God has performed *only if* we already have in mind a standard of goodness by which God's actions can be judged. But if this is true, Nielsen concludes, then it can obviously no longer be claimed that the ethical principles that originate in God provide the ultimate ethical standard. Rather, our own ethical intuitions must be acknowledged to be the ultimate standard.

The other option, Nielsen informs us, is to claim that the statement "God is good" is true by definition or, more correctly, to claim that "goodness" is a necessary defining characteristic of "God." God's attitudes (and actions) are then good simply because God possesses (or performs) them. But this response generates another question: upon what basis do theists label the being they worship "God"? Or, to state Nielsen's question in a somewhat different fashion: how do theists know that the being from whom they have received those ethical principles that they accept as authoritative is actually God?

Theists, Nielsen points out, cannot justifiably claim that such a being is God simply because this being says it is good. The question then simply becomes the following: upon what basis can the claims of such a being be believed? Nor, he argues, can theists claim that the actions of the being they worship are good, and thus that the being can justifiably be considered God, just because they believe this being is the omniscient, omnipotent creator of the universe. It may be true that it would be unwise not to follow the commands of such a being, but it is also not impossible for an omnipotent, omniscient creator to be wicked. The only valid response, we are told, is for theists to admit that the being they worship is called "God" because they possess an independent ethical standard of goodness with which the actions and attitudes of this being are consistent.

An analogy may help clarify this important point. Let us assume that someone declares the statement "All puppies are young" to be a definitional truth. This alone does not allow her also to maintain justifiably that a dog that has just entered the room is a puppy. To make this claim justifiably, she must first determine whether the dog is young. To do this she must already have in mind the characteristics that young dogs possess—for instance, oversized feet and an excitable personality. Likewise, Nielsen is arguing, theists can claim that the being whose commands they follow is God, and thus is an acceptable ethical authority, only if they can determine (possibly in addition to other things) that this being is good. But this can be accomplished only if they already have in mind a concept of goodness by which this being can be judged. Thus, again, theists must admit that their own ethical intuitions are the ultimate ethical standard.

Is Nielsen correct? First, it must be emphasized that Nielsen's argument applies only to those theists who maintain that ethical truth originates totally in God—for example, in God's nature. His comments are not relevant to those theists (noted earlier) who maintain that although ethical truth is in some sense dependent on God, it is also in some sense independent of him.

What, though, of those theists who hold that ethical truth *does* originate totally in God? Is Nielsen's argument compelling in this case? It may well be true that many theists maintain that God is good because the attitudes and actions of the being in question are consistent with their own ethical sensibilities. That is, it may well be true that many theists generally judge God to be good by ethical standards possessed before this judgment is made. But to grant Nielsen this much seems innocuous. The crucial part of his thesis is his contention that the ethical criteria used by theists to evaluate God's goodness constitute an ethical standard that is separate from, and more fundamental than, the basic ethical beliefs of the divine code-giver being judged.

However, it is not clear that theists need grant Nielsen this point. The ethical criteria by which theists judge the goodness of God are "separate" and "more fundamental" in the sense required by Nielsen only if they are formulated by each theist apart from divine influence. But Judeo-Christian theology, for example, has traditionally maintained that humans are divine creations. More specifically, it has traditionally been held that the basic ethical principles that we as humans find ourselves affirming, as creatures made in God's image, are actually divine in origin. In exactly what sense this is so, as we shall see, differs among theists. Yet if such principles are in any sense divine in origin, then it is not clear that theists need grant in the last analysis that they judge God by an ethical standard that is separate from, and more ultimate than, God's. They can claim, rather, that they judge God by a standard that they possess because God has brought it about. In short, it appears that by affirming the "divine" origin of their own ethical sensibilities, theists can grant that they judge the goodness of God by their own ethical standards and yet justifiably deny that their own personally formulated ethical code is the final seat of ethical authority.[13]

Nielsen, of course, does not accept this religious understanding of the origin of humanity's basic ethical intuitions. But this is not relevant. Nielsen is not assessing the truth or falsity of theists' beliefs concerning God's existence, attitudes, or actions. His contention, rather, is that theists cannot consistently maintain that their ethical decisions are based on an ethical standard ultimately independent of human thought, even if they make certain religious assumptions. However, it seems this contention can be countered successfully.

THE ACQUISITION OF RELIGIOUSLY BASED ETHICAL TRUTH

Let us assume, then, for the sake of argument, that theists can justifiably maintain not only that ethical truth originates in God but also that such truth is authoritative for this reason. This still leaves us with the question of how theists acquire this ethical insight.

Three distinct, although not mutually exclusive, methods of acquisition are mentioned most frequently. First, theists often claim that God has communicated ethical truths through some form of written revelation—for example, the Bible or Koran. Opinions differ widely on the extent to which God is thought to have been directly involved in the production of this revelation. Some believe God is directly responsible for every word; others believe God is responsible for the basic concepts; and still others believe that God is responsible only for helping to collate the most accurate human ethical insights. But many, if not most, theists hold that written revelation is a very important source of information about the ethical principles by which God wants us to live.

It is here, though, that conservative Jewish and Christian theists—those who believe the Torah or Bible to be a clear, direct communication from God—run into a well-known dilemma. The problem is that, at face value, some of the actions attributed to God appear to be ethically questionable. For example, in Numbers 31 it is God who declares that all members of an enemy tribe are to be killed by the Israelites, and then decides how to divide up the thirty-two thousand virgin girls who were not destroyed. And in I Chronicles 21, it appears that God brings it about that seventy thousand individuals die solely to punish King David, and not because of any wrong-doing on their part.

Some conservative theists respond by separating the ethical principles by which God operates from those applicable to human behavior. God, it is argued, has created a consistent, thoughtful ethical standard for humans—a standard that, if followed, will bring about what God desires and the greatest fulfillment for all. But God is not bound by such a standard. God can do whatever he wants for whatever reasons he possesses, and such actions are ethically justifiable simply because he has performed them.[14]

Of course, this contention generates obvious questions. If God operates by a different ethical standard, how can God remain the object of our ethical admiration? We might well obey a being who has created rules for us because we recognize that these rules maximize human fulfillment or because we fear the rule-giver. But could we truly worship or revere a being who not only could but did violate the most basic ethical concepts by which we have been told (and created to feel) we should live?

Many theists think the answer is no. They deny that two distinct standards exist. Of course, they grant, God has created some ethical tenets that apply only to humans. For example, rules related to the well-being of our physical bodies are not relevant to God because God has no such body. However, the basic ethical principles God has communicated to us are the same ethical principles that also "guide" God's activity. Accordingly, they conclude, any seeming violation of these principles must ultimately be a problem of human perspective. If we could see the whole picture from God's perspective—if we were aware of all the contextual factors—we would see that everything God has actually said and done is consistent with God's nature, which is loving in the basic manner in which we understand the term.[15]

Second (to return to our primary question of how theists acquire their ethical beliefs), some theists, in the "natural law" tradition of Thomas Aquinas (c. 1224–1274), continue to believe that human reason is capable of discovering divine ethical truth. According to this perspective, God is the ultimate source of all ethical knowledge. That is, God establishes the ultimate distinction between good and evil. However, as the result of being created in God's image, we as humans possess the rational capacities to comprehend those aspects of this ethical standard that have been revealed in nature. That is, from our observation of the natural order, we can deduce how human beings are to act and be treated.

We have, for example, a natural tendency to preserve ourselves, to produce offspring, and to live in a social setting with others. From these principles we can deduce that God sanctions self-defense. From the fact that we have a natural tendency to protect young children and the fact that we all desire to avoid pain, we can deduce that God does not sanction the killing of innocent children.

Thomistic natural law theorists are quick to point out that such ethical reflection is not a more trustworthy avenue for discerning ethical truth than written revelation. In fact, many have acknowledged that written revelation must be given precedence in the event of a conflict. However, although written revelation is *sufficient* for giving us God's basic ethical perspective, it is not *always necessary.* Human reflection on the nature of things, it is held, can discover much about God's basic ethical standards and their application to our daily lives.[16]

Third, as has been implicitly stated, some theists also claim that divine ethical truth is at least in part innate. Each of us, they maintain, has been created in the "image of God," including God's "ethical image." This means that our basic ethical intuitions—for example, the belief that we should not kill innocent children—automatically mirror God's basic ethical perspectives. As Gottfried Leibniz (1646–1716) and others rightly noted, such innate intuitions may require some external illumination before we become consciously aware of them.[17] We may, for instance, need to understand what a child is, and what killing means, before we become consciously aware of the fact that killing children is wrong. Moreover, not all available ethical insight comes to us in this fashion. Written revelation and reason are also necessary. But some of the basic ethical principles we believe to be true, these theists argue, were not "learned." We, as divine creations, were simply "born" with them.

There is, however, a seemingly serious problem that proponents of all three of these modes of acquiring divine ethical truth must face. Why is there so much ethical diversity among theists? That is, why do seemingly sincere, knowledgeable theists differ significantly on so many issues related to human thought and action? If theists have access to basic ethical truth, as they claim, why is there not greater ethical consensus?

Some of this diversity can, of course, be reasonably attributed to the diversity in religious perspectives themselves. It is true that proponents of almost all religions claim to have access to ethical truth through written revelation, reason, and/or inborn awareness. However, given that religious perspectives differ not only with respect to the content of their "written revelations" but also with respect to the role that innate awareness and rational reflection can play in the discovery of truth, it should not be surprising that there exists a great deal of ethical diversity in the general religious community.

What can be said, though, about the significant amount of ethical diversity that remains *within* various religions—for instance, within the Judeo-Christian perspective? Such diversity can be explained in part by distinguishing between basic ethical principles and their practical application. Consider, for instance, the question of whether we should allow physicians to help terminally ill patients end their lives. There will be little debate within most religious perspectives at the level of principle. Conscientious theists, it will be held, ought to respond in a just, caring manner. But what does this mean in practice? Does it mean theists ought to work to ensure the legal right of those in unbearable pain to be helped to end such suffering? Or should theists fight any attempt to legalize a "right to die" that might ultimately cause those in the final stages of death to feel morally obligated to end their lives? Since either can reasonably be construed as a just, caring response, it should not be surprising that sincere theists within almost all religions disagree (sometimes strongly) on the appropriate response in this case. In short, since the general ethical principles of most religions allow for varied application, the fact that we encounter some diverse ethical behavior, even within a given religious perspective, is to be expected.

Ethical diversity within a given religion is also at times clearly a function of differing "factual" assumptions. Abortion is a good example. Most in the Judeo-Christian tradition affirm the same relevant ethical principles: for instance, that taking an innocent life is wrong. What they differ on is whether a fetus is sufficiently human to fall within the protective bounds of this principle.

Even granting, though, that some diversity can be explained in these ways, the basic tension remains in that some theists within any given religious tradition differ on the *basic* "innate" or "rational" principles themselves. For example, whereas some Christians believe it is never right to use life-threatening force, others believe this is justified in times of war or to defend an innocent person. As an additional example, whereas some proponents of given religions believe that men and women should function as equals in all contexts, other adherents to the same religions maintain that men must still exercise authority over women, especially in the home and church. Can diversity of this fundamental sort justifiably be viewed as compatible with the contention that the proponents of a given religion have access to authoritative ethical truth?

In response, many theists emphasize the important distinction between affirming *different* basic ethical principles and ranking the *same* basic ethical principles differently. Take, for example, the case of Christians who were hiding Jews in their homes during World War II. When the Nazis came to ask if Jews were within, some Christians thought it right to lie while others did not. But the issue here was not primarily one of principle. All of the Christians involved thought it was their God-sanctioned duty both to protect innocent lives *and* not to lie. They differed on the question of which principle was properly to be given precedence in this case.[18]

Other theists hold that the human ability to identify divine ethical principles accurately has been severely damaged by "the Fall"—that is, by a break in the relationship between humans and God that was precipitated by an act of rebellion by humans. Thus, they claim that although many of us at times are able to discern with relative accuracy the ethical principles affirmed by God, some of us will inevitably be unable to do so, or at least be unable to do so consistently.[19]

Finally, those theists who maintain that some ethical truth is "inborn" often emphasize the significance of cultural conditioning. It is one thing, they argue, to say that each human has some basic understanding of the divine ethical law, but quite another thing to say that such an understanding will always be consciously felt as predominant. Individuals are greatly influenced by their culture. If, for instance, they are raised in a culture where stealing, cheating, or lying is condoned, they will have a strong disposition to believe it is right to engage in such activities. They might have some vague feeling that such actions are wrong, but it need not be held that this "divine perspective" will always be most influential.[20]

Of course, even if all this is granted, pervasive ethical diversity among and within religious perspectives still leaves us with the following question: which religious ethical standard most closely resembles God's standard? This surely is an important question in that much strife historically has been the result of individuals or groups acting on what they perceived to be the correct set of divinely sanctioned ethical principles. In fact, it is so important that it may well be true that the reality of pervasive diversity stands as a good reason for theists to periodically reassess their ethical beliefs (and the behavior such beliefs generate). That is, such diversity may well stand as a real challenge to ethical dogmatism, especially in action.

We must be careful, though, to keep all this in perspective. There is diversity in the methods used by theists to acquire ethical truth *and* in the "truths" allegedly acquire. However, just as the reality of diversity in political opinion does not necessarily require us to become political relativists or skeptics, the reality of ethical diversity does not necessarily require us to become ethical relativists or skeptics. Ethical diversity ought to be recognized and considered by theists as they put their ethical beliefs into action, but it does not follow from the fact that theists acknowledge the reality of ethical diversity that they cannot justifiably claim that there exists any ethical truth, that such truth is divine in origin, or even that they have access to it.

THE SIGNIFICANCE OF RELIGIOUSLY BASED ETHICAL TRUTH

What does all this mean for those individuals who are not religious? If theists are correct in holding that ethical truth originates in God and that they have access to such truth, what are the implications for those who do not believe in God (or at least deny that ethical truth is in any sense dependent on God)?

Does it mean, for instance, that those who do not believe ethical truth is in any sense dependent on God cannot meaningfully communicate about matters of moral significance with those who do? Most theists do not hold this to be the case. That is, they do not claim that one must believe in God (or believe ethical truth is dependent on God) to be aware of any of God's basic ethical beliefs. Most maintain, rather, that God has created all individuals with an "inborn" understanding of, or the rational ability to discover, certain basic ethical principles, and that the mutual possession of these principles allows for meaningful ethical dialogue between the two groups, even if nontheists do not recognize the "divine" origin of their basic ethical beliefs.[21]

However, a significant question remains: can a nonreligious person, or anyone else who does not believe ethical truth to be dependent on God, justifiably affirm ethical absolutes? That is, can someone who does not ground ethical truth in God justifiably claim that some actions are wrong (or right) for all persons at all times and places? In reality, of course, most non-religious individuals do affirm ethical absolutes. The vast majority believe, for instance, that innocent children ought, in principle, never to be tortured. But can such absolutes be justifiably affirmed? Most theists ground absolutes in an objective, external standard: God's nature. But if there is no God, are not all ethical beliefs ultimately human in origin? That is, if there is no God, how can it be said justifiably that one human or group of humans has the right to dictate how all others *ought* to live? Does it not follow rather, in the words of Jean-Paul Sartre (1905–1980), that "everything is permissible if God does not exist?"[22]

In response, Nielsen argues that the "nonexistence of God does not preclude the possibility of there being an objective standard on which to base moral judgments." There are, he tells us, "good reasons, of a perfectly mundane sort, why we should have the institution of morality as we now have it. . . . Morality has an objective rationale in complete independence of religion."[23]

So what is this "objective rationale" that is "independent of religion"? Such objectivity, Nielsen maintains, can be founded on ethical beliefs such as "happiness is good" and "all persons should be treated fairly" since such beliefs are not only ethical principles that most persons intuitively know to be true, but are also principles that, if put into practice, are normally most advantageous for all involved.

Suppose, however, that it is pragmatically advantageous for individuals to treat others unfairly—for example, to cheat on their taxes—and that they therefore do so. Or suppose that individuals claim to have radically different ethical intuitions—for example, claims that lying and stealing are right. On what basis can such persons be judged ethically wrong? Nielsen is aware of such difficulties. For instance, he admits that he cannot prove that happiness is good, arguing that he "can only appeal to our sense of psychological realism to persuade us to admit intellectually what in practice we acknowledge." Furthermore, He admits that he cannot prove that fairness is always the most advantageous principle to employ, but argues that "to be moral involves respecting [human] rights."[24] As he phrases this point in another context, unless such a principle is affirmed, there can be "[no] understanding of the concept of morality, [no] understanding of what it is to take the moral point of view."[25]

Is Nielsen correct? Has he offered us a sound nontheistic basis for objective morality? As we consider this question, it is first important to realize that Nielsen is clearly not defining "objective morality" as it is usually defined by theists. For most theists, absolute (objective) ethical principles are nonexperientially grounded (a priori) statements that are true for all persons at all times in all places. For Nielsen, "absolute" ethical principles are experientially grounded (a posteriori) statements that ought, on the basis of rational considerations, to be affirmed *at present* by everyone. Thus, while most theists see "Thou shalt not kill" as a timeless truth affirmed by, but not founded on, human reasoning, Nielsen sees this ethical principle as a truth that all individuals ought to affirm, at present, on the basis of rational thought.

However, does this not make Nielsen's "objective" ethical perspective quite relative to the obvious variations in human thought and the amount of relevant data being considered? In response, Nielsen is willing to admit that if ethical principles are solely the product of human thought, then they are to a certain degree relative in this sense. However, to maintain that ethical truth is relative can also be taken to mean that there is no objective basis for preferring one ethical perspective to another—that what is *right* in every case is solely a function of what each individual personally thinks is right. It can be taken to mean, for example, that there is no stronger *objective* basis for favoring capital punishment than for opposing it. Obviously, Nielsen does want to deny that his ethic is relative in this sense. He believes, as we have seen, that given the human desire for happiness, and given that there are good pragmatic reasons for believing that certain forms of behavior will generally help us reach this goal, nontheists do have an objective basis in some contexts for saying most people should behave in certain ways most of the time.

Some continue to claim, though, that to base ethical beliefs on common elements in human thought or experience is to confuse factual and ethical issues—to deduce unjustifiably that people *ought* to affirm certain ethical norms solely from the observable fact that such norms *are* affirmed. In response, Nielsen grants that we cannot simply "deduce that people ought to do something from discovering that they do it or seek it any more than we can conclude from the proposition that a being exists whom people call God that we ought to do whatever that being commands." However, he adds, "we do justify moral claims by an appeal to factual claims, and there is a close connection between what human beings desire on reflection and what they deem to be good."[26]

It appears that Nielsen is at least partially correct on this point. The majority of philosophers agree that neither the religious nor the nonreligious individual can directly deduce an *ought* from an *is*. But it does seem that religious as well as nonreligious individuals justify their ethical claims at least in part by appealing to factual contentions—for example, by appealing to certain claims about the nature of God, natural human desires, or shared ethical intuitions.[27]

Moreover, even if we reject Nielsen's basis for an objective nonreligious morality, it is not clear that a nonreligious person is committed to radical ethical relativism. It may be that nonreligiously based ethical norms must be somewhat relative to the context to which they apply, or must at least be more relative than religiously based norms. However, to establish the total relativity of nonreligiously based ethics—to establish that ethical truth for the nonreligious person is nothing more than personal preference—it must be demonstrated that there exists no rational basis for humanity (all rational individuals) in general to affirm any given ethical norm. It does not appear that this has yet been done. In fact, even some theists think it is misguided to attempt to do so. Louis Pojman, for instance, agrees with Nielsen that "secular morality based on a notion of the good life is inspiring in itself, for it promotes human flourishing and can be shown to be in all of our interests, whether or not God exists."[28]

Even granting this fact, if ethical truth is solely a human invention—if there exists no ultimate standard of value apart from our human perspective—can life have any real meaning? To state the question differently, is it at least true, as some theists have claimed, that belief in God is necessary if life is to have any significant purpose?

To answer this question, we must more clearly understand what theists have in mind when they claim that ethical relativism leads to "meaninglessness." Most argue at the very least that nontheists can posit no ultimate purpose for the universe as a whole. Hans Küng (b. 1928), for example, maintains that "by denying God, man decides against an ultimate reason, support, and end of reality."[29] This contention, however, has limited significance. Although it may be true that some nontheists need to be reminded that a godless universe is ultimately nonpurposeful, thoughtful nontheists readily acknowledge this fact.

Some theists, however, have wanted to go further. They have wanted to argue that once nontheists realize that there exists no ultimate purpose for the universe as a whole, they will no longer experience any personal meaning. Rather, in the words of Küng, they will be exposed "quite personally to the danger of an ultimate abandonment, menace and decay, resulting in doubt, fear, even despair."[30]

Not surprisingly, however, most nontheists do not find this line of reasoning compelling. First, while they grant that some nontheists may experience a loss of personal meaning when they come to recognize that there exists no ultimate cosmic meaning in a godless universe, they deny that this is the case for most.

More importantly, however, nontheists argue that this type of "head-counting" approach to the question of personal meaning begs the question by its very nature. They do not deny that many theists have found in their own experience a significant tie between cosmic and personal meaning. They do not deny, for example, that many theists truly hold, with St. Augustine (354–430), that the human "heart" is restless until it finds its rest in God. In fact, many nontheists do not even deny that theists are justified in maintaining that some such connection exists.

The key issue, they point out, is not what the theist can rationally affirm; the issue is what the nontheist can rationally affirm. Here, it is argued, the burden of proof clearly lies with the theist. What the theist must establish is not that she is justified in claiming that she would possess no personal meaning if there were no God or even that some nontheists also feel this way. What the theist must establish is that nontheists who deny cosmic meaning but still claim to possess personal meaning are not justified in maintaining this position. This, most nontheists contend, the theist has not done. In fact, given that there appears to be no widespread scientific (psychological or physiological) or logical support for the claim that one cannot justifiably claim to have personal meaning if one denies cosmic meaning, most nontheists do not see how the theist could even attempt to establish such a connection in a non–question-begging manner.

It appears the nontheist is correct, at least given the manner in which he has structured the debate. A nonreligious worldview may require some reworking of the traditional concept of personal meaning. Some nontheists may in fact not experience personal meaning. But it does not appear to follow necessarily from this that nontheists cannot justifiably affirm an enduring sense of personal meaning. A separate argument is needed for this end, an argument that does not already assume the truth of what is to be proved.

CURRENT ISSUES

One approach to ethics to which philosophers have recently been giving considerable attention is called *virtue ethics,* and this has carried over into the religious realm.[31] To understand any aspect of this discussion, we must first bring to the forefront the well-known distinction between *what* individuals do and *why* they do it. Consider, for example, the following situations.

Case A: One day while walking to the Post Office, Grandmother Smith trips and falls. Tim is cycling past on his way to a ball game and sees what occurs. Because he is late, he momentarily considers riding on. But this thought is quickly replaced by his concern for Grandmother Smith's welfare. Thus, he stops, helps her up, and makes sure she is not hurt before continuing on his way.

Case B: One day while walking to the Post Office, Grandmother Smith trips and falls. Bill, who is cycling by on his way to a ball game for which he is late, observes the event. But he has no intention of stopping. He is late for his game, but even more importantly, he dislikes Grandmother Smith. Thus, he is actually pleased that she has fallen. However, just as he is ready to leave the scene, he notices at a distance a person who looks very much like the pastor of his church, and he fears that this person has seen Grandmother fall and will see him riding away without helping. Thus, Bill stops, helps her up, and makes sure she is not hurt before riding on.

The observable behavior in each case is identical. Grandmother Smith has fallen, and a young man has stopped to help. Hence, any ethical theory stating that ethical judgment should be based solely on observable behavior would have to consider the actions of Tim and Bill as ethically equivalent. But for many of us in the Western ethical tradition, this would not be acceptable. We are happy with the "ethical output" in each case—we are glad Grandmother Smith has been helped. But our ethical assessment of Bill and Tim would not solely, or even primarily, be based on their observable behavior.

It would be based primarily, or at least significantly, on our assessment of their "ethical input"—their motivation or intentions. In this regard Bill and Tim do differ significantly. Tim wanted to help; Bill did not.

It is possible, however, to discuss this difference in ethical input in terms of either *duty* or *virtue (virtuous character)*. In terms of duty, we might say that Tim's behavior is praiseworthy because he desired to act in accordance with the recognized ethical duty to help those in need, while Bill deserves no commendation because his actions were not motivated by this or any other relevant ethical duty. In terms of virtue, we might say that Tim alone deserves praise because his behavior was an expression of a virtuous character trait—for example, benevolence.

Of course, these two ways of describing ethical input are not mutually exclusive. In fact, it seems to many that both are necessary to a full understanding of ethical behavior. However, there has recently been a great deal of interest in whether we should view duty or virtue as the more basic (or primary) ethical concept. Those wanting to emphasize duty argue that it is because we have a duty to do something that our intention to do it is virtuous. To state this point more formally, they argue that it is because we have a basic disposition to want to act in accordance with recognized duties that we can be said to have a praiseworthy character. In terms of our current illustration, this would be to say that Tim's desire to help Grandmother Smith is virtuous because he acted in accordance with the recognized duty to help those in need.

Those wanting to emphasize virtue argue instead that we have the ethical duty to act, or refrain from acting, in certain ways because such duties are expressions of virtuous character traits. In terms of our illustration, this would be to say that Tim can be praised for fulfilling his ethical duty to attempt to help Grandmother Smith because this duty is the expression of his benevolent character. Still other philosophers see neither duty nor virtue as primary, but rather as two partially overlapping and mutually interdependent perspectives on ethics.

The relevance of this question for religious ethics is obvious. The discussion of traditional ethical issues in this chapter has generally been couched in terms of ethical principles, which can quite plausibly be understood to be statements describing ethical duties. That is, it might appear from the tone of this chapter that to be ethical from a religious perspective is to act in accordance with the revealed rules (duties) that have their grounding in God. But the recent interest in virtue ethics has led some to conceive of religious ethics differently. Specifically, they no longer conceive of ethical activity primarily in terms of doing what God wants, or even wanting to do what God wants, but rather in terms of being the type of person God wants us to be.[32]

To help make this distinction clearer, let us consider the common religious belief that we should love one another. In the traditional framework of a duty ethic, the theist's primary task is to apply this principle to each aspect of daily life. Such a process, of course, is in part contextual. For instance, how one responds in love to a three-year-old throwing a tantrum or to an unhelpful store clerk is allowed to differ from situation to situation. But in each case the theist's task is to determine consciously what would be the most loving response.

Under a virtue ethic, however, the situation is fundamentally different. The essence of ethical activity is not seen as conscious adherence to a set of duties. Specifically, the key to ethical living is not thought to be something that can be abstracted from the religious tradition and rationally applied to culture. The essence of ethical living is to *be* religious—for example, to be Christian or to be Islamic. We must become part of a tradition, a faith community, in which the character of this community—its intentions, desires, and values—becomes our own. We will then quite naturally find ourselves living as we should. Stated differently, once we *become* religious, we will act in a proper religious manner. The development of our religious character occurs prior to the realization of our religious duty.

This perspective also leads, not surprisingly, to a deemphasis on the traditional philosophical responses to ethical issues. For example, many theists have traditionally thought it important to respond to the problem of evil: why does there exist so much seemingly unnecessary pain and suffering in a world allegedly created by an omnipotent, omniscient, perfectly good being? In fact, in the words of one influential Christian "virtue ethicist," for a Christian to even attempt to answer this question "is a mistake." Evil is not "a metaphysical problem needing a solution" but rather a "practical challenge needing a response." The appropriate response is a "community of care which [makes] it possible to absorb the destructive terror of evil that constantly threatens to destroy all human relations."[33]

There are, of course, many theists who think both duty and virtue are important ethical concepts. But the emphasis on virtue ethics appears to be something that will have an impact on the nature of religious ethics for the foreseeable future.

Another approach to ethics to which philosophers are also giving increasing attention has come to be called *feminist ethics*. Given the widely divergent interpretations of what constitutes feminism itself, it should not be surprising that there is no unambiguous understanding of what constitutes this approach to ethics. But there are some points on which almost all who claim to be doing ethics of this type agree.

All feminist approaches to ethics maintain that the traditional ethical theories—whether utilitarian or rights-based—are inadequate. Most important, it is argued that traditional Western ethical theories are male-biased in the sense of uniformly "representing the experiences of men, not women."[34] Specifically, Alison Jaggar tells us, these theories have "either devalued or ignored issues or spheres of life that are associated with women . . . women's virtues have been seen as less significant than those associated with men; women's work has gone unrecognized or its creativity has been unappreciated; the abuse of women and children, especially girls, has been ignored."[35]

Moreover, while feminists differ on the extent to which any ethical system needs general moral rules from which we can deduce appropriate behavior in specific contexts, there is general agreement that traditional ethical

systems rely too heavily on abstract generalized principles applied to hypothetical situations, often at the expense of the immediate needs of actual
individuals.

Finally, feminists hold that the recognition of, and respect for, women's
moral experience is indispensable in that such experience enables us to identify "previously unrecognized ethical issues . . . introduce fresh perspectives on issues already acknowledged as having an ethical dimension . . .
and [counter] traditional stereotypes of women as less than full moral
agents, as childlike or close to nature."[36]

It should not be surprising, accordingly, that feminist ethics is overtly
"political"—that is, it is concerned with the actual rules and regulations that
govern our human interaction. This should not be construed to mean that
proponents of feminist ethics do not concern themselves with theoretical issues. They explicitly acknowledge the need to "develop theoretical understandings of the nature of morality that treat women's moral experience re-
spectfully but not uncritically."[37] But "fully feminist ethicists are committed,
first and foremost, to the elimination of women's subordination—and that of
other oppressed persons—in all of its manifestations."[38] In other words, feminists desire not only to theoretically "unmask and challenge the oppression,
discrimination and exclusion that women have faced," but also to influence
relevant public policy.[39]

As is true of feminist ethics in general, religious or theological feminist
ethics is quite divergent in nature and scope. But again several common factors are apparent.

First and foremost, religious feminists believe it is necessary to identify
in the traditional theological ethical systems those "powers and forces, the
structures and practices that oppress women."[40] Many, if not most, religions,
it is argued, continue to deny equal ethical status to both men and women.
Within a few branches of conservative Christianity, for instance, women are
still viewed as the ones ultimately responsible for evil. But even within
those religions where this is not the case, men are still often considered more
"rational" than women and thus more responsible for creating and/or interpreting the ethical standards by which we are to live, standards that are often
quite different for women than for men. Men are told not to take advantage
of others as they strive to accomplish their goals; women are often explicitly
or implicitly told to give of themselves so that others (especially men) can accomplish their goals. Men are asked to control their sexual behavior; women
are still often encouraged to remain totally pure in thought and deed. Men
are encouraged to make the ultimate decisions; women are encouraged to
offer helpful advice. Moreover, religious feminists emphasize, it is not
enough simply to identify this sort of male bias in religious ethics. Such bias
must be openly challenged.[41]

In addition to this "deconstructive" project, there is also the desire on the
part of most religious feminists to "reconstruct" a religious ethical perspective compatible with basic feminist tenets. Specifically, there is an attempt to
construct an ethic that not only frees women from patriarchal oppression, but
also encourages women's self-affirmation as equal participants in the reli-

gious and ethical arenas. Such attempted reconstruction, though, takes various forms. Some religious feminists base their efforts on the assumption that since "all men and all male thought and action are different from and opposed to all women and all female thought and action," what men have said and done in the area of religious ethical theory (as in all other areas) must be repudiated. Accordingly, they have as their goal to create a wholly new religious ethic, one based on the concepts and language that arise from women's experiences.[42]

Other feminists, however, reject the contention that the traditional theological ethical systems are necessarily hostile to the interests of women. Some Christian feminists have argued, for instance, that aspects of the manner in which the early Christian church envisioned the relationships among those with unequal power are quite compatible with contemporary feminist thought.[43] Thus, as those in this camp see it, what must be done is to identify and challenge those aspects of the traditional systems that discriminate on the basis of gender, while retaining those aspects that are inclusive of women's experience.[44]

There are, not surprisingly, some theists who feel that theological feminists place too much emphasis on gender equality—that is, that they wrongly identify gender equality as the primary factor in assessing the value of a religious ethical tradition. But few theists today deny that male bias continues to exist to some extent and thus that the feminist concerns noted must be taken seriously.

STUDY QUESTIONS

1. What do you think most theists really mean when they say that ethical truth has its origin in God? Given this interpretation, are theists still open to the charge that God's commands could be arbitrary and capricious?

2. How do you make ethical decisions? What part, if any, does belief in God play in this approach to ethical decision making?

3. Why does Kai Nielsen believe that the religious person's ethical standard is ultimately based on her own ethical intuitions, not God's commands? How do theists respond?

4. Why does ethical pluralism—the wide variety of ethical perspectives—pose a challenge for religious ethics? Which of the responses to such pluralism discussed in this chapter do you find most convincing?

5. Is belief in God necessary for life to have ultimate meaning?

6. Why do some claim that ethics must be totally relative if there is no God? Briefly outline and assess Kai Nielsen's response to this claim.

7. Those theists who consider the Torah or Bible to be a trustworthy source of information about God must grapple with the seemingly questionable behavior sometimes attributed to God in these texts. Which of the responses discussed did you find most convincing? Why?

8. What is "virtue ethics"? Do you think "virtue" or "duty" is the more basic ethical concept? Why?

9. Do you think that religious individuals behave more ethically than nonreligious individuals? If not, is the opposite true?

10. Is the world, on balance, a better place because of the role religion has played in ethical behavior?

11. Do you agree with religious feminists that the traditional ethical systems have been (and continue to be) male-biased? Why or why not?

NOTES

1. See, for example, A. C. Ewing, "The Autonomy of Ethics," in *Divine Command Morality*, ed. Janine Marie Idziak (Lewiston, N.Y.: Edwin Mellen Press, 1979), pp. 228–30.

2. Louis P. Pojman, *Ethics: Discovering Right and Wrong* (Belmont, Calif.: Wadsworth, 1990), p. 188.

3. See, for example, Emil Brunner, *The Divine Imperative* (Philadelphia: Westminster Press, 1947); Carl F. H. Henry, *Christian Personal Ethics* (Grand Rapids, Mich.: William B. Eerdmans, 1957).

4. William of Ockham, *On the Four Books of the Sentences*, bk. 11, question 19, in Idziak, ed., *Divine Command Morality*, pp. 55–59.

5. See, for example, Patrick Nowell-Smith, "Religion and Morality," in the *Encyclopedia of Philosophy*, vol. 7 (New York: Macmillan, 1967), p. 156; A. C. Ewing, *Prospect for Metaphysics* (London: George Allen and Unwin, 1951), p. 39.

6. See, for example, Robert Adams, "A Modified Divine Command Theory of Ethical Wrongness," in Louis Pojman, ed., *Philosophy of Religion* (Belmont, Calif.: Wadsworth, 1987), p. 527.

7. Adams, pp. 533–4.

8. It is sometimes argued that Adams's "modified" divine command theory is actually just a "modified" version of the "autonomy thesis," since it appears that some independent ethical principles are accorded preference over God's commands. In one sense, this appears true. Adams does maintain hypothetically that if God were to utter certain commands, we could appeal to a higher, independent ethical standard in refusing to obey such commands. But Adams denies that it is possible for God to utter such commands, and concludes, therefore, that God's actual commands can justifiably be viewed as the actual basis of our ethical principles.

9. Bruce Reichenbach, "The Divine Command Theory and Objective Good," in *Georgetown Symposium on Ethics*, ed. R. Porreco (New York: University Press of America), pp. 219–31. It should be noted that Adams is not necessarily in agreement with all aspects of this line of reasoning.

10. Adams, pp. 525–37.

11. Alasdair MacIntyre, "Which God Ought We Obey and Why?" *Faith and Philosophy* 3 (1986): 359.

12. Kai Nielsen, *Ethics without God* (London: Pemberton, 1973), chap. 3.

13. E. I Carnell, *Christian Commitment* (New York: Macmillan, 1957), p. 134.

14. See, for example, Gordon Clark, *Religion, Reason and Revelation* (Philadelphia: Presbyterian and Reformed Publishing Company, 1961), pp. 221–41.

15. Adams, pp. 525–37.

16. See, for example, R. E. O. White, *Christian Ethics* (Atlanta: John Knox Press, 1981), pp. 124–35; Garth L. Hallet, *Christian Moral Reasoning* (Notre Dame, Ind.: University of Notre Dame Press, 1983), pp. 83–4, 114–5; E. Albert, T. Denise, and S. Peterfreund, *Great Traditions in Ethics*, 5th ed. (Belmont, Calif.: Wadsworth, 1984), pp. 106–25.

17. Gottfried Leibniz, *New Essays on the Human Understanding* (1765), bk. 1, chap. 2, sec. 5.

18. See Norman, Geisler, *The Christian Ethic of Love* (Grand Rapids, Mich.: Zondervan, 1973), pp. 76–127.

19. See Mark Talbot, "On Christian Philosophy," *Reformed Journal* 34 (September 1984): pp. 19–20.

20. John Hick, "The Philosophy of World Religions," *Scottish Journal of Theology* 37 (1984): 231–6.

21. Adams, pp. 535–7.

22. Jean-Paul Sartre, "The Humanism of Existentialism," in *Philosophy: A Literary and Conceptual Approach*, ed. Burton Porter (New York: Harcourt Brace Jovanovich, 1974), pp. 70–1.

23. Nielsen, pp. 48, 64.

24. Nielsen, pp. 86, 62.

25. Kai Nielsen, "On Religion and the Grounds of Moral Belief," *Religious Humanism* 11 (Winter 1977): 33–4.

26. Nielsen, *Ethics,* p. 56.

27. Reichenbach, p. 230.

28. Pojman, p. 191.

29. Hans Kung, *On Being a Christian* (Garden City, N.Y.: Doubleday, 1976), p. 75.

30. Kung, p. 75. Some theists make a weaker claim. To Louis Pojman, for instance, "it seems plausible to assert that in some ways the world of the theist is better and more satisfying than one in which God does not exist" (p. 194).

31. See, for example, Alasdair MacIntyre, *After Virtue* (Notre Dame, Ind.: Notre Dame University Press, 1981); Stanley Hauerwas, *The Peaceable Kingdom* (Notre Dame, Ind.: University of Notre Dame Press, 1983).

32. Stanley Hauerwas, *The Peaceable Kingdom and a Community of Character* (Notre Dame, Ind.: University of Notre Dame Press, 1981).

33. Stanley Hauerwas, "God, Medicine and the Problems of Evil," *Reformed Journal* (April 1988): 19.

34. John D. Arras and Bonnie Steinbock, "Moral Reasoning in the Medical Context," in *Ethical Issues in Modern Medicine*, ed. John D. Arras and Bonnie Steinbock, 4th ed., (Palo Alto, Calif.: Mayfield, 1995), p. 28.

35. Alison M. Jaggar, "Feminist Ethics: Projects, Problems, Prospects," in *Feminist Ethics,* ed. Claudia Card (Lawrence: University of Kansas Press, 1991), p. 85.

36. Ibid., pp. 86, 91.

37. Rosemarie Tong, "Feminist Ethics," *Stanford Encyclopedia of Philosophy,* http://plato.standford.edu/entries/feminis-ethics, p. 12.

38. Jaggar, p. 98.

39. Arras and Steinbock, pp. 28–9.

40. Sally B. Purvis, *The Power of the Cross: Foundations for a Christian Feminist Ethic of Community* (Nashville, Tenn.: Abingdon Press, 1993), p. 14.

41. See, for instance, Sally Purvis; Linda Woodhead, "Feminism and Christian Ethics," in *Women's Voices: Essays in Contemporary Feminist Theology,* ed. Teresa Elwas (London: Marshall Pickering, 1992); Marilyn J. Legge, *The Grace of Difference: A Canadian Feminist Theological Ethic* (Atlanta: Scholars Press, 1992); McClintock Fulkerson, *Changing the Subject: Women's Discourses and Feminist Theology* (Minneapolis, Minn.: Fortress Press, 1994); Denise Lardner Carmody, *Virtuous Woman: Reflections on Christian Feminist Ethics* (Maryknoll, N.Y.: Orbis Books, 1992).

42. Woodhead, p. 58.

43. Purvis, pp. 13–4.

44. Woodhead, p. 58.

SUGGESTED READING

Carmody, Denise Lardner. *Virtuous Woman: Reflections on Christian Feminist Ethics.* Maryknoll, N.Y.: Orbis Books, 1992.

Daly, Lois, ed. *Feminist Theological Ethics: A Reader.* Westminster/John Knox Press, 1995.

Donagan, Allan. *The Theory of Morality.* Chicago: University of Chicago Press, 1977.

Frankena, William. *Ethics.* 2d ed. Englewood Cliffs, N.J.: Prentice-Hall, 1973.

Fulkerson, Mary McClintock. *Changing the Subject: Women's Discourses and Feminist Theology.* Minneapolis, Minn.: Fortress Press, 1994.

Gill, Robin. *A Textbook of Christian Ethics.* Edinburgh: TPT Clark, 1985.

Hare, John. *The Moral Gap.* Oxford: Oxford University Press, 1996.

MacIntyre, Alasdair. *After Virtue.* Notre Dame, Ind.: University of Notre Dame Press, 1981.

McClendon, James W., Jr. *Ethics: Systematic Theology.* Vol. 1. Nashville, Tenn.: Abingdon, 1986.

Mitchell, Basil. *Morality: Religious and Secular.* Oxford: Oxford University Press, 1980.

Mow, Richard. *The God Who Commands.* Notre Dame, Ind.: University of Notre Dame Press, 1990.

Nielsen, Kai. *Ethics without God.* London: Pemberton, 1973.

Outka, Gene, and John P. Reeder, Jr., eds. *Religion and Morality.* Garden City, N.Y.: Anchor Books, 1973.

Pojman, Louis, ed. *Ethical Theory: Classic and Contemporary Readings.* Belmont, Calif.: Wadsworth, 1989.

———. "Ethics: Religious and Secular." *Modern Schoolman* 70 (November 1992): 1–30.

Quinn, Philip. *Divine Commands and Moral Requirements.* Oxford: Oxford University Press, 1978.

Siddiqui, Daniel J. "Ethics in Islam." *Asian Journal of Theology* 10 (1996): 105–17.

CHAPTER 15 THE CONTINUING QUEST: GOD AND THE HUMAN VENTURE

Oxford philosopher J. L. Mackie (1917–1981) writes:

> It is my view that the question whether there is or is not a god can and should be discussed rationally and reasonably, and that such discussion can be rewarding, in that it can yield definite results. This is a genuine, meaningful question, and an important one—too important for us to take sides about it casually or arbitrarily. Neither the affirmative nor the negative answer is obviously right, but the issue is not so obscure that relevant considerations of argument and evidence cannot be brought to bear upon it.[1]

These words begin Mackie's book, *The Miracle of Theism*. As the title suggests, Mackie takes it to be astonishing—or, to speak in hyperbole, "miraculous"—that theism has endured for centuries as a credible idea in the minds of intelligent people. For him, when the arguments and evidence are fairly evaluated, it is more reasonable to believe that theism is false than that it is true.

Mackie echoes the judgment of numerous influential philosophers, both past and present: Lucretius (c. 99–55 B.C.), David Hume (1711–1776), Friedrich Nietzsche (1844–1900), W. K. Clifford (1845–1879), Bertrand Russell (1872–1970), Antony Flew (b. 1923), Michael Martin (b. 1932), William Rowe (b. 1931), and many more. On the other side, there have been equally distinguished philosophers who think that, when all of the relevant considerations are weighed, it is indeed rational to believe that theism is true. The names of Augustine (354–430), Anselm (1033–1109), Aquinas (c.1224–1274), René Descartes (1596–1650), Richard Swinburne (b. 1934), William Alston (b. 1921), and Alvin Plantinga (b. 1932) merely begin the list of highly esteemed theistic philosophers.

As we have seen throughout this book, a number of important issues within the philosophy of religion are relevant to a full-scale discussion of theism: the significance of religious experience, the viability of arguments for and against God's existence, the question of whether rational argument is relevant or necessary to the acceptance of theism, the problem of how religious statements are meaningful, the difficulty of making sense of the concept of miracle, the extent to which the plurality of other religious belief systems affects the appraisal of theism, and many more. Other areas of philosophy that have a bearing on issues in religion could also be explored, making a thorough consideration rich and complex undertaking.

THE INTELLECTUAL PROCESS

All of the issues related to theism discussed in this book—religious experience, miracles, evil, and the like—are of enduring interest. Every generation and every thoughtful person must raise and ponder them afresh. Fortunately, we are not without help in our investigation of religion since great thinkers of past and present have left a legacy on which to build. They have helped clarify key problems, identify options, show where burdens of proof lie, and suggest the most reasonable positions. We need the wisdom of past and present in addition to the best thinking we can bring to the task.

In other words, we have been engaging in a great dialogue, a dialogue that inquiring minds have carried on for centuries. It will continue as long as people raise philosophical questions regarding religious belief. This is an exciting intellectual process of argument and counterargument, of carefully considering alternatives, and of trying to gain deeper insight into the issues surrounding religious belief. This text itself serves, along with other classic and contemporary works in philosophy of religion, as evidence that human reason can meaningfully consider matters of religion. All important issues in human life must be subjected to responsible, reflective reason. This holds for beliefs associated with a particular theistic religion, beliefs drawn from theistic religions generally, or beliefs maintained by nontheistic religions. If religious beliefs are not subject to the earnest, objective approach of reason, then prospects for the human venture are bleak indeed.

If rational analysis is appropriate, are there *limits* to the philosophical investigation of religious belief? The answer here depends on precisely how one takes the question. If this question is about *psychological limits*, the answer may well be *yes*. Obviously, each individual or personality-type will have some idiosyncratic limitations. There may be points at which a given individual's cultural background, family upbringing, religious convictions, capacity for abstract thought, and the like will surely produce real limitations. There may even come a point at which a particular person simply says that she can press the investigation no further.

However, if the question is about whether there are *theoretical limits* (or perhaps *logical limits*) to the rational investigation of religious belief, then the answer must be *no*. In principle, there is no fixed terminus or predetermined point at which investigation must stop. We may grant that certain individuals reach their own idiosyncratic limits, and these vary widely among people.

However, we must also recognize a fundamental a lesson of intellectual history: when someone declares a limit to thought in some area of human endeavor, someone else eventually goes beyond it. No person or group can prescribe for others the limits to their rational search, not even in matters of religion.

Some will object that the vast mystery of God or Brahman or Nirvana or some other Ultimate Reality is inaccessible to finite human minds. Even if God is beyond our thoughts in certain respects, rational investigation is simply an inquiry into *concepts* of God and *beliefs* about God. It is the enterprise of trying to make our thoughts about God and related subjects clear and coherent, informed and reasonable. God may well be infinite, but concepts and beliefs about God are not infinite and are entirely open to rational investigation.

To maintain, though, that there are no theoretical limits to the examination of religious belief is not to say that the process is in any way infallible or complete. The nature of the human rational quest seems to be that of bringing our best thinking to bear upon the problems we face, realizing full well that our results are tentative and incomplete, revising and moving ahead cautiously. Yet this process is all we have. Even if some revelation is true or if a certain religious vision is authentic, its credentials still must be rationally evaluated, and it must stand or fall in light of the arguments and evidence. The recognition of our own fallibility, as well as the strong proclivity of some religious dogmatists to claims of infallibility, suggests to us that the hope is brightest for progress when we strive hard for objectivity, fairness, and tolerance.

PHILOSOPHICAL ACTIVITY AND RELIGIOUS FAITH

Although many will admit that religion is subject to rational appraisal, some would insist that the results of philosophical inquiry are irrelevant or antithetical to authentic religious faith. Some will claim, for instance, that the sacredness of the subject makes critical, penetrating inquiry disrespectful or blasphemous, or that it encourages unwholesome doubt. But while the subject matter may be deemed sacred, every major religion recognizes and encourages responsible thought. The major world religions have long histories of debate and discussion of their key doctrines and themes. Besides, nothing encourages intractable doubts as much as forbidding free and open inquiry. Consider the opening words of Pascal's Memorial (dated November 23, 1654) which makes a strict distinction between "the God of Abraham, God of Isaac, God of Jacob," on the one hand, and the God of the "philosophers and scholars," on the other. For Pascal (1623–1662) and many other people, even if the existence of God could be validly inferred from acceptable premises, it would be of merely academic interest. Deeply religious people often claim that they already live in a dynamic relationship with God and thus that rational argument and other intellectual exercises are patently beside the point. The proper response to their claim runs along two lines.

First, it is quite right to distinguish carefully between philosophical activity, on the one hand, and vital religious faith, on the other. *Philosophical* interest in God is simply different from *religious* interest in God, another mode of human activity. In general, we can say that engaging in rigorous analysis and argument is neither a necessary nor a sufficient condition for a robust religious faith. Philosophical understanding is not a *necessary condition* for faith because some persons may not have the mental ability to engage in the sophisticated intellectual study of religion—and thus cannot produce any persuasive argument, say, for the existence of God—and yet may clearly possess religious faith.

Second, other persons may be quite skilled in philosophical matters, able to advance impressive arguments in favor of God's existence, and not have religious faith at all. They might be intellectually persuaded, for example, that Christianity is true and yet not commit themselves to or find themselves in relation to the God worshiped in that religion. Likewise a person might be intellectually persuaded that Hinduism is true and yet not be personally devoted to Shiva or Vishnu. The same holds for all who merely assent to the truth of other religions. Thus, the philosophical examination of religion is not a *sufficient condition* for religious faith, either.

Although the rigorous philosophical examination of religion is neither necessary nor sufficient for religious faith, we must not suppose that faith is entirely divorced or separated from the rational process. It seems, rather, that religious faith (conceived as trust in a divine being and the like) is predicated on at least some amount of rational thought—and perhaps on more thought than some might initially suspect. The particular form of rational thought involved is belief that a statement or proposition is true. Many such beliefs that are taken to be true constitute a religious believer's set of intellectual commitments, conscious or unconscious.

As we have seen, having faith in God involves having certain beliefs about God and how God relates to the world. Granted, many ordinary religious believers may not be fully conscious of their own beliefs or may not critically attend to those beliefs when acting as one of the faithful. However, those beliefs are present and operative nonetheless, and much the same general rules and constraints for reasonable believing apply to them as to other human beliefs. This point is often punctuated when some religious believers realize that their own intellectual integrity depends on their beliefs conforming to some basic standards of rationality. They intentionally decide to probe and make good sense of their beliefs, to have their beliefs comport well with both *logic* and *fact*. Their religious faith is not, as Mark Twain once remarked, "believin' what you know ain't so."

Whether or not religious believers are aware of the beliefs that undergird their faith, these beliefs nevertheless can be abstracted and systematized for philosophical examination. Philosophy of religion applies standard methods of analysis and argument as well as insights from metaphysics, epistemology, and other fields of philosophy to these abstracted beliefs. Of course, this means that concerns such as consistency, coherence, and correspondence to the facts really do pertain to religious believing. It means that matters of plausibility and truth are relevant.

Nonbelievers may also fail to recognize the intellectual or belief-component of faith. They can mistakenly characterize faith as purely emotional response or as socially conditioned behavior and thus fail to perceive the underlying beliefs that are subject to intellectual investigation. They may reject religious belief without engaging it in a responsible rational process. Thus anyone, believer or nonbeliever, considering the viability of a religious perspective must maintain a conscientious respect for the general intellectual standards that philosophy employs. These kinds of rational considerations figure prominently into the decision as to whether a religious faith is sensible and warranted or confused and misguided.

WHERE DO WE GO FROM HERE?

The present study merely scratches the surface of philosophy of religion. Each issue could be pursued in much more depth and detail. Then, as one moves beyond the standard core of issues, other fascinating topics also invite further reflection on *classical theism.* For example, the "hiddenness of God" would be a fascinating topic to pursue at greater length. Still other kinds of topics pertain more specifically to the doctrines and beliefs unique to specific historic religions. Many key theological conceptions within Christianity— such as atonement, trinity, heaven, and hell—need further philosophical attention.[2]

Another area for philosophers of religion to explore is the relationship between philosophy and theology as disciplines. Although philosophy and theology had an intimate relationship in the medieval period, dialogue between philosophers and theologians in modern times has become problematic. This is in part because of differences in how the assumptions and methods of their two disciplines are conceived.[3] Theologians may claim revelation or church tradition as the final authority and arbiter in religious matters, whereas philosophers would recognize only reason. One interesting controversy revolves around the use of modern logical techniques and conceptual analysis by philosophers, leading some theologians to insist that such methods cannot do justice to human experience and history. Although the insularity of the two fields of theology and philosophy continues in many quarters, there are encouraging signs that some thinkers are attempting to break down old barriers.[4]

While many theologians—particularly those associated with historical theology and biblical exegesis—have largely avoided contact with academic philosophy, other theologians have consciously shaped their perspectives around certain philosophical concepts. These "new theologies" cover a wide range: *process theology, liberation theology, feminist theology, environmentalist theology, postmodern theology,* and other new theologies supply the substance for much philosophical thought and reflection.[5]

The philosophical scrutiny of other major religious conceptions offers another direction for further study and reflection. For example, some specific nontheistic religion—its particular beliefs and living practices—could be a fruitful object of philosophical scrutiny. In this text, for example, Hindu pantheism (or panentheism—God including the world as a part of his being) was mentioned from time to time for the primary purposes of comparison and contrast with Western theism. But it would be wholly appropriate for a text analogous to this one to be written on the religious beliefs emerging primarily from Hinduism. A more complete treatment of Hindu beliefs would, for example, discuss the precise shape of the problem of evil as it arises for Hinduism. Also, the implications of the Hindu belief system for human morality could be traced out. Fundamental Hindu theological conceptions—such as *karma* and *samsara*—could be analyzed and their logical structure clarified.[6] In fact, it would be possible to provide a careful, philosophical treatment of the beliefs of any other world religion following the approach used in this book. Of course, one complicating factor of great philosophical interest itself is that each major religion has its own philosophical tradition, a tradition that may not endorse the approach we have used.[7]

Ideally, the serious study of religion will lead eventually to other disciplines: anthropology, sociology, and psychology. The additional perspectives that these other disciplines offer on the complex reality of religion allow the philosophical scrutiny of religion to be relevant and informed. In fact, the whole question of the bearing of these other disciplines on religion or on philosophy of religion is itself a philosophical question.

All of this shows that philosophy of religion is a dynamic and growing field, filled with stimulating and important issues. It appears that the whole issue of how to find grounds for theological-philosophical dialogue will be in the forefront for some years to come. Serious thinkers will find that the perennial problems continue to offer an inexhaustible supply of possibilities for research and reflection. They will also devise new strategies and approaches, providing countless permutations on old issues. Virgin territory always remains to be pioneered, opening up new and important problems for consideration. All of this taken together, then, becomes part of growing edge of philosophy of religion.

Those interested in the important problems related to theistic belief can do additional background study in philosophy of religion and follow the new developments in the field. This process is intellectually stimulating because we cannot always predict the outcome of classic issues, nor can we perfectly anticipate the direction of future debate. However, to understand the value of the rational appraisal of religious belief is to take a large step toward being able to navigate religious issues and to fulfill one's intellectual responsibilities. We will show ourselves willing, as Aquinas put it, "to inquire, in a rational way, into the things human reason can disclose concerning God."[8]

STUDY QUESTIONS

1. Discuss the kinds of attitudes appropriate to the fair and objective discussion of religious beliefs.

2. After engaging in the analysis and appraisal of religious belief throughout this book, how would you assess the reasonableness or the truth of classical theistic belief?

3. In light of all you have read so far, try to make the best case you can for theistic belief.

4. In light of all you have read so far, try to make the best case you can against theistic belief.

5. What topics in philosophy of religion covered in this book would you be interested in pursuing more thoroughly?

6. What issues in fields related to philosophy of religion would you be interested in pursuing?

7. In what ways, if any, has studying the issues presented in this text changed your approach to religion? Changed you?

NOTES

1. J. L. Mackie, *The Miracle of Theism* (Oxford: Clarendon Press, 1982), p. 1. Also see pp. 11–12 for a further explanation of the title of the book.

2. Fred Freddoso, *The Existence and Nature of God* (Notre Dame, Ind.: University of Notre Dame Press, 1983); Nicholas Wolterstorff, "The Remembrance of Things (Not) Past: Philosophical Reflections on Christian Liturgy," in *Christian Philosophy;* ed. Thomas Flint (Notre Dame, Ind.: University of Notre Dame Press, 1990), pp. 118–61. The volume in which this essay appears is devoted entirely to exploring the philosophical ramifications of a variety of Christian ideas (e.g., the effects of sin) and practices (e.g., creedal affirmation).

3. Note the differences between theology and philosophy assumed in such pieces as Gordon Kaufmann, "Evidentialism: A Theologians's Response," *Faith and Philosophy: Journal of the Society of Christian Philosophers* 6, no. 4 (1989): 353–77; Maurice F. Wiles, "Review of *The Logic of God Incarnate,*" *Journal of Theological Studies* 38 (April 1987): 272; Thomas V. Morris, "Philosophers and Theologians at Odds," *Asbury Theological Journal* 44, no. 2 (1989): 31–41; William Abraham, "Oh God, Poor God," *The American Scholar* (Autumn 1989): 557–63.

4. One piece of evidence that there is some interchange is the conference on "Philosophical Theology and Biblical Exegesis," at the University of Notre Dame, March 15–17, 1990. Theologians and biblical scholars are also starting to invite philosophers to speak at their professional conferences (e.g., American Academy of Religion, Society of Biblical Literature). Another piece of evidence of the contact between philosophy and theology is the Cornell Studies in Philosophy of Religion series of scholarly monographs and the Library of Religious Philosophy series from the University of Notre Dame Press. The Society of Christian Philosophers continues to sponsor conferences and seminars on topics related to theology. *Faith and Philosophy: Journal of the Society of Christian Philosophers* continues to seek dialogue with major theologians

(e.g., see the October 1989 issue, which is devoted entirely to the topic of the Bible and philosophy).

5. For a good survey of modern theological movements, see R. Kliver, *The Shattered Spectrum* (Atlanta: John Knox Press, 1981). Some classic sources of feminist theological thought include Carol P. Christ and Judith Plaskow, eds., *Womanspirit Rising: A Feminist Reader in Religion* (New York: Harper and Row, 1979); Mary Daly, *Beyond God the Father: Toward a Philosophy of Women's Liberation* (Boston: Beacon Press, 1973); and Rosemary Ruether, *New Woman—New Earth: Sexist Ideologies and Human Liberation* (New York: Crossroad, 1975). For the impact of postmodernism, see Jean Luc Harion, *God without Being*, trans. T. Carlson (Chicago: University of Chicago Press, 1991).

6. For an example of how the philosophical examination of concepts in a nontheistic religion might be carried out, see Bruce Reichenbach, *The Law of Karma: A Philosophical Study* (London: Macmillan, 1990).

7. A notable example is Nagarjun's Madhyamfia Buddhism. Another example would be Dogen's Zen Buddhism.

8. St. Thomas Aquinas, *Summa Contra Gentiles*, trans. Anton C. Pegis (Notre Dame, Ind.: University of Notre Dame Press, 1975), vol. 1, chap. 9.

SUGGESTED READING

Alston, William P. *Divine Nature and Human Language: Essays in Philosophical Theology.* Ithaca, N.Y.: Cornell University Press, 1989.

Audi, Robert, and William Wainwright, eds. *Rationality, Religious Belief, and Moral Commitment: New Essays in the Philosophy of Religion.* Ithaca, N.Y.: Cornell University Press, 1986.

Freddoso, Fred. *The Existence and Nature of God.* Notre Dame, Ind.: University of Notre Dame Press, 1983.

Mackie, J. L. *The Miracle of Theism.* Oxford: Clarendon Press, 1982.

Martin, Michael. *Atheism: A Philosophical Justification.* Philadelphia: Temple University Press, 1990.

Plantinga, Alvin, and Nicholas Wolterstorff, eds. *Faith and Rationality: Reason and Belief in God.* Notre Dame, Ind: University of Notre Dame Press, 1983.

Ross, James. *Philosophical Theology.* Indianapolis, Ind.: Bobbs-Merrill, 1969.

Stump, Eleonore, and Thomas Flint, eds. *Hermes and Athena: Biblical Exegesis and Philosophical Theology.* Notre Dame, Ind.: University of Notre Dame Press, 1993.

NAME INDEX

SUBJECT INDEX

Advaita vedanta, 66, 74n. 13, 120
Allah, 5
American Humanist Association, 6
Analysis, rational and reflective, 8, 11–12.
    See also Philosophical analysis.
Anthropic principle, 94, 260
Anti-evidentialism, critical, 49–50
Apologetics, 16n. 5, 41, 50
Apophatic tradition, 235
Arguments for God's existence. *See*
    Theistic arguments.
Association of American Atheists, 6
Atheism, 87, 101–2, 129, 130, 133, 138.
    See also Atheist
Atheist (antitheist), 6, 11–12, 114, 139

Beliefs
    basic (properly basic), 110–19. *See also*
        Reformed epistemology.
    belief-forming practice, 118–20
    derived (nonbasic), 109–11
    incorrigible, 110–11
    justification of, 8, 26–29, 272–73
    religious beliefs justified, 8, 312–16
    self-evident, 110–11
Bible
    inclusion of feminine images for God,
        235–36
    God portrayed in, 15, 222, 235
    literalistic use of, 248–50
    as revelation from God, 117
Biblical exegesis, 315
Big Bang Theory, 85–88, 93, 255
Blik, 227
Brahman, 7, 58, 66

Buddhism and Buddhists, 6, 16, 18, 12,
    33, 195, 268
    Mahayana, 197, 257
    Theravada, 269
    Zen, 5, 33, 267–68

Calvinism (theological determinism),
    158–63, 167–69
Causal principle, 84, 88–89, 92
Causation
    divine, 132, 173–77, 183–86
    natural, 132–33, 173–77, 180–82
Christian
    Anonymous, 281–82
    thinker, 312–14
Christianity, 7, 270–71, 280–82, 285,
    306, 314
Classical theism. *See* Theism: classical
Cognitive component to faith. *See* Faith:
    as involving beliefs (cognitive)
Cognitive faculties, 121–22
    proper function, 121–22
Coherentism, 112
Commitment (of faith). *See* faith:
    commitment
Compatibilism, 131–32, 143
Completist fallacy, 90
Confucianism, 194, 268
Contingency, 3, 63, 88–91
Cosmological argument. *See* Theistic
    arguments: cosmological
Counterfactuals of freedom, 160–63
Creation
    fundamentalist understanding of, 250
    Judeo-Christian doctrine, 254

Properly basic belief. *See* Beliefs: basic
Prophecy, 169
Protestantism, 158, 249, 257
Providence of God, 154–69

Rationalism
  critical rationalism, 49–53
  strong rationalism, 41–44, 52–53
Re-creation of persons after death, 195,
  205–7
Reason, human power of, 9–10, 12,
  39–57, 316
Reformed epistemology, 109–23
  as consideration against viability
  of theodicy. *See* Theodicy:
  viability of
Reincarnation, 195
Religion, definition, 6–8
Religious belief-system, 40–41, 48
Religious commitment. *See* Faith: as
  commitment
Religious diversity, 30–31, 268–70
Religious ethics
  acquisition of, 295–99
  authoritative basis for, 293–95
  as commands of God, 292–93
  of duty, 303–5
  feminist, 305–7
  innate sense of, 297
  natural law tradition, 296
  relation to God's goodness, 293–95
  relation to the meaning of life,
  299–303
  source of, 290–93
  of virtue, 303–5

Religious experience, 41
  common core to, 31–35
  interpretations of, 19–24
  justification of belief by, 26–29,
  116–20
  kinds of, 16–19
Religious language
  analogical use of, 222–25, 242n. 4
  equivocal use of, 222
  falsification of, 226–27
  feminist interpretation of, 234–35
  literal use of, 223
  symbolic use of, 232–34
  univocal use of, 222
  verification of, 235–26
  Wittgensteinian interpretation of,
  230–32
Resurrection
  of the dead, 195, 197
  of Jesus, 186–88, 212

Revelation, divine
  Bible as. *See* Bible: as revelation from
  God

Scientific materialism, 248–50. *See also*
  Scientific naturalism
Scientific naturalism, 44. *See also*
  Scientific materialism
Self, as psycho-physical, 204–5. *See also*
  Soul
Sensus divinitatis, 122–23
Simple foreknowledge, 163–67, 69
  providentially useless, 166–67
Skepticism, 45
Soft facts, 165–66
Soul, 195–96, 198–99, 201–3, 214
  critique of the concept, 202–4
  immaterial entity, 198–201
Special theory of relativity, 71–72
Strong rationalism. *See* Rationalism:
  strong rationalism
Sustainer, God as. *See* God: attributes of:
  sustainer

Teleological argument. *See* Theistic
  arguments: teleological
Theism
  classical, 2
  cumulative case for. *See* Theistic
  arguments: cumulative case
  argument expanded
  expanded, 136
  process, 59, 66–67, 70, 146, 156–57,
  169
  restricted, 9
  traditional, 59–73, 155–69
Theistic arguments, 108–9, 123
  cosmological argument, 83–91
  atemporal argument, 88–91
  Kalām argument, 83–86
  cumulative case argument, 100–101
  moral argument, 98–100
  ontological argument, 79–83
  Anselmian version, 83–91
  contemporary version, 82–83
  teleological argument, 91–98
  analogical argument, 91–92
  anthropic argument, 93–95
  intelligent design, 95–98
Theodicy
  Augustinian, 144
  best-of-all-possible-worlds, 140
  free will, 143, 145
  Irenaean, 144–45
  natural law, 145
  process, 146–48